FAR EAST

TRAVEL DIGEST

3rd EDITION

CHARLES & BABETTE JACOBS

India • Sri Lanka • Nepal
by ROBIN LYNN

•

Virginia Bleier — Editor

•

Paul Bleier — Graphic Arts

Copyright © 1979
by Charles & Babette Jacobs

Library of Congress Catalog Card No. 75-113820
ISBN 0-912640-15-4

TRAVEL DIGESTS, Division of
PAUL, RICHMOND & COMPANY — PUBLISHERS
73-465 Ironwood, Palm Desert, CA 92260
Phone: 714/346-4792

Address Mail Orders to:
30695 Ganado Dr., Rancho Palos Verdes 90274
Phone: 213/541-6161

Book Trade Distribution by
Rand McNally & Company
Chicago • New York • San Francisco

Chinese New Year, a time for visiting relatives, requires dressing the children in formal clothes to pay their respects to their elders. Boy on right is giving the traditional Kung Chi greeting. Peach blossoms betoken prosperity for the New Year.

Contents

All There Is To Know
About the Far East

In Cantonese Opera, symbolism of costume color and pattern has always played a leading role. To-day, the more ornate the costume, the more important the character. Here the actor is wearing the plain dress of an old, somewhat indigent man.

Floating Market of Bangkok

Foreword

For at least 800 years, nothing has proved more intriguing to the Occidental world than the Orient, nothing rivaled it in exotic, lurid, lavish splendor. Where else, except for Greece, such early flowering of the delicate arts? Where else has a more fascinating list of romantic names and things echoed thru the ages?

Marco Polo and the Great Khan. Sultans, Shoguns, Radjas and Emerald Buddhas. Ming and Ch'ing. Dynasties and Emperors. Madame Butterfly and Suzie Wong. Opium dens and ornate palaces. Red-roofed temples, golden-domed mosques, many-tiered pagodas, elaborate wats. Gunpowder and Gunboat Diplomacy. Silks, spices and porcelains. King of Siam, Charley Chan and, ah so, Mr. Moto.

Curiously, much of this allure remains today to fascinate the Western mind and eye. For to most of us, despite the vast inroads of modern technology and adoption of Western modes of living, the Far East is still mysterious, a vast melting pot of alien cultures, religions and races about which and whom we know next to nothing. Certainly some of the lessons of Vietnam exposed our bigotry and ignorance, our inability to assess Indochina accurately, our failure to react properly to alien situations. Shouldn't all of us move to react positively to what many feel is a rather self-evident

5

global situation: the steady westward movement of economic and political, even cultural, power?

Even the term Far East is antiquated, a relic of sailing days when travel was eastward from Europe. Yet for the past four hundred years, westward has been the way of history: Spain and Portugal to the Caribbean and South America; England, France, Holland and Spain to North America; Portuguese, Dutch and English into the Far Pacific, China Seas and Indian Ocean, Commodore Perry to Japan. There was the English Century (1775-1875) of economic domination, followed by the American Century, and now, as freely predicted by the pundits, the Pacific Century begins.

Certainly the ingredients are there: resources, economic know-how, political integration and, above all, manpower which is finally being used effectively and with consideration. Yet at this important moment, there's been a long step backwards in affluence and prestige for the English-speaking world. The power of the Commonwealth is minimal, U.S. prestige and dollars not what they used to be — the latter conspicuously in the hands of hordes of Japanese and European tourists who buy them at bargain prices with their upgraded national currencies. Canadians, especially, suffer from the decline of their dollar. A strange and disturbing sight to Americans, Canadians and English alike, yet one that bears investigation by any discerning, inquisitive person.

THE FAR EAST TODAY

Completely aside from elements of national prestige and self-interest, there are valid personal reasons for traveling thru the area. Of course, Vietnam, Cambodia and Laos are out of bounds, but otherwise there are no travel restrictions nor any reason, from a safety standpoint, not to travel anywhere in the Orient — including People's Republic of China (if you can get a visa).

It's a fascinating melting pot, a multi-racial and religious mix of Chinese, Japanese, Thais, Malays, Koreans, Indonesians, Indians and whites — Buddhists, Hindi, Muslims, Christians. And because of increasing middle-class affluence, they're traveling from one country to another as never before, a radical change in the tourist composition that's distinctly beneficial to Americans — we're no longer *the* ugly tourist. European charter groups, mostly German and French, are large and frequent with Thailand a special target. Australians invade Singapore and Malaysia in strength. The Japanese are everywhere.

An interesting by-product of a trip here is the political and social views one picks up from newspaper articles, editorials and news items quite impossible to obtain back home. They provide an insight into what the various countries think, how they live and what they hope to become.

Despite inflated hotel, restaurant and sightseeing prices (and the decline of the US dollar), economy-conscious tourists can live better for less money than many areas closer to home, thus reducing the impact of higher air fares. By careful planning — especially by spending more time in less expensive countries — Far East trips are competitive, price-wise, with any faraway area.

But the ultimate reason for coming here is simply this: there's nothing quite like it anywhere else. One is so very conscious of being in a different world. One still sees feudal Japan in Kyoto, the regal splendors of Siam in Bangkok, the gorgeousness of Chinese arts in Taipei, the dignified remains of English colonialism in Hong Kong and Singapore, the imposing rituals of Islam in Malaysia and Java, the complete blending of beauty between man and nature in Bali. And finally, most importantly, one begins to discern Chinese from Japanese, Koreans from Filipinos, Thais from Malays. They come into focus thru their arts, dances and lifestyles as more than quaint, odd, brown-skinned, slant-eyed individuals. Suddenly they are nationals of different countries which are coming into their own in the world hierarchy.

You'll enjoy meeting them. And you'll encounter nothing but friendliness.

GENERAL MAP OF THE PACIFIC AND EAST ASIA

COPYRIGHT BY PACIFIC TRAVEL NEWS

7

GUIDELINES TO THE FAR EAST

Or How To Use This Book

Most Successfully

The *Travel Digest* series has proved to be far more than mundane guides. Thru our personal travels, thousands of contacts within the international travel trade and hundreds of conversations with, as well as letters from, travelers themselves, each *Travel Digest* has become a Travel Planner — primarily for travel agents but equally useful for individual travelers. Incidentally, *you* in the text includes both travelers and travel agents.

We don't for a moment believe that our assessments and recommendations reflect the likes and desires of *all* travelers. However, 15 years of successful publication of 28 separate editions does insure satisfactory performance for at least the majority of our readers and, in the case of the travel trade, a large number of steady subscribers. For every *Travel Digest* has been published with complete freedom to express things as we see it. This edition is no exception.

Read carefully our assessments of the touristic appeals of the various countries, our recommendations for trip planning within each country. In this way, travel agents who have not made such surveys on their own may determine which destinations to include for independent travelers (FITs) or which tour packages are most suitable for group-minded.

For first-time visitors to the Orient, there is no question in our minds that the most important destinations are Japan, Taiwan, Hong Kong and Thailand. Any FIT trip of 21 days or less should not attempt to see more; allowing for travel times, this breaks down to only three to five days in each country — bare minimum for only the essentials.

To the foregoing Most Important Destinations, we'd include Bali — definitely an illuminating experience — were it not so far out of the mainstream.

Although once across the Pacific distances between destinations are not great, a combination of jet lag and unaccustomed sights, sounds and food necessitates scheduling that allows plenty of rest, minimum of early morning departures following late night arrivals. Read tour brochures with such in mind; if they don't list flight times, inquire. We saw one that brought a group into Singapore at 11 p.m., woke them up at 5 a.m. for next day departure. FIT schedules should never inflict such punishment. Nor, if at all possible, should 16- to 20-hour flights be scheduled on the homeward leg of any trip without a stopover; friends returned from a rigorous 30-day trip on a non-stopover flight from Hong Kong and were in bed a week recuperating.

MAKING YOUR TRIP MORE ENJOYABLE

That's really quite simple: *come prepared.*

We are well equipped to make that suggestion for on our first trip out here, we definitely were not — and suffered the consequences. We then had little idea of the relative importance of various sightseeing trips, about the same amount of appreciation of what we were seeing and practically no idea of what we were missing. Reason was that friends called at almost the last moment to ask us to join them on their second trip, so off we rushed on what we thought was a pure vacation — though as you see, thru sheer enchantment with what we saw it became our fifth travel book. Fortunately, our friends helped orient us to the Orient in what otherwise could have been a lost opportunity.

We have always found careful preparation and anticipation half the fun of any trip. This is doubly important in an area with which, as already noted, most of us have no cultural ties, where life is so alien. Hence, you'll find herein brief sketches of some of the more interesting and curious facets of Asian life: cuisines, customs, religions. Those with the urge to know considerably more about the places and peoples they're about to see should read considerably more. We have another friend who's never been to the Far East but is so widely read (and such an avaricious reader) that should she go, we know she'd know all the history, the arts and not only the dates of the Chinese Dynasties but the names of each emperor, how many wives and children they had, what was done during their reigns and, it wouldn't surprise us, what they ate for breakfast.

Your Far East adventure starts from the nearest public library.

ASIAN TRAVEL TIPS

With exception of Korea and the Philippines, all traffic moves on the left. So when crossing streets, look the wrong way. And walk on the left-hand side of sidewalks.

Asians drive like maniacs. With trishaws, motorcycles, cars, minibuses, big buses, trucks and bicycles all over the streets, it's a madhouse on wheels — or so it seems to the Westerner. Let pedestrians beware!

When taking cabs, ask the hotel doorman how much it will cost to where you're going. If it sounds high, tell him it's too much — use him to help you bargain. Best to always have your destination written in native script; likewise the name of your hotel. If picking up a cab in the street, use your fingers to determine how much the ride will cost. Learn to say "how much?", "too much" and, most needful of all, "drive slowly." Latter won't do any good, just makes your wife feel better.

In bars and nightclubs, credit cards can usually be used to pay for food and drink *but not for charges due hostesses.*

In larger hotels, there are standard (usually for groups), superior and possibly deluxe class rooms which relate to size (standard rooms can be *very* small) and location. Generally the rates rise with the floor. You can escape some, not all, of the inconveniences of being engulfed by large groups by staying at the best hotels in superior class rooms — but even deluxe spots may be group-oriented.

At Naha International Airport, Okinawa, a sign warns, "Beware of Pickpockets." Hong Kong and Bangkok, we understand (though not from personal experience), might use the same.

AIR TRAVEL

The importance of traveling at the *right times* cannot be overemphasized. The right time weather-wise, the right times to enjoy colorful festivals and events (these alone can make your trip), the right time to economize on GIT air fares (Nov.-May) should always be considered. Of course, more than one of these factors may not always be reconciled, though they usually can be compromised; this applies particularly to reconciliation of weather conditions in these wide-flung areas.

The key, of course, is *careful advance planning*. Read this book carefully to decide which countries interest you the most, then consult following Routing suggestions before scheduling. Check our listing of festivals in the countries you have scheduled (these are merely highlights — there are many more), what the weather should be like during the season under consideration.

Intra-country Trip Planning is included in each country section.

GATEWAYS TO THE FAR EAST

From North America, Tokyo is the closest destination and, of course, the fastest routing — flown almost entirely with 747 jumbos. From Vancouver, it's a 9-hour, 40-minute non-stop run (CP and JL). From Seattle, Tokyo is only 8:55 away (NW), San Francisco 10:45 via JL and PA (CI, JL also fly 1-stop). From Los Angeles, JL and PA fly non-stop from New York (13:40), JL and NW 1-stop flights. NW jets from Washington to Chicago, then non-stop (12:50) or one-stop to Tokyo.

Two alternative gateways, though with less frequent services, are Taipei and Seoul. China Airlines flies 747s non-stop to Taipei from San Francisco in 12 hrs., from Los Angeles by one- and two-stop flights (Honolulu, Tokyo). Seoul is a one-stop flight from Los Angeles via Korean Airlines (15:55), non-stop from Honolulu (9:30).

To Hong Kong, PA jets non-stop from San Francisco (12:40), one-stop from Los Angeles (17:10). NW flies to Hong Kong from New York (2-stop) and Seattle (1-stop; 13:15). From Vancouver, CP does it 1-stop in 15:50; from Honolulu, PA has 1-stop service.

As of April 1979, Singapore Airlines has three and four weekly flights (DC-10s) from SFO and HNL non-stop (from latter) to Hong Kong, then on to Singapore. After Sept. 1, it's 747 service.

Several tour operators are operating charter flights thru 1979: Creative World Travel to Hong Kong, SITA World Travel to Bali — and undoubtedly there will be others to those destinations, possibly Manila, only ones thus far to permit low-fare charter operations.

Southern gateway to the Orient is Manila. From San Francisco, PR flies direct, one-stop, in 16:55; PA two-stop. Same carriers fly to Manila from HNL (PR non-stop in 10:10).

Big advantage in flying westward is you're following the sun. Leave our West Coast from 1 to 2 pm, arrive in Tokyo by mid to late afternoon — but because you crossed the International Date Line, it's the next day (see Time Chart, Page 29) — in time for a light snack before a good night's sleep, thus catching up with jet lag.

But if you don't relish these long flights (we avoid them whenever possible), plan to layover in Hawaii, make it part of your vacation (at no extra cost in air fare). From there, the Far East gateways are relatively closer, the flights less tedious.

GLOSSARY OF TRAVEL TRADE ABBREVIATIONS

ABC—Advance Booking Charter
CAB—Civil Aeronautics Board
F—First Class
FIT—Foreign Independent Traveler
GIT—Group Inclusive Tour Fare
IAC—Intra-Asian Charter Fare
ITX—Inclusive Tour Fare
OTC—One-Stop Tour Charter
OW—One Way   RT—Round Trip
Y—Economy Class
YE—Economy Class Excursion Fare

FAR EAST AIRLINE ROUTES
(With Mileages and/or Flight Times)

To Tokyo From (and vice versa):

Bangkok — IA*, JL*; other lines 1-stop via HKG (2849)

Guam* — JL, PA (3:35; 1557)

Hong Kong* (4:00) — AI, AZ, BA, CP, CX, JL, LH, NW, PA, SR (1788)

Jakarta¹ — GA. JL

Kuala Lumpur — JL¹, MH²

Manila* (4:00) — JL, KL, MS, NW, PK, PR, SK, SN (1862)

Peking — AF*, CA, IR*, JL*, PK* (2:50; 1298)

Seoul* (2:00) — CX, JL, KE, NW (725)

Shanghai — CA*, JL¹ (1104)

Singapore — JL* (6:00), SQ²

Taipei* (3:00) — CI, CX, EG, MH, NW, PR, SQ, TG (1304)

To Taipei From:

Bangkok¹ (4:00) — CI, KE, SQ, TG (1564)

Hong Kong* (1:30) — CI, CX, EG, KE, MH, SQ, TG (501)

Guam¹ — CO, NW

Jakarta — CI²

Kuala Lumpur¹ (6:00) — CI, MH

Manila* (1:50) — CI, EG, PR, TG (731)

Okinawa — CO, NW (389)

Seoul (2:10) — CI, CX, KE, SQ (917)

Singapore — CI¹, SQ* (4:15)

To Seoul From:

Bangkok² — KE, SQ, TG

Hong Kong — CX¹, KE* (3:10), SQ¹ (1295)

Manila — KE* (3:40), TG¹

Osaka* — JL, KE (1:30; 511)

To Hong Kong From:

Bangkok* (2:40) — AF, AI, AZ, CI, CX, LH, JL, KE, SQ, SR, TG (1065)

Denpasar* — GA (4:40; 2149)

Jakarta — CX¹, GA* (4:35; 2030)

Kota Kinabalu* (2:15) — CX, MH (1140)

Kuala Lumpur* (3:30) — CI, CX, JL, MH, SQ (1575)

Manila* (1:40) — CX, PR, QF (702)

Okinawa* — JL

Osaka* (3:45) — AI, CX, JL, SQ (1545)

Penang — CX¹, MH* (3:00; 1501)

Singapore* (3:35) — CI, CX, SQ (1607)

To Bangkok From:

Delhi* (3:35) — AF, AI, AZ, JL, KL, LH, TG (1815)

Denpasar — TG2

Jakarta — KL* (3:15), TG¹ (1451)

Kathmandu — RA* (2:45), TG¹ (1369)

Manila* (3:30) — AF, JL, KL, MS, PK, PR, SK, TG (1368)

Osaka¹ — AI, JL, SQ, TG

Penang* (1:30) — CX, MH, TG (596)

Rangoon* (1:05) — TG, UB (363)

Singapore* (2:05) — CI, CX, JL, KL, QF, SK, SQ, TG (897)

To Singapore From:

Delhi* (5:45) — KL, SU (2581)

Denpasar¹ — GA, TG (1044)

Jakarta* (1:30) — CX, GA, JL, SQ, TG, UT (557)

Kota Kinabalu* — MH (896)

Kuala Lumpur* — CX, JL, MH, SQ (204)

Kuching* — MH (445)

Manila* (3:15) — PR, SQ (1481)

Medan* — GA, SQ (392)

Osaka — JL¹, SQ²

Penang* (1:05) — CX, MH (371)

Rangoon* (3:15) — UB (1198)

* means Non-Stop; ¹ One-Stop; ² Two-Stop

AIR MILEAGES FROM U.S. & CANADA

LAX—TYO	5478	YVR—TYD	4699
Via HNL	6402	HNL—TYD	3849
LAX—GUM	6350	HNL—GUM	3797
LAX—MNL	7849	HNL—MNL	5296
SFO—TYO	5149	HNL—SEL	4543
Via HNL	6246	HNL—LAX	2553
SFO—GUM	6194	HNL—SFO	2397
SFO—GUM	7693	HNL—SEA	2678
SEA—TYO	4793	HNL—YVR	2706

CITY ABBREVIATIONS

BKK—Bangkok	OSA—Osaka
CHI—Chicago	PEK—Peking
DEL—Delhi	PEN—Penang
DPS—Denpasar	PUS—Pusan
GUM—Guam	RGN—Rangoon
HKG—Hong Kong	SEA—Seattle
HNL—Honolulu	SEL—Seoul
JKT—Jakarta	SFO—San Francisco
KTM—Kathmandu	SHA—Shanghai
KUL—Kuala Lumpur	SIN—Singapore
LAX—Los Angeles	SYD—Sydney
MNL—Manila	TPE—Taipei
NYC—New York	TYO—Tokyo
OKA—Okinawa	WAS—Washington

AIRLINE ABBREVIATIONS

AF—Air France	LH—Lufthansa
AI—Air India	MH—Malaysian
AZ—Alitalia	MS—Egyptair
BA—British Air	NW—Northwest
CA—CAAC	PA—Pan American
CI—China Air	PK—Pakistan
CO—Continental	PR—Philippine
CP—CP Air	QF—Qantas
CX—Cathay Pacific	RA—Royal Nepal
EG—Japan Asia	RG—Varig Brasil
GA—Garuda	SK—SAS
IA—Iraqi	SN—Sabena
IR—Iran	SQ—Singapore
JL—Japan Air	SR—Swissair
KE—Korean Air	SU—Aeroflot
KL—KLM Dutch	TG—Thai Int'l
	UB—Burma Air

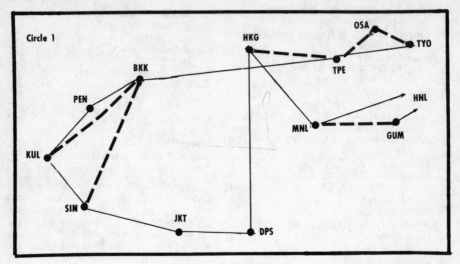

FAR EAST ROUTINGS

Circle 1 represents the Grand Tour — the way to see everything, or almost so. Missing is Burma, Eastern Malaysia and Brunei; Burma is best reached out of Thailand, the other two as side trip or cruise from Singapore. Diagram is counter-clockwise from Tokyo; broken lines (— — —) indicate alternative or ground routings.

After taking excursions out of Tokyo, you can leave from Osaka (if in Kyoto) rather than backtrack. From Bangkok, a good alternative to flying is to take bus or train to Penang, Kuala Lumpur and/or Singapore, the only area in the Far East (except Hong Kong to Canton) where international ground travel is possible. The Grand Tour could be made clockwise by first flying to Manila. It could also be altered to return to North America from Denpasar (instead of Manila) via the South Pacific, in which case Hong Kong would be visited after Taipei, before Bangkok.

Circle 2 is an abbreviated, yet representative, Grand Tour. Korea could be added between Osaka and Taipei, while East Malaysia and Brunei can be seen between Singapore and Manila (Kuching-Brunei-Kota Kinabalu-Manila).

Both Grand Tours presuppose the use of F, Y, ITX or GIT fares as it would not be practical, even impossible, to compact them into 21 days. Ideal trip length: 28 to

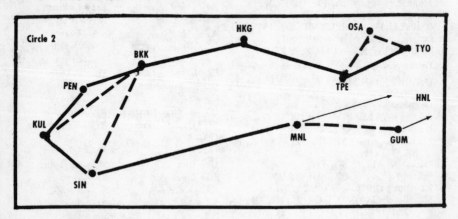

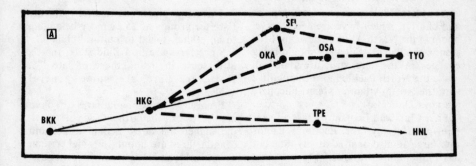

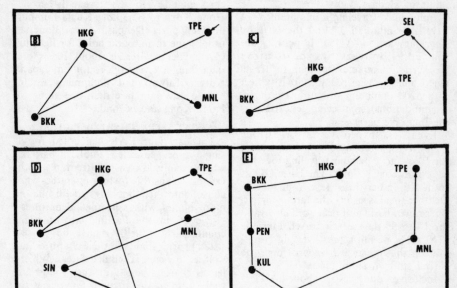

35 days minimum, longer if possible.

People's Republic of China has not been included since tours to this country are special packages with Hong Kong and/or Tokyo the normal gateways. For full details, refer to pages 166-169.

Routings A, B and C use Bangkok as turn-around point, are most adaptable to shorter vacations and, most importantly, concentrate on two or three of the more economical countries.

Routings D and E use Denpasar and Singapore as turnarounds.

We are quick to point out that all of these routings can commence with Japan — as we've seen, Tokyo is closest to North America. In many ways, Japan is one of the most interesting countries and certainly should be visited. In the final analysis, it's a question of expense; if you can afford it, see it. Actually, the same pertains to other of the world's star attractions.

Those interested in economical travel should use ITX or GIT fares, concentrate a good portion of their schedules in those countries that are comparatively inexpensive: South Korea, Taiwan, Thailand, Indonesia and Philippines — and reduce time in big cities in favor of touring the countryside. That's our advice — which we ignore when we come to Hong Kong, our favorite city.

NORTH PACIFIC AIR FARES

As of late '78, low-cost air fares, regular and charter, which have created a travel boom in the North Atlantic have not been seen in the Pacific. But 1979 should bring changes in the fare structure that will make the North Pacific more competitive with the North Atlantic. Meanwhile, here are your choices:

First Class and Economy Class all-year fares good at any time. Economy Excursion fare can also be used at any time but has a minimum duration of 14 days, maximum of 21 days.[1]

Individuals traveling a minimum of 14 days, maximum of 35 find the *Inclusive Tour* fare a good value. It permits unlimited stopovers on customized itineraries, complete freedom to travel where and when desired; the fare is subject to a $200 minimum pre-purchase of accommodations, sightseeing, etc. (that is the Inclusive part).

Even less expensive is the *Group Inclusive Tour* fare, used by tour operators for 10 or more persons traveling together as a group at all times. The basic GIT is from November thru May; from June to October (peak season), the fare is higher. These two, basic and peak, are also valid for 14 to 35 days of air travel. Like the ITX, GITs permit a "restover" in Honolulu on the homeward leg providing the carrier stops in Honolulu.

Inclusive Tour fares are about 4½% less than 21-day Excursions, but they permit 14 additional days of travel.[2] ITXs are 15% to 20% lower than regular Economy fares.

GIT peak season fares are 19% to 26% less than ITXs — with *basic period fares 15% to 20% less than peak*. Obviously, taking a tour between November and June saves a lot of air fare, though the land portion remains the same.

[1] Exceptions: 30-120 days to Manila, Hong Kong or Bangkok, India or Sri Lanka, and 15-120 days to Pakistan. All are less than the Inclusive Tour fare but are valid only to a single destination (two in India), allow no other stopovers.

[2] Limitations start from day *after* departure with return leg beginning no later than midnight of the last day. Hence, on a 21-day limit, you can actually return any time before midnight of the 22nd day.

There's a single destination Affinity Fare for groups of 25 or more belonging to an ethnic, social or cultural club.

Since fares are in a fluid state, there's little sense in listing those of late '78. However, here are some general guidelines:

From U.S. and Canada, fares to Tokyo are the lowest; the farther west you travel, the higher the fares. Seoul, Taipei and Manila fares are about 16% higher than Tokyo's, Hong Kong's 22%-25% more. It costs some 16% to 18% more to fly beyond Hong Kong to Bangkok, Kuala Lumpur or Singapore. Denpasar, in Indonesia, usually the turnaround point for figuring Circle Pacific fares, is about 10% more than Bangkok. Thus, a routing of Japan, Korea, Taiwan and Philippines would have a lower air fare than one going to Hong Kong and beyond.

WHAT'S THE CHARTER PICTURE?

Unclear. Our CAB has opted for a single type, so-called Public Charters, which permits low-cost charter fares, both OW as well as RT, by tour operators who consolidate their bookings to fill one or more planes with scheduled departures. However, in the Pacific, most foreign counterparts of the CAB have thus far resisted charter flights to their countries (as well as low-cost scheduled fares). Which leaves charters largely on the ground (as well as up in the air with few places to land).

Thus far, only Hong Kong, Manila and Bali permit charter flights. To these destinations, it is no longer necessary to belong to a club to buy low-cost transportation. Tour operators, who charter planes from airlines, offer charter fares to the public thru travel agents. These flights, to a single destination, are usually limited to 7-14 days duration, a great way to get a glimpse of the Orient. Land arrangements are optional, though sponsoring operators will probably offer various options, including trips to other countries via pre-arranged Intra-Asian Charters. However, it requires careful analysis to determine if one of these charters, plus one or more IACs, is more or less costly than GITs to the same destinations.

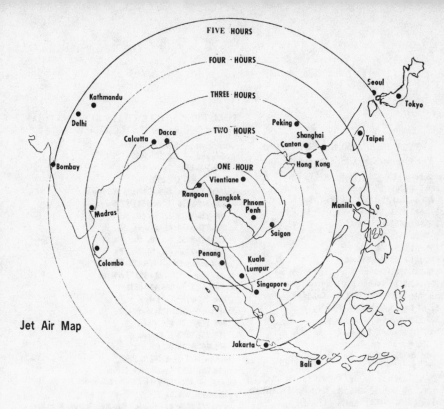

Jet Air Map

Creative World Travel, San Francisco, and Windsong Express, Los Angeles, have charter programs to Hong Kong. SITA World Travel, Los Angeles, has charters, to Bali and Manila.

In a break-thru of sorts, the Japanese Transport Ministry is permitting the introduction of Inclusive Tour Charters to and from Japan on an experimental basis thru March 1980. However, these will not be allowed at Narita and Osaka, thus carriers must use smaller airports such as Kagoshima, Nagoya, Fukuoka and Nagasaki. ITC fares are projected at 60% lower than regular fares, 40% less than present package fares.

By the way, CAB does not permit airlines to offer charter fares directly to the public, only thru tour operators and their agents.

BUY CAUTIOUSLY

Shop carefully *before* you sign up for a charter. Not all travel agents offer every charter. Nor are charter fares the same, even to the same destination. Too, they vary according to the season; travel off-season to save the most.

Brochures should be read *very carefully* before signing up and paying down, *particularly the cancellation clause;* invariably a cancellation will cost you anywhere from a few dollars (for cancellation insurance) to the full fare. Check into the possibility of a price increase *after* signing up.

ASIAN AIRLINES

We're not exaggerating when we say that one of the delights of Far East travel is submitting to the tender ministrations of a group of superbly serviced airlines: Cathay Pacific, China, Japan, Malaysian, Singapore and Thai International — listed alphabetically, not in order of excellence (which would be difficult to rate). Decor and food, even in economy class, are usually outstanding; cabin attendants, often exotically garbed, hover solicitously with plush restaurant desire to please. Many provide free booze.

Japan Air Lines, the largest foreign operator of 747s, flies that super-jet from

Continued on page 17

15

TOLL FREE 800 RESERVATIONS
For Continental U.S. (Except As Noted)

Air India — 800-223-7776 (Ex NY)
  800-442-8115 (NY State)
CP Air — 800-426-7007 (US West, SW)
  800-663-3566 Alberta
  800-663-3502 B. Columbia
  800-663-3516 Saskatchewan
  800-361-8635 NB, NS, PEI
  800-361-8740 Newf'dland
  800-261-8561 Ontario
  800-361-8026 Quebec
Japan Air — 800-421-8262 Az, Co, Id, Nv, Nm, Or,
  Tx (El Paso County), UT, Wa, Wy.
  800-252-0071 Ca (Ex LA, SF)
  800-223-5405 Al, De, Fl, Ga, Me, Md,
    Ms, Nc, Sc, Va, DC.
  800-223-5030 Ct, Ma, Nh, Nj, East Pa,
    Ri, Vt.
  800-621-8353 Ar, In, Ia, Ks, Ky, La, Mi, Mn,
    Mo, Nb, Nd, Sd, Oh, Ok, West Pa, Tx, Wi, Wy.
Korean Air — 800-421-8200
  800-252-9038 S. Ca.; 800-227-4810 N. Ca.
  800-621-1128 Midwest (Ex Ill.)
  800-223-5262 East (Ex NY)
  800-392-3380 Tx
Malaysian Air — 800-421-8641 (Ex Ca)
Northwest Orient — 800-792-0764 N. Ca.
  800-252-9041 S. Ca only
  800-552-0775 Wa only
  800-421-8282 Az, Nv, Nm, Ut
  800-426-0380 Id, Or, Mt
  800-328-4480 Ia, Nb, Nd, Sd
  800-972-9008 Il; 800-362-2122 Oh
  800-621-7311 In, Mi, Wi
  800-424-9380 Md, Pa, Va, Wv
  800-522-2177 Ny; 800-552-1290 Mn
  800-221-7300 Ct, De, Ma, Nh, Nj, Ri, Vt
  800-432-1210 Fl
  800-327-4511 Al, Ga, Ms, Nc, Sc, Tn
Pan American — 800-792-0740 N. Ca
  800-252-9081 — S. Ca
  800-426-0390 — Id, Mt
  800-621-7107 Nb; 800-972-1634 Il
  800-621-2909 In, Ia, Ks, Ky, Upper Mi, Mn,
    Oh, Wi; 800-621-0595 Nd, Sd
  800-522-7400 NY (W of Albany)
  800-452-1050 Fl; 800-282-1690 Ga
  800-241-4276 Sc, Tn
Philippine Air — 800-227-4500
  800-622-0850 Ca

TOLL FREE HOTEL CHAIN RESERVATIONS
For Continental U.S. (Except As Noted)

Americana — 800-228-3278
Goodwood — 800-223-5652
  800-352-6680 Ca
Hilton — 800-542-6101
Holiday Inns — 800-453-5555 W. States
  800-942-9090 Il; 800-542-5270 Tn
  800-238-5400 Dc, Fl, La, Md
  800-238-5210 Al, Ar, Ga, Ky, Nc
  800-323-9050 In, Mi, Mn, Oh, Wi
  800-243-2350 Ma, Nj, Ny, Pa, Ri
Inter-Continental — 800-621-1155 (Ex Il)
Mandarin — 800-223-6800 (Ex Ny)
Regent Int'l — 800-421-0530
  800-252-0277 Ca only
Sheraton — 800-325-3535
  800-329-3500 Mo
  800-261-9393 E. Canada
  800-261-9330 W. Canada
Western Int'l — 800-228-3000
  800-261-8383 Canada (Ex Toronto)
Oberoi — 800-252-0171 Ca (Ex 213 area)
  800-392-3908 Tx
  800-227-4139 Az, Co, Id, Mt, Nv, Or, Ut, Wa, Wy
  800-621-0530 Ks, Mi (Ex Detroit), Mo, Nb, Ok
  800-521-0780 Il (Ex Chi), In, Ia, Mn, Wi
  800-521-5930 Oh (Ex Cleveland)
  800-462-4949 Pa (Ex Phil)
  800-882-1618 Ma (Ex Boston)
  800-225-1739 Me, Ny (Ex NYC, Nassau Co.)
  800-225-1726 Ct, Nh, Ri, Vt
  800-523-9000 De, Nj
  800-424-9200 Md (Ex Balt), Va, Wv
  800-241-8847 Al, Ar, Fl (Ex Miami), Ky, La, Ms,
    Nc, Sc, Tn

U.S. ABBREVIATIONS

		Nd—N.D.
Al—Alabama	La—Louisiana	Oh—Ohio
Az—Arizona	Me—Maine	Ok—Okla.
Ar—Arkansas	Md—Maryland	Or—Oregon
Ca—Calif.	Ma—Mass.	Pa—Penn.
Co—Colorado	Mi—Michigan	Ri—Rhode I
Ct—Conn.	Mn—Minn.	Sc—S.C.
De—Delaware	Ms—Miss.	Sd—S.D.
Dc—D.C.	Mo—Missouri	Tn—Tenn.
Fl—Florida	Mt—Montana	Tx—Texas
Ga—Georgia	Nb—Nebraska	Ut—Utah
Id—Idaho	Nv—Nevada	Vt—Vermont
Il—Ill.	Nh—N.H.	Va—Virginia
Ia—Iowa	Nj—N.J.	Wa—Wash.
In—Indiana	Nm—N Mex.	Wv—W Va.
Ks—Kansas	Ny—N York	Wi—Wisc.
Ky—Kentucky	Nc—N.C.	Wy—Wyoming

Tokyo to Seoul, Hong Kong, Bangkok and India, DC10s to Hong Kong, Bangkok and Singapore, DC8s on other routes. Korean has a fleet of 747s, DC10s and Airbuses; Cathay Pacific 707s and Lockheed 1011s; China 747s, 707s and 727s; Malaysian DC10s, 707s, 737s; Singapore 747s, 707s and 737s; Thai DC8s and 10s.

All tourist destinations are connected by frequent daily flights, *yet heavy traffic necessitates advance reservations.*

Fun cruising in Indonesian-Malaysian waters aboard the "Prinsendam."

SEA TRAVEL

Aside from occasional World *(Queen Elizabeth 2, Rotterdam* and *Sagafjord),* Circle Pacific (Royal Viking *Sea)* and Trans-Pacific *(Prinsendam)* cruises, the only regularly scheduled services to the Far East from the U.S. and Canada are by 12-passenger freighters. However, there are passenger services out of Australia to various parts of the Orient; see South Pacific Travel Digest for details. Also, cruising out of Singapore has been highly successful (details follow).

Having thoroughly enjoyed last year's cruise on the very deluxe Royal Viking *Star,* we can heartily recommend her sister, the 22,000-ton *Sea,* to those who'd like to visit Bali, Singapore, Hong Kong, Japan's Inland Sea and Yokohama as part of a 70-day Circle Pacific Cruise which first sails thru the South Pacific. Departure from San Francisco/Los Angeles on Feb. 7/8 in '79, about the same time in 1980. On space available basis, certain segments can be taken as Air/Sea packages; turnaround point is Sydney, Australia.

On April 30, 1979, Holland America's *Prinsendam* (9,000 tons, 427 ft. long, 62 ft. wide) sails from Singapore on a 29-day voyage across the Pacific to Vancouver with calls at Manila, Hong Kong, Shanghai (2½ days with shore excursions), Yokohama, four stops in Alaska. On October 2, 1979, there's a 27-day crossing in reverse. Cruise prices include air fare between Singapore and any West Coast gateway (and vice versa).

"Prinsendam" passengers visit the jungle village of Bawomataluo on the Island of Nias where they may witness ancient war dances in the village square.

FREIGHTER-PASSENGER SERVICES

These are generally sold out at least a year in advance due to popularity and comparatively low cost. Here's a quick rundown of lines with frequent departures:

American Mail Line — Deluxe C-6 Containerliners; weekly sailings from Seattle to Kobe, Nagoya, Yokohama and return with 1-2 days in each port. About 24 days RT; OW passage available. Can stopover, rejoin later vessel. 1010 Washington Bldg., Seattle 98101.

American President Line — Weekly Orient service out of San Francisco, Los Angeles to eight ports in Japan, Korea, Okinawa, Taiwan, Hong Kong. 601 California St., S.F. 94108.

Barber Steamship Lines — Norwegian cargoliners sail twice monthly from Pacific Northwest-California to Japan and Southeast Asia ports (60 days). From Houston, 75-85 days; from East Coast, 100-108 days (latter includes Bangkok). All cabins outside w/bath. 17 Battery Place, New York 10004.

Orient Overseas — From East Coast, New Orleans, Houston and Galveston to Singapore and Malaysia about once a month. Island Navigation Corp., Maritime Bldg., Singapore.

States Steamship Line — Cargoliners from Pacific Coast call at Honolulu, Yokohama, Manila, Bangkok, Hong Kong, Taiwan, Okinawa and Korea. No stopovers on thru tickets; OW fares depend on vessel classification. Schedules projected six months in advance. 320 California St., S.F. 94104.

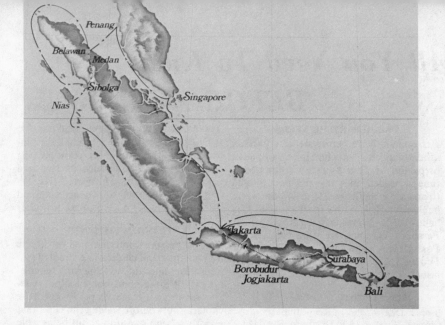

CRUISING OUT OF SINGAPORE

Becoming increasingly popular each year is a series of 7-, 10- and 14-day cruises in Indonesian-Malaysian waters developed by Holland America's air-conditioned, fully stabilized *Prinsendam* sailing out of Singapore from the end of October to the end of April. During the past season, the ship carried 40% Americans, 50% Europeans (this cosmopolitan mix is one of the ship's most pleasant aspects); 55% of these boarded in groups, mostly of 10 to 25 persons.

Christened in 1973 and custom-designed for Asian shallow water ports, *Prinsendam* is very modern in look, decor and fittings. Of 201 staterooms (small), all but 14 are outside ones. It boasts of a movie theater, 200-seat dining room (two sittings), Lido Terrace (pool) and Lounge, a forward bar-lounge and central lounge for entertainment and dancing (live orchestra), gift and beauty shops. There's a hospital with doctor/-nurse in attendance.

A cruise director directs daily events (sports, bingo, card games, et al), there are nightly movies, entertainment and dancing, shore trips (extra) at all ports of call. Lido Deck buffet available at lunch, Promenade Deck buffet at midnight. All cabins are nicely appointed, have wall-to-wall carpeting, telephone, two-channel music, individually controlled AC. Staffed by Dutch officers, the ship has an Indonesian service crew that draws rave notices from passengers.

But, undoubtedly, top billing goes to the unusual, fascinating ports of call. Sailing from Singapore, the ship visits Penang (4 hrs.), Belawan (11 hrs.) and Sibolga (5 hrs.) in northern Sumatra, then Nias (7 hrs.), Jakarta (11 hrs.), Bali (30 hrs.) and Surabaya (10 hrs.) before cruising back to Singapore via Jakarta. There are optional overland trips from Belawan to Sibolga to see famed Lake Toba, from Surabaya to Jakarta to visit fascinating Yogyakarta and incomparable Borobudur.

The 10-day segment is from Singapore to Bali, 7-day from Jakarta to Bali and return to Singapore, 14-day the entire Singapore-to-Singapore circle. Rates thru April '79 are about $117 per day minimum (inside double) to $190 daily (deluxe outside double). Prices include gratuities but not an $8.25 port charge. Air/Sea packages (cruise and other parts of the Orient) are available from the U.S. and Canada.

Although the *Prinsendam* is small and not ultra deluxe, reports we have received from wealthy, world travelers indicate that both ship and cruise have proved one of their most rewarding travel experiences.

All You Need To Know
BEFORE You Go

PRE-DEPARTURE NEEDS

Passport: A birth certificate or notarized affidavit of birth vouched for by a relative or person who has known you for a long time is needed, plus two passport photos (front view 3x3" or 2¼x2¼" on white background). U.S. passport costs $13, is valid for 5 years. Apply in person at Passport Agencies. In other cities, some Post Offices issue them, as do Clerks of Federal Courts. Passports issued within 24 hours cost an extra $2.

U.S. PASSPORT AGENCIES

Boston 02203—John F. Kennedy Bldg.
Chicago 60604—219 S. Dearborn, Rm 244A
Honolulu 96813—Federal Bldg., Rm 304
Lawndale 90261 (Los Angeles area)
  15000 Aviation Blvd.
Los Angeles 90071—World Trade Center
  350 S. Figueroa.
Miami 33130—51 SW First Ave.
New Orleans 70130—2 Canal St.
New York 10020—630 Fifth Ave., Rm 270
Philadelphia 19108—401 N. Broad
San Francisco 94102—450 Golden Gate
Seattle 98101—500 Union, Rm 225
Washington, DC 20524—Dept. of State

Passports obtainable by mail *providing you have had a passport within past eight years* and it was issued *after your eighteenth birthday.* To apply, write your Passport Agency for pink application form DSP-82. Upon receipt, return same accompanied by old passport, 2 photographs and $10 fee (personal check or money order). Allow two weeks for return.

CANADIAN PASSPORT

Costs $10 for 5 years (businessman $12), non-renewable. Persons born in Canada must have birth certificate or proof of citizenship (voter registration, expired passport, armed forces identification) and signature of guarantor. Persons not born in Canada must have guarantor and documentary proof of citizenship. Applications available from travel agencies and carriers; passports issued in Ottawa, Montreal, Toronto, Vancouver.

INTERNATIONAL VACCINATION CERTIFICATE

Doctor's certificate of smallpox inoculation within past three years proving immunity must be recorded on standard yellow certificate of World Health Organization and approval stamped thereon. Same form used to record other inoculations.

ENTRY REQUIREMENTS

Valid passport, international certificate for smallpox and cholera (see country sections for specific vaccination requirements). We maintain our smallpox vaccinations every three years, always have cholera shots before leaving the U.S.; that way there's no question about being able to enter any country.

Visa regulations vary; Japan, Indonesia, India, Nepal, Burma, Taiwan and People's Republic of China require them, other countries don't. Visas obtainable from respective consulates and/or embassies in U.S. and Canada or, for a service charge, thru visa service agencies in major cities; look for them in the yellow pages under Visas. Tour operators usually obtain necessary visas for those booking their tours. Best to enclose your International Certificates of Vaccination with visa applications as proof of compliance with entry regulations.

Always have with you a memo of your passport number, date of issue and expiration so a duplicate can be obtained thru nearest embassy or consulate in case of passport loss. By registering at consulate or embassy upon arrival in a country, you're entitled to an on-the-spot replacement (instead of waiting for one from Washington).

Within reason, there are no customs restrictions on what personal clothing and effects you can bring with you; in fact, inspections are usually token affairs — if at all. 200 to 400 cigarettes, 50 cigars, one to three bottles of liquor per person, one still and one movie camera with appropriate film are the usual limits. Written declarations required by some countries.

U.S. CUSTOMS REGULATIONS

$300 duty-free exemption (fair retail value) is allowed each U.S. citizen, including minors, on purchases brought with them providing no prior exemption was claimed in 31 days. Oral declaration sufficient if under the $300 limit — but have purchase receipts handy. You can mail back, duty free, bona fide gifts of $25 or less per day and per recipient to relatives, friends. Write *"Unsolicited Gift — Value Under $25"* in large letters on outside of package. Such gifts do not have to be declared on return. Merchandise purchased abroad and mailed to your home *cannot be included in your customs exemption.*

Additional purchases up to $300 can be brought in duty free if made in U.S. island possessions (Guam, American Samoa, Virgin Islands). Gifts to the value of $40 can be mailed from them.

Above the $300 duty-free limit, a flat 10% will be levied on the next $600 worth of purchases (5% if purchased in island possessions). Above that, various percentages of duty apply.

Merchandise purchased in Duty Free Shops abroad must be declared and included with all other purchases.

Antiques (100 years or older) are duty free; obtain proof of antiquity from seller. Art is also free if hand-drawn (original or copy) — but frame is dutiable. No duty on genuine pearls if loose or temporarily strung without clasp. Unset diamonds and other precious stones have lowest duty rates.

Not more than one liter of liquor, 50 cigars or 200 cigarettes are permitted duty free. Liquor is also restricted by state limitations. For example, New York allows 4 quarts to be brought in (duty must be paid on 3 qts.), California only 1; a Californian returning to the country by way of New York can bring in 4 quarts by declaration, only one (legally) when he eventually enters his home state. Best to ascertain your state limits before departure. Internal Revenue Tax on hard liquors is $10.50 per U.S. gallon (128 fluid ounces), plus 50¢ or more customs duty, if under 100 proof.

Among things you *can't bring into the U.S.* is a little-known category — endangered wildlife species (dead or alive). This means no alligator shoes and purses, jaguar or leopard skins or coats, vicuna cloth and a host of others, including bird plummage. For a complete list, write Fish & Wildlife Service, Department of Interior, Washington 20240.

Penalties for smuggling are severe: 100% of the value and, if illegal, confiscation of the merchandise.

IMPORTANT CUSTOMS INFORMATION FOR TOURISTS RETURNING TO U.S.

Certain items *intended for personal use only* may be brought back with you, or shipped, *completely duty free.* And you may still claim your duty-free exemptions for articles not on the GSP* duty-free list.

What Can Be Brought In Duty Free?

Most likely articles on the GSP (General System of Preference*) merchandise list are the following, *all of which must be made and acquired in country of origin:* bamboo items (except furniture), candy, cigarette lighters, earthenware tableware or stonewear (77-pc. sets at no more than $12 per set), bone chinaware (also nonbone but not tableware), China figurines,

* A system used by the U.S. and other developed countries to help developing nations thruout the world improve their financial/-economic condition thru export trade. There are different regulations for commercial importers.

21

THE WEATHER

Generally, the Far East can be visited year 'round though in the tropical countries such as Indonesia, Macau, Malaysia, Philippines, Singapore (rain Oct-Feb), Thailand, it's rainy from May-October, though exact months vary with the countries. In subtropical countries such as Republic of China and Hong Kong, rain is usually heaviest in summer. Korea and Japan have seasonal climate (cold in winter). In the tropical regions, you find more rainfall, humidity and higher temperatures — snow in the mountains of Japan, Korea and Republic of China. See the various countries for full details.

artificial flowers, furs (but not endangered species), board games, golf balls/-clubs, cottage handcrafts and wood carvings, ivory (except from Hong Kong), jade (but not if set in jewelry), jewelry of precious metal, stones, other types (except from Hong Kong), gem stones (but not emeralds, diamonds; nor sapphires, rubies from Thailand), musical instruments (no pianos), paper items, cultured or imitation pearls (loose or temporarily strung w/o clasp), records/tapes, shell products (except from Philippines), silver tableware, flatwear, toys (not including dolls) except from Hong Kong.

Foregoing can be brought in duty free from all countries covered in this book *except Indonesia, Japan and People's Republic of China.* Binoculars and camera equipment are duty free *but not if made in Japan;* so are solid-state radios (except car radios) *if not made in Taiwan, Hong Kong, Korea, Singapore or Japan.* Tape recorders, other than from Japan, Indonesia, are duty free. However, bear in mind that the above exceptions are only for the Far East; merchandise from developed countries in other parts of the world are also excluded.

For articles valued at more than $250 each, the District Director of U.S. Customs *may* require a Certificate of Origin (Form A), whether shipped or brought back in person; if shipped, both Form A and an invoice must accompany the goods. Form A, normally obtained from the seller, must be signed by an authorized official of the country of origin. If you're contemplating such purchases, best to contact the nearest U.S. Customs Service *before departure,* or else the American Embassy or consulate in the city of purchase.

Remember, all articles acquired abroad, free of duty or not (including those entitled to GSP) must be declared on your return to the U.S. (we believe all of the foregoing also applies to Canada) — orally if under $300, in writing if over. Be sure to have all sales receipts/invoices to substantiate your purchase.

For more detailed information, obtain *GSP & the traveler* and *Custom Hints for Returning U.S. Residents* from your local U.S. Customs Service or from its Office of Information and Publications, Washington 20229. Military and civilian personnel of the U.S. Government should obtain *Customs Highlights for Government Personnel* before returning from extended assignment abroad. *U.S. Customs Trademark Information* (10¢) lists brand names restricted from entry. *U.S. Import Regulations* is a free guide to entry papers, invoices, bills of lading, certificates of origin.

It's wise to register foreign-made personal articles, such as cameras, jewelry and other valuables, with Customs *before departure.* To obtain certificates of registration, take the articles to the nearest Customs office or one at an international airport in the U.S. — but allow sufficient time prior to departure. If you don't register your imports, at least have proof of prior ownership: bill of sale, insurance policy, repair receipts.

CANADIAN CUSTOMS REGULATIONS

$250 per year allowed duty free, divided thusly: after 48 hours abroad, $50 during two quarters of the year; after an absence of 7 days or more, $150 allowance once a year. One bottle of liquor, one carton of cigarettes permitted. Purchase shipped to Canada, excepting gifts under $10, are not includable in exemptions.

WHAT TO WEAR

Coordination is the key. Remember he who travels best travels light.

In Tokyo, dress as you would seasonally in New York City. Always suit or jacket/tie for men. Japanese dress somberly and in conformity.

Taipei is informal except for special dinners/functions when a suit, cocktail dress is best.

In Hong Kong/Singapore, sports clothes; jacket/tie at night. Same in Bangkok/Kuala Lumpur better hotels.

Only heavy clothing needed as for Japan/Korea in winter. Otherwise spring/summer clothing.

WOMEN'S WARDROBES

Winter travel usually means carrying both heavy and lightweight clothing. We found the add-to and take-off method most feasible. For Japan, we wore thermal underwear when it was cold, added a turtleneck shirt and sweater under our knit suit and mediumweight coat. Woolen socks kept our feet warm, wool-lined gloves did the same for our hands. An all-purpose, waterproof jacket with fold-under hood is helpful, particularly since you can add to its warmth with a heavy wool cardigan underneath. Except for Peking and the ski slopes of Japan, that should do the trick.

For the rest of the year, normal resort and city wear are in order. A color coordinated assortment of long sleeve (protection against insects) and sleeveless blouses, tops, slacks, shorts, shifts and dresses should be chosen — with emphasis on the washable, no-iron fabrics for carefree vacations. Stockings unnecessary except for cocktail and travel wear. Here's what we pack:

Three pairs of slacks and four blouses of varying colors, three dresses (one long sleeved), sandals, shoes, a head scarf, one or two swimsuits with a long sleeve jacket which doubles as a robe. We find three bras, two nylon gowns, two lycra girdles suffice for our longest trips; make a habit of washing them nightly so they're dry by morning.

For the sophisticaed places, add a knit suit with matching coat, a spring weight wool coat or all-purpose silk one. Plus one or two cocktail dresses and/or slack suits (which can be worn anywhere).

Of course, there are accessories — but keep them on the light side, both weight and quantity. And take only the jewelry you normally wear, not the state occasion kind. Saves time and worry looking for the heirloom we've just mislaid (don't we all?).

Include a pair of tennis shoes, sport socks, plastic raincoat, hood and boots (kind you buy at notion counters). Surprising how people goggle when I whisk them out of my purse.

Do bring skin creme (in plastic tube) and Woolite (not usually sold abroad). And folding slippers are handy for beach, plane and room wear. As protection from the sun, you can always buy an inexpensive straw hat on arrival — or a fur one in Peking.

Most important — *bring your own hair formula* as the right color is not always available, particularly when traveling by ship; also saves time and explanations.

We've seen many women waste half a day packing and unpacking at each destination. Don't let that happen to you. Travel light!

MEN'S WARDROBES

We usually take one suit, several medium weight jackets and slacks that can be worn interchangeably, a top coat that can double as raincoat and also, with a zip-in lining, as a cold weather garment. For northern winters, you'll want a pair of warm gloves, woolen socks, heavy sweater and thermal underwear.

Other than winter, regular resort and city wear suffice. Pack a lightweight, weatherproof coat or jacket. Rely heavily on wash-and-wear shirts, slacks, shorts, tops. Jockey shorts are cooler than boxers. In the sub-tropics, bring lightweight, light colored clothes with possibly one jacket; in the Philippines, *barongs* (embroidered native shirts) are worn for the most formal occasions.

23

LUGGAGE

Most international air carriers allow economy class passengers to check two bags with total dimensions of both not to exceed 106 inches (length + height + width), with larger one not to exceed 62"; some carriers permit a 62" and 55" bag. No bag may weigh more than 70 lbs. A carry-on bag (up to 45") is also allowed if it can be stowed under the seat.

Unfortunately, these allowances have not been adopted by all carriers. Also, in some areas the dimensional allowances are applied on flights from the US, the old (and lesser) weight allowances on return flights. Best to check in advance which are applicable to each leg of your journey.

Regardless, each of us travels with one hanging wardrobe bag and a single piece of carry-on luggage. Pleasure of traveling light is inestimable — to say nothing of money saved in tips. Careful planning, color coordinating before packing is the key. Plus reliance on wash-wear clothing and wrinkle-free knits.

LUGGAGE TIPS

Do not check luggage thru to final destination if transfer from one carrier to another is required; recheck it yourself at transfer point.

Always count number of claim checks to make sure each piece has one — and watch each one being tagged. Determine, too, that your luggage has been routed to correct destination — you can tell by abbreviation letters on claim checks.

Keep luggage free of all tags except the one for current destination, otherwise baggage handlers might be confused. When you reach your hotel after a flight, remove the destination tag.

Tag each piece of luggage, *both inside and out*, with your name, address, phone number so that it's easily identifiable in case of loss. An outside luggage tag is required by airlines.

Take an extra flight bag, preferably plastic that folds into a compact square —

mighty handy for carrying things you buy along the way.

If luggage is damaged, report immediately to nearest office of the responsible carrier so Baggage Damage Report form can be filed. Report lost luggage immediately (before plane departs) at the airport; if carrier can't locate same within 3 days, claim forms will be furnished and settlement made between 4-6 weeks — but don't expect full amount you paid for your effects as deductions are made for depreciation.

WHAT NOT TO TAKE WITH YOU

Formal dresses, furs, expensive jewelry — and anything else you wouldn't want to lose.

Electrical gadgets (hair curlers, etc.) are a nuisance. Don't pack breakable bottles (transfer contents to plastic containers), pressurized spray cans (can explode during flights). When filling containers with liquids, leave air space at top.

AIRLINE LUGGAGE LIABILITY

Airlines' luggage liability is limited — up to $750 maximum per paying passenger on U.S. domestic flights, by baggage weight on international (amount printed in your ticket) — so best to take out luggage insurance before departure. Put your name, address, phone number on both outside and inside of each piece of luggage, then lock it. *Best to carry cash, travel checks, jewelry, passport, other valuables on your person.*

To learn about denied boarding compensation due you, how to avoid being bumped, what amenities you may expect from an airline because of flight delays/-cancellations and other such matters, get *Air Travelers' Fly-Rights* from Publication Services, Civil Aeronautics Board, Washington 20428.

Any complaint against an airline flying in, to or from the U.S. which has not been resolved by the airline to your satisfaction should be submitted in writing to Office of Consumer Advocate, Civil Aeronautics Board, Washington 20428 — but that's no guarantee you'll obtain satisfaction.

HEALTHFUL TRAVEL

Diarrhea or dysentery, the more severe form, *may occur anywhere in the world* as a result of a combination of unaccustomed living and eating conditions: different mineral contents of water, new types of food and seasoning, altitude, eating and drinking too much at other than usual hours, jet lag and, especially, excitement — but, of course, always be alert as to whether or not eating conditions are sanitary.

In the Far East, you won't have to worry about altitude except in the Himalayas and northern Japan's ski areas. Water and ice in first class hotels are potable — but bottled water, plain or carbonated, is readily available if desired.

Don't patronize sidewalk food vendors, snack shops. Never eat anything that can turn bad from lack of proper refrigeration: potato salad, cole slaw, cream puffs, cream, etc. Eat only cooked food (unless fruits, vegetables are peeled), drink only bottled water and/or soft drinks in out-of-the-way places.

By taking things easy at first, staying in good hotels, eating only in good restaurants, you should not experience any discomforts. But should you have symptoms of stomach upset, take *Lomotil* immediately for prompt relief; a prescription drug in the U.S.

Carry prescription medicines in original containers to identify them as legal drugs when returning home. Have an extra pair of prescription glasses and/or the prescription itself; test plastic frames before departure — they have a tendency to dry out and crack after several years' use.

In Indonesia and other tropical or semitropical areas, an insect repellent (Cutter's is good) proves a pleasant companion. Our doctor advises four vitamin B-1 tablets daily; resulting perspiration odor is repellent to mosquitos and other insects (but not fleas). Too, wear light colored clothing — mosquitos more attracted to dark skins, dark outer wear. If you do get bitten, Decaspray (prescription) soothes and cures quickly.

MEDICAL ASSISTANCE

In cases of emergency, better hotels thruout the Far East can usually obtain a doctor for you. However, the most valuable travelers' medical aid organization we know of is the International Association for Medical Assistance to Travellers (sic), or IAMAT, which coordinates the services of doctors and clinics thruout the world — 450 cities in 120 countries. A non-profit organization, it guarantees members qualified medical assistance 24 hours a day from an English-speaking physician in all cities listed in its Directory.

A tax-deductible contribution to IAMAT[1] entitles you to a year's membership, a membership card and current Directory; latter lists a center in each foreign city which furnishes, on request, a daily list of approved doctors (both internists and specialists) from a panel on 24-hour duty. Individual doctors have agreed to a uniform fee schedule (US currency): Office visits, $15; Hotel call, $20; Nights (10 p.m. to 7 a.m.), Sundays and holidays, $25. Those rates do not apply to special consultations.

You can obtain immediate assistance in Japan (7 cities), Korea (2), Hong Kong, Bangkok, Singapore, Rangoon, Taipei, Macau, Malaysia (4 cities), Indonesia (5), Philippines (5), India (15), Sri Lanka, Kathmandu and Pakistan (4).

PERSONAL ASSISTANCE KITS

Were we to tell you to be sure to pack 26 emergency items, 12 first-aid items — plus 10 to help you recover from a too-festive fiesta — you'd probably say, "Bully for you but who's got the time and space?

Well, Hartford House[2] has the time to assemble those items in three handy kits that anyone can pack in a jiffy, for they measure just 4 ½ x 3 ½ x ½ *inches*. They're priced at about $1.25 each in gift, drug, specialty and variety stores.

We wouldn't go anywhere without the Crisis Kit!! with its 26 grooming, sewing and first aids — invaluable things like spot remover, rain bonnet, shoe shiner, thread (6 colors), needles, buttons, sterile bandage strips. First Aid Kit includes amonia inhalant (who'd ever think of that?), adhesive tape, bandage strips and others. Recovery Kit has a couple of headache remedies, antacid tablets, mouth wash, instant beef broth and mixes for a Bloody Mary and Screwdriver.

[1] 350 Fifth Ave., Suite 5620, New York 10001; 4950 Queen Mary Rd., Suite 225, Montreal, Que. H3W 1X3.
[2] Brookfield, RR3, Conn. 06804.

TRAVEL WITH THE U.S. DOLLAR

Biggest problem since the double devaluation for Americans as well as Canadians is how to cope with rising costs of travel abroad. Except for the handful of countries in the world maintaining parity with the dollar, travel costs have increased 15% or more due solely to devaluation *without taking into account rising prices of food, hotel rooms, etc.* Which makes $10 A Day as extinct as the Charleston.

From our travels, on which we keep detailed records, we know that deluxe or first-class accommodations, meals and sightseeing coupled with economy air fares, the way most Americans and Canadians go, is very expensive and getting more so each year. "Go Now, Pay Later" is better advice than "Go Later, Pay More."

Inflation is the villain. Air fares, hotel and sightseeing rates, food prices are spiraling; hotels are experiencing an annual 8% increase in overhead, meaning you'll pay at least 10% more each year for rooms — a $40 rate today will be $80 (or more) in the early 1980s.

Here are some ways to mitigate this trend without curtailing scope: 1) Use promotional air fares. 2) Stay longest in countries where U.S. dollars buys the most. 3) Travel with a group or another couple to reduce sightseeing expenses; Fly/Drive programs are money-savers, particularly when car costs are shared by two couples. 4) Step down a grade in choice of hotels, stay longer in smaller cities, resorts where rates are lower. 5) Buy duty-free booze for drinks in your room.

U.S. TRAVEL CHECKS

They may or may not bring a higher rate of exchange than cash (depends on the country), but they're certainly more convenient and safe, usually easier to convert into foreign currency. Be sure to copy check numbers (in case of loss); keep list separate from the checks.

U.S. CREDIT CARDS

American Express, BankAmericard and Diner's are prevalent in all countries; Master Charge seems to be coming on strong. Avis and Hertz cards can be used at their respective branches.

FAR EAST CURRENCIES

One country's currency may be exchanged for another's — at a loss to the seller. So leave each country with as little of its money as possible.

Except for Japan, Hong ·Kong and Singapore, the dollar has remained fairly stable. All in all, the Far East has been a lot kinder to us than the Middle East and Europe.

Obviously, the exchange rates quoted herein for the various countries are subject to change at any time.

Unlike some other parts of the world, hotels give the same official exchange rates as banks in most instances — but best to check that on arrival. In case they don't, pay by credit card (which converts at official rate) or with cash obtained from a bank. You'll always find a bank or currency exchange at international airports.

Hotels do not cash or accept personal checks without prior arrangement — although we've often found it easier to do so than in many places in the U.S.

Singapore Hilton

THE HOTEL PICTURE

As they once sang about Kansas City, everything's up to date in Tokyo, Taipei, Hong Kong, Bangkok, Kuala Lumpur, Singapore, Jakarta and Manila (as well as in a lot of other places). In fact, we don't know of any area of the world outside North America that can boast of more outstanding hotels. Their facilities are, for the most part, ultra-modern and luxurious. They invariably offer a variety of restaurants serving surprisingly good food, often at very reasonable prices. In some instances — Indra Regent in Bangkok, Hilton in Kuala Lumpur, the Bali Beach come readily to mind — the architecture and decor are literally sensational.

Just as the Dorchester and Savoy of London, Ritz of Paris and Lisbon, Gritti Palace of Venice and Excelsior of Rome and Florence symbolize the essence of luxury and tradition, so do the Peninsula of Hong Kong, Grand of Taipei, Imperial of Tokyo and Oriental of Bangkok carry on the finest traditions of the Orient.

There are also many other establishments with superior ambience, cuisines and service. Some of our favorites: the Hiltons of Kuala Lumpur and Singapore, President of Taipei, Indra of Bangkok and last, but far from least, Hong Kong Island's Mandarin — room service, decor and cuisines are perfection, the view from its harbor rooms the most exciting we've ever experienced.

We'd like to report that famed Raffles in Singapore is just as romantic as yesteryear and that Sydney Greenstreet sits in the lobby in white suit and broad-brimmed hat sipping Singapore Slings. It's not and he doesn't.

The foregoing are merely some of the highlights — there are many others (too many to list). Refer to the Hotel Directory in each country section for complete details. Particularly note that at peak seasons, reservations must be made at least several months in advance.

There are as many excellent first-class hotels, at correspondingly low rates, as deluxe ones. Almost without exception, service is cheerful and good. Housekeeping standards are high in all types of establishments.

Far East hotels are highly oriented (no pun intended) to group tourism, their rates realistically low. Which means that individuals on package tours or charters are traveling as economically as possible.

HOTEL ABBREVIATIONS

DL—Deluxe
FC—First Class
MOD—Moderate
DL+—Extra Deluxe
FC+—Superior FC
Inexp—Inexpensive

AP—American Plan (three meals)
MAP—Modified AP (breakfast & one other meal)
CP—Continental Breakfast
FB—Full Board (same as AP)
B—Room and breakfast
D—Double Occupancy   S—Single
DT—Downtown location
EP—European Plan (room only)
R—Room   SU—Suite
Rsv—Reservation   Rst—Restaurant
Refrig—Refrigerator

Chinese Sword Dancers, part of Singapore's elaborate dance shows that entertain tourists nightly.

MUCH ENTERTAINMENT?

And how! Some of the most lavish, lurid, licentious, lovely, exotic, exciting and tantalizing as any anywhere in the world. Whatever you're looking for, you'll find. And whatever that is, for us it was the Thai and Balinese dances, Chinese operas, Japanese drama and drum dances, the . . . . . . but we could go on and on. In all of our travels, we haven't seen anything to match these acts of Oriental splendor. They and the temples and wats and pagodas are what makes the Far East oriental.

What makes it pleasurably earthy, however, is best pointed up by this occurrence:

On arrival at an Asian hotel, an official of the World Council of Churches was asked, as men often are, if he wished female companionship for the night. He declined, but the hotel porter persisted in his persuasions, finally asked why he wasn't interested in one of his beautiful young women. "Because I'm a minister of a Christian church," was the reply. The porter left abruptly. Soon came a knock on the clergyman's door. Enter smiling porter. "Evelything okey-dokey now. Chlistian woman, she be here soon."

WHAT ABOUT GAMBLING?

Casinos in Korea, Macau, Malaysia – and horseracing everywhere.

HOW'S THE FOOD & BOOZE?

The former great, the latter usually expensive (sometimes, like in Japan, outrageously so); keep an inexpensive supply on hand by buying your favorite brands at Duty Free Airport Shops.

There's no area in the world where there are more varied cuisines: Japanese, Chinese, Korean, Thai, Malaysian and Indonesian along with any and every type of western food. Dining in a few countries (notably Japan) can be quite expensive, but most are relatively moderate in price, a few (Taiwan particularly) quite inexpensive. But all provide delightful experiences, even sensations, that highlight any Far East trip.

Until we traveled to Taiwan, Hong Kong and Singapore, we could take so-called Chinese food or leave it, mostly the latter. But now that we've had the real thing — and know something about ordering it — we are mad about it, though we must admit that the farther away we get from the Big Three (we haven't been to the People's Republic), the less mad we become.

Under each of the countries will be found a brief guide to the outstanding native dishes. But because we regard the various styles of Chinese cooking as preeminent, we follow with a brief roundup of what and how to eat — designed to increase greatly your enjoyment of meals, as well as things Chinese, if read carefully beforehand. Put aside any Chop Suey prejudices (an American dish that doesn't exist in the Orient) and come prepared to return a delighted convert.

LANGUAGE A BARRIER?

English is a second language in all countries, particularly in Hong Kong and Singapore; in Tokyo, many directional signs are in English as well as Japanese. Only with cab drivers and when asking directions in the street will you have difficulties, but such can be avoided by carrying written directions in native script. If you are caught short, make inquiries of a young person — good chance that he knows some English.

All better hotels and restaurants have plenty of English-speaking employees. Tour guides are usually fluent but oft times a bit difficult to follow; v's tend to become w's (willages, wegetables, wessels) and, as in Japan, r's are pronounced as l's and vice-versa — which makes a fun scrabble game when you try to duplicate same (sample: Deal Lichald).

FAR EAST — NORTH AMERICA TIME ZONES[1]

E	D	C[2]	B	A	HST	PST[3]	MST[3]	CST[3]	EST[3]
2400	0030	0100	0200	0300	0700	0900	1000	1100	1200
0100	0130	0200	0300	0400	0800	1000	1100	1200	1300
0200	0230	0300	0400	0500	0900	1100	1200	1300	1400
0300	0330	0400	0500	0600	1000	1200	1300	1400	1500
0400	0430	0500	0600	0700	1100	1300	1400	1500	1600
0500	0530	0600	0700	0800	1200	1400	1500	1600	1700
0600	0630	0700	0800	0900	1300	1500	1600	1700	1800
0700	0730	0800	0900	1000	1400	1600	1700	1800	1900
0800	0830	0900	1000	1100	1500	1700	1800	1900	2000
0900	0930	1000	1100	1200	1600	1800	1900	2000	2100
1000	1030	1100	1200	1300	1700	1900	2000	2100	2200
1100	1130	1200	1300	1400	1800	2000	2100	2200	2300
1200	1230	1300	1400	1500	1900	2100	2200	2300	2400
1300	1330	1400	1500	1600	2000	2200	2300	2400	0100
1400	1430	1500	1600	1700	2100	2300	2400	0100	0200
1500	1530	1600	1700	1800	2200	2400	0100	0200	0300
1600	1630	1700	1800	1900	2300	0100	0200	0300	0400
1700	1730	1800	1900	2000	2400	0200	0300	0400	0500
1800	1830	1900	2000	2100	0100	0300	0400	0500	0600
1900	1930	2000	2100	2200	0200	0400	0500	0600	0700
2000	2030	2100	2200	2300	0300	0500	0600	0700	0800
2100	2130	2200	2300	2400	0400	0600	0700	0800	0900
2200	2230	2300	2400	0100	0500	0700	0800	0900	1000
2300	2330	2400	0100	0200	0600	0800	0900	1000	1100

[1]From right to left, standard times in North American zones (Eastern, Central, Mountain, Pacific, Honolulu) show corresponding times *one day earlier* in: Zone A-Guam (same as Australian East Coast); Zone B—Japan, Korea; Zone C—Hong Kong, Taiwan, Philippines, Vietnam, Shanghai-Peking; Zone D—Malaysia, Singapore; Zone E—Indonesia, Thailand, Laos, Cambodia. Burma is one-half hour earlier than Thailand. Thus, when jetting from the Pacific Coast or Honolulu on the first of the month, it's already the second in the Far East.

[3]Plus 1 hour during Daylight Savings. On this chart, 0600 is 6 a.m., 1200 is noon, 1800 is 6 p.m. and 2400 is midnight.

CHINESE COOKING

According to Charles Lamb, 19th-century English essayist, an ancient Chinese manuscript said it began, after the first seven thousand ages when men ate raw meat, when the cottage of Ho-ti, a swineherd, burned down with all the pigs inside cooked to a fragrant, delicious crisp. Whereupon cottages all over the country burned, one after another. Not until two centuries later was the grill invented, thus eliminating the burning of cottages and inaugurating the art of cookery.

Governing factors of Chinese cuisine are "harmony, contrast and accent . . . the selection, blending and harmonizing of textures, color, aroma and taste."[1] To achieve the ideal effect, flavors are blended in such a way that one ingredient is toned down in order to bring out the flavor of another. Textures are mixed to complement each other; colors should be pleasing to the eye.

The principal of contrast, or dynamic balance, is one of the more interesting aspects. Fish and meat are fried together, sweets played against salts, smoothness against crunchiness. The well-balanced meal should have contrasing tastes and textures — a crisp dish followed by a smooth one, a spiced one after a bland. Hence, Chinese cuisine excels in an inexhaustible variety as chefs cleverly vary their combinations of meat, vegetables, seasoning accents and other ingredients. One constant is soya sauce, used in every dish. Other condiments are black bean paste, oyster sauce, wined bean curd and sesame oil.

Chinese are adventurous, open-minded eaters. As long as food is pleasing and not harmful, no reason it should not be attempted or become the main feature of an elaborate recipe. Some food is valued for its nutrition, others for their quasi-medicinal functions. Shark's fin helps to prolong youthfulness, snake dispels rheumatism, bird's nest preserves the skin, whelk (a mollusk) increases vitality — the list is long.

The belief that food is the most satisfying part of good living makes it a favorite topic of conversation; passionate arguments take place over who has the best *won tons* in town. The numerous festivals are no more than occasions for eating particular kinds of food: fried dumplings and rice cakes for the Chinese New Year, for example. Respect paid to one's ancestors means a generous spread in front of the shrine or grave, from golden suckling pigs to elaborately garnished rice cakes; after a suitable display period, the array is put to more practical use.

Probably nowhere in the world is food so prevalent as gifts. *Hand messages,* as these are called, may be fruits, cakes, dried seafood, sausages depending on the season. In imperial days, bestowal of food by the royal family was a mark of high honor.

REGIONAL CUISINES

In China, inhabitants north of the Yellow River had as their staple food wheat and other grains, resulting in a variety of noodles, steamed bread and dumplings. On the other hand, rice was the mainstay of the south. Additionally, cuisines varied from east to west, resulting in six principal, regional styles.

A Chinese saying held that the ideal life was to be born in Soochow (renowned for the beauty of its women), die in Laochow (its sweet-smelling timber made the best coffins) and in between eat in Kwongchow (Canton). To westerners, Cantonese (southern) food is almost synonymous with Chinese cooking, possibly because it's less spicy, more subtle and the least greasy. At its best, it costs more than other styles because of the use of highly concentrated chicken bouillon as the basis of soups, steamed or fried dishes. Besides, the most expensive ingredients are served, resulting in the best shark's fin and turtle soups, the most delicious roast suckling pig, bird's nest (both as soup and dessert), steamed fish and shellfish (abalone and whelk are great delicacies) stir-fried, crispy chicken, steamed chicken (marinated in ginger), sweet-sour pork, fried beef (with oyster sauce) — the list is endless.

A delightful Southern eating habit, prevalent in all Chinese communities in the

[1] *The Fine Art of Chinese Cooking* by Dr. Lee Su Jan.

Far East, is a *dim-sum* breakfast and *yum cha* (drink tea) lunch where "little somethings" — an array of steamed dumplings stuffed with meat and/or seafood, chopped meat patties, fluffy pastries — are served from loaded trays by teahouse waitresses who often call out the names of their dishes. A *dim-sum* meal may be a very social, or business, occasion for an hour or more. Westerners are well advised to take a Chinese friend or guide to "interpret" the dishes which, by the way, are paid for on departure by the number of plates and containers piled on the table.

Peking (or Peiping) food, featuring mild, northern dishes, is also popular, largely because of its famed Roast Duck. Fried shredded pork, fried meat balls, sliced fish with yeast sauce, bean sprouts and shredded pork, sour and hot (pepper) soup are some favorite types. Barbecued meats, particularly mutton, cooked at the table are popular during the winter.

Shanghai (eastern) cooking specializes in highly seasoned sauces; its seafood — famed Yangtze estuary crab (in the Fall), fish, shrimp, prawns, eel and frog legs (called fried cherries) — is outstanding. Other specialties are: chicken with chestnuts, pork with preserved bean curd, Lion Head (large meat balls), braised shark fin, live shrimp with ginger and sauces, steamed crab, mushroom and bamboo shoots, salted vegetable and bamboo shoot soup. All are lightly spiced, always cooked in plenty of sauce.

Hunan (central China) food is rich, either spicy and hot or sweet and sour; its sweet-sour Yellow River carp is world famous. Meat and chicken dishes are popular, steamed dishes a specialty.

Szechwan (western) cuisine is distinguished by its hot, peppery taste. Because of the mountainous terrain and humid climate of that province, most dishes are liberally laced with red hot chili (considered an antidote to dampness). Roast duck with camphor leaves, pork steamed in rice flour, fried prawns and fish with soysauce, ox-tail soup are some of the specialties.

Fukien and Swatow cuisines, more or less the same, feature many steamed and stewed dishes accompanied by thick soya sauce and a sweet plum sauce. Swatow roast goose, dipped in white vinegar, is popular. By the way, the smoky flavored, Yunnan ham is considered the best in China.

Mongolian Barbecue appeals to most westerners. Usually cooked outdoors on a grill, guests select food and sauces from a buffet spread of beef, mutton, pork, venison, peppers, onions, leeks, tomatoes, cabbage, hot sauces, rice wine, ginger water, vinegar, shrimp and sesame oils, then hand their combinations to the chef for barbecuing. Hot sesame cakes and millet gruel are also served.

HOW TO ORDER

A good Chinese dinner is usually designed for eight or more persons seated around a circular table. The number of diners is important in order to contend with the eight to 12 courses that should be included in a well-proportioned dinner. A well-chosen meal usually begins with four cold plates, followed by up to eight main courses, last of which will be a fish that's followed by a final soup, pastries and seasonal fruits. Diners help themselves to each dish as it's placed in the center of the table (on a Lazy Susan).

Tea is usually served at the beginning and end; many banquets included Chinese wines (yellow rice wine, served warm, is popular) and liquors for toasts; beer may also be offered. Two Chinese toast phrases you should know: *gan bei* (bottoms up) and *sui bien* (as you wish).

Obviously, lone couples, even two, won't dine as sumptuously in Chinese restaurants as four or more.

Menu Recommendations For Four Persons

Cantonese — Onion Marinated Chicken; Sweet-Sour Pork; Crab Meat with baked vegetables; Double Boiled Chicken Mushroom Soup; Fried Rice.

Peking — Fried Mutton; Fried Cabbage w/mushroom; Peking Duck eaten three ways (soup included).

Shanghai — Yellow Croaker cooked two ways; Wine Chicken; Bean Curd Pork; Green Cabbage stewed w/mushrooms.

Recommendations For Eight Diners

Cantonese — Paper Wrapped Chicken; Fried Minced Pigeon; Shark's Fin w/Shredded Abalone; Deep Fried Shrimp Balls; Steamed Pomfret; Baked Vegetables w/cream sauce; Mashed Chicken/Cream of Corn Soup; Fried Noodles.

Peking — Fried Sweet Pork; Fried Shrimp w/tomato; Fried Chicken w/hot pepper; Fried Cabbage w/Ham; Duck eaten three ways (with soup).

Shanghai — Steamed Crabs; Bean Curd Pork; Wine Chicken; Yellow Croaker cooked two ways; Fried Shrimp w/pea shoots; Stewed Bean Curd w/mushrooms.

Suggestions For 12 Persons

Cantonese — Cold Meat Combination; Sliced Beef in oyster sauce; Fried Minced Pigeon; Fried Frog Legs w/garlic; Mushrooms in Oyster Sauce; Grilled Spring Pigeon; Fried Duck Webs with oyster sauce; Deep Fried Fish, sweet-sour sauce; Double Boiled Chicken Feet and Mushroom Soup; Pastries and Sweet Soup; Fruits.

Peking — Four Appetizers (fried mutton slices; honey ham; sweet fermented rice w/fish slices; sweet fried cashew nuts); Shark's Fin w/chicken gravy; Fried Chicken Leg; Fried Prawns; Peking Duck; Mushroom and Corn; Vegetable Mix; Sweet-Sour Fish; Candied Banana; Abalone w/asparagus; Silver Fungus Soup.

In Taipei, Hong Kong and Singapore, menus are printed in English as well as Chinese; you can rely, too, on the waiters to make the proper suggestions.

CHOPSTICKS

Although you can always obtain knives and forks, you'll enjoy being part of the scene if you use chopsticks when dining in Chinese and Japanese restaurants. A little practice, after some amusing interludes, makes perfect. Note: chopsticks become very ornery after the third martini.

Chopstick control requires only light finger movement, very little strength or force. Here are the three basic steps:

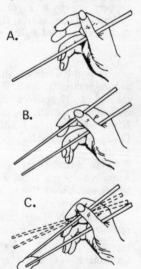

A. The stationary stick is held with slight pressure between the second joint of the thumb and a half-curled fourth finger, just above the tip. The thumb is about two-thirds from the end of the stick.

Always keep the chopstick ends even.

B. The moving or pinching stick is held and positioned between the thumb, fore and middle fingers, as you would hold a pencil. Then the thumb becomes a pivot point while the fore and middle fingers are bent inwards, thus bringing the points of the chopsticks closer together.

C. The chopsticks are held loosely in a relaxed hand, with the sticks slightly apart. When a morsel is desired, an inward bending of the fore and middle fingers will bring the two points together.

With practice, the chopsticks will meet in a positive straight movement.

At formal dinners, don't rest your chopsticks across the bowl; use the plate or a chopstick rest (if there is one).

IT'S POLITE TO MAKE A MESS

A Chinese dinner, formal or informal, is a relaxing, often boisterous, occasion with less ritual than a Western dinner party. In fact, Chinese consider it a greater honor to entertain guests in a restaurant, where facilities and ingredients are best, than in the home.

"Shut our your worries, open your chopsticks" captures the spirit of a Chinese dinner. Menus are often presented to guests, the courses described so poetically as to remain a mystery until their appearance: Shrimp on Golden Sand; White Moon Over Pastures Green; Gem-bestrewn Snow are some of the delightful inventions. Welcoming guests to the table, the host will, with traditional modesty, apologize for the inferior food they're about to eat. This was once written on a menu: "Honorable Guests: We solicit your toleration of this frugal and insipid meal of which you are about to partake with us. Verily we are emboldened by one of our sages who said, 'Let the flower of amity bloom from the heart, not from the stomach.' "

At informal dinners, help yourself with chopsticks or spoon as the Lazy Susan revolves; at formal dinners, your host or hostess serves you. The guest of honor is always placed to the left of the host. It is the height of Chinese good manners to favor honored guests (which includes Westerners) by depositing choice morsels in their bowls. At a banquet, never start to eat any course until a formal toast has been proposed.

With the "nimble brothers" (chopsticks), pick up the food, place it in your small bowl and then start it on its way to your mouth. If desperate, use the spoon to scoop up the food your chopsticks can't handle (slippery things like button mushrooms are hard to handle). Correct way to eat rice is to hold the bowl between thumb and middle finger, bring it up to the lips and then, with chopsticks, shovel the rice into your mouth. It's okay to use your fingers on food like shrimp, spareribs.

The plate found at your place setting is used for discarding bones and shells. Don't be surprised to see Chinese spit them directly onto their plates, even on the tablecloth. To them, dragging something out of mouths with fingers, or using chopsticks to do so, is unsightly and unsanitary. By the way, a soiled tablecloth means everyone is having an enjoyable time, so don't worry about dropping things.

Besides the bowl and plate, you'll have a condiment dish of soy sauce for dipping, a teacup and wine glass at your left. Don't ask your neighbor to pass you anything, though you can comment that you like vinegar in shark's fin soup and hope he gets the hint. Passing things with both hands is considered polite; you should accept them in the same fashion. Further, Chinese believe that enjoyment of food and drink begins at the lips, not on the tongue, so loud sipping of soup and noisy slurping of noodles are commonplace sounds.

Napkins aren't usually served, but you can request one at restaurants. Instead, hot towels in winter and iced ones in summer are brought before and after eating; don't be surprised to see Chinese, after wiping their hands, use the towel on their face, back of neck and, on necessary occasions, to blow their nose into.

You're not expected to eat all your food; in fact, it's considered good etiquette to leave some as a gesture of having had more than enough. Your host and hostess will implore you to eat and probably will serve you regardless of protestations. Yet it's quite correct not to eat any more — only then are they convinced you're surfeited. By the way, eat rice and noodles with restraint (no more than two bowls); otherwise you'll give the impression you didn't like the other courses.

Smoking is permitted thruout the meal, conversation around the table is spirited — but avoid the subject of death or any inauspicious topic, such as divorce at a wedding feast. Toasts of rice wine, beer or tea occur thruout the meal to honor the guests and praise the dishes as they appear. At formal and traditional dinners, the main toast is drunk when the shark's fin soup is served. If you are toasted, you should also drink; if the toasters stand, so do you. Always hold the wine glass or teacup with both hands, placing one around the glass or cup, the other on the bottom.

After several hours eating and drinking, people leave almost immediately after the last course, at which time they praise the food (not a delightful evening). A typical Cantonese expression of thanks is, *"Ho ho sic, ho doh sic"* — "Good food, plentiful food."

And that's what you'll have, what you'll enjoy.

Chang Chun Ching versus Ching Chang Chung
or
WHAT'S A CHINESE NAME ALL ABOUT?
by Kai-Yin Lo[1]

Most Chinese names have three characters: family name comes first, then the individual's name (usually in two characters).

I was once called Lo Kai Yin, Lo being my surname, but the hyphen was introduced (my name is not Kai, as my Western friends like to abbreviate it, but Kai Yin) and Lo transferred to last place after my luggage was lost twice, and airline officials accused "Miss Yin" of confusing the issue.

In traditional Chinese families, members of one generation are often called by the same character, and it is only the last word that's actually a person's own name. My third cousin is Kai-Ching, a second cousin Kai-Ming and my brother Kai-Yiu.

All Chinese names have a meaning. Literally, my name is Lo the Dazzling Revelation. In having my name translated phonetically, I showed less imagination than my friend, Chan Yue Mei, known as Moonbeam Chan. On the other hand, look at poor Hip Fat Chueng, whose Chinese name should translate Harmonious Expansion.

Foreign friends often complain of the difficulty in remembering Chinese names. Why is it that a mere apostrophe is enough to distinguish the Ming Emperor Chia-Ching from the Ch'ing Emperor Chia-ch'ing? And as for the episode when General Chang Chung Ching fought Ching Chang Chung, and Chang won while Ching lost because of the desertion of Chang Ching Chung, I really can't blame my friends who wish all three had died in battle.

The Chinese language lends itself readily and expressively to neat, compressed names which can sound amusing in translation. Like Milky Way Brassiere Co., Fat Fun Company, Gravel Steak House, Hang On Scaffolding Co. Peaceful View Terrace overlooks the slums of Happy Valley in Hong Kong, and Perpetual Repairing Service for Cars and Everlasting Flower Shop are located next to the Hong Kong Funeral Home. Finally, there's the Ever Ready Tailor whose sign assures all that "Ladies can have a fit upstairs."

The other side of the story must be told as well. Chinese versions of Western names can sound equally ridiculous. Despite adulation of Jacqueline Kennedy, few Chinese girls name themselves after her as Jacqueline sounds dangerously close to the Cantonese expression *chic hak lien,* meaning "instant shrink." Yet there are an increasing number of Chinese who've taken on English names: Esquire Ip, Huckleberry Ng, Jason Fung, Rock Ho (after Rock Hudson), Napoleon Ng, Samson Sun, Catalina Choy, Sonata Ch'ing and Alexander Hamilton Young. A legal friend is toying with naming his firstborn Jurisprud Ngan.

Why not?

Excerpted and condensed from Vol. 1, No. 11, of "The Mandarin, Hong Kong."

Actually, there are many festive occasions thruout the Chinese year, like this Tin Hau Festival in Hong Kong's New Territories. Celebrated on the birthday of the Goddess of the Sea and Protector of Fisherfolk (April or May), Joss House Bay is crowded with gaily decorated junks and lighters.

CHINESE NEW YEARS

The Chinese lunar New Year commences on the first day of the first moon of a Chinese Calendar that began 46 centuries ago in 2698 BC — predating our Gregorian Calendar by 4280 years (it replaced the Julian Calendar introduced by Julius Caesar in 46 BC).

The next New Year's begin at zero hour on January 29, 1979, when the year of the Sheep chases out the Horse, and on February 16, 1980, the year of the Monkey. They are followed by the Year of the Chicken, Dog, Pig, Rat, Ox, Tiger, Rabbit, Dragon, Snake, Horse — recurring 12-year cycles.

Preparations for the new year commence weeks ahead to prepare for the heavenward ascent of the Kitchen God. His departure five days before the New Year is symbolized by a drawing of the god being burned after his lips are covered with a sweet substance — to ensure a favorable account, or silence, of the family's doings in the year past. A new drawing of the Kitchen God is placed on the wall. Feasts are lavish, families clad in their best, children are given red envelopes containing money; they may gamble, stay up as late as they wish — all an integral part of a joyous and festive occasion.

Religions of the Far East

BUDDHISM

You'll encounter various forms or creeds thruout the area: Hinyana in Thailand and Burma (plus a modified form in Laos), the more liberal Mayayana in Japan and among Chinese outside the People's Republic, Zen (which originated in China) and its Japanese variation, Bushido, the code of chivalry.

The last and greatest of a succession of historical Buddhas, the Enlightened One who preaches the true doctrine, was Siddhattha Gautama, born some 500 years before Christ. Essentially, the essence of Buddhism is ". . . the wise man conceives disgust for the things of the senses, and being divested of desire he removes from his heart the cause of suffering."

Buddhism owes its development and permanence to its many thousands of monasteries where men may retreat from the materialistic world, teach the principles of Buddha *(Dharma)* by exemplary lives unfettered by desire, unbound by social ties, devoted solely to serving mankind, becoming integral to the Order *(Sangha)*.

The saffron-robed, shaven monks you'll see in the streets live in the monasteries, are not priests, take no vows, follow no strict rules of obedience (though there is discipline), may leave the *Sangha* at any time. Their possessions consist of a robe, razor, water strainer, needle and begging bowl. Many join when older after raising a family, earning a living; in Thailand, living as a monk for weeks, months or even years has become a form of Youth Service in which young men learn the discipline of holy life, the value of meditation.

A notable feature: Buddhism is the only religion which contends that salvation can be attained on earth, not in life after death, though there is the doctrine of transmigration of the essence of man into other bodies — men, beasts or gods.

There is no designated leader of Buddhism, no ecclesiastical council or organizations, yet thru the Order it maintains a powerful hold on millions thru its tradition of spiritual truth.

Temples (see What's A Wat? in Thailand section) contain the Buddha image or images, are sanctuaries of silent worship punctuated, perhaps, by the chanting of monks in low monotones. Worshippers remove their shoes, offer flowers and candles to Buddha, sit on mats and extend their hands towards the image in rituals concerned with the attainment of harmony.

SHINTOISM

The Way of the Gods, a form of Buddhism, is the religion of Japan that is more an expression of national solidarity than a religious feeling since the Japanese are not particularly religious by nature. Shintoism involves the worship of gods, *Kami,* in nature, ancestor worship and the belief in an afterlife. There are little moral teachings.

Shrines are not places of worship but are venerated as the dwelling places of the gods. As such, public rituals and festivals center about the large, important state or city shrines, though the vast majority — 100,000 or so — are small, simple shrines of village or family. But large or small, they are approached thru the simple yet distinctive *Torii* (gateway) of wood, usually painted red, consisting of two uprights joined overhead by double cross-beams, the upper one projecting over the uprights on both sides. Adjacent to some of the larger shrines are monasteries.

There are a number of splinter groups, or sects, some of which have been influenced by Western thinking. One has to do with faith healing, another is monotheistic, others identify with Mt. Fuji as representing the original creation-deity.

CONFUCIANISM AND TAOISM

Like Buddhism, these religions are largely ethical systems. The well-known Chinese conception of the basic duality of the universe, Yang (positive) and Yin (negative), profoundly influenced Taoism.

Confucius, a Westernized form of K'ung Ch'iu, or Master K'ung, was born in the province of Shantung, China, in 551 BC and died 72 years later. His teachings were social rather than religious. He tried to forge some sort of controlling instruments by imposing rigid formalism, rules and regulations for a bureaucratic state. He wanted order in the system so that his way of life could be brought to bear on state problems.

For about 2,000 years, Confucianism was the state religion of China. Today, it exists in the Republic of China in Taiwan, in Chinese enclaves around the globe but has been strongly opposed and all but obliterated in Red China, together with the family clans based on ancestor worship. Yet this Chinese religion always tried to maintain an appropriate and correct conduct under all circumstances, a way of life, *Tao,* neither mystical nor theocentric but practical. According to famed scholar Lin Yutang, the spirit of Chinese humanism is based on the teachings of Confucious, which he describes as ". . . the end of life lies not in life after death, for the idea that we live in order to die . . . is incomprehensible; nor in Nirvana, for that is too metaphysical; nor in the satisfaction of accomplishment, for that is too vainglorious; nor yet in progress for progress sake, for that is meaningless. The true end, the Chinese have decided in a singularly clear manner, lies in the enjoyment of a simple life, especially the family life, and in harmonious social relationships. . . . There is no doubt that the Chinese are in love with life, which is so sad and yet so beautiful, and in which moments of happiness are so precious because they are so transient."

Taoism, founded in the 6th century BC by Lao-tse, was a pacifist faith and, essentially, a philosophy of inaction. It had its own mental discipline, a technique of achieving complete relaxation by Yogi-type exercises, making the mind a blank. Corresponding to the first Christian centuries, Taoist religion became a search for ways of conquering death and disaster and included practices of divination, sorcery and, believe it or not, archery. It utilized demons and ghosts, and its priests became specialists in exorcising evil spirits.

As is happening in so many parts of the globe, orthodoxy is rapidly losing ground, and even in the Chinese world outside of Red China, Confucianism is far from thriving, and Taoism has degenerated into a series of superstitious (and mercenary) practices.

ANCESTOR WORSHIP

Implicit in Chinese and Japanese religions is the veneration of the family, a sense of solidarity that includes the dead as well as the living. For the spirits of one's ancestors require that they be remembered and honored by their descendents. The Chinese, particularly, have the most elaborate burial ceremonies and mourning rites. Family clans may erect imposing shrines (often included as an outstanding sight on city tours) that are both beautiful and costly. Most homes have their humble shrine, usually a small niche in which stand wooden tablets lettered with the names of the departed.

ISLAM

The creed that states "there is no god but Allah, and Mohammed is his prophet" is one that has crossed all national frontiers, is primarily significant in the Far East in Malaysia, Singapore, Indonesia and the southern islands of the Philippines. It has a code of ethics with simple yet well-defined rules, a firm conviction that the Prophet has retained all that was best in previous revelations. It is a religion of a Book, the Koran, which is co-eternal with Allah. The rewards of a sensual paradise are great, the horrors of hell terrifying. Traditions of the Prophet are imitated. Diets are regulated, gambling and alcohol forbidden, almsgiving is essential. Men may have four wives and concubines — but just in case, divorce is easy (for the man).

To the Western eye, Eastern temples are lacking in devotional ceremonies albeit rich in festivities. Not so with mosques. The faithful are called to prayer by the muezzin at sunset, night, dawn, noon and afternoon. Worshippers do not uncover their heads but remove shoes or sandals. Prayers, consisting primarily of words of praise with requests for forgiveness and guidance, are recited facing Mecca along with stipulated prostrations and other postures. Prayers are led by an Iman, a pious and scholarly person. If not in a mosque, a Moslem (or Muslim) spreads his mat, faces east and goes thru his devotions alone or with his family. Once in a lifetime, he's supposed to make a pilgrimage to Mecca.

Of the five basic teachings of Mohammed, the third, concerning the future state of man, is most interesting to the unbeliever. On judgment day, the dead have their bodies restored before passing over a narrow bridge to heaven or hell. The true believer is resurrected with eternal youth and strength, enjoys all the luxuries of a sumptuous heaven, including wine and hordes of lovely *houris*. But hell, a place of eternal fire for unbelievers in God's unity, is divided into seven chambers to receive Christians, Jews, idolaters, hypocrites and others.

Basically, Islam has been adapted to the average man's needs without the excessive demands of Christianity, involving explicit and limited commands that are easily obeyed. It has nothing comparable to the Christian requirement for reformation of character.

HINDUISM (BRAHMANISM)

Like the Chinese, East Indian enclaves exist in many parts of the Orient, particularly in Malaysia and Bali. Wherever they exist, you're sure to find beautiful temples and shrines, some covered with pornographic carvings and drawings, and a rich, entertaining source of colorful festivals.

Hinduism, which originated and thrives in India, has the richest mythology of any religion. Described as a "living example of a great national paganism," it's far too complex to describe here. Suffice to say that it embodies a trinity of gods: Brahma, the creator; Vishnu, the preserver; Shiva, the destroyer — often depicted as one body with three heads.

Temples are the abodes of the gods, not places for congregational worship. Here the gods sleep, awaken, bathe and feed (thru offerings brought to the temples by worshippers).

As a religion, it is largely indifferent to fact or fancy, incorporates both. Customs are ancient; the veneration of cows is almost impossible to overcome. Devout Brahmins spend much time in rituals, baths and scripture reading, have strong feelings of self-denial and caste observance. According to the Karma doctrine, rebirth after death depends on thoughts, words and deeds while living; a man of low caste may be reborn in a higher caste (or vice versa).

After 5,000 years, Brahmanism is remarkably complex yet lacking in unity and exceedingly contradictory. It's said to require both self-mortification and orgies; demands human sacrifices while counting it a sin to crush an insect or eat meat; severely rejects all externals yet has more images, rites and priests than Babylon at its raunchiest.

This ancient bas relief masterpiece in Mahabalipuram, India, features over 400 figures in its 80-foot length, 20-foot height.

Relating Oriental and Occidental Art

To attempt even a beginner's course in Oriental Art is beyond our scope, but thanks to *A History of Far Eastern Art,*[1] here are some guidelines for relating Eastern art, timewise, to well-known periods of Western artistic development.

The arts of China, an obvious leader in Oriental achievements, developed at approximately the same time as in the West. Neolithic cultures of Early Mesopotamia and the Old Egyptian Kingdom dated from about 3500 BC to 2000 BC; in China it began somewhat later, lasted to about 1500 BC when the Bronze Age began; it had already begun in the New Kingdom of Egypt in 2500 BC, lasted until the Iron Age started in 1100 BC. China's Iron Age began around 650 BC (Late Chou Period), approximately at the time early Greek art began to flower. By the end of the Eastern Han Dynasty (220 AD), Roman art had peaked and was in decline. Romanesque art of 1000 AD corresponded to the stylistic Heian Period in Japan, Five Dynasties and Northern Sung Period in China, while Japan's remarkable Kamakura Period and China's Yuan Dynasty occurred when Gothic art was in vogue in the West. China's Ming Dynasty and Indonesia's Majaphit art (its finest) coincided with our Renaissance and Baroque periods; Japan's Momoyama Period, possibly its best, came between 1573 and 1615. The latter part of the Ch'-ing Dynasty coincided with Manet and the Impressionists; the latter, surprisingly, had much in common with Japanse artists of the Meiji (Modern) Period.

Chinese art seems, in the beginning at least, to have influenced Korean artists first, Japan's somewhat later. Nara, Japan, is an outstanding example of Chinese culture influencing another race, even up to the present. Much of the same happened in Korea.

It should be emphasized that Far Eastern art is concerned with multi-media. Not just paintings and sculptures and vases and urns but also shrines and temples, ceramics and lacquerware, ivory and jade. Too, styles and media differed in importance from country to country, from century to century.

In our Foreword, we stressed the importance of advance orientation. Certainly your appreciation of Oriental arts, which contribute so much enjoyment to a trip, plus the pleasure of visiting places you've learned to identify with those arts, will be heightened by reading beforehand "Chinese Painting and Ceramics of the Sung Dynasty" and "Japanese Art of the Kamakura Period."[2] Moreover, we advise visits to museums with Far East collections before you depart. Just think how you'll impress your group with a knowing nod and an airy remark such as, "Ah, Eastern Han, no doubt."

By Sherman E. Lee, Director and Curator of Oriental Art, Cleveland Art Museum. Prentice-Hall, Inc., Englewood Cliffs, N.J. 527 pgs.

[2] Two of the chapter headings, *A History of Far Eastern Art.*

CHINESE DYNASTIES

The earliest exactly known date in Chinese history is 841 BC. According to calculations made by a number of scholars on the basis of probable reign lengths, the date of the founding of the Shang Dynasty has been put between 1766 and 1523 BC, that of the Chou conquest between 1122 and 1018 BC.

SHANG			c. 1550–c. 1030 BC
CHOU	Western Chou	c. 1030–771	c. 1030–256
	Eastern Chou	770–256	
	'Spring and Autumn' period	722–481	
	Warring States period	480–222	
CH'IN			221–207
HAN	Former (Western) Han	202 BC–AD 9	202 BC–AD 220
	Hsin	9–23	
	Later (Eastern) Han	25–221	
THREE KINGDOMS	Shu (Han)	221–263	221–265
	Wei	220–265	
	Wu	222–280	
SOUTHERN (Six Dynasties)	Chin	265–316	265–581
	Eastern Chin	317–420	
	Liu Sung	420–479	
	Southern Ch'i	479–502	
	Liang	502–557	
	Ch'en	557–587	
and NORTHERN DYNASTIES	Northern Wei (T'o-pa)	386–535	
	Eastern Wei (T'o-pa)	534–543	
	Western Wei (T'o-pa)	535–554	
	Northern Ch'i	550–577	
	Northern Chou (Hsien-pi)	557–581	
SUI			581–618
T'ANG			618–906
FIVE DYNASTIES	Later Liang	907–923	907–960
	Later T'ang (Turkic)	923–937	
	Later Chin (Turkic)	937–946	
	Later Han (Turkic)	947–950	
	Later Chou	951–960	
	Liao (Khitan Tartars)	907–1125	
	Hsi-hsia (Tangut Tibetan)	990–1227	
SUNG	Northern Sung	960–1126	960–1279
	Southern Sung	1127–1279	
	Chin (Jurchen Tartars)	1115–1234	
YÜAN (Mongols)			1260–1368
MING			1368–1644
CH'ING (Manchus)			1644–1912

JAPAN

Famous scarlet Torii of Miyajima on the Inland Sea

A balanced, unbiased introduction to Japan has proved more difficult to write than that of other countries, probably because Japan is a complex tourist problem for which there is no simple solution.

After spending a total of 22 days in this country, it was tempting to write, "Skip Japan." It's an expensive, ofttimes tiring experience. Cities, at best, are dull and unimaginative, and some are plain ugly. Even Kyoto is unimpressive when first glimpsed from the train station. But then we remember our first days in Japan, how goggle-eyed we were, how busy we were soaking up all the Oriental atmosphere and watching the incredible vitality and activity and being excited by our first bullet train ride and awed by the splendor and *differentness* of temples and pagodas and . . . oh, let's face it, like it or hate it, there's no way one can pass up Japan — if one can afford it.

To use the old phrase that the country and its people are puzzles wrapped in an enigma is trite enough yet, to most western eyes, true. A Japanese similarly described his nation as a bamboo pole sheathed in steel and wrapped in plastic — the veneer and the strength can be seen, but the real, enduring core of Japan is unseen. That's what fascinated us. Traditional sightseeing, though interesting, was secondary to sizing up the Japanese and their society.

Japan is an industrial oligarchy, an Establishment, with paternalistic trappings. Employees join one of the big trusts for life, as we would a private club, and in return the employer assumes a protective, paternal attitude in providing life security — a welfare state run by industry with government approval. Has industry been so successful because of greater efficiency and know-how? Or is it due to superior motivation of the average worker and his dedicated absorption in doing a better job? Yet the living standards of these people, workers and young executives, have decades to go before they begin to equal those of the average U.S. worker, especially in housing.

It is the wide range of contrasts seen on all sides that intrigue the foreigner. We are led to believe by their economic strides, their immaculate Western dress, their adoption of Western ideas, international floor shows, girlie bars and what not, that the Japanese have become westernized. Not so according to those who've lived with them, studied them. When day is done, businessmen return to their walled-in homes, shed the western veneer, put on a kimono and sit on tatami mats, become what they've always been and, as far as can be foretold, always will be — utterly Japanese in thought, feeling and inclination. So, here are a few of the things you should know about all those dark-suited, attache-cased, earnest young men you see bustling with western determination:

They represent a very unified people living in a closely knit society with the same basic traits and beliefs wherever they live, particularly that of conformity — it's important not to stand out individually, one of the reasons they travel in groups, why you'll rarely find Japanese, no matter how long you've known them, to become personal. Chinese friends make you feel at ease, laugh and slap you on the back in high good humor; Japanese smile politely, laugh with control, nod vigorously and seem to fawn upon you, yet you always sense a gulf, a feeling of withdrawal. Does it mask lack of understanding, indifference or hauteur?

If still available on Japan's newsstands, buy a paperback book, "JAPAN — Images and Realities" by Richard Halloran, an American newspaperman who lived there for years. Invaluable insights into what makes the country and its people tick; will add much to your appreciation of what you see, what goes on around you. The publisher, Charles E. Tuttle Co., advised book was no longer distributed in the U.S.

Marriages are still arranged by families, today usually with the consent of son and daughter[1]. Home life is very important and well knit, consists of three generations, grandparents to grandchildren, when living quarters suffice. Men take foreigners to nightclubs, geisha houses (without wives along), almost never to their homes.

Status is more important than money (witness those ridiculous expense accounts). Homes are small, crowded and, compared to western standards, somewhat primitive — yet the Japanese, despite their sophisticated products, seem not to mind. Nonetheless, the visitor wonders what would be the effect on the people and the country if Japan were to turn its efforts to building better houses and roads instead of concentrating on exports. Of course, since they import all their oil they must be able to pay in exports, so. . . .

People are, for the most part, well and neatly dressed. They seem controlled — not as much laughter and boisterousness as you'd see in western streets, restaurants, bars, probably because it's not considered polite or refined. Women hide their laughs and titters with hand to mouth. A wall of the coffee shop at the Imperial Hotel was usually lined with gossipy, tittering, teen-age waitresses looking as though they were saluting — with hands over mouths.

Wizards at electronics, Japanese TV color is excellent, programs elementary. During winter, hotel room "air-conditioning" only heats, and even with it turned off, one can swelter as windows usually aren't made to open. Many Japanese hotels have large, even huge lobbies and small, even tiny, rooms. In a Kyoto hotel, the washbasin was so low a tall man would have to kneel.

Auto traffic is chaotic; Tokyo's traffic rate is said to be the world's highest. Yet there are probably fewer slums, less povery than in other large cities elsewhere in the world. And Japan has the world's highest literacy rate: 85% finish high school, 55% college or university.

It's still a man's world with much ego and exhibitionism of virility involved. When drunk, they tend to be the happiest men in the world, become very sentimental, forget their inhibitions. But there's a growing number of young, very-with-it women attending universities. Some work for awhile after graduation, a few go into the professions and business, though businesswomen, aside from clerks and waitresses, are relatively few. More go into journalism, some are active in politics, and a few have been elected to the Diet. High school graduates are the saleswomen and secretaries, elementary schools supply the workers for textile mills, electronic plants, etc. But marriage is the name of the game; to become a wife, mother and center of the family is the basic desire. After marriage, many women help their shopkeeper husbands.

HISTORICAL BACKGROUND

Legend states that Japan was born from the union of the god Izanagi and goddess Izanami; the sun goddess was given the power of the heavens, her brother, the lord of storms, ruled the oceans. Because the goddess became frightened of the ocean storms, she hid in a cave, and the world was enveloped in darkness. Because the darkness worried the gods, they hung a necklace and a mirror on a tree near the cave to lure the goddess from her cave, and the world was once again bright. Her brother, banished to the land of darkness, the earth, slew a monster in Japan and found within it a sword which he presented to his sister as a peace offering. The mirror, necklace and sword became the Imperial Regalia of Japan and were presented to the sun goddess's grandson when he descended to earth to rule Japan.

This legend was believed and taught in Japan until the end of the Second World War when the emperor denied his divine status.

Boy's family make sure that the girl comes from a good family, is healthy (so she can bear children), has good education and morals. Many middle-class families hire an investigator to make a careful check; this is considered a smart thing to do, is not at all shameful, will cost about Y25,000 or so. Divorce, though legal, is a disgrace for it signifies failure of the original investigation.

Partial view of Imperial Palace, Tokyo.

For centuries, although Japan isolated herself from the world, she did feel the influence of other cultures in art and religion. In the sixth century, Buddhism came from China, Chinese writing and architecture were adapted to Japanese thinking. From the 12th century, Japan was ruled by divine emperors, and Shoguns (military leaders), who controlled *samurai* warriors, became the most powerful men in Japan and ruled it thru their Shogunates. In the sixteenth century, the Portuguese brought Christianity and guns to the Japanese who, intrigued by the latter (but not the former), soon were producing their own weapons. Because Jesuit missionaries were felt to have had a corrupt influence on the people, a wave of anti-Christian sentiment swept the country, and the Shogun forced all foreign traders to leave the country except the Dutch, who were confined to an island base. However, with 250 years of peace followed by the strong military rule of the Tokugawa Shogunate, uprisings declined, and feudal warfare almost came to an end. There was an artistic revival; woodblock printing became popular during this period.

In the middle of the nineteenth century, Commodore Perry forced trade with Japan and negotiated a treaty opening up two ports for trade. Later, Japan granted the privileges to Britain, France and Russia. Some Japanese welcomed the foreigners, others resented them and felt that Japan showed a weakness in submitting to foreign demands.

In 1867, the dual role of Emperor and Shogun ended, and Japan's most enlightened Emperor, Meiji, came to power. Foreigners were welcomed at the court which had moved from Kyoto to Tokyo (formerly Edo). By the end of the Meiji reign in 1912, Japan had become a world power. With the organization of the army, only regular soldiers were permitted to carry swords; a bloody rebellion was staged at Kagoshima by the samurai who were defeated. But this event did not end militarism in Japan. The conquest of Korea, Manchuria, China and Southeast Asia followed, did not end until August, 1945.

MacArthur gave Japan a constitution, a parliamentary form of government and a set of basic laws designed to prevent the return of militarism, yet allowing the Japanese to preserve their way of life. Today, economic development has earned the average Japanese less than $2,000 a year, a car, color television, refrigerator and radio, a tiny house or apartment in which, as we've seen, he is supposed to be content. Perhaps you may wonder, as we did, after visiting Japan, "Will he be content to continue this way much longer into the future?"

TRIP PLANNING

For all practical purposes, foreign tourism is confined to the west of Japan, the Tokyo — Island of Kyushu Route as defined by the Japan National Tourist Organization. Except for skiing at Sapporo, nothing of importance has been done to develop foreign interest in the north. Which is just as well seeing there are enough problems involved scheduling a cross section of Japan within the time limitations imposed by the usual Far East trip.

Assuming arrival in Tokyo, logical since it provides the shortest flight from North America, plan a departure from Osaka, Fukuoka or Okinawa depending on how far west/southwest you go. This is an important time and money-saving flow compared to the tendency to make sorties out of Tokyo — for the obvious reason that Tokyo has enough hotel rooms to support large-scale group movements, other cities less. Obviously, then, our advice could be nullified by too many groups following it — but until that happens, we're sure your enjoyment of Japan will be increased and costs of seeing it decreased; after all, hotels are less expensive outside Tokyo and return rail or plane fares are eliminated.

Before getting into suggested itineraries, we must remark on the efficiency of tour operators and their escorted tours. They're run on time in first-class equipment and with adequate, persistent guide service; it's a sight to see docile foreigners being herded thru Tokyo Station by the little man with the red flag — like sheep avoiding slaughter. Anyway, the tours are good — but arduous when taken as a continuous series; they can be deadly tiring when combined with constant bus and rail travel each day. Avoid too fast, too far packages that cram a number of places into a few days. Instead of two days, take three — five instead of four. Or go on your own. Any experienced traveler can do so without undue difficulties, enjoy the pleasure of setting his own pace.

The tourist heart of the country lies between Tokyo and Kyoto, the famed Tokai Route, with Kyoto, Nara and Kamakura the centers of ancient imperialism — three of the world's leading cultural cities. If it's feudal Japan you want to see — and that's by far the most intriguing aspect — then these are where you want to be.

Tour operators[1] offer a variety of preplanned tours between Tokyo and Kyoto by train and/or bus. Most, we feel, include too many stops enroute which results in Kyoto, the main destination, receiving an inadequate amount of sightseeing. We opt only for Kamakura enroute — if that. Had we just five days in Japan, we'd spend two in Tokyo, take the bullet train directly to Kyoto for three days, depart from Osaka. Too much time is usually wasted going to Nikko, Hakone, Atami and Mt. Fuji; we took a day trip to the latter, could have spent the time to much better advantage in Kyoto. The famed volcano, symbol of Japan, is best seen from a distance — if, indeed, you see it at all; as good a seat (and chance) as any is to sit on the right-hand side of the bullet train taking you to Kyoto.

With more than five days, there are several interesting tours to be made from Kyoto,[2] others that cruise the Inland Sea, go west and south to Kyushu Island or further westward to Okinawa.

In this section, we follow that westward progression in proper sequence.

A final observation. Of what we've seen of central Japan, only Kurashiki to Hiroshima and other regions bordering the Inland Sea provide glimpses of beauty. On a world scale, this area ranks with, say, our Midwest in minimum grandeur, maximum boredom — and in winter it's particularly drab (Spring and Fall are best).

[1] JNTO furnishes an annual bulletin that lists (by code, duration, price) Japan Holiday Tours (jointly operated by 14 wholesalers), Imperial Coachman Tours (Fujita Travel) and Sunrise Holiday Tours (Japan Travel). These cover all popular destinations in Japan.

[2] Best is a circle trip (described later) to Kurashiki, Okayama, Hiroshima and Miyajima, then departing from Osaka or continuing to Fukuoka; excellent routing if you have time.

Five-story pagoda on lovely Shrine Island

Japan Facts

CLIMATE & CLOTHING

Climate and seasons are similar to the mid-Atlantic states of U.S. In northern Honshu and Hokkaido, winters are cold with lots of snow. Tokyo, on other hand, is virtually snow-free, while Shikoku and southern Kyushu are quite mild all year.

In Tokyo and vicinity, spring temperatures average 46⁰ in March to 64⁰ for May, 70⁰ to 80⁰ during summer (highest was 92.6⁰) which tends to be humid and with tropical storms in June. March thru July and September thru November average 5 days of rain monthly with occasional typhoons in the latter three months. December thru February are coldest (38⁰ to 43⁰ with lowest of 21.7⁰) but little rain.

Lightweight clothing is the rule except in winter when a warm coat, suits and sweaters are needed. A raincoat or all-weather coat is always needed, as are heavy woolen socks if dining Japanese style or staying in Japanese inns.

For night dining, women should wear dresses, men suits or conservative jacket and slacks with tie.

TOURIST INFORMATION

Japan National Tourist Organization dispenses information (but does not book tours) very efficiently, has a wealth of booklets/folders (almost an overkill). Offices in U.S.: 45 Rockefeller Plaza, NY 10020 (757-5640); 333 N. Michigan, Chicago 60601 (332-3975); 1420 Commerce, Dallas 75201; 624 S. Grand, L.A. 90017 (623-1952); 1737 Post, S.F. 94115 (931-0700); 2270 Kalakaua, Honolulu 96815 (923-7631).

In Canada, 165 University, Toronto (366-7140).

Japan Convention Bureau occupies same offices as Tourist Organization.

JNTO Tourist Information Centers are in the Arrival Bldg. of Narita International Airport; near Yurakucho Station in DT Tokyo (phone 502-1461 or 2; open 9 to 5 Mon. thru Sat.); in Kyoto Tower Bldg. in front of Kyoto JNR Station (same hours; phone 371-0480). Last two offices closed at noon. Additionally, JNTO has Teletourist Service — free tape recordings of events being held in and around Tokyo; phone 503-2911 for English tape.

Japan Airlines has an excellent *VIP's Guide — Tokyo* (about $2), these helpful booklets: *Parlez-vous Japanese?* and *Businessman's Language Guide to Japan* (both phoneticized), *Businessman's After Hours Guide to Japan* and *JAL's Guide to Budget Dining in Tokyo*.

RULE OF THE TOWEL

The bathing hour is still a social event in Japan. Though most spas now offer separate facilities for men and women, community bathing remains perfectly natural, evidently on the assumption that nude bodies are more or less the same, no matter to whom they belong.

First rule of etiquette is to hold your towel across the midsection — on the theory that nudes can be seen but not looked at. Holding the towel thusly is natural, not obvious. Scrub yourself and rinse off the soap before entering the steaming pool; there are no showers, just tiny faucets placed close to the floor for filling the rinsing basins.

After a thorough soaking, ring out your towel upon emerging and again place it around you.

OTHER JAPANESE CUSTOMS

1. When beckoning you, Japanese wave their hand with the palm out toward you. When meeting you, they bow their heads several times, do not shake hands.
2. When writing an address, they begin with the name of the country, followed by the city, ward or block, number and then name of the person.
3. When writing their names, they first write the family name and then the given name.
4. Japanese say "Yes" when Westerners would say "No." For instance, "Isn't that your custom?" would be answered, "Yes, it isn't."
5. When carpenters plane a board, they pull the tool downward; when sawing, they pull a saw backward instead of pushing a saw away.
6. At formal banquets, a speech is given *before* dinner.
7. When receiving a gift, the receiver does not open it in front of the giver.
8. When giving change, cashier does the mental substraction and hands you the change without counting it out.

ENTRANCE REQUIREMENTS

Passport, visa (no charge, no photos; valid for multiple entry for four years) issued by Japanese consulate or Embassy to U.S. citizens; Canadians do not need a visa for visit of up to three consecutive months (if not engaging in business); multiple visas valid for 12 months are issued to Canadians at no charge. Air travelers transiting Japan may be granted an excursion permit for up to 72 hours without visa providing onward reservation and ticket are confirmed.

Ship passengers may land in transit for sightseeing up to 15 days providing they leave by same ship, travel a pre-designated route.

Maximum period of stay is 15 days for in transit travelers, 60 days for tourists, performers; a year allowed students, artists and skilled labor, 3 years for businessmen, educators, missionaries, correspondents and technicians. Application for extension must be made to Immigration at least 10 days in advance.

Foreign air travelers need make only an oral Customs Declaration; go to counters illuminated by white lamps (red and green for Japanese). Written declaration required of ship passengers or for unaccompanied baggage. Reasonable amount of personal effects may enter without duty, including 3 bottles liquor, 400 cigarettes, 2 oz. perfume — but don't bring more than 2 watches each (unless you wish to pay duty on the others).

If you intend to drive a car, *have an International Driving Permit* (state license not acceptable).

On leaving Japan, surrender your Alien Registration Certificate and have passport stamped.

TRANSPORTATION TO & FROM NARITA INTERNATIONAL AIRPORT

Efficient bus services are available from Narita to Central Tokyo or to Haneda Airport (now used for domestic flights). Downtown buses take at least 1½ hrs. to City Air Terminal, charge Y1,900 per person; from Terminal to hotels, taxis cost from Y500 to Y1,500 depending on location. Bus schedules are posted at central ticket counter outside customs area.

Keisei Lines run express trains to DT at 30-minute intervals; fare is Y1,050. Shuttle buses run between Arrival Bldg. and Keisei Station; fare is 60 yen.

By taxi to DT via toll roads takes from 70 to 90 minutes, costs approximately Y12,000 including tolls.

DEPARTURES FROM NARITA

Plan on leaving hotels *at least four hours before flight time* — or, preferably, plan itinerary to include departure from Osaka. Check in is at Tokyo City Air Terminal where luggage is checked, an airport service fee of Y1,000 (Y500 for children age 2-11) is collected and reservation made for seat on bus to Narita. Information desks with English-speaking personnel are located at Terminal entrances.

AUTO TRANSPORATION

Taxi meters start at Y330 (for first 2 km), then Y60 for each additional 410 meters — plus a time charge for waiting or slow traffic, all meter totalled — 20% more if taxi responds to a phone call; also between 11 p.m. and 6 a.m. If cruising cab is unoccupied, a red light shows on its left side; usually plentiful except late at night or rainy days when they're choosy and want extra fare (so what's new?). Best bet: get a cab at street stands (DT only), in front of hotels, railway stations.

Chauffeur-driven hire cars (Ha-i-ya) are available thru hotels, travel agencies, by phone and at airport (by hour, trip or day) and are your best private car bet. Driving yourself is advised only for the most experienced — or suicidal.

DOMESTIC AIR TRAVEL

Japan Air Lines (JAL), All Nippon (NH) and Toa Domestic (JD) link Tokyo with the rest of the country. To Osaka, Fukuoka and Okinawa, JL and NH are the main carriers; NH flies to/from Hiroshima. These companies provide airport bus service to/from city ticket offices.

Include as much domestic routing as possible in the international ticket.

SHIP TRAVEL

Numerous ferry routes make travel by car possible thru the four major islands.

Most popular, enjoyable boat trip is from Osaka to Beppu across the Inland Sea with stopovers at Kobe and other ports on the north coast of Shikoku Island. Takes about 14 hours on well-equipped steamers (3,500-5,000 tons) with cabins/private bath. There are numerous other services (hovercraft, hydrofoil, steamer) on the Inland Sea, really a chain of five seas linked by channels stretching for 311 miles.

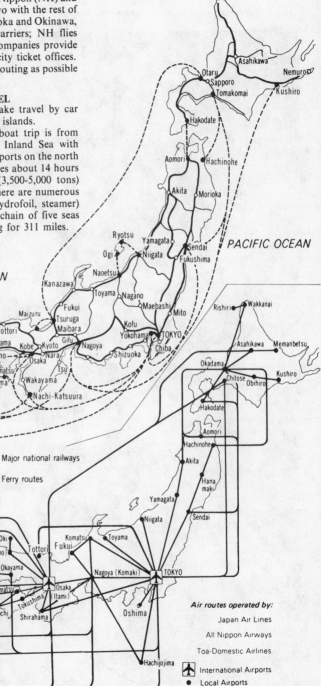

PACIFIC OCEAN

SEA OF JAPAN

Major national railways

Ferry routes

To Okinawa

Air routes operated by:

Japan Air Lines

All Nippon Airways

Toa-Domestic Airlines

✈ International Airports

● Local Airports

51

Green Car of the Hikari Super-Express. Larger-size luggage is stored at the front of the car.

BULLET TRAINS

Usually the means of getting to Kyoto, this is a don't-miss deal. Not that it's ultra deluxe: the four abreast Green Car reserved seats, the best, are comfortable but not plush while cars with five abreast seats are barely comfortable. Nor is it any longer inexpensive. But it's the speed (up to 130 mph) and precision (electronically controlled, the train always stops precisely as marked on station platform) that impresses. And woe to the tardy — trains are programmed for a minute or two for loading and unloading and away they go, with or without you. Yet serious accidents are almost unheard of; strangely enough, we were held up by one (derailed car, nobody hurt) — first time in years.

Most interesting part of the ride is the opportunity to observe fellow passengers at leisure — and the houses (we call their architecture neo-shrine) and apartments in which they live. Noticeable is the lack of color — drab monotones of brown and grey — except for some blue tile roofs. No squalor nor slums — just depressing mediocrity. Meals are served in dining-buffet cars, but watching people buying ice cream, beer, soft drinks, candy and sandwiches from vendors in the aisles is the most fun.

There are two types of super-express service on the Shinkansen (New Trunk Line) between Tokyo and Hakata (Fukuoka City): *Hikari,* which makes the 730-mile run in 6 hours, 56 minutes with only six stops (Nagoya, Kyoto, Osaka, Okayama, Hiroshima and Hakata); *Kodama,* which covers various segments of the run, stops at all stations. Takes 2 hours, 53 min. for the 319-mile run from Tokyo to Kyoto.

On the Hikari Super Express, cars 1 thru 4 have non-reserved seats (Y200 less), cars 5 thru 7 and 10 thru 16 reserved seats. One of those cars are set aside for non-smokers (76% of Japanese men smoke, only 15.5% of the women). Green Cars (with four-leaf clover emblem) are 11 and 12. In case you're wondering about 8 and 9, they're the dining and buffet cars. All cars are numbered as are the station platforms where cars come to rest, making it easy to board.

Super-Express fares (both Hikari and Kodama) include reserved seat charge; Green Car, if desired, is an extra 20%. Fares from Tokyo, including Green Car charge, are: Nagoya, Y9,300; Kyoto, Y12,800; Osaka, Y13,100; Hiroshima, Y18,500; Hakata, Y21,300 — or roughly $49 to $110. Air fares, except to Hakata, are 20% to 28% less.

Since you're allowed stopovers, best way to see southern Japan by train is to continue from Kyoto or Osaka to Okayama (1 hr.), Hiroshima (58 min.) and then Hakata (1:45; 175 miles).

Prospective Bullet Train riders can make reservations thru the U.S. and Canadian sales offices of Japan Air Lines (if they fly JAL to Japan) up to two months in advance. In Japan, best way to make reservations, buy tickets is thru Japan Travel Bureau or Nippon Travel Agency offices in major hotels.

Don't throw away your tickets after boarding; they must be surrendered to platform gatemen at final destination.

You're allowed to board with two large pieces of luggage (don't know how carefully the restriction is policed); additional bags can be checked thru (preferably day in advance) and, for an extra fee, delivered to your hotel.

Strict rule: no tipping on trains. In stations, porters charge Y200 to Y250 per bag; worth it to see them carry bags fore and aft by head straps. Locker available for Y100-Y400.

For night travel, there are A class sleepers with roomettes, lower and upper berths; cost Y11,500, Y9000, Y8000, respectively (plus train fare). B sleepers (3-bunk berths) cost about two-thirds less.

Japanese National Railways' Super-Expresses depart from Tokyo Central Station (Nihonobashi), northern trains from Ueno Station. In addition to JNR, there are private railways operating deluxe limited-express trains to Hakone, Nikko and Nara — with English-speaking female guides. Japan National Tourist Organization's *Train Guide* lists all JNR, private railway schedules, stations from which trains depart.

This little girl is dressed in her New Year's finest, perhaps to call on her grandparents or on January 2, to greet the Emperor. For closing out the old year, celebrating the new covers a span of six weeks in Japan with everything closing down for a week beginning December 28th. On New Year's Eve, people bathe and dress up and, before midnight, fill the temples and shrines to make their first obeisances of the year; at midnight, those up front throw coins into huge nets spread to catch them; this shower continues all night and thru the next day. *Bonen-kai* (year forgetting) parties are held prior to the first, *shennen-kai* (welcoming) parties afterwards. Exhausted from having such a good time, people settle down to work about mid-January in order to recover.

CURRENCY

Yen floats in relation to U.S. dollar. Was as low as Y180 to $1; *check current rate.* Notes come in 100, 500, 1000, 5000 and 10,000 denominations; coins in 1, 5, 10, 50 and 100 yen.

When buying yen, foreign exchange record is attached to your passport. Upon departure, you can repurchase dollars with yen, though $1000 or more requires your yen purchase record.

Airport currency exchanges are open 24 hours daily.

Hotels give full, current exchange rates. In less traveled areas of the country, you might have difficulty cashing U.S. travel checks.

GENERAL INFORMATION

Auto Traffic — Left-hand side of road.

Bank Hours — 9 to 3; 9-12 Sat.

Barber, Beauty Shops — Use those in hotels.

Business Interpreters — Y13,000 half day; Y15,000 per day (8 hrs.).

Cigarettes — A government monopoly. Imports available but expensive. Most popular domestic brands: Hi-lite, Hope, Seven Stars (all filtered) and Peace. Y75-Y220 a pack.

Credit Cards — American Express, Bank-Americard, Diner's, Master Charge are acceptable.

Current — 100v, AC. 50 cycle in East Japan, 60 in West (Kyoto). Hotels usually provide 110 and 220v outlets.

Embassies — Phone 583-7141 for U.S.; 408-2101 Canadian.

Emergencies — Dial 119 for Ambulance; 110 for Police (useful if you're lost).

Film — Fuji and Sakura are major brands; Kodak, Agfa also readily available (have developing labs in Tokyo).

Guides — Available in all languages thru hotels, travel agencies or Japan Guide Assoc. (213-2706 in Tokyo). Standard fees: Y13,000 half day, Y15,000 for 8 hrs. (plus expenses) for 1-4 persons.

Lost & Found — Your hotel can locate articles left in taxis, trains thru their respective L & F departments.

Medical Services — Excellent. Protestant and Catholic hospitals are recommended.

Population — 112 million. Tokyo, world's largest city, has 12 million.

Police Assistance — Many speak some English. Look for them near a Police Box at busy intersections, in railway stations.

Porters — Rates are fixed and posted at airports and stations. No tipping.

Postage — Airmail letters (10 gr.) cost Y120 to U.S., Canada. Air postcards Y80. Aerograms Y100. Buy stamps from hotel front desks.

Press, Radio — Four daily English-language newspapers, plus U.S. Services' Far East Network (FEN; 810 KHz).

Public Phones — Small red phone, Y10 (3 minutes only). On larger red, blue and pink phones, talk as long as you want providing you deposit enough Y10 coins; blue takes up to ten Y10s. Dial anywhere in Japan using area codes. Calls to North America (about $22 for three minutes, less on Sun.) placed by hotel operators.

Shoeshine — Leave shoes outside hotel room door at night; usually no charge.

Telegrams — Letter cablegrams (22-word minimum, including address) to N.A. are cheapest. Domestic telegrams should be sent Urgent if in a hurry (costs twice as much as Ordinary).

TV — Major hotels in Tokyo, Osaka have English-language programs (cable).

Tipping — Rarely necessary (including taxi drivers). Hotels add 10%-20%, bars/restaurants 10%-15% for service. Not done in barber/beauty shops. Hire car guide-driver expects a tip. So does your tour guide, but amount depends on how good he or she is; on extended tour, wait until the end and pool your tip with others in the group.

Toilet Facilities — Outside hotels, best places to look for Western-style toilets are department stores, large office buildings.

Water — Tap water is potable, safe thruout Japan.

NATIONAL HOLIDAYS

Jan. 1 — This is *the* festival of festivals, celebrated with solemnity, though streets are gay with New Year decorations. People, dressed in their best, visit shrines, friends, relatives.

Jan. 15 — Adults' Day, celebrating those who have reached adulthood (20).

Feb. 11 — National Foundation Day.

Mar. 20 or 21 — Vernal Equinox Day, known as Higan. Buddhist temples hold special services, people pray for the souls of the departed for 3-4 days before and after.

April 29 — Emperor's Birthday.

May 3 — Constitution Memorial Day.

May 5 — Children's Day. Families with small boys celebrate with paper (or cloth) carp hoisted over their houses while a set of warrior dolls are displayed inside.

Sept. 15 — Respect for the Aged Day (how nice).

Sept. 23 or 24 — Autumnal Equinox Day.

Oct. 10 — Health-Sports Day.

Nov. 3 — Culture Day — to encourage the nation to cherish the old, create new cultures.

Nov. 23 — Labor Thanksgiving Day.

ANNUAL EVENTS (Partial List)

Jan. 6 — New Year Parade of Firemen; Harumi, Tokyo.

Feb. 1-5 — Snow Festival in Sapporo.

Feb. 3 or 4 — Setsubun, a Bean Throwing Ceremony (to celebrate last day of winter) at shrines, temples thruout Japan.

Feb. 25 — Beginning of Plum Blossom Festival (until Mar. 12) at Yushima Tenjin Shrine (near Yushima station, Chiyoda subway), Tokyo. Tea ceremony, dances on Sat., Sun. from 1 p.m.

March 3 — Hina Matsuri, a Doll Festival (everywhere). Mothers wish their daughters to grow up as beautiful as Hina dolls.

March (2nd Sunday) — Fire Walking Ceremony, Mt. Takoa. Interesting train trip from Tokyo sponsored by Japan Travelers Club, 1 Marunouchi, Tokyo; full day. Includes visit to Mogusa-en to see plum blossoms in bloom.

March 18 — Golden Dragon Dance of Sensoji Temple in downtown Asakusa, Tokyo.

April — Cherry Dances (usually from 1st on); Azuma Odori at Shimbashi, Tokyo; Ashibe Odori at Dotombori, Osaka; Miyako Odori at Gion, Kyoto.

April 8 — Hana Matsuri, floral festival at all Buddhist temples commemorating Buddha's birthday.

April (2nd Sat., Sun.) — Tea Party, Saidaiji Temple, Nara. Humorous.

May 15 — Aoi Matsuri (Hollyhock Festival) at Shimogamo and Kamigamo Shrines, Kyoto. Extremely important, colorful — reproduces an elegant, old court procession.

May 17-18 — One Thousand Warriors' March of Toshogu Shrine, Nikko, dressed in traditional Samurai costumes. Also in mid-May, Sanja Festival of Asakusa Shrine, Tokyo.

June 7 — Night Festival of Torigoe Shrine, Tokyo.

June 14 — Rice Planting Festival, Sumiyoshi Shrine, Osaka.

July 1-17 — Gion Festival, Yasaka Shrine, Kyoto. Largest and gayest of the year; climaxes on 17th with gorgeously decorated floats.

July 25 — Tenjin Festival, Temmangu Shrine, Osaka.

Aug. 13-15 — O-bon (thruout Japan) when dead revisit their former homes. Buddhist ritual to return them to the other world on Aug. 16 is the Daimonji-yaki Bonfire at night on sides of five mountains surrounding the Kyoto basin.

Oct. 11 — Antler Cutting, Deer Park, Nara; outstanding attraction.

Oct. 11-13 — Oeshiki Festival, Hommonji Temple, Tokyo.

Oct. 17 — Autumn Festival, Toshogu Shrine, Nikko.

Oct. 18 — One Thousand Warriors' March, Nikko.

Oct. 22 — Jidai Matsuri, Heian Shrine, Kyoto. last of the big three festivals. Main feature is unique costume procession representing 10 centuries of historical epochs.

November — Month of the Chrysanthemum, crest of the Imperial family. Exhibitions of the flower (dolls often covered with them) begin in mid-October. Best exhibits: Yasukuni Shrine, Hibiya Park, Shinjuku Gyoen, Meiji Shrine in Tokyo. In Kyoto at Maruyama Park, Daikaku-ji Temple, Heian Shrine and Nishi-Hongan-ji Temple. Momiji Festival is also celebrated at this time in Kyoto as the hillsides around scenic Arashiyama sector blaze with tinted maple leafs. In Tokyo particularly in front of Otori Shrine, Asakusa, tens of thousands celebrate Tori-no-Ichi on Tori (zodiak bird) days with bamboo rakes decorated with dolls, other ornaments (sold in markets).

Nov. 15 — Shichi-go-san (literally 7-5-3) is shrine visiting day for girls 3 and 7, boys 5; parents pray for their healthy growth. Mothers and daughters often dress in colorful kimonos; children eat long red/white candy (chitose-ame). In Tokyo, Meiji and Hie Shrines are most popular (great for photo snapping).

Nov. 3 — Daimyo Procession, Hakone; feudal lords parade in Edo period (1615-1867) costumes from Soun-ji Temple at 10 a.m.

Dec. 14 — Gishi Sai, Sengakuji Temple, Tokyo. Ceremonial rite for 47 faithful Samurai warriors buried here after honorable Hara-kiri deaths.

Dec. 17 — On Matsuri (The Festival) at Kasuga Shrine, Nara, is a gala, old-time costume procession.

Dec. 17-18 — Toshi-no-ichi (Year End Market) held in street leading to Torigoe Shrine in Asakusa, Tokyo.

JNTO's folder, *Annual Events In Japan*, lists everything, everywhere.

SHOPPING TIPS

As a foreigner, you're entitled to shop in Tax Free stores and eliminate excise taxes on Japanese manufactured merchandise. Stores must enter your purchases in a form "Record of Purchase of Commodities Tax Exempt for Export" which they furnish. Keep all such Records for presentation when leaving the country.

When purchasing electric/electronic appliances, be sure you receive *export models* to avoid electrical problems back home.

Tax Free items include: pearls; jewelry of precious metals, precious/semi-precious stones; furs; cameras, projectors and accessories; radios, transistorized TV; record players, tape recorders, etc.; watches, clocks; articles of tortoise shell, coral, amber, ivory, cloisonne, autos.

In Tokyo, Akihabara Bargain Street stores offer discount prices on electric/electronic products; reached by Yananote-elevated, Akihabara Station (2nd stop from Tokyo Station). Another is Nishi-Ginza Electric Center between Imperial Hotel and Ginza Subway Station.

If looking for local products, you don't have to run all over Japan to find them. 29 districts display/sell such products in Tokyo showrooms located in the Kokusai Kanka Kaikan Bldg. (in front of east entrance of Tokyo Central Station); 13 more are in the station building partly occupied by Daimaru department store.

Pearls, as is well known, are outstanding buys, should be judged by weight, size, luster and color. By using the tongue test, you'll find that real ones are not as smooth as the synthetic. But, unless you're an expert, buy only from the large, reputable dealers (upon whom you can rely without question). After purchasing pearls, keep them clean by dipping them frequently in mild water and soap suds; have them restrung as soon as knots become soiled.

It's interesting to know that when experiments for seeding oysters began, *powdered* pearls were most popular in China where they were sold to make women beautiful, men virile. Thus, it was for their medicinal properties, not decorative, that the search for cultured pearls was launched.

Oysters are harvested every three years. Women, clad in white (once they were naked), dive for only 10 days during the summer; balance of year, when pearl diving is prohibited, these women earn their living by diving for scallops, fish, etc.

You can buy Japanese dolls at any price — up to Y70,000 ($370) or more. Most famous, beautiful and eye-popping are the Kyoningyo of Kyoto and Hakata of Fukuoka; both are less expensive in their home towns than in Tokyo. Wooden Kokeshi dolls with painted features are far less expensive but still attractive.

If you want to be the envy of your friends, return with a fine, silk kimona (but inexpensive ones aren't worth packing) — they are utterly gorgeous. Old ones, with family crests, are the finest. But don't wear your purchase on the streets — very few Japanese women, except some of the older ones, do except for weddings and festive occasions. If you have the chance, see one of the department store exhibits featuring the dressing of a bride — it's sheer art. Their kimono departments, by the way, are the ones to shop.

Kimonos are classified, roughly, in these categories: *Homongi,* for formal occasions; *Furisode* with up to three-foot sleeves; *Edozuma* or *Tomesode* for married women; *Uchikake,* especially gorgeous, for weddings. An ordinary *Homongi* or *Furisode* of silk will cost at least $210 — and there is no upper limit for the finest kimonos. However, *Happi,* a kimono-type slipover, is inexpensive and very popular with visitors.

Japanese chinaware can be exquisite. Most famed are *Arita-yaki* and *Imari-yaki* of northern Kyushu, *Kutani-yaki* of Ishikawa Prefecture, the products of Kyoto and Seto, latter near Nagoya.

Shinto wedding with traditional bridal kimonos

Red and black lacquerware is also outstanding. But learn how to care for your purchase. Dry heat and air are lacquer's enemies. Never soak in water — moisture under the lacquer coating will cause it to crack.

You'll find many more things that attract you. Good-looking *shippo* (cloissone) accessories are generally reasonable. So are the handsome, traditional (*Ukiyoe;* 1603-1867) multicolored woodblock prints — reproductions, of course, of original Ukiyoe artists: Utamaro (glamorous courtesans), Sharaku (Kabuki actors), Housai (scenes of Mt. Fuji), Hiroshige; latter meticulously illustrated 53 scenes along the Tokaido, road linking Edo (Tokyo) and Kyoto.

Beautiful, handpainted fans of silk, cloth or paper can prove to be collector's items. Or perhaps you need a stone lantern for the garden?

Of course, silks of all types are available everywhere, some mediocre but many gorgeous. If you'd like something very unusual, there's *amagata,* a rich, two-sided weave — like black satin on one, royal blue on the other — designed for kimono-covering rainwear.

Shops and stores are generally open Saturdays, Sundays and holidays from about 10 a.m. to 8 or 9 p.m. Department stores usually close at 6 p.m. and one day a week (Mon., Tues., Wed. or Thurs.). Stores are one-price with merchandise clearly marked. It's bad taste to even consider bargaining.

The area surrounding the city of Nagoya is famous for porcelain, cloisonne, lacquerware and fans. The International Shopping Center, 6th floor of Meitetsu Department Store, Nagoya, carries all of the best.

Don't miss the huge underground shopping plazas in Tokyo (Tokyo Central Station), Nagoya, Kobe and, above all, Osaka (near Umeda Station).

BUSINESS & INDUSTRY INFORMATION

Obtainable by contacting any of the following in Tokyo: Japan External Trade Organization (JETRO); phone 582-5511. Chamber of Commerce & Industry; 283-7617. Tokyo Trade Center, World Trade Center Annex Bldg.; 435-5394.

There's the Display Hall of Japan General Merchandise Promotion Center at the International Trade Center, Harumi; 531-8331.

If you wish to see the manufacturing of any of Japan's representative products, contact Tourist Section, Tokyo Metropolitan Government, 8th floor of Tokyo Kotsu Kaikan Bldg. (near Yurakucho Station), Tokyo (phone 212-2403). No charge for plant inspection.

In Osaka, the following charge for plant inspections: Osaka Tourist Association, Osaka JNR Station (345-2189); Trade & Tourist Section, Osaka City Gov't (231-6647).

TOKYO... Head and Heart of Japan[1]

Even by Japanese accounts, it is a city of superlatives, not many laudatory. It's a cosmopolitan city — the biggest, most populous and chaotic, busiest, ugliest, noisiest, gayest and, possibly, the most fascinating on earth. And the most expensive — ofttimes shockingly so. It's a daytime of interesting sights, a nighttime of both conventional and illicit pleasures. And more than any place else in the country, it heightens the illusion that Japan is Westernized. Yet for every Western adoption there remains a corresponding traditional legacy — in plain view and in daily use.

From the days of the shoguns, it's been an incomprehensible jumble. Even rebuilding after the War was done in helter-skelter fashion; one wag called it "Plan for the Unplanned." There are few street names, no systematic house and building numbers; people locate them by area names and major cross streets. In residential areas, houses are numbered by the order in which they were built. No. 1 may be in one block, No. 2 a hundred yards away — or many as 10 houses built at the same time on the same plot will have the same number.[2] Yet the intent observer can find rare moments of beauty in the myriad small streets.

Most Tokyo neighborhoods are mixtures of rich and poor, middle class and laborers. Zoning laws are apparently nil, or unobserved if adopted. Very few neighborhoods are distinctive. Most are a melange: houses, garages, machine shop, school, doctor's office, the man who sells bamboo poles, coffee and food shops.

Every Tokyo *machi* (town) is self-contained. Most shopping is done in specialized stores: rice from the rice man, milk from the milkman, meat from the butcher, perhaps chicken from another, fish from the fish shop. From habit, older housewives shop before each meal. Younger women, who have refrigerators, may shop every other day. Vendors of special items, like noodles and bean curds, sell from door to door. Each has a distinctive trade cry: a horn, the clack of heavy scissors, the rhythmic beat of sticks, even a transistorized bullhorn (the sweet potato men).

These *machi* retain some of the feeling of small towns in rural areas; each has its own shrines and festivals. You'd do well to get directions to such from your hotel porter, spend time enjoying a Tokyo that lies well beyond the Ginza.

However, even if you don't, you'll probably enjoy all the unfamiliar sights and people, the omnipresent electronic time signs in the streets and on TV — time must be the tyrant of the Japanese, possibly because 8,000,000 of them commute to and from the city each day. And if France is a nation of shopkeepers, Japan is the supernation of same; we've never seen so many.

---

[1] In actuality a cluster of small cities and towns within a bigger city of some 13,000,000 persons governed as a special political entity, a superprefecture. Greater Metropolitan Tokyo (which takes in Yokahama, Kawasaki and other outlying cities, towns) probably embraces 20,000,000 — about one-fifth of Japan's total population.

[2] More specifically, street addresses are determined by this system: *ku* (ward), *machi* within the *ku, cho* (village) within the *machi, chome* (block, or even several square blocks) and *banchi* (number).

The ritual and drama of Sumo wrestling

GETTING TO KNOW YOU, TOKYO

Best way is to take the combination City Tour (morning and afternoon) as you save money, and they're both necessary. Then if you have the time, you can do some of things we suggest in the pages that follow.

Sightseeing bus tours[1] leave daily from all major hotels, are precisely run, cover everything the average tourist wants to see. Of course, sightseeing by private car with guide (expensive) can also be done; best to have two couples share expense.

After the familiarization program, you'll want to walk, shop and, if you have plenty of joie de vivre, ride the subway and elevated trains which we'll tell you how to do.

Where you walk and shop will be determined largely by where your hotel is, but certainly at least once you'll want to rubberneck around Central Tokyo between the Imperial Palace and Ginza, the famed shopping and entertainment center. Start with the 250-acre grounds of the Palace (you can't miss it — it's the only large spot of beauty here) and walk east from Imperial Palace Plaza[2] thru the financial district of Marunouchi (13 acres of hi-rises), into Tokyo Station (handles 1½ million passengers daily) with its five underground levels, emerging in the Nihombashi district[3] to turn south into the more crowded Ginza.[4] Turning right (west) at Harumi-Dori or Miyuki-Dori brings you to Hibiya Park, another lovely oasis in a desert of grey concrete across from the Imperial Hotel. This is a fun stroll at any time, particularly on Sundays and holidays (see Always On Sunday); allow a half day or more.

North of Hibiya Park, in Kasumigaseki, are the governmental offices and ministries. Near the Diet is revered Hiye Shrine. South is Shiba Park and Tokyo Tower, Zojoji Temple. West of here is Azabu, Tokyo's green belt, with posh residences, embassies and hi-rise apartments (mostly for foreigners at $2,000 per month and up). Directly north is Roppongi, entertainment center for the young in-crowd.

North of Kasumigaseki is the Akasaka district with some of the major hotels, the Versaille-type Akasaka Detached Palace. This, too, is extremely walkable territory, for there are many attractive side streets and lanes, lots of shopping-dining-drinking action. Way west, by Freeway No. 4, is the Meiji Shrine, a major showpiece. It was dedicated to Emperor Meiji (1852-1912) and his Empress, occupies a huge, landscaped expanse.

Nearby, to the northeast, is Shinjuku district, a youth city, a fun place for university students, more typically New Japan than the Ginza. Here, too, is a large, governmental development (in which the Keio Plaza Hotel, reputedly the world's tallest, is located) that will become the center of a second Tokyo city. The Japanese-style part of the 144-acre Shinjuku Gyoen Garden is one of Japan's most beautiful.

On the other side of downtown, northeast of Nihombashi, are the districts of

As we've said, all tour operators do an excellent job, but we must particularly commend Japan Travel Bureau, operators of Sunrise Tours, for their efficiency. Whether taking care of Americans at the Imperial Hotel or Japanese at the Beverly Hilton, they are invaluable for every type of tour arrangements and domestic transportation (including Tokyo train tickets). Offices in major hotels and stations; also in U.S. and Canada.

Best vantage point for viewing the Palace, expansive grounds, stone embankments and moats. Higashi-Gyoen (East) Garden, opposite Palace Hotel, is open to the public daily (except M, F) from 9:30 a.m. to 3 p.m. It covers about one-third of the compound, was the site of Edo Castle (1457). To visit other parts, phone 213-1111, Ext. 485, several days in advance for a permit. Palace itself is open to the public only on January 2 and April 29 (Emperor's birthday). Overlooking the Palace (to the west) is the Diet (Parliament).

[3] Quality shopping and restaurant area, the original geographic center of the country.

[4] About half a square mile split by eight east-west streets (plus a myriad of small lanes) and in half by wide Chuo-Dori (Ginza-Dori). See Entertainment and Shopping for further details.

Kanda (four universities) and Akihabara, the noisy wholesale and discount store shopping center. Further north is Ueno Park and, to the east, Asakusa. Latter is the site of Asakusa Kannon Temple, one of the major tourist attractions that's quite startling to first-time visitors. Nakamise, the street leading to it, is lined with shops, stalls and counters selling everything. Kokugikan, the sumo stadium with its Sumo Museum, and the 4,000-seat Kokusai theater are nearby.

We spent interesting hours in Ueno Park. If time permits, take the Green Line from Yurakucho station (track 1 or 2), return on tracks 3 or 4 (see Elevated Train map). At the park entrance is the Museum of Western Art. Then comes the Science Museum, straight ahead the National Museum, to the left the Tokyo Metropolitan Fine Art Gallery (Japanese old masters, modern artists) and in between some ponds and fountains. We found the Eastern Art wing (the modern one to the right) of the National Museum fascinating: marvelous pottery, figurines dating to the 2nd and 3rd centuries; Buddhas, wall plaques, glazed bowls in variegated colors, ancient relics are but a few of the treasures. To the west is the fun area — the Zoo — and Toshogu Shrine.

Another of the joys of coming here is the opportunity to see Japanese of all ages enjoying themselves, the Zoo, the lovely gardens, the tall bamboo trees. In Japan they say, "My, you're growing like a bamboo" because it takes only six months for bamboo to grow from seedling to full height.

OTHER MUSEUMS OF INTEREST
(**Open 10 to 4-5 p.m. Usually closed Mon.**)

Newest is the Maritime Museum on land reclaimed from Tokyo Bay, a six-story structure shaped like a passenger liner which features an 85-ft. mast for spectacular views of the Bay. A marine park with sea bird sanctuary and an amphitheater adjoins. From Takeshiba, there's passenger boat service every 20 minutes to the Museum; costs about $1 for the 15-minute ride. Bus service eventually will line all main points on this reclaimed waterfront.

National Museum of Modern Art (contemporary Japanese) and Folkcraft

Yomeimon Gate of Toshogu Shrine in Nikko

Museum (excellent displays, particularly pottery and wood) are in Kitanomaru Park directly north of the Imperial Palace (Takabashi subway station). Bridgestone Gallery, near Tokyo Station, shows Japanese and foreign paintings. For splendid Chinese bronzes, ceramics, etc., visit Nezu Art Museum in Aoyama; truly exquisite scrolls can be seen but only by appointment. Okura Museum of Antiques, Hotel Okura, also has exciting collections.

There are museums of Science, Transportation, Electric Science and Communications.

JNTO's excellent, detailed *Tourist Map of Tokyo* will guide you safely anywhere you wish to go. Get one before arrival in Tokyo, study in conjunction with our recommendations, and you'll see twice as much in half the usual time.

CITY TOURS

Morning — Tokyo Tower, Imperial Outer Garden, Marunouchi District, Ueno Park, Asakusa Kannon Temple, Nihombashi and Ginza.

Afternoon — Imperial Palace Plaza, Pearl Gallery, Asakusa, Meiji Park and Shrine, Olympic Gym, Shibuya Park, Visit Japanese Family.

Sunrise Tours have variations of above with tea ceremony in a.m. tour, Bridal Kimono Show or Japanese Dance Performance in p.m. Of others by JTB, we'd recommend Art Around Town, Village Life and Crafts (both with lunch).

There are several combinations of Night Tours.

DAY EXCURSIONS

No. 1 in our opinion is to Nikko; in fact, it's the only one we recommend since the other destinations seen on one-day excursions from Tokyo are covered enroute to Kyoto. However, for those who have hearts set on seeing the Mountain of Eternal Life fairly close up, Fuji (12,365 ft.) and Hakone are paired in a day trip. By the way, July is the best month for climbing. JNTO has all the climbing information.

EXCURSION TO NIKKO

Nikko, about two hours north of Tokyo by train, is internationally famed for its natural beauty (a wilderness park of lakes and volcanic mountains), resorts and particularly for fabulous temple architecture. If this combination is appealing and you have the time, by all means visit here on a day or overnight trip.

Nikko City's Toshogu Shrine is a multi-colored architectural gem with wooden columns and walls exquisitely lacquered, gilded and painted, a sharp contrast to most shrines which are unpainted. There are over a dozen buildings, including the imposing Yomeimon Torii, which form an exquisite blend of man-made and natural beauty. This shrine is dedicated to Tokugawa-Ieyasu, founder of the Tokugawa Shogunate (last 300 years of the feudal period). 13,000 stately Japanese cedars line the main approaches for 23 miles. It's along this road from nearby Futarasan Shrine that 1,200 men in Samurai warrior costumes parade on May 18 and October 17 each year.

YOKOHAMA

Southwest of Tokyo (½ hr. by elevated train) on Tokyo Bay is Yokohama (pop. over 2½ million), an important and bustling trading port, a gateway to Japan with an interesting mixture of many cultures.

The business center is Kannai where most of the shipping and trading offfices are located. On Isezaki-cho, shops abound as they do in the Motomachi Shopping Center. The Silk Center is located near the south pier at Yokohama Port and boasts an outstanding silk products museum.

For dining, don't miss Chinatown with over 80 excellent restaurants — a mecca for residents from surrounding areas as well as visitors.

Other points of interest: Minato no Mieru Oka Park for its outstanding, panoramic view of the Port; Sankeien Garden with historic 16th-century buildings set amidst quiet, Japanese gardens; Marine Tower, said to be world's tallest lighthouse.

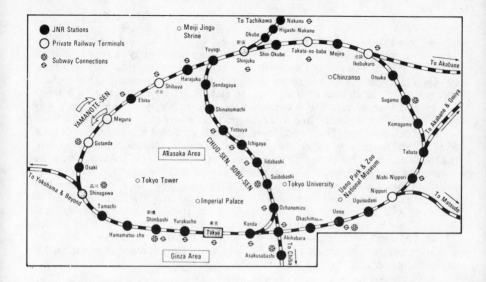

ELEVATED (Kokuden) TRAINS

For tourists, Yananote-sen Loop Line (green coaches) is a terrific way to see most of Tokyo, operating both clockwise and counter-clockwise. Stations well marked with English names, but, unlike Subway, tickets difficult to purchase unless you read Japanese. Again the advise is: buy a minimum Y50 ticket, pay later (if you and the guard understand each other). We overcame in a different way — purchased our tickets from English speaking personnel at Japan Travel Bureau's office in the Kotani Bldg. near Yuracucho Station (see map); for a 12% service charge (and at these prices who cares?), you're told what track to go to, how many stops to where you you want to go, etc. *Be sure to buy return ticket at same time* if getting off enroute. Full circle trip takes about an hour.

If you want to cut across town to Shinjuku, take the orange (Chuo-sen) or yellow (Sobu-sen) coach lines. Ship passengers can use the Kokuden to/from Yokohama.

Other electric trains feed suburban areas, towns from stations along the Yamanote-sen loop — including Hakone, Nikko — but be sure to have written directions (English and Japanese) before you try them.

SUBWAY (Chi-ka-teh-tsu)

The eight lines that criss-cross Tokyo provide quickest, cheapest way to get around though, of course, you see nothing as you go. Operate from 5 a.m. to midnight; beware of a.m. and p.m. rush hours. At each station, routes are mapped with English names and cost (Y80 minimum). Most stations have automatic ticket vending machines; deposit coins (either exact amount or more), push correct denomination lever (if in doubt, deposit Y80 and pay difference when you get off) to receive ticket and change. Show ticket to guard on entry to train platform, surrender it upon completion of trip.

BUSES

Because of route confusion, local buses (Y80) are not advised. But Inter-City buses are something else — cheapest way to Nagoya, Kyoto, Osaka and Kobe is via Japanese National Railways' Expressway Bus which leave Tokyo Station at night, arrive in a.m. Buses are air-conditioned, have reserved and reclining seats. Reservations (up to 3 weeks in advance) made by dialing 215-0489; ticket office is next to Shinkan-sen Green Window on Yaesu side of Tokyo Station.

As in all cosmopolitan centers, you can eat your way around the world, from Texas-style steak houses (*Angus Ranch* in the Ginza has cowboys/cowgirls to serve you, a couple of sheriffs to ride herd) to Russian samovars. Rooftop restaurants (World Trade Center, Kasumigaseki Building, Hotel Keio Plaza and other hi-rises) and revolving restaurants abound; the one atop Hotel Pacific is called a Moving Museum of Transportation as it overlooks the port, railway yards and Haneda Airport. A Bulgarian restaurant and pub occupies three floors and a basement of a Shinjuku district building. Then, too, there are such cordon bleu names as Colonel Sanders, McDonald's, Wimpy's, Burger Chef and Dunkin' Donuts. With exception of the last five, they all have one thing in common: expensive menus. Tokyo can be more expensive than New York. We know people who paid $3 for a glass of fresh orange juice, $14 for a room service breakfast (not elaborate) for two. That doesn't mean you can't get reasonably priced continental/American breakfasts in hotel coffee shops — you can. And a dinner doesn't have to cost a fortune. Approved International Restaurants[1] (by Dept. of Tourism) serve, along with a la carte menus, what's called "Tourist Menus" — table d'hote Japanese, Chinese and Western meals — for around $10, including tax and service charges.[2] A la carte, it'll cost quite a bit more. Service always polite, efficient.[3]

Since Tokyo is not an easy town in which to find places, particularly at night, restaurant hopping is usually, among tourists, restricted. Which is really not too much of a restriction as larger hotels have a number of restaurants: Western, Chinese and, above all, Japanese; if uninitiated in this style, by all means become initiated in a Sukiyaki, Sushi, Tempura or Teppan-yaki hotel restaurant before trying others. Here are the basics for:

DINING JAPANESE STYLE

Chawanmushi — Custard of egg and fish, or meat, steamed in a small bowl.

Dango — Steamed dumplings, a popular snack, of ground rice or other grains with soy sauce, sweet bean paste, etc.

Kabayaki — Eel cut to small lengths, skewered and steamed, then broiled over charcoal with repeated dippings into special sauce. *Unagi* is similar.

Kaiseki — Originally served before a tea ceremony, today considered the most as a traditional cuisine. Features seasoned vegetables only served in a variety of unusual bowls, plates (some like leaves, fans), arrangements. Every dish designed to highlight *sake* flavor.

Kamameshi — Rice cooked with shrimp, crab, salmon, chicken or mushrooms in miniature *kama* (traditional rice cooker), served steaming hot in same pot.

Mizutaki — Chicken, beef or pork slices, vegetables and soup stock (from seaweed, dried bonito) boiled in earthenware pot with water. Eaten by dipping in special sauce. *Shabu-shabu* and *shippoku* are similar styles.

Noodles — Very popular. *Soba* is made from buckwheat, *udon* from wheat flour. Both eaten from soup-filled bowls or by dipping into soup. Cool noodles are eaten in summer. Quite proper to slurp noodles and soup — Japanese think you odd if you don't.

Oden — Food that appears in street stalls: fish cakes, vegetables, hard-boiled eggs, octopus and anything else that can be boiled.

Sashimi — Raw fish (also meat, chicken) with rice; goodies that go on top vary from fried egg to sea urchin.

Sukiyaki (*ski-yah-key* is way to say it) — Thinly sliced beef (or pork, chicken) cooked with vegetables in special sauce laced with *sake*. Served very hot. Diner should place a portion in a small bowl containing a whipped, raw egg — adds flavor, cools it off. Variations in cooking method: *butter-yaki, oil-yaki.*

Sushi — Methods of preparing rice. Most common is *nigirizushi*, small rectangular balls of rice seasoned with vinegar and topped with caviar or a thin slice of fish, shrimp, etc. Dip into horseradish and soy sauce, eat by hand with a bit of pickled ginger. Cucumber, pickled radish, sweet egg omelet are also used as toppers. Other types include *nori-maki (wrapped in seaweed)*

[1] JNTO's "Restaurants In Japan" lists them for all cities.

[2] Restaurants must add 10% eating/drinking tax to all bills exceeding Y2000 per person. 10% to 15% service charge also added.

[3] And fast. In a hotel coffee shop, hold onto your plate, or it might be whisked away before you're finished.

*THREE
JAPANESE
DINING STYLES:*

Sushi

Sukiyaki

Tempura

and oshi (sandwich form). Westernized sushis use ham, cheese, etc.

Tempura — Shellfish or fish, mushrooms and vegetables deep-fried and served piping hot with special sauce. Should be eaten only in a top tempura restaurant.

Teppan-yaki — Prime cuts of beef grilled to order on open grill. Variation is *Ishi-yaki* — beef, vegetables cooked on heated stones.

Yakitori — Small pieces of marinated chicken skewer-barbecued, often with vegetables.

Yose-nabe — Japanese-style chowder.

A final word about Japanese food — fruits. Japan has some of the world's finest. In season there are giant strawberries, canteloupe, apples, peaches, tangerines. Or more exotic kinds: Nijusseiki pears, loquats, pomegranates, persimmons and shaddocks (grapefruit-like).

TOKYO RESTAURANTS

For gourmands and those who love the impeccable, the sine qua non is a traditional Japanese restaurant. For this you'll need the guidance of an erudite Japanese if you are to obtain the necessary attention to not only the preparation of food but also the manner of presentation — an appeal to both the sense of taste and sight. Dishes should be carefully selected to set off the food to greatest advantage; such a display of exquisite porcelains, earthenware and lacquerware is truly an artistic achievement and delight. With a price tag to match.

When the weather is mild, you'll enjoy the spacious, serene garden settings of *Chinzanso, Hannyaen* and *Happoen.* Former is a favorite of tour groups, particularly for lunch; noted for Genghis Khan (Mongolian) barbecue.

Moderately priced restaurants are found in department stores (always a good bet), stations (Tokyo Station's underground center has 77 eateries open from 9 a.m. to 9 p.m.), large office buildings. Highly regarded are the places in the Yuraku Food Center at Yurakucho Station. Restaurants display plastic models of what they serve (and what they cost); efficient (tell cashier the number of plate you wish, pay for it, receive a chit which you give to waitress) but unappetizing. Many are seafood-oriented. Price range: Y700-Y1400 for lunch; Y1500 to Y2500 for dinner. No service charge but 10% tax is applicable on checks of Y2000 or more.

The best sushi, we've heard, is served at *Tsujitome,* basement of the Nikkei Bldg., Ginza, from noon to 8 p.m. For tempura, *Ten-ichi,* Sony Bldg., Ginza (11 a.m.-9 p.m.), and *Inagiku,* 2-6 Kayabacho, Chuo-ku, are recommended. In most districts, sushi shops are open until late at night; some restaurants keep sushi plates coming at you on a miniature train track — pay for the number of plates you wind up with.

Of course, there's always Big Mac. One of the liveliest spots in town on weekday afternoons is in front of Mitsukoshi Department Store, Ginza Dori, where hordes of kids gobble hamburgers and milk shakes.

Coffee shops *(Kissateh)* that provide music, not stools, are everywhere. For the price of a cup (Y280-Y300) of coffee or tea, plus toast or sandwich if desired, one can sit at a table for hours listening to taped music — trick is to choose the coffee shop that plays type of music you want; high-class places with live music may charge Y500 or more per cup.

JAPANESE HOME VISITS

Phone Tourist Information Center (502-1461) in Tokyo at least a day in advance to visit a Japanese family. No charge except for cost of getting there — and it's polite to bring a gift. When entering a typical (non-Westernized) home, take off your shoes and don slippers; when entering a *tatami* (mat covered) room, take off the slippers. Squatting Japanese style (formal) is difficult, even painful, for a foreigner; squatting Indian style is an acceptable alternative.

In Yokohama, apply to Yokohama International Welcome Assoc. (641-5824). In Kyoto, phone 761-0016, Dept. of Cultural Affairs & Tourism; in Osaka, the Osaka Tourist Assoc., 261-3948.

ENTERTAINMENT & RECREATION

Traditional Theater

There are three forms, of which the *Bunraku* and *Kabuki* are the most enjoyable for foreigners.

Beautifully costumed, 40" Bunraku Puppets, manipulated by three artists in lifelike manner, act out 300-year-old folk art stories against a musical background. In Tokyo, Bunraku is staged in Feb., May, Sept., Nov.; in Osaka during Jan., April, July and Oct.

Kabuki delights because of the gorgeous period costumes, stylized dancing and acting (by all-male cast, including female roles), colorful and symbolic stage settings, haunting music. It's the way you secretly hoped Japan might look — though knew it couldn't.

Noh is an extremely sophisticated, slow-moving drama (mostly tragic), performed by costumed, masked actors, dating back to the end of the 14th century; it is narrated to a musical accompaniment of drums, flutes. A farce form of Noh is called *Kyogen*.

During cherry blossom season (usually by early April), Cherry Dances are presented in leading theaters thruout Japan — a show of classic dance play in gorgeous settings, often with a plot, by colorfully kimonoed dancers to gay music.

We found that the most enjoyable way to get to know "Old Japan" was thru a Drum and Folklore Show, usually presented at hotels during conventions or other group functions, also at theaters. *Taiko Odori* (Drum Dance) is terrific — quite unlike anything you've seen; the comical puppet show, with Japanese music, is indeed humorous and the folk and Kabuki dances — all beautifully costumed — delightful. Don't miss such entertainment — worth a hundred nightclub acts. *Matsubaya* (Geisha show) and *Shichigosan,* entertainment spots in Asakusa district, Tokyo, specialize in the traditional.

If you wish to penetrate the mysteries of a geisha party, you'll need the introductory services of a Japanese customer of geisha houses, which are declining in popularity and number.

Another traditional form of entertainment is available (for men) in so-called Turkish Baths *(toru-ko)* — massage parlors. Admission: Y1500-Y6000 (for an hour), plus "tip." Saunas provide non-sexual massage.

Tea Ceremony (Chanoyu)

An aesthetic pastime originating as a monastic custom imported by Buddhists from China (729 AD), Chanoyu is, today, a social institution peculiar to Japan. As such, it is well worth witnessing. For tea represents tranquility, the utensils cleanliness of soul and mind; the entire ceremony is an appreciation of subtle beauty in art and nature, the harmony of the participants. The ceremony embodies nearly all phases of etiquette observed by educated Japanese, hence brides to be are encouraged to take lessons in Chanoyu.

The hostess, beautifully kimono-clad, places powdered tea in a large bowl, adds hot water, beats the mixture with a bamboo whisk, later pours. Guests are offered a sweet wafer so that the bitter tea is more palatable. Incidentally, it's polite to admire the utensils and flower arrangements but never the kimono.

Only the choicest green teas are used, now produced in Uji (near Kyoto) by an evergreen plant; these large bushes provide four pickings a year (unless over a hundred years old when shoots are picked only twice) beginning in May and June.

Attend a Tea Ceremony at Imperial Hotel (10 a.m. to 4 p.m.) or Hotel Okura (11 to 5); closed during lunch, Sundays, holidays. Department stores often put on a Ceremony accompanied by a lavish display of kimonos.

Flower Arrangement (Ikebana)

So well known is this intrinsic Japanese art form it needs little elaboration. Established in the 15th century, it's so endeared itself that over 30,000,000 Japanese practice it; along with the tea ceremony, it is part of a young woman's preparation for marriage.

Displays of the floral art can be seen in florist windows and by attending department store exhibitions. Ikebana classes in English are held at the Ohara Center, one of the numerous schools, in Tokyo (phone 478-3312), Ikenobo Institute (293-3710) or Adachi School (463-4192). Admission free (for visit) but by appointment only.

Department Store Culture

Unique to Japan is the role of department stores *(depatos)* in dispensing *free* cultural entertainment. For example, in one week of 1975 there were 22 separate exhibits in Tokyo stores (all have Craft Salons, Galleries) ranging from pottery, lacquerware, calligraphy, carvings, paintings to Japanese dolls, tea utensils, excavations of districts along the Mediterranean, TV prop art and Scandinavian furniture. Culture, it seems, is one of the few inexpensive items in Japan. By the way, a good way to keep up with it and other events is thru the columns of *Tour Companion,* an excellent tourist tabloid weekly (free).

Bonsai Nurseries

Neighboring Omiya City (about 35 min. by train) has Bonsai Village where those marvelously twisted miniature potted trees are raised; nurseries are open daily except first and third Thursdays of each month. A Village Life & Crafts Tour (Wed., Sat. Mar.-Nov.) by JTB includes Bonsai Village, Osembei (rice cracker), Daruma (papier mache) workshops, a farmhouse.

Traditional Sports

Judo and karate, of course, are most familiar. In Tokyo, the Kodokan trains and presents exhibitions of the former. *Kendo* is a form of fencing; if interested in watching or training, phone 561-8251 (Metropolitan Police Center).

But the sport you've probably always wanted to see is *Sumo* wrestling by professionals weighing from 250 to 350 pounds. Rules are simple. Two wrestlers wearing only loin cloths enter a sanded, 15-ft. ring set up on a square mound; when any part of either's body, except feet, touches the ground, or when one steps or is pushed out of the ring, he's the loser. 15-day tournaments are held at Kuramae Kokugikan in Tokyo during Jan., May and Sept., in March at Osaka, July at Nagoya and in Nov. at Fukuoka. Tickets cost Y500 to Y5500 get them well in advance.

Baseball has also become traditional — biggest spectator sport in Japan. There are two leagues that, thru the Japan Series at the end of October, produce the national champion. Admission to professional ball is Y400 to Y1800.

Night Life

It's probably correct to say that Tokyo has the most extensive and expensive forms of after-dark pleasures and palaces of any city in any country — thanks to the Japanese corporate status symbol, the Expense Account, which can, without a qualm or quiver, cover a $2000 (not yen) nightly tab. Many executives, both junior and senior, enjoy monthly expense accounts far exceeding their salaries.

In Tokyo, it's mostly over by 11 p.m. — the time commuting citizens (and most are) leave in order to make the last trains (which stop running at midnight).

There are more than 20,000 bars, cabarets and clubs (employing 150,000 hostesses — all beautiful according to the ads) of every description, from small, informal drinking spots to very glittery establishments, located in various districts; most popular with foreigners: Ginza (11 p.m. closing), Akasaka with its internationally oriented spots (and later closing), Roppongi, Tokyo's Greenwich Village, where the action continues the latest, and Shinjuku, less expensive and hangout for a younger crowd.

The hostess system is simple: an hourly rate of $10 and up for companionship (conversation, dancing), plus drinks; trouble is, you rarely know the cost until you get the final tab. After hours companionship, if any, is a separate and private deal. And lest Women's Lib feels slighted, there are clubs with hosts.

Nightclubs have hostesses, entertainment but no dancing; some are exclusively private. Cabarets have hostesses, dancing and elaborate international shows; you can easily spend $65 to $200 each during one to two hours. Popular Ginza spots: *Crown* (phone 572-5511 for rsv.), very expensive; *Monte Carlo* (571-5671); *Queen Bee* (573-7251) where a yen-filled wallet is needed; *Mikado,* block from New Japan Hotel, has 1,000 hostesses in three tiers of noise and booze, provides the painless use of credit cards. In Akasaka, *New Latin Quarter* (581-1326) and *Copacabana* (558-5811), two of the city's flashiest, will extract your money in no time.

Theater restaurants, like the Imperial Hotel's and *Cordon Bleu,* are more sedate, provide good food/entertainment (no hostesses) at comparatively reasonable prices (though still expensive).

Exceptions to the high-priced spots: *Tame,* small and intimate, behind the Ginza's Nikko Hotel, where for a set price (about Y15,000 weekdays, Y10,000 Sat.), you drink what you want, stay as long as you want watching a topless show, talking to one of two dozen young hostesses. In Akasaka, *Byblos,* combination disco-dance hall, has mobs of young people enjoying latest American/British rock; good for the modest price. *Berni's Inn* (also in Roppongi), featuring inexpensive steak/beer, is an English-style pub for foreigners and locals. So is *Gaslight* for steak and Dixieland band.

DRINKING SCENE

Imported booze is *very* expensive. For business or personal gifts, bring Johnny Walker Black with you; a status symbol, it costs $40 a fifth here. And while you're at it, bring bottles of your favorite brand for your own consumption.

Domestic gin, vodka and whiskey sell for about the same bottle prices as in U.S. Japan's rice wine, *sake,* served both warm or cold, requires acquiring a taste. Suntory scotch, which comes in a number of grades, is quite good in its Genuine or Very Rare stages. So is Asahi, Kirin and Sapporo beer (small, medium, large bottles). By the drink, domestic scotch costs Y450-Y600 — imported brands are two and three times as much.

To keep bar tabs to a minimum, don't wander beyond hotel bars. Most others have hostesses, can cost you an arm and leg in no time; an American friend told us that he and an associate were taken to a bar by a Japanese businessman, had *one drink each* and the company of hostesses — for a mere $100.

Beer halls and gardens, on the other hand, are reasonable. During the summer, beer gardens atop the roofs of tall buildings are crowded after work. Small, medium, large mugs of beer cost Y250 to Y700; appetizers available. There are beer halls and gardens and so-called Mammoth (or Campa) Bars (companionable places) featuring bands, go-go girls that also serve hard liquor; these are very popular with young people as they are inexpensive — Y1000-Y2000 is a normal cocktail hour tab. White- and blue-collar workers also patronize the *taishu sakaba,* Japanese equivalent of a pub.

Tour operators provide 5-hour night tours of various combinations: Sukiyaki dinner, Kabuki drama, cabaret and/or nightclub shows, Geisha show; usually include a drink at each spot. About $55 or so per person.

TOKYO SHOPPING

A list of stores is as necessary as bringing sand to a beach. Generally, best selections of quality merchandise are found in hotel arcades and in Nihombashi, the district immediately north of the Ginza. Of particular note, however, is the *Boutique Julien Sorel* on Miyuki Dori and *Wako's* at corner of Harumi Dori and Namiki Dori. The former has a very "in" coffee shop where fashion showings are given at tea time. The latter is an oh-so-exclusive men's, women's and home accessory store with exquisite merchandise at correspondingly exquisite prices; plastic handbags for $600, jewelry and watches at Y1,000,000 and more, vases at (to us) unheard-of prices. Whatever you've heard of the Japanese economy, you can't appreciate how much individual wealth there must be until you shop here. An experience.

But the Ginza is where the fun is, particularly the department stores — or the crowds around a fast-spieling vendor. Night time is great, also on Sundays when families are out. If you can't get downtown, then shop the Asakusa, Shinjuku, Shibuya districts, whichever is nearest your hotel; all have department stores.

ALWAYS ON SUNDAYS

Pedestrians' Paradise, closed to traffic on Sundays and holidays, stretches along Chuo-Dori (Ginza Street) from, roughly, one Matsuakaya Department Store (at Miyuki-Dori and Chuo-Dori) to another in Ueno (near Ueno-Hirokoji Station, Ginza Subway) — better than two kilometers. Since this stretch is connected at both ends with similar traffic-free streets, there are about 5½ kilometers, or 3.4 miles, of Paradise in all. Other sections in Tokyo have similar deals.

This is a real treat not to be missed. Tables and chairs are set up under colored umbrellas, vendors sell balloons, ice cream, et al — a holiday atmosphere and a perfect setting for observing Japanese families enjoying their fun and games.

Always on Sunday in the Ginza .

GINZA DEPARTMENT STORES —
A One-Stop Lesson in Japanese Life

Nowhere else can you obtain, so quickly, an insight into the entire gamut of daily life in Tokyo as in one of the huge *depatos,* open six days a week including Fridays, Saturdays and Sundays.

On entering any large depato, you can usually pick up a directory in English showing what's on each floor; there's also an Information Counter. As you step onto the escalator, a young Japanese beauty bows and bids you welcome with the oft-heard *Irasshaimasu.*

Starting in the basement, you find groceries, fresh meat and fish, snack shops, bakeries — a chance to see all the ingredients the housewife uses in her daily cooking.

On other floors and departments, you look into the Japanese kitchen, living room and bedroom as you encounter array of thousands of cooking utensils, the low-to-the-floor furniture appropriate to the national life style on tatami mats, and mounds of cotton-stuffed futons and multi-colored futon covers used for bedding.

You may get lucky and see one of the frequent demonstrations of how to dress in kimonos, which takes a Westerner into another world, another era — yet still traditional and viable in modern Japan. An entire floor may be devoted to kimonos.

Near the upper floors, there are galleries and museums. Here great numbers of Japanese, young and old, view the treasures of the world and learn about the history and culture of their own and other countries. And on a nearby floor, in case you're hungry, you'll find dozens of small, informal restaurants (each specializes in different foods), even a very plush one.

And don't miss the rooftops. Hordes of children, as well as adults, are drawn to the penny (ten yen) arcades and playgrounds. In the summer, after business hours, these rooftops turn into festive beer gardens abounding in tasty snacks, camaraderie and, of course, freely flowing draught beer.

Back on the main floor, you may not wish to leave until you have your finger-nails buffed to a glossy, natural shine by a pert P. Shine girl — a demonstration of a nail-care kit which, incidentally, is a good buy (similar kits sell for much more in the States). P. Shine girls love to practice their English while buffing away — and you'll get a kick out of the conversation.

TOKYO-KYOTO PLANNING

As already stated, those with but four or five days in Japan should go by bullet train direct to Kyoto. But with more time available, take one of the two excursions (two days each) that follow. Matter of fact, if returning to Tokyo after seeing Kyoto, both could be taken — one in each direction.

VIA KASHIKOJIMA-PEARL ISLAND-NARA

We took this two-day trip from Kyoto, and it was a most pleasurable one. We recommend it highly, though it may not be available as a regular package tour.

From Tokyo, take the bullet train to Nagoya where transfer is made for the lovely train ride south to Toba, famed for Mikimoto Pearl Island where the pearl cultivating process, including the highlight, an oyster operation, is demonstrated. 80% of Japan's cultured pearls are produced in this area. We had an excellent lunch (conch au gratin was superb) at the attractive, beautifully sited Toba Hotel. Toss up as to whether you stay here overnight or at the really lovely resort hotel of Shima Kanko near Kashikojima, also beautifully sited amidst hills and overlooking a lovely bay in which strings of bamboo rafts for cultivating pearls are anchored.

Toba and Kashikojima are connected by the winding Ise Shima Skyline Drive that affords sweeping panoramas of pine-clad mountains and island-dotted waters of the Pacific. A stop is made at Ise Jingu Shrine, dedicated to the Imperial Ancestress and one of the most venerated in Japan; lovely setting, too, amidst huge, towering pines.

By train to Nara on the second day. After reveling in the treasures here, it's only a 25-mile drive to Kyoto via Uji, noted for its tea bush plantations and rice fields (usually two crops a year).

VIA KAMAKURA-HAKONE-ATAMI

By motorcoach thru the suburbs of Yokohama to Kamakura, a seaside summer resort noted for the *Daibutsu* (Great Buddha) a huge bronze Buddha cast in 1252, the Tsurugaoka Hachimangu Shrine and other ancient temples (Kenchoji, Engakuji), shrines and artistic treasures of the Kamakura Period (1192-1333) when this was the seat of the Shogunate. By train, Kamakura is but 55 minutes from Tokyo.

The *Daibutsu*, second largest in the country, is 44 ft., 3 in. high, weighs 133 tons. On September 16, *yabusame* (target shooting by horsemen in warrior attire of the 13th century) is a feature of the annual festival at Tsurugaoka Hachimangu Shrine.

Continue thru the mountains of the Fuji-Hakone National Park to Hakone for a cruise on Lake Ashi, a ride on the 2,600-ft.-long Komagatake cableway, then overnight in either a nearby hotel or one in Atami. On the morning of the second day, take the bullet train to Kyoto for early afternoon arrival (in time to take the Afternoon Tour).

Hakone, a popular resort between Mt. Fuji and the Izu Peninsula, is where you see lots of volcanic topography and hot springs. Scenic but spurious as far as foreigners are concerned. Same applies to the Fuji Five Lakes and Atami, a hot-springs spa on the Izu Peninsula with 360 hotels and inns.

Those two excursions can be combined by this combination: Tokyo-Kamakura-Hakone-Atami-Nagoya and then on to Kyoto as previously described. This takes three days, though the usual tour offered for this routing *does not include Nara* (but should).

Glimpses of "old" Japan, like this Kyoto vignette, are pure delight.

KYOTO — Cradle of Japanese Civilization

Much of the charm of its ancient past when it was Japan's capital (794-1868) remains in this "spiritual home of the people" — providing you overlook the far from spiritual modern parts of this center (1,150,000 pop.) of production of fine silks, embroidery, porcelain and lacquerware.

Spared from bombing, Kyoto has about 1,600 Buddhist temples and 200 Shinto shrines, nearly a third of the national treasures and is a literal repository of most of the nation's cultural heritage. It would take several weeks to thoroughly absorb it and certainly should be given more time than normally allotted by package tours.

On our first visit, we did as most tourists do — took day trips out of Tokyo. This results in seeing nothing more of Kyoto than what's shown on the afternoon tour, of which we later remembered little because it was such a jam-packed day. Second time here, attending a Pacific Area Travel Association Workshop, sightseeing tours within Kyoto and to the west of it were taken *prior* to reaching Tokyo. We were able to appreciate and enjoy Japan much better.

Minimum stay, including Nara, should be three days. You need at least the morning and afternoon tours[1] to see the major attractions, another day to roam and shop at leisure, a third for the Nara day tour. During April-October, there's a very worthwhile Garden Tour,[2] while during the same period a Spirit of Samurai & Gion Corner Tour[3] is offered. During July-August, you can go cormorant fishing on the Oi River. Of course, if you're here at festival times (see Annual Events), you'll really hit the jackpot, particularly in October-November when the maples are in their glory.

Nara is a full-day excursion always taken out of Kyoto. Trouble with a Tokyo-Hakone-Kyoto-Nara tour is that it provides only a half day of sightseeing in Kyoto.

As you can see on the map, many of the temples and shrines are central and within reasonable range of each other. Here are the standouts:

Higashi Honganji Temple (3), headquarters of the Buddhist Jod Shinsu sect, was built in 1895, is largest wooden structure in the city. Nishi Hoganji (2), headquarters for the Shinsu sect, was moved here in 1591; has several National Treasures, including Hiunkaku Pavilion in the southeast corner.

Most striking to the western eye is Sanjusangendo Temple (5) with its wooden Thousand-Handed Kannon (Buddhist Goddess of Mercy), 28 followers and 1001 smaller images. We've seen it twice, were fascinated both times. Nearby (4) is the Kyoto National Museum exhibiting art treasure of various shrines and temples.

[1] Morning includes Gold Pavilion, Old Imperial Palace, Nijo Castle and Higashi-Honganji Temple (Sun., national holidays only). Afternoon: Sanjusangendo, Heian Shrine, Kiyomizu Temple, Handcraft Center.

[2] T, Th and Sat. mornings to three temple gardens: Saihoji (moss), Ninnaji (landscape), Ryoanji (rock).

[3] Daily for demonstrations of Kendo, Karate, Aikido and Judo at an arena, flower arranging, a tea ceremony, puppet show and court music at Gion Corner. Costly but fascinating and a good way to see it all in a half day.

Toji Temple (41), has impressive collection of ancient art. A five-story pagoda about 183 feet tall, it's the tallest in Japan and an important relic of the Heian Period (794-1192). Nijo Castle (29), with its landscaped garden and rippling streams, was a residence of the Tokugawa Shogun; gorgeously decorated with screen paintings and carvings of the Momoyama Period, considered the flowering of Japanese culture.

Old Imperial Palace (27) is the heart of the old city; originally built in 794, the present building only dates to 1855, but the Shishin-den and Seiryo-den halls are of Heian architecture.

Yasaka Shrine or Pagoda (7), revered for centuries, is the focal point of the July 17 Gion Festival. In this district, one often glimpses geisha and maiko dancing girls. Nearby Gion Corner in Yasaka Hall (8) features samples of traditional stage and cultural arts. Twice-daily programs (8 and 9 p.m.) have flower arranging, tea ceremony, Kotu music, ancient court music, dances and comedy, Kyoto dance and Bunraku puppets.

Heian Shrine (14), another standout, is the epitome of what you expect shrines to be. This gorgeous structure, completed in 1895, is an exact replica on reduced scale of the original Imperial Palace, and its garden and bridges have been exquisitely fashioned. You're reluctant to leave. The same, possibly more so, is true of Kiyomizudera Temple (6), perched steeply hillside with a superb city view, built in 1633 *without the use of a single nail.* You'll be intrigued and awed by this wooden structure. The long climb up is less than rigorous as you're always stopping to shop the shops that line the approach; for our granddaughter, we bought a gorgeous doll, case and all, for much less than in Tokyo, had it shipped — and it arrived safely without delay.

Nanzenji (Zen) Temple (16) has beautiful paintings by artists of the 16th-century Kano school, an equally beautiful landscaped karesansui-type garden of rocks and white sand.

Kinkakuji Temple (30), the Gold Pavilion, another popular attraction, is a modern (1955) three-story pagoda, the

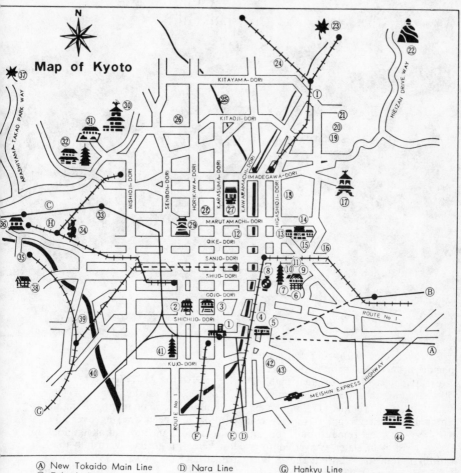

Map of Kyoto

N

A New Tokaido Main Line
B Tokaido Line
C San-in Line

D Nara Line
E Keihan Line
F Kintetsu Line

G Hankyu Line
H Keihuku Line (Arashiyama Line)
I Keifuku Line (Hieizan, Kurama Line)

① Kyoto Station
② Nishi Hongan-ji Temple
③ Higashi Hongan-ji Temple
④ Kyoto National Museum
⑤ Sanjusangendo Temple
⑥ Kiyomizudera Temple
⑦ Yasaka-no-toh Pagoda
⑧ Gion
⑨ Maruyama Koen (Park)
⑩ Chion-in Temple
⑪ Shoren-in Temple

⑫ Kyoto Shiyaku-sho (City Hall)
⑬ Kyoto Kaikan
⑭ Heian Jingu Shrine
⑮ Okazaki (Park)
⑯ Nanzen-ji Temple
⑰ Ginkaku-ji Temple
⑱ Kyoto University
⑲ Shisen-do Jozan-ji Temple
⑳ Manshu-in Temple
㉑ Shugaku-in Rikyu (Imperial Villa)
㉒ Mt. Hiei-zan

㉓ Ohara Village
㉔ Kyoto Int'l Conference Hall
㉕ Botanical Garden
㉖ Daitoku-ji Temple
㉗ Kyoto Old Imperial Palace
㉘ Kyoto Fucho (Prefectural Office)
㉙ Nijo-jo Castle
㉚ Kinkaku-ji Temple
㉛ Ryoan-ji Temple
㉜ Ninna-ji Temple
㉝ Myoshin-ji Temple

㉞ Koryu-ji Temple
㉟ Arashiyama
㊱ Tenryu-ji Temple
㊲ Takao Valley
㊳ Saiho-ji Temple
㊴ Nishikyogoku Sports Center

㊵ Katsura Rikyu (Imperial Villa)
㊶ To-ji Temple
㊷ Tofuku-ji Temple
㊸ Sennyu-ji Temple
㊹ Daigo-ji Temple

first two covered with gold foil and a splendid bronze phoenix atop the third — an exact replica of the original building 550 years old when destroyed by fire in 1950. Ginkakuji Temple (17), not to be confused with the foregoing, was erected in 1489 as a retirement pad for an Ashigago Shogun, later converted to a Buddhist temple. Called the Silver Pavilion, it isn't silver despite the Shoguns' original intention to cover the interior with silver foil.

Further out (40) is Katsura Detached Palace, an architectural masterpiece built for an Imperial prince in the early 1600s. On the opposite side of town (21) is Shugakuin Palace, or Imperial Villa, consisting of three detached palaces. Both Katsura and Shugakuin command lovely views of the surrounding hills, both require a permit (in advance) to visit.

Near Shugakuin is the Kyoto International Conference Hall, first extremely modern facility of its type in Japan and a real beauty. We recommend it unqualifiedly to any conference or convention group.

MOTION PICTURE VILLAGE

Located next to the Koryuji Temple in Uzumasa (No. 35 on map), this unique attraction has been drawing over 100,000 visitors, foreign and national, monthly. For here you go backward into the Edo feudal days of 1603 to 1867.

Uzumasa was the Hollywood of Japan before TV. Of its dozens of movie studios, only one, the Toei Company, remains. It is here that you see the sets used for filming the Edo period films which, for Japan, were the same as our Westerns. In this vast area (28,000 sq. meters) are a huge variety of sets, each reproducing an Edo-period establishment and all arranged in precise Japanese order. There's the old Nihombashi Bridge spanning Tokyo's Sumida River; Nihombashi Street, once the city's commercial hub, with its cherry-adorned quarters; shops and stores representing the daily life of the townsfolk, great mansions of ranking samurai warriors, magistrates' offices, back court tenements. There are buildings that housed wholesalers' products, willow-lined canals, inns for ship passengers. Comparatively modern-looking, Western-style buildings are included in a Meiji era (1868-1912) street scene, along with an old city tram and rickshaws.

If you have the time, Motion Picture Village provides a fascinating opportunity to see old Japan in miniature, one otherwise unavailable except thru prints. Open from 9:30 a.m. to 5 p.m. daily from April thru November; 10 a.m. to 4 p.m. December thru March (closed Dec. 26-Jan. 3). Admission: Y700 (Y400 for children) weekdays, Y150 Sundays, holidays. Take bus from Kyoto Station to Koryuji Temple, a 5-minute walk from Village.

SHOPPING IN KYOTO

Everyone loves it since there are outstandingly beautiful silks, embroideries, porcelains and pottery, dolls and folding fans. You'll not want to skip the Handcraft Center (open 9 to 6) which also carries tax-free items.

If interested in traditional folk crafts, for which Kyoto is noted, then visit the Municipal Center for Traditional Industry, 10 minutes by car from Kyoto Station, where there's a display of traditional handcrafts, demonstrations and exhibits of production processes and a display of an old Kyoto house. Crafts shown include dyed fabrics, embroidery, porcelain, lacquer ware, cloisonne, dolls, folding fans, bamboo and metal, wood block prints. Open daily (except Wed.) from 9 to 5; Y200 entrance.

Kawashima Textile Mill, 25 minutes by car, or Tatsumura Silk, 15 minutes, offer one-hour factory tours to see weaving of tapestries, brocades and designing of obis and draperies.

DINING

Ajibil — Japanese dishes, barbecued steaks. Open daily from noon 'til 4 a.m.

Kani-Doraku — Near Kyoto Royal Hotel. Specializes in seafood, crab tempura.

Manyoken — Popular at lunch or dinner for French cuisine. Exp.

Minokichi — Near Miyako Hotel. Traditional Japanese, country-style rst. Mod. and attractive.

Suehiro — Steaks, sukiyaki are specialties.

HISTORIC NARA

The first permanent, settled capital (710) of a country in the process of being unified, Nara (now a city of almost a million people) represents the influence of a magnificent era of Chinese civilization, hence was, and still is, more culturally Chinese than Japanese. Viewed in the light of Japanese history as well as the interest it holds for visitors, it is most assuredly an important and fascinating destination.

During the height of its glory (until 784), towering temples, shrines and residences of priests and notables covered the area, which was larger than today's. Fortunately, some of these buildings remain, principally in wooded Nara Park with its tame deer. Here are the most important sights:

Todaiji (Great Eastern) Temple, world's largest wooden building (current one is the third, now 282 years old), houses in the Hall of Great Buddha the black, bronze image 53 feet high, weighing 500 tons; its crown contains 16 gold Buddhas symbolizing the 16 phases of Buddhism.

Horyuji Temple, oldest wooden complex in the world, has 33 buildings built from 552 to 1868, a beautiful five-story pagoda.

Byodoin Temple, built in 11th century, is noted for its Phoenix Hall, the Image of Amitabha (represents Buddhist concept of harmony).

Fushimi Inari Shrine is dedicated to Goddess of Rice and Food. The 10,000 red shrine gates were donated by believers. During festivals, girls in red skirts perform sacred dances.

Kasuga Shrine, set amongst huge trees with steps leading to shrine above, has 3,-000 stone lanterns lining the pathways; lanterns are lit by candles on Aug. 15th and Feb. 3rd.

Nara Museum in Nara Park has Buddhist works of art dating from 645-785 AD. Over 400 deer believed to be divine messengers roam the 1,200 acres. Deer Horn Cutting Ceremony takes place the middle of October.

Hall of the Great Buddha in Nara

OSAKA

Japan's second largest city (8,000,000), located at the mouth of Yodo River, is the center of commerce for every type of product from all over the country. In ancient days, with its many canals as the main means of transportation, it was known as the Venice of the Orient. Today, highways and railways, subways, hi-rises have changed its appearance. Now it is divided into two sections: new Kita business area in the north, the old Minami district to the south.

A fifteen-minute walk from Osaka Station is Naknoshima Park between the Tosabori and Dojima Rivers. Here, surrounded by a moat, is the famous, reconstructed (1931) Osaka Castle with a delightful museum and a dazzling view of Osaka from the top. The Castle still retains much of the history of the original, once a defensive network and city in itself.

Osaka's most celebrated shrine is Temman-gu originally built in 949 (reconstructed in 1901) and dedicated to Sugawara Michizane, patron saint of learning. In July, the colorful Tenjin Festival is held here. 3,000 men carrying portable shrines dance thru the streets. Climax is the evening boat procession and fireworks.

Founded in 593, the Shitenno-ji Temple, near Tennoji Station and Park, is a complex of buildings dominated by a pagoda. This sanctuary is a welcome relief from the bustling commerce of the city. The melodic sound of bells you hear pealing out over the city comes from here.

Similar to the Ginza in Tokyo is Shinwaibashi-suji, the shopping, theatrical, restaurant and bar area.

If you're here at night, attend a performance at the Doll Theater (Ningyo Shibai) in the Dotombori amusement section. The early writings of Chikamatsu (17th-century Japanese Shakespeare) are scripts used for the puppet shows.

Osaka is primarily a businessman's destination; few tourists spend more than a half day here before departing the country.

KYOTO TO HIROSHIMA

If time's limited, go direct (via Okayama) via bullet train. Otherwise make a three-day trip out of it, as we did: overnight in Okayama, by bus to the provincial town of Kurashiki and then by train — a gorgeous ride along the Inland Sea, past rushing streams and between pine-clad hills to Hiroshima.

One can live without Okayama despite its traditional Korakuan Gardens, considered one of the finest in Japan, but it's a necessary stop enroute to Kurashiki, a delightful spot unlike anything else we saw in Japan, featuring an outstanding Ohara Art Museum (excellent collection of Impressionists, plus early Jackson Pollack abstractions) and Kurashiki Folk Museum (Japanese and foreign handcrafts), Archeological and Historical Museums. After lunch another train ride and the chance to see a section of Japan such as you always visualized it should be.

Being new, Hiroshima is a splendidly planned city with broad avenues — but interesting only in the sense of being a modern phoenix. Peace Memorial Museum (open 9 to 4:30) is something else — its pictures and exhibits are a gruesome testimonial to man's inhumanity. As you watch healthy, happy children frolicking in Peace Memorial Park, you think ever so strongly of the futility and senselessness of war. Diplomats and politicians should be required to make annual treks here.

A delightful contrast, however, is the bus and ferry excursion to nearby Miyajima, the Shrine Island, with its photogenic, scarlet Torii and beautiful Itsukushima Shrine, a heavenly spot where violence would seem impossible. It has always been considered one of the most scenic places in Japan, noted for cherry blossoms and autumnal tints.

The Shrine itself is very old, its origins as far back as 811. The main shrine and several subsidiaries are connected by wide

There is nothing in the English captions or the tapes to indicate that the bombing was anything but an unprovoked assault on a blameless Japan. No background of the war is given. History is rewritten thru omission.

galleries; when tides roll in on both sides, the entire complex and its Torii seem to be floating on water. Festival dances are performed on a large, open-air platform, ordinary shrine dances in the area set aside for public worship.

TRIP EXTENSIONS FROM HIROSHIMA

There are a number of options: by train or plane to Osaka or Tokyo, by limited express train to Beppu, the spa on Kyushu Island, by train to Hakata (Fukuoka) on Kyushu. Those with sufficient time should at least go to Beppu for the opportunity to return to Osaka by excursion liner on the Inland Sea.

Another way to cruise the Sea is by ferry from Takamatsu, which is on the south shore in a line with Okayama; this is an afternoon run with dinner aboard before arrival in Osaka. In this case, one goes directly to Hiroshima, returns by way of Kurashiki, ferries across to Takamatsu for an overnight stay and morning sightseeing before departure for Osaka.

KYUSHU ISLAND

After taking the bullet train from Hiroshima to Hakata, a motorcoach tour covers Nagasaki, Unzen, Shimabara, Amakusa, Kumamoto and Beppu, followed by the cruise (14 hours) on the Inland Sea to Osaka. Or else go by motorcoach from Beppu to Fukuoka. This segment is usually done in four days, provides for exiting from Japan from either Osaka or Fukuoka.

If looking for scenery, Kyushu, southernmost major island,[1] has it: majestic mountains, rugged seascapes, beautiful inlets and national parks, particularly Aso National Park and its stunning Mt. Aso and awesome crater, Kyushu's most popular tourist spot. Climate varies from severe in winter on north side facing the Korean Straits to sunny in the southeast. In the east is the popular hot-springs resort, Beppu, with its boiling ponds (*jigoku*), largest acquarium in the Orient, Monkey Hill (*Takasaki-*

---

[1] The chain of Japanese islands runs for about 1,860 miles from the north to southwest.

yama). Nagasaki, within encircling hills, is a similar experience to Hiroshima.

Shimabara is reached by a picturesque drive over 3,500 ft. Nitta Pass in Unzen, and from there a ferry is used to reach Amakusa Islands, set in the mirror-smooth Sea of Ariake, thence over the Five Amakusa Bridges (which link the islands) to Kumamoto and its Castle, followed by the drive to Mt. Aso. Final drive is over picturesque Yamanami Highway (beautiful highland country) to Beppu.

Extensions can be made to Kirishima National Park and the southern city of Kagoshima, 90 miles from which is the lavish seaside resort and spa of Ibusuki with its ultramodern Ibusuki Kanko Hotel set in a botanical garden with more than 3,000 birds, a "jungle bath" where guests can soak themselves in any of 59 mineral water pools or tubs, be entertained in a 5,000-seat theater restaurant, take off weight in the world's only natural sauna bath — hot sands in which you're buried (all but the head).

According to Copley News Service travel editor, Phil Sousa, Kyushu is rarely seen by foreigners. And deserves to be if you like "palm trees, hibiscus and other flowers galore . . . slow-moving and easygoing folks . . . clean, quiet beaches at the edge of lush forests . . . uncrowded roads, unpolluted rivers and sparkling creeks . . . beach and mountain resorts Las Vegas would find impressive."

OKINAWA

Okinawa, two hours by air from Tokyo, lies at the southernmost end of the Japanese archipelago, the largest of over 70 islands in the Ryukyuan group. Naha, the capital (over 400,000 pop. and connected with Okinawa City), is situated in the south. The island is surrounded by emerald blue waters, beautiful coral reefs and lovely beaches. Climate is semitropical, and the vegetation is both tropical and sub-tropical. January is cherry-blossom time, in April cliffs are covered with white lilies, scarlet deigos bloom in May.

People are hospitable, particularly in rural villages and in the northern part of

Okinawa and on the offshore islands where traces of ancient Japanese culture remain. From ancient days, Okinawa has been a crossroad of Japanese, Chinese, Southeast Asian and, after 27 years of U.S. occupation, American cultures. Now, as one of the 27 prefectures of Japan, it is entering a new era as less than enthusiastic Japanese.

Handcrafts are closely connected with the daily life of the people. Ceramics, Ryukyu dolls, lacquerware and the sanshin (3-stringed musical instrument) are well known and reasonably priced. New resort hotels have been opened.

Festivals seen here are completely Okinawan. On July 13th to 15th, the popular *Eisa Bon Dance* takes place. There's a *Tug of War, Juri Uma* (music festival) and *Kaijin-sai* (sea festival).

Part of the former International Ocean Expo site, 55 miles from Naha (2 ½ hrs. by bus), has been opened as Okinawa Emerald Park, world's largest national tropical park. Currently open are an Aquarium, Okichan (Dolphin) Theater, Oceanic Culture Pavilion, Seashore Park, Expo Beach and other buildings; from the 1975 Expo is Expo Land, Okinawa Ocean Center and Aquapolis, sea-city of the future. Open 10-6 daily (except M).

HOW TO GET HERE

Naha is the southernmost gateway to Japan. JAL and All Nippon Airways fly from Fukuoka, Kagoshima, Nagoya, Osaka and Tokyo. There are direct flights by international lines from Guam, Hong Kong, Honolulu, Manila, Seoul and Taipei.

HELPFUL TRAVEL HINTS

Bring some sturdy handkerchiefs, or plenty of hand tissues, as there are no hand towels in public toilets.

Business cards are extremely important, even on social occasions. Present yours promptly upon introduction.

When seeking directions, ask a young person (English is studied in school from 12 years of age onward) or, preferably, write your request — he'll most likely read better than he understands spoken English (or speaks it).

LANGUAGE

For a phonetic shortcut approach to a difficult language, buy *Sight and Sound* ($2) from JAL, Box 618, Old Chelsea Station, N.Y. 10011.

The following might be of some help. Phonetic pronunciation is in italics.

1-*each;* 2-*knee;* 3-*seing;* 4-*she;* 5-*go;* 6-*rock;* 7-*city;* 8-*hatse;* 9-*que;* 10-*ju each;* 20 *knee ju.*

Change the money — *Okane o kaete kudasai*
Get me a doctor — *Isha o yonde kudasai*
Good; great — *Kek-koh-des*
Good morning — *Oh-high-oh*
Good afternoon — *Kohn-NEE-chee-waw*
Good evening — *Kohm-BAWN-waw*
Goodbye — *Sah-yoh-nah-rah*
He — *Kah-reh*
Haircut — *Sampatsu*
Hello — *Kohn nee-chee-wah*
How do I get to the rest room — *Toilet wa doko desuka*
   washroom — *Toire*
How much — *Ee-kuhrah deskah*
Hotel — *Hoteru*
Hurry up, please — *Isoide kuh-dah-sigh*
I — *Wah-tahk-shee*
I am sorry — *Sume-masen*
I don't understand — *Wah-kah-ree mah-sen*
I want that (be sure to point) — *Ah-ray gah ho-shee des*
I will take this — *Kore wo kudas*
Paper — *Kami*
Pen — *Borupen*
Pencil — *Enpitsu*
Pillow — *Makura*
Please — *Doz-oh; kudasai*
bring — *Wo motte kite kudasai*
   bring — *Wo motte kite kudasai*
   have this pressed (washed) — *Kore wo puresu (sentaku) shite kudasai*
   give me some water — *Mee-zuh o kudasai*
   give me a receipt — *Reshiito o kudasai*
   take me to — *Made itte kudasai*
   show me the way to — *e yuku michi wo os-hiete kudasai*
She — *Kah-noh-joh*
Shampoo — *Shampu;* set — *Setto*
Stop there — *Soko de tomatte kudasai*
Take me to — *Made itte kudasai*
Taxi stand — *Takushi noriba wa doko desuka*
Today — *Kyo*
Today — *Kyo*
Toilet—Toilet; *toire*
Tomorrow — *Ashita*
Wait for me here — *Kokode maggeite kudasai*
Where is — *Wa doko desuka*
   railway station — *Tetsudo no eki*
   subway station — *Chicatetsu no eki*
   bus stop — *Basu noriba*
   beauty shop — *Biyoh-in wa doko desuka*
   barber shop — *Tokoya wa doko desuka*
Yes — *Hai*

Hotel Directory

Difficult to find one that isn't completely modern, efficiently run, immaculate, and hasn't extremely polite, willing service. And just as difficult to find (outside of Tokyo) hotels with other than small scale, bland rooms. Lobbies and public rooms are usually large, even huge, and attractive, shopping arcades extensive, restaurants many and varied, from coffee shops to elaborate entertainment — but as can be expected from the average Japanese stature, bedrooms, baths and closets are usually small, ceilings low.

Rooms in better hotels (European Plan) are usually priced as Standard (meaning very small), Superior or Deluxe — plus Suites/Jr. Suites. *10% to 15% service charge and 10% tax are added to room rates* (don't faint when you get the bills).

HOTEL RATES

As projected for the 1979 season, but subject to change, herewith the range of EP rates for twin-bedded/double-bedded rooms with bath, double occupancy:
DELUXE (DL) — Y13,000-Y23,000; SU Y23,000-Y200,000; Jr. SU — Y17,000 up.
FC+ — Y10,000 to Y20,000; SU — Y23,000-Y135,000.
FC — Y8,000-Y16,000; SU Y17,000-Y125,000.
MODERATE — Y9,000 to Y15,000.

In deluxe Tokyo hotels, robe and slippers are placed on turned-down beds — a nice touch. Outside Tokyo, slippers, robes and toothbrush kits are usually furnished — with a polite suggestion, "Please, not to take with you."

King or queen size beds are rare. Better hotels have central heating, complete air-conditioning, TV, radio and, often, small refrigerators in the rooms.

Most of the newer hotels have Japanese-style accommodations (indicated herein by *JS*), usually at higher rates than western style.

Best to reserve well in advance during May, October, November and late December-early January; during latter period, rooms are apt to be booked a year in advance.

For a complete listing of 263 members of Japan Hotel Association, get JNTO's *Hotels in Japan*.

Japanese Inns

To get the feel of traditional Japan, do try to spend at least one night in a home-like, personalized *Ryokan*. Of the 80,000 inns, only 158 members of the Japan Ryokan Association have conveniences suitable for Western tourists; a *Ryokan Guide* is available from JNTO. Central heating, Western baths are featured in many modernized inns; smaller ones have room heaters.

Ryokan rates, on a per person basis with two meals (breakfast, supper), range from Y7000 and up without bath (use communal bath), anywhere up to Y22,000 with bath — *per person*. Rooms are usually spacious, some like suites. There are no beds, possibly no chairs (a genuine Ryokan provides cushions); at bedtime, your personal maid brings out bedding from a closet, spreads it on the floor (one for each guest). She also carries luggage, serves the table d'hote meals in your room and may even sit by your table to pour tea, help you to second portions of rice, etc. This personalized service extends to serving tea each time you return from outside, hanging up your clothes, helping you put on a *yukata* (Japanese bathrobe) provided by the inn.

When you enter a ryokan, sit on the higher floor of the vestibule to change into slippers; leave your shoes pointing outward. Before stepping onto the *tatami* (straw matting) floor of your room, slip out of the slippers. On departure, don't put your coat on until you're outside the room.

Bathtubs are not meant for washing but for warming and relaxing the body. Tub water will not be changed for each bather. Here's how to proceed: wash the body without soap, soak in the tub, climb out and wash thoroughly with soap, then rinse by pouring water over the body, then climb back in for another good soak. To be done before meals, if possible, for relaxed enjoyment of the food.

Another Japanese contrivance requiring expertise is the toilet, made for aiming, not sitting. The bidet-shaped receptacle with hood at one end (from which water is flushed) is usually imbedded in a raised floor, open end towards the entrance. Climb up, face the hood, squat down, aim carefully (too far out and you miss the bowl); not comfortable, perhaps, but sanitary. A male, needing only to urinate, stands on the lower floor. By the way, when asking for the rest room, just say, "Ben-joe do-ko?" (Toilet, where?).

Inexpensive Accommodations

JNTO (Japan National Tourist Organization) has information on over 250 youth hostels all over the country. Charges for bed, breakfast, dinner, sleeping sheet and heating range from Y1200 to Y1700 a day per person. Reservations, which should be made well in advance, especially during July-August, are made direct with the hostels.

JNTO lists *Inexpensive Accommodations* in

Tokyo and other cities. But these are inexpensive only by Japanese standards. For example, rates for YMCAs and YWCAs are Y3500 single, Y5500 double *without bath*. There are also Budget Ryokan listings. Efficiency Hotels (Western style, no frills) are in the Y6000 to Y8500 range. Tokyu Inns, Sun Route Hotels and Hokke Clubs are well-known chains in this category.

People's Lodges *(Kokumin Shukusha)*, Japanese or bunk-style rooms, are located in national parks, hot springs resorts. Average cost: Y2900-Y3400 per person with two meals. Japan Travel Bureau has Green Coupon Reservation system. Also for National Vacation Villages *(Kokumin Kyuka Mura)*, public Club Med type facilities in 21 parks.

Family Inns *(Minsnuku)* are where foreigners can enjoy real Japanese home life — for Y3000 and up with two meals. Write, visit or phone Minshuku Center, Tokyo Kotsu Kaikan Bldg. (near Yurakucho Station), Tokyo; phone 216-6556. Weekdays 10 a.m.-7 p.m.

For monthly lodgings, students should make inquiries of: Japan Student Assoc., 9-21-2, Misaki-cho, Chiyoda-ku, Tokyo; International Student Assoc., Ito Bldg., 10-12, Shibuya 2-chome, Shibuya-ku. Tokyo.

TOKYO HOTELS

No. 1 hotel area, in our opinion, is the downtown area — Ginza-Marunouchi-Uchisaiwai-cho districts — because of its accessibility to all the action. Too, most of Tokyo's beauty surrounds it: Imperial Palace Plaza and grounds, Hibiya Park, Hibiya-Dori, Tokyo's Fifth Avenue and one of the few thoroughfares with charm and distinction.

Most of the other top hotels ring the downtown area to the west, northwest and north — either a long walk or a taxi/subway ride away. Between the World Trade Center and Haneda International Airport to the southwest are the Pacific and Takanawa Prince hotels. To the northwest, in a newly built district, is the Keio Plaza.

DOWNTOWN AREA

IMPERIAL (DL) — A superb hotel that's always been synonymous with fine service, prestige. Large, stunning lobby and fine shopping arcade, nine restaurants (including good coffee shop, splendid Theater Restaurant), five bars, top convention facilities. Older bldg (less exp.) has old-world charm where you receive kimona, slippers, etc. Newer bldg has modern rooms with coffee-maker. Suggest Superior or Deluxe rooms. 1281 units. *Conv:* 2500.

MARUNOCHI (FC) — Japanese decor; old world charm with modern conveniences (remodeled). 152 R, SU in main building, 58 AC R w/refrig. in new; green tea served complimentary. Several rsts, bar; roof garden dining in summer. Their John Bull Sky Restaurant, across street atop Ashi-Taokai Bldg., serves fabulous food. Well located between and near Imperial Plaza and Tokyo Central Station.

MIYAKO (FC) — 400 R (some JS) opened fall '77 in upper floors of Kintetsu Motors Bldg. Rst, bar, cocktail lounge.

PALACE (FC+) — Another distinguished hostelry beautifully sited across from Imperial Palace grounds. 407 continental style (mostly large) R and SU. Excellent Crown Restaurant, Simpson Grill, plus Japanese rst; several bars. Popular lunch spot. Newer GRAND PALACE, round the corner, is modern hi-rise w/500 R. Several rsts, bars, 23rd-floor Crown Room serves fine French cuisine. Conv. facilities.

NOT FAR FROM DOWNTOWN

OKURA (DL) — Residential area adjacent to U.S. Embassy. Beautiful hi-rise with 980 rooms, suites; 7 rsts, 5 bars, 2 pools, shop arcade. *Conv:* 3000 (37 meeting rooms).

SHIBA PARK — Near Tokyo Tower, Shiba Park. 300 AC R, Western and Chinese Rsts, bars. Mod.

SHINJUKU PRINCE (FC) — In Kabukicho, Shinjuku-ku. Opened '77 with 600 AC R, 3 rsts, several bars.

TOKYO PRINCE (FC) — 510 R with huge public areas; all types of rsts; bars. Pool. Daily tours start from here. *Conv:* 1500 plus 25 meeting rooms. Airport/hotel transfer.

TOKYO URASHIMA (FC) — 1000 R, coffee shop, rsts (Japanese, Chinese, Int'l), bars, pool, bowling alley. South of Ginza. *Conv:* 300. Well priced.

Mid-Town (Akasaka Area)

NEW JAPAN (FC) — 506 R, SU (30 JS). Many rsts, including Polynesian, Tempura, and bars. Well located for nights of fun.

NEW OTONI & TOWERS (DL) — One of the world's largest with 2100 AC R, SU. 2 pools, 3 pavilions serving barbecue specialties within 10-acre Japanese gardens. 4 tennis courts. Over 20 rsts. 17th-floor revolving rst serves a marvelous Chinese buffet. Nightly entertainment, dancing. Over 100 shops. *Conv:* 50 banquet rooms. *Rsv:* Sheraton.

TOKYO HILTON (DL) — What you imagined a charming 475 AC R Japanese hotel would look like. Japanese gardens, pool, fine shops; delightful rsts, bars, cocktail lounge. In fashionable Akasaka area.

OUTLYING

HOLIDAY INN OF NARITA (FC+) — ¾ mile from airport. 254 AC R, four rsts, rooftop rst, bars, pool.

HANEDA TOKYU — Few blocks from Haneda Airport (not to be confused with Terminal Hotel). 297 small R (also JS rooms). Rsts, coffee shop, bar, pool Economy class.

KEIO PLAZA INTER-CONTINENTAL (DL) — 47 stories agleam with glistening chandeliers, flashing chrome and complete with every modern convenience. 1057 attractive R, SU, plus 11 rsts, 9 bars, pool, shop arcade. Service reported good. Said to be one of world's most completely fireproof bldgs. *Conv:* 3000.

NIKKO NARITA (DL) — 5 minutes from airport, 15 from rail terminal. 535 R, rsts, bars, pool.

BEPPU

NEW GRAND (FC) — Mountain hot springs spa 30 miles from Beppu. 111 R. Rst, grill, bar. Pool, golf, tennis. *Conv.*

SUGINOI (FC) — Near station. 606 R. Dining room, nightclub, cocktail lounges, pool, bowling, ice skating. *Rsv:* JTB.

FUKUOKA (Hakata)

NISHITETSU GRAND (FC) — DT. 308 R, 5 rsts, several bars. *Conv:* 800.

HAKONE
(Japanese style rooms recommended)

FUJIYA — Attractive inn with 189 R (some w/o bath) located in many annexes. Rsts, bar, indoor/outdoor pool, golf. Good lunch spot. Mod.

HAKONE HIGHLAND (DL) — Beautifully situated at foothills of Mt. Fuji. 60 R with all amenities. Opened '77.

HAKONE KANKO (FC) — Mountain side. 114 R (few JS). Japanese rst, grill, cocktail lounge. Golf, fishing, skating, swimming available.

HAKONE PRINCE (DL) — Overlooks Lake Ashi in National Park. Continental buffet, French and Japanese rsts, bars, niteclub; pool, tennis, golf, boating. 96 R.

KOWAKI-EN — Hot springs resort w/300 R, some AC, both Western-Japanese. Dining room, bars, nightclub, bowling alley. Hillside above Lake Ashinoko, below Mt. Fuji. Pool and Polynesian bath. Mod-FC.

HIROSHIMA

HIROSHIMA GRAND (FC) — Good DT location. 404 very attractive R w/rfg. Older section, with more spacious rooms, completely renovated. Garden, Japanese, Chinese rsts, sky bar. Shop arcade. EP, AP rates.

KASHIKOJIMA

SHIMAKANKO (DL) — Surrounded by lovely green mountains and superbly sited on Ago Bay, this is a delightful pagoda-style resort. 145 large R are well appointed with TV, tea table (and thermos), couch and balcony; 55 large ryokan rooms with or w/o bath overlook flowered roofs, gardens, pool (open summer). Excellent Western/Japanese food. Cruiser tours Bay daily at 9:30; tours to Ise-Shima National Park arranged. Golf at two nearby courses. FC rates.

KUMAMOTO

NEW SKY — 201 R, SU. Rst, coffee shop, cocktail lounge. Inexp-Mod.

KYOTO

FUJITA (FC) — 15 min. from station on Kamo river. 195 R, several rsts, bars. Lovely gardens. Shopping arcade.

HOLIDAY INN (FC) — NE section, 20 min. from station. 180 R. Rst, bar, pool, bowling alley, ice-skating rink. *Conv:* 200.

INTERNATIONAL HOTEL KYOTO (FC) — Across from Nijo Castle, 10 min. from station. 332 AC R. Main dining room has nightly entertainment. Japanese rst, 3 bars. Pool.

KYOTO (FC) — 15 min. from station. 520 Japanese/Western style R within 3 sections — the newer the room, the smaller it is. Continental-style dining room w/paneled walls is huge. Small grill serves good food. Bar.

KYOTO GRAND — Near railroad station, overlooking old Kyoto. Dining room serves Chinese, French, Japanese cuisine. Bars, pool, shops. 403 R. *Conv:* 800. Popular w/groups. Japanese style.

KYOTO STATION — At railroad station. Convenient for overnight. 130 plain R, with or w/o baths. Rst, bar. Mod.

KYOTO TOWER — Across from station. Space needle at top. 148 R with or w/o bath. Dining room, cocktail lounge.

MIYAKO (DL) — Ideally located in residential area just moments away from shrines, temples and palaces; 3 sections (one Japanese style) are within 16-acre Japanese garden. 480 R, SU some w/rfg; those in newest section best. Scandinavian Rst least expensive and good; others frightfully expensive. 4 pools. *Conv:* 1000. Rooms with city view more exp. than garden view. *Rsv:* RW; Western. *NEW MIYAKO,* in front of station, opened '75 with 714 AC, soundproof R.

NIBANKAN — Recently opened DT with 96 R for women only. Inexp. Built as an annex to 238 R New Kyoto, near Nijo Castle. Inexp-Mod.

Kyoto Ryokan
Tawaraya — Anekoji, Fuya-cho (211-5566)

NAGASAKI
NAGASAKI GRAND — 126 AC R, 2 dining rooms, Sky Rst. Mod.

NAGASAKI TOKYU — 226 R, 2 SU, 2 rsts, 2 bars. Pool. *Conv:* 200. Mod.

NAGOYA
KANKO (FC+) — Newest; 505 R modern hirise. French, Chinese, Japanese rsts. 2 bars, cocktail lounge, grill. Shopping arcade. *Conv:* 1300.

MIYAKO (FC+) — 5 minutes from RR station. 400 R. 3 cocktail lounges, Western-style rst. Shopping arcade. *Conv:* 1000.

NAGOYA CASTLE (FC+) — ½ hr. from airport. 254 AC R, SU. Rst. Sky Lounge, 3 bars, nightly entertainment. Pool. Meeting rooms.

NARA
NARA — Near Deer Park. Charming pagoda-style hotel w/attractive grounds. Japanese decor. Dining and grill room, bar. 73 R (5 Japanese). Golf club privileges. Conv.

NEW NARA ANNEX — At Kintelsu station. 107 R modern hi-rise lacks charm of older Nara. Sky lounge and grill.

YAMOTO SANSO — 5 min. from station, near Todaiji Temple. 51 R, SU. Dining room, bar, lounge. FC+ rates.

NIKKO
NIKKO KANAYA — 95 R older hotel. Dining room, bar, pool. Mod-FC.

NIKKO LAKESIDE — On Lake Chuguji. Japanese garden, dining room, cocktail lounge. Cruiser. FC rates.

NIKKO PRINCE (DL) — Shobugahama, Chugushi. Plush lake resort hotel. 60 R, SU and villas. Pool, tennis, fishing. Dining room, cocktail lounge. Exp. Rates from Nov-July less.

OKAYAMA
OKAYAMA PLAZA (FC-) — Overlooks Korakuen garden and castle. Opened '72 w/smallest modern R we've ever seen. Attractive ground floor coffee shop, private main-floor dining rooms; rooftop dining. Good service and food. Inexp.

OKINAWA
GRAND CASTLE (FC) — 305 R are cheerful, spacious, more attractive than public rooms and pool area.

HILTON (DL) — 308 w/balcony in semicircular design in beautiful, landscaped park. Panoramic view of China Sea, Pacific and Koza City. 2 rsts, bars, discotheque. Pool, mini-golf. 15 miles N of Naha.

MIYAKO (DL) — 329 R, SU. 20 min. from airport. Rooftop revolving rst. Bar. Pool.

OKINAWA HARBOR VIEW (DL) — 346 AC R and Japanese SU. Rsts serve Chinese, Japanese and Western cuisine. Entertainment. Pool. Few minutes from ocean terminal.

KUME ISLAND
EEF BEACH — 50 miles W of Okinawa. New 38 R and cottage resort along sandy beach.

OSAKA
DAI-ICHI (FC) — Opened in '77 with 500 R; half hour from airport or ocean terminal. Rst, bars.

ROYAL (DL) — 870 R in old wing, 730 in new. 15 rsts, 4 bars, Sky Lounge, huge shopping arcade. 20 min. from airport, 10 from station. *Conv:* 6000. *Rsv:* JTB.

TOYO (DL) — Great location — few minutes from station, 15 from airport. 641 R. Several rsts, bars; good conv. facilities, shops. FC-DL rates. *Rsv:* U.

SAPPORO
(Advance Reservations for Feb. Festival)
DAICHI (DL) — Opened early '75 with 500 R, all the trimmings.

NEW MIYAKOSHI — 124 R, some JS. Rst w/French specialties. Tea ceremony. Water sports, skating. 5 min. from station.

SAPPORO GRAND (FC-Mod) — DT. 521 R, SU. Chinese, Japanese Rst. Cocktail lounge and bar w/traditional music. Several shops. *Conv:* 1000.

SAPPORO INTERNATIONAL — In front of station. Several dining rooms, bar, coffee shop. 100 R with various type accommodations. *Conv:* 2500. Moderate.

SAPPORO PARK — Suburban, mile from town. 225 R (8 Japanese). Several rsts, bars, bowling alleys, ski rental. *Conv:* 1000 in 12 meeting rooms.

SAPPORO PRINCE — Dt. 228 R. Dining room, Japanese rst, cocktail lounge. Golf and skiing rentals. *Conv:* 1000.

SAPPORO ROYAL — DT. 88 R (some Japanese). 6 rsts serving every type cuisine. Car rentals, souvenir shops.

SAPPORO TOKYU — Dt. 270 R, dining room, bar, cocktail lounge.

SOUTH KOREA

GETTING TO SEOUL

Korean Airline (both 1- and 2-stop flights) and Northwest Orient (2-stop) from Los Angeles via Honolulu (747s, DC10s). From San Francisco, NW (2-stop once weekly). There's frequent service from Japan and Hong Kong so that it's easy to include Korea in any circle trip.

There's a ferry from Shimonoseki, Japan, that crosses to Pusan (8 hrs.) on M, W, F at 5 p.m.; lvs. Pusan T, Th at 5 p.m., Sat. at 10 a.m. First-class fare about US $36 OW; 10% discount RT.

ENTRY REQUIREMENTS

Passport, tourist visa (free for up to 60 days), smallpox certificate. No visa required for transit passengers (up to 5 days).

You can bring in two bottles of liquor w/o duty *if opened*, otherwise subject to 151%-205% tax. 400 cigarettes or 50 cigars allowed. Undeveloped film not allowed out (according to the rule book; don't know if enforced).

CURRENCY

485 Korean Won (W) equal $1 US. Won notes come in denominations of 1,510, 50, 100, 500, 1,000, 5,000 and 10,000 ($20.60). Coins are W1, 5, 10, 50 and 100. Foreign currency must be declared on entry; readily exchangeable at airport, banks and hotels (but don't cash too much at a time or pockets will be stuffed with W notes). Won may not be brought in or taken out; you can reconvert up to $200 worth of Won into dollars.

CLIMATE & CLOTHING

September to early November is the best time to visit. Spring is inclined to be stormy, and summer is hot and humid with rain during June-July. Winters are dry and not excessively cold (Dec.-Jan. coldest). Seoul's climate is similar to Denver's; winters in Pusan are less chilly. Dress is fairly formal at clubs, restaurants, hotels. Bring northeastern U.S.-type clothing — heavy for winter, lighter for fall and spring. And don't forget rainwear.

Sort of as a foreword, note that names translated from the Korean into English may have different spellings, such as: Taegu or Daegu; Kyongju, Kyungju or Gyeonju; Pulgak-sa; Sokkuram, Sokguran or Seoggulam; Pusan or Busan, etc.

The Republic of Korea, occupying the southern portion of a mountainous peninsula with uniquely beautiful scenery, has been described as a "Museum Without Walls" — a nation with relics over 4,000 years old.

The 31,500,000 South Koreans are descendants of numerous migrating tribesmen originating in Asia, and despite terrific pressures at various times by China and Japan have kept their distinctive Korean culture, language, alphabet, cuisine and arts. Today you find them charming, gregarious, courteous and friendly.

Korea owes much of its culture, religion, art and writing to the Chinese; from here, it was passed along to Japan. The country, however, was a unified one under various indigent kingdoms (notably Silla) from the fifth century AD until its annexation by Japan in 1910 despite numerous incursions by Mongols, Chinese and Japanese, including a 200-year period of complete isolation from the rest of the world following its subjugation by Manchus in 1627. But the previous 200 years or so were a Golden Age when Korean arts and culture flourished.

Beginning in 1883, numbers of Western missionaries (mostly American) came to Korea, but the land continued to be a battleground between China and Japan, later Russia and Japan with the latter the final victor. In 1945, the country was divided at the 38th parallel into American and Russian zones of occupation. The Korean War began in June of 1950 with the invasion of South Korea, ended with the signing of an armistice in July of '53. Today, of course, South and North are still divided at the 38th parallel.

South Korea rarely fails to surprise, then please, its foreign visitors. Being one of the more uncommon destinations (except during the war), it is still, comparatively, an uncontaminated culture with a distinctive, national flavor that tourists find thoroughly enjoyable. However, with Korea National Tourism Corporation and Korean Airlines vigorously pushing tourism, obscurity is soon to be but a memory.

Folk dancing in the Changdok Palace complex.

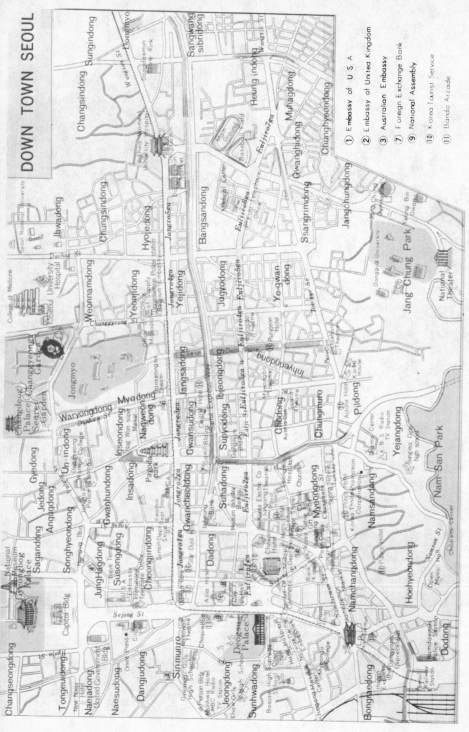

DOWN TOWN SEOUL

① Embassy of U S A
② Embassy of United Kingdom
③ Australian Embassy
⑦ Foreign Exchange Bank
⑨ National Assembly
⑩ Korea Tourist Service
⑪ Bando Arcade

SEOUL

A modern city of 7,500,000 with skyscrapers, good hotels, nightclubs and kisaeng houses, it is also an ancient city (capital of Korea since 1392) with stately palaces, gracious gardens, temples and shrines, imposing gates piercing ancient walls. From the Great East Gate (Ton Dae Mun), a 20-minute walk covers a great many of these old-time splendors. Overall, the city covers 102 sq. miles.

Subway sightseeing can be very rewarding. First stop should be the Toksu Palace Compound with its gracious, old buildings and the newer National Museum of Modern Art. Two stops further along bring you to the Chongmyo Royal Shrine, built to honor the spirits of the 27 Yi Dynasty monarchs. Annually, on the first Sunday of May, descendents of those Yi kings do just that.

A causeway brings you into Changkyong-won Park with its charming little houses, once retreats of royal ladies, a crystal pavilion and boating pond, botanical gardens and zoo.

Ride the subway to its eastern terminus, then hop a bus for a half-hour ride to the Royal Tombs.

Or start a day's sightseeing by riding an aerial tram to the summit of Mt. Namsam for a superb view of the city. Visit Changdok Palace and the Secret Garden, shop the East Gate Market.

Plan an afternoon at the Folk Museum and National Museum (closed Mon) on the same grounds as the Kyongbok Palace (open daily 9:30-5). The National Museum houses thousands of relics, many 4,000 years old, in eleven exhibition halls. On Sat, Sun afternoons between 3 and 4, attend the cultural dances at Korea House — no charge. On weekdays, special concerts of Confucian music can be arranged for groups of 150 or more at the National Classical Music Institute.

If you're on your way to Walker Hill to gamble or sun and bathe, drive thru Grand Children's Park — really something with its specially designed Coney-Island amusement area, lovely wooded paths among pavilions, forests where small animals roam and fish ponds with a variety of fish.

There are small admission fees (W150-200) for the Palaces, Secret Garden and Changkyong-won Zoo. Open 9:30 a.m. to 5 p.m. daily. Thruout Korea, museums are closed on Mondays.

If doing it on your own is not for you, KNTC (Korea Nat'l Tourism Corp.) has daily guided tours from 10 a.m. to 1 p.m. and 2 to 5 p.m. Morning tour (W4500) covers Changduk Palace, Secret Garden, Namsan Mt. and East Gate Market. In the afternoon (3500) the National Museum, Korea House and Pugac Skyway drive.

Seoul Tourist Information offers a free, daily minibus tour of the city.

SIGHTSEEING TOURS OUTSIDE SEOUL

Little question but that the two most important are to the Korean Folk Village and Panmunjom.

The Folk Village is a re-created country town in which every province of the country is represented, and all but two of the 180 buildings are authentic and traditional. Koreans actually live in these thatched-roof houses, follow rural ways of life, wear traditional clothing while tilling the soil and plying their crafts. Dramas and puppet plays are presented, folk dances have farmers swinging and swaying to the accompaniment of drums and gongs, while even mock funerals and weddings take place. Particularly interesting for those who haven't the time to tour the rural countryside, dine in a typical Korean restaurant. Admission is W1000; only additional charge is to see the palatial Yangban House — a 10-building compound representing an ancient nobleman's way of life. An hour's drive from Seoul to Yong-in by scheduled express bus (W800) or tour buses, it's open daily, 10 to 6.

A visit here should be combined with one to Suwon, an old fortress town that's still approached thru an elegant, seven-arched Rainbow Gate, the walls still linked by gates and watchtowers. Nearby is Yongju-sa, a fine Buddhist monastery.

KNTC has daily (except Sat, Sun) conducted tours to the demilitarized zone of Panmunjom, a 1½-hr. drive northwest of Seoul. Reservations by name, nationality and passport number must be made two days in advance. Cost of W7000 includes lunch.

Korean war veterans wishing to revisit the country can do so at very attractive tour prices (including half-price RT air fare from Los Angeles) thru May 1979; contact KNTC Los Angeles or New York offices for details.

DINING KOREAN STYLE

Specialties include: *Kimchi* — peppery, fermented pickle stored underground in earthen jars thruout winter. *Pulgogi* — strips of beef marinated with soy sauce, sesame and spices and charcoal roasted; *Sinsallo* — vegetable and meat casserole cooked at table. Delicate rice cakes are served with almost every meal.

Korea House, Pil Dong (27-7244), serves top Korean food; reservations a must. One of the famous fast-order restaurants is *Hanil Kwan,* adjacent to Cosmos Dept Store; known for red snapper, short ribs (kal bi). Upstairs are two beer gardens where a singer entertains. A grotto in the basement houses *Heart and Heart,* a dimly lit fun spot. Two blocks from Chosun Hotel is *Nam Gang,* specializing in sushi and sukiyaki — inexpensive, too. If your mouth is watering for roast beef, *Pine Hill,* in center of town, is the place. There are, of course, many Chinese and Japanese restaurants.

ENTERTAINMENT & NIGHT LIFE
Curfew midnight-4 a.m.

Not to be missed is the *kisaeng* party. A kisaeng is a young gal who serves as entertainer and hostess — and for much less than a Japanese geisha. Major hotels can arrange a party for you; the more attending the better as that makes it less expensive. Alone, an evening will cost from $60

on up. Upon arrival at a top restaurant, leave your shoes at the door; on being seated, you're served ginseng liquor (national drink). Your kisaeng leads you to a banquet table where you sit together on the same cushion. There will be plenty of food, drinking and dancing — balance of evening is up to you.

Most of the night life in Seoul is in the Itewon section which teems with bars, live music and dancing. There's a large selection of nightclubs, one of the favorites being *Pacific Nightclub,* San 21 (550181); dinner/show about W9000. The Myung Dong district, center of town, boasts of good entertainment spots. *Alte Liebe* and *Pago Pago* are two lively beerhalls, popular with the young crowd — a glass of beer or whisky about $1.50. Imported booze is sky high. Drink rice wine or ginseng.

Korean folk dances are being revived and can be seen at many hotels. Saturdays, Sundays at 3 p.m., there's a performance at Korea House; admission is free.

Native Korean music is divided into Confucian ritual music (ceremonial Chinese court music) and varieties of military, chamber and vocal music. Then there are Buddhist chants and the folk music of common people. Court music is slow, instruments ancient, singing is accompanied by drum only. Dances are stately. Folk music is fast and lively with athletic-type dancing. Music depends largely on metal gongs, *changgo* (drum) and a trumpet-type oboe.

There are lively mask dramas, the tragi-comic Lion Dance, spectacular Drum Dance and traditional Fan Dance performed on a revolving stage. The stunning National Theater, opened in '73, has helped revive Korea's native arts. Symphonies, operas, ballet are performed here. Near the National Theater, on eastern slope of Mt. Namsan, is the Institute of Classical Music, home of Royal Court Orchestra. Try to attend a *kayagum* (string instrument) concert.

Pan Korea Theater-Restaurant, downtown off Ulchi-ro, puts on three shows nightly. Korean performances from 7:20-8:30; Western at 9 and 10.

Chinese/Western dinner. About US $18 each. Open from 7 to 11 p.m.

There are night tours which include Yangban entertainment, a Pulgogi dinner and gala stage show, or an Arirang Night (where you make merry with singing and dancing) a Pulgogi dinner and, usually, a theatrical performance. From 6 to 11 p.m.; around W11,000 each.

Considered the best (and biggest) night spot is the Walker Hill complex southeast of DT Seoul. Las Vegas style, 24-hr. gambling (a new, lavish *Casino Continental* as of April 1978), the *Pacific* Theater Restaurant (two shows nightly), *Rainbow Night Club* (open all night) and all types of restaurants, bars are found here.

WHAT & WHERE TO BUY

Good bargains are still to be found here. From toothpaste at 30¢ to cashmere at $5 per yard (60" width), shopping is both good and varied. In the gift shops and arcades of major hotels, English-speaking personnel are found — but not in department stores and underground arcades. And don't forget, haggling is the way to buy.

Best buys are dolls, 24 kt. gold jewelry, white porcelain pottery, inlaid lacquerware, bamboo and rattan furniture, silks, brocades, musical instruments, leather goods, wood carvings, custom tailoring, transistor radios. But check everything closely for quality. Genuine antiques, such as paintings, handcrafts, must have authorization and certificate from Bureau of Cultural Property before export is permitted.

There are tax-free shops in all major cities; valid passport and foreign currency (no Won) required.

Best shopping areas: Chosun Hotel Arcade, Bando Arcade, Pagoda Park Arcade, Saewoon Arcade and East Gate Market. Shinsegye, Midopa, Saerona, Sin-Sin, Cosmos and Koreana are the department stores.

Korean Ginseng is the mysterious herbal medicine known thruout the world as a rejuvenator and elixir of life. There are red and white ginsengs as well as ginseng tea, extract, powder and drink preparations. Red Ginseng is available only from Korea Ginseng Industrial Co., west exit of Bando Arcade; white from any tax-free store. When purchasing ginseng, check for government guarantee seal on label. Amounts for export limited.

THE SPORTING LIFE

Not only are modern sports very popular but traditional folk games still survive in rural communities. National Folk Arts Contest occurs last week of October; provinces vie for top honors. Particularly colorful is *Kosam-nori,* a group game recalling ancient battles. *Taekwondo,* a deadly art of self-defense, originated in Korea. Also, men dressed in long white robes, black hats compete in archery.

In Seoul, there's horse racing at Tuksom Track. There are 14 golf courses in the country, several of championship caliber. There's snow skiing at Taekwallryong Highland (ski lifts, bungalow accommodations), mountain climbing at Mt. Pukhan, near Seoul, Mt. Sorak on the east coast and Mt. Halla on Cheju-do; the island is also popular for top pheasant shooting.

SEOUL TRANSPORTATION

From airport to hotels, there are several ways to go. Public limousines charge W250 per person. By taxi, it's about a W2000 ride.

Basic taxi fare is W200 for first two kilometers, W30 each additional 500 meters. Hourly rates flexible — bargain. Don't tip (unless driver handles luggage, waits for you).

Private car with guide-driver runs about $50 a day.

DOMESTIC TRANSPORTATION

KAL has daily flights to Pusan, Kangnung, Cheju Island, Samchok, Pohand, Chinhae, Sokcho, Chinju from Seoul, direct flights between Pusan and Cheju.

By train, there's service to all major cities from Seoul, a super-express with reclining seats, dining car to Pusan (4½ hours). Tickets for train and bus travel are sold OW only; obtainable day in advance at stations or from qualified agents.

Highways are good, bus service frequent. 5- to 5½-hour run to Pusan via toll road. Rental cars readily available; motels being constructed thruout country.

KYONGJU

Anyone wishing to absorb the underlying culture of Korea should plan to visit Kyongju, for it is here in the heart of the thousand-year-old Silla Kingdom, founded in the days of the Caesars, that the Land of Morning Calm continues to live the true beauty of its name.

This is an ancient, walled city of royal gold crowns, castle ruins, highly painted temple walls, carved stone monuments and tombs, age-incrusted pagodas that take you back 1,500 years. Bearded old men walk the roads, younger men and women pull handcarts over them.

In this town — it's really not a city despite its 90,000 inhabitants — the Kyongju National Museum has a priceless collection of Silla artifacts, jewelry of untold wealth, crowns of kings and queens, ancient pottery (still being discovered as more tombs are unearthed). In fact, the entire town is an open-air museum of shrines and pagodas by willow-swept ponds, not to mention the ruins of a legendary Palace of the Crescent Moon. Thruout this valley, you see dozens of royal burial mounds, 60 ft. high and 200 to 300 feet in length, beneath which are the burial chambers.

Twenty minutes away, at Pulguk-sa in beautiful Songni National Park, is Korea's most famous Buddhist Temple with its intricate stonework and archways. Ten minutes up the mountain from Pulguk-sa, the Great White Buddha (Sakya) is enshrined within the Sokkuram Cave Temple, a place of reverence for Buddhist pilgrims for the past 12 centuries. Silla Folk Festival is celebrated in Kyongju in mid-October.

Tour operators have regular tours out of Seoul and Pusan. An easy way to get here from Seoul is by air-conditioned, express buses which depart for the 4½-hr. scenic trip over a super-highway every 1½ hours from Dongdaemun bus terminal near the East Gate. KAL has 45-minute flights to Taegu or Pusan for transfer by car or bus (50 min.) to Kyongju. Or take a deluxe train to Taegu (3 hrs.).

Beautiful Sejong Cultural Center, in central Seoul, has a 4,200-seat auditorium equipped with film and convention facilities and rotating, elevating and sliding stages that accommodate up to 500 performers. Complex includes a 500-seat auditorium, conference halls and meeting rooms. Hotel Lotte is also well equipped for major conferences.

Kyongju's Tourism Center, part of the Bomun Lake Resort, has a 900-seat auditorium, three seminar rooms, all modern equipment.

PUSAN

Korea's largest port is interesting to those arriving from Japan by air or ferry, to Korean war veterans and, most of all, to visitors to Kyongju, just 50 miles away (1½-hr. drive).

A day tour should include visits to the U.N. Cemetery, where the fallen of 16 allied nations lie, the lovely Pomo-sa Temple, founded some 1,300 years ago, and equally delightful Tongdo-sa complex of shrines and grand halls.

Thirty miles away is Haeundae Beach — white sands, mild surf, spa and casino.

From Seoul, Pusan is an hour's plane flight, four hours by Kwan Kwang Express train or five and a half by express bus.

CHEJU ISLAND

The "Hawaii of the Orient" is a volcanic island dotted with orange groves, pineapple fields and charming villages of straw-roofed houses. Once an independent kingdom, the people still retain their own identity — in fact, the landscape is quite different from the mainland 60 miles to the north. Here beneath the lofty slopes of Mt. Halla, Korea's highest, are miles of inviting beaches, sub-tropical temperatures and the famed diving women who supply Korea with abalone and edible seaweed. An encircling highway gives easy access to the forests, waterfalls, caves and villages.

In spring and fall, Samsonghyol Cave Festival takes place here, as does the Halla Folk Festival in October.

With the opening of KAL's Hotel Cheju, the island has become a lovely year-'round resort just an hour's jet flight from Seoul, 40 minutes by air from Pusan.

Hotel Directory

Most hotels have central heating, AC and TV. Many serve Korean, Chinese, Japanese as well as Western-style food.

Hotel rates are quoted below in U.S. dollars for double occupancy. Korean-style rooms slightly higher than Western style. Some hotels add from 10%-20% tax depending on hotel and city.

If without advance reservations, Tourist Information Center at Seoul airport can make them on arrival.

SEOUL

DL: $36-$49; SU: $60-$275.
FC+: $30-$45; SU: $47 up.
FC: $25-$38; SU: Up to $80.
MOD: $25-$27; SU: $35 up.
INEXP: $15-$20.

AMBASSADOR (FC+) — DT. 170 R, SU, plus 300 R, SU in new wing. Attractive Sky Lounge, several bars. Chinese, Japanese, Korean, French Rsts. Nightclub. *Conv:* 1700. US $36-$44.

CHOSUN (DL) — DT. Definitely best, most luxurious to date. 500 R, SU (uniquely Korean). Top service. French rst, Italian coffee shop, Chinese rst and terrific noon buffet. Posh Tomorrow Nightclub. 2 cocktail lounges. Pool, large shopping arcade. *Conv:* 800. *Rsv:* Americana. US $37-$52.

HAN YUNG (FC) — Near Han River, 10 min. from DT. 15-story hi-rise with 417 R, several rsts, nightclub. Opens late '78.

HILTON HOTEL (DL) — 600 R. Opens 1980.

HYATT REGENCY (DL) — Should be great. Opens '79 at foot of Mt. Namsan. 720 R.

KING SEJONG (FC) — Older, spacious hotel has been refurbished. 222 older R, 100 in newer wing. Dining rooms serve several different cuisines. Coffee shop, bar. Korean dances on request. *Conv:* 1000.

KOREANA (FC) — 268 R, SU. Japanese rst, grill, coffee shop, bar. Nightclub features Korean dancing, music and Western show. *Conv:* 400.

LOTTE (DL) — Opened DT in '78 with 940 R. Indoor pool, several rsts, outside glass elevator, large convention facilities.

PRESIDENT (FC) — 33-story DT hi-rise with great views. 303 R (some Korean style); excellent Jumbo Steak House, bar, cocktail lounge. 31st-floor nightclub. Well priced for top hotel. US $25-$29.

ROYAL (FC) — DT. 320 R, SU. Sky view dining in one of several rsts. Discotheque. Nightclub features Korean dancing, drama, music. *Conv:* 300.

SEOUL MIRAMAR (DL) — Great view of Han River, near San Park. Opened early '78 with 659 R, game room, pool, tennis court. Several rsts, bar, nightclub.

SEOUL PLAZA (DL) — DT, near Duksoo Palace. Opened '76 with 540 R, SU (some Korean style). Several rsts, tea lounge, coffee house, bar and shopping arcade. Well priced.

SEOUL TOKYU (FC+) — DT. 210 R, SU. Starlight nightclub, Japanese rst, tempura corner. Crystal Grill (French specialties). *Conv:* 500.

SHILLA (DL) — 10 min from DT near Namsan Hill adjacent to Yongbing-wan (official Government guest house). 700 luxurious R. 4 rsts, 2 bars, cocktail lounge and nightclub. Pool, tennis courts. *Conv:* 1500. Opened '78.

TOWER — Residential area, 15 min. from railway terminal, 30 min. from airport. 243 R, some Korean style. Skyview lounge, rst and nightclub. Pool. Mod.

SHERATON WALKER HILL (DL to FC) — 800 R, SU and villas. Limousine service to DT (20 min), airport (30 min). Casino, kisaeng house. Hilltop Bar, Rainbow Nightclub, Pacific Theater Rst, plus many more. Indoor and outdoor pool, tennis, golf riding; water sports during summer. Korean folk dances. Secluded atmosphere.

CHEJU-DO ISLAND
(10% service & 10% tax added.)

CHEJU-KAL (FC) — 310 AC R, SU and Korean-style R (rates same). Casino, nightclub, Kisaeng, pool, bowling. Several rsts, cocktail lounge. Cheju traditional entertainment. *Rsv:* KAL. Mod-FC rates.

INCHEON

OLYMPOS (FC) — Popular weekend gambling casino resort, 40 min. from Seoul, 25 min. from Kimpo airport. Several dining rooms, bars. Kisaeng house (Korean music on request). Pool. 191 AC R overlook port and beach. Mod. rates, plus 20% tax.

KYONGJU

KYONGJU PARK (FC) — 238 R; opened April '78. Near Pulquk-sa Temple.
BOMUN LAKE — Opens Spring '79 with 600 rooms. An American project.

PUSAN

CHOSUN BEACH (DL) — Haeundae Beach, 25 min. from DT. Beautiful lobby, many rsts, bars. Pool. 350 AC R, SU have ocean view. Opened late '77. *Rsv:* Americana.
KUKDONG — Hot springs resort on beach. 125 R, dining room, bar, cocktail lounge, nightclub. Pool. Rsv. difficult in summer.
PUSAN (FC) — DT, near station and ferry. Opened Jan. '78 with 130 R, rsts.
PUSAN PLAZA — Economy class opened '77. Popular with Japanese. 124 R, 2 rsts, nightclub.

OTHER KOREAN FACTS

Airport Departure Tax — $2.50 US.
Current—100v AC, 60 c.
Embassies—US at 82 Sejong-ro (722601). United Kingdom (for Canada), 4 Chong-dong (757341).
Gambling Casinos—At Walker Hill, Incheon, Pusan, Cheju-do Island.
Language — Korean; English quite widely spoken.
Medical Service—Good. Hospitals staffed by competent, well-trained doctors, nurses.
Population—32 million; Seoul 7+ million.
Time — Same as Japan.
Tipping — Lightly if at all. Taxi drivers, waiters, bellboys not usually tipped. Hotels/restaurants add 10% service. Baggage porters get W100 per load.
Tourist Information — Korea Tourist Board in Los Angeles (510 W. 6th St.; 213-623-1226) and New York (460 Park Ave.; 212-688-7543).
Visas — Obtainable from Korean Embassies in Washington and Ottawa, from Consulates in Atlanta, Boston, Chicago, Cleveland, Dallas, Denver, Honolulu, Houston, Los Angeles, Miami, Minneapolis, Mobile, Montreal, New Orleans, New York, Oklahoma City, Phoenix, Portland, San Antonio, San Diego, San Francisco, St. Louis, Seattle, Vancouver.

CALENDAR OF EVENTS

Traditional festivals are based on lunar year; holidays of recent origin according to the solar almanac.

January 1st — Offerings to senior family members. Memorial services for the spirits of ancestors.
March 1st — Commemorates Independent Movement against Japan.
Late May — Buddha's Birthday observed with lantern festival; festive parades in Seoul.
June 10th-15th. Farmers' Day. Colorful dances, music and much drinking of *makkolli* (rice wine).
July 17th — Constitution Day. Military parades.
August 15th — Liberation Day. Parades celebrate liberation from Japan in 1945.
October 1st — Armed Forces Day. Colorful pageants, air show, military parade. 3rd — Founding of Korea by Tangun, 2333 B.C. Late Sept. or early Oct. — Moon Festival, a great national holiday — Korean version of Thanksgiving; visit tombs for a day of remembrance and feasting. Mid-October — Silla Cultural Festival. 5-day celebration with parades, mask dances, folk music. 24th — United Nations Day. Tribute to all who took part in Korean War.
December 25th — Christmas is celebrated in much the same manner as Western countries.

TAIWAN
Republic of China

Bridge of Motherly Devotion, Taroka Gorge, is also known as the Marble
Bridge (rails and lions of marble).

Republic of China

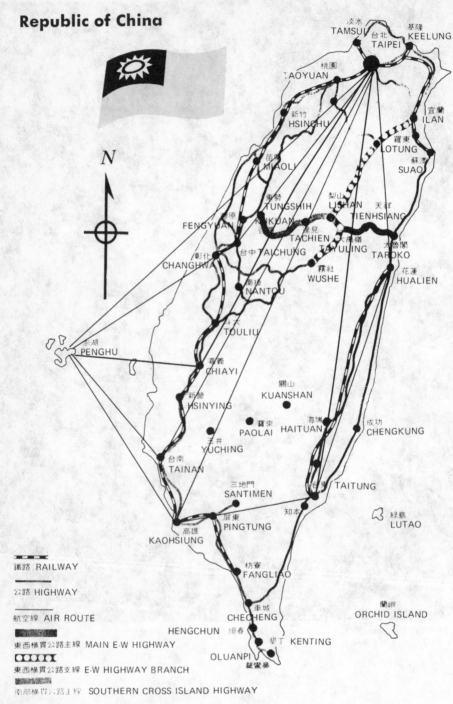

N

淡水 TAMSUI
台北 TAIPEI
基隆 KEELUNG
桃園 TAOYUAN
宜蘭 ILAN
新竹 HSINCHU
羅東 LOTUNG
蘇澳 SUAO
苗栗 MIAOLI
東勢 TUNGSHIH
梨山 LISHAN
天祥 TIENHSIANG
豐原 FENGYUAN
谷關 KUKUAN
大甲 TACHIEN
台中 TAICHUNG
大禹嶺 TAYULING
太魯閣 TAROKO
彰化 CHANGHWA
霧社 WUSHE
花蓮 HUALIEN
南投 NANTOU
斗六 TOULIU
澎湖 PENGHU
嘉義 CHIAYI
關山 KUANSHAN
新營 HSINYING
寶來 PAOLAI
海端 HAITUAN
成功 CHENGKUNG
玉井 YUCHING
台南 TAINAN
三地門 SANTIMEN
台東 TAITUNG
綠島 LUTAO
屏東 PINGTUNG
知本
高雄 KAOHSIUNG
枋寮 FANGLIAO
蘭嶼 ORCHID ISLAND
車城 CHECHENG
恆春 HENGCHUN
墾丁 KENTING
鵝鑾鼻 OLUANPI

鐵路 RAILWAY

公路 HIGHWAY

航空線 AIR ROUTE

東西橫貫公路主線 MAIN E-W HIGHWAY

東西橫貫公路支線 E-W HIGHWAY BRANCH

南部橫貫公路主線 SOUTHERN CROSS ISLAND HIGHWAY

100

"To the people of Free China the fact that they are able to celebrate the lunar New Year in the traditional manner is a matter of great significance. It means that we are a free people, and, being free, we can do anything that is legally permissible. In the meantime, we are well aware that our compatriots on the mainland no longer have such freedom. During the last quarter of a century the Chinese Communists have turned them into slaves in the truest sense of the word. Being hardly able to keep body and soul together, they cannot afford to celebrate the lunar New Year as we do, even if they could obtain the permission of their Communist rulers, who are bent on the destruction of Chinese culture."[1]

The foregoing, though naturally biased, is essentially valid. Some United States congresswomen, after spending two weeks in Red China in early 1976, were thoroughly disillusioned and depressed by the condition of the masses. Yet in the Republic of China — very possibly the most misunderstood and underrated nation in the world — per capita income is the second highest in the Orient, the economy is surging ahead,[2] people are well fed, well dressed and obviously happy. One had only to view the Special Exhibit on Agricultural and Rural Development in Taipei's Sun Yat Sen Memorial to appreciate how far the Republic of China has progressed since the old War Lord days — and how far behind this tiny progressive country has left the hulking, clumsy Red Giant on the mainland.

On our third visit to Taiwan, we spent two weeks becoming reacquainted with Free China — a totally pleasant, fascinating and enjoyable experience we can recommend to any freedom-loving person. For it is our firm conviction that only here will you see the real China of old.

HISTORY OF TAIWAN, Republic of China

Taiwan, meaning *Terraced Bay*, has been familiar to the West as Formosa, the result of being sighted in the 16th century by a Portuguese galleon and the sailors exclaiming rapturously, "Ilha Formosa" (beautiful island) — which it is.

But long before that, it had a colorful history. It was a protectorate of the Chinese Empire in 1206, the year the Mongol conqueror, Genghis Khan, founded the Yuan dynasty. In 1684, it became a prefecture of Fukien province on the mainland, and in 1887, during the Ching or Manchu dynasty, China's last, was proclaimed a separate province of China.

The Dutch invaded in 1624, remained as colonists for 37 years until driven out by invading forces from the mainland. Previously, the Spanish had occupied northern-most Taiwan in 1626 but were driven off by the Dutch in 1641.

In 1884, it was France's turn to occupy the north following a dispute with China over the Yunnan-Indo China border, and in March of 1885 they also took the Pescadores but withdrew completely from both areas three months later under terms of a treaty with China.

Following the 1894 war over Korea, China ceded Taiwan and Pescadores to the Japanese, Korea was declared independent — and subsequently annexed by Japan. Of course, as of 1945 Japan lost everything and Taiwan and the other small islands once more belonged to China, later to become the stronghold of the Republic of China when 2,000,000 mainlanders emigrated in 1948-49.

Actually, this mountainous island has, for centuries, been settled by Chinese from the mainland and thus became a true center of Chinese culture long before 1948. Except for some 260,000 descendents of original island dwellers, called aborigines, Taiwanese are essentially Chinese.

Buddhism and Taoism are the predominate religions. There are around 600,000 Christians, divided equally between Catholics and Protestants, and some 40,000 Moslems.

[1] Editorial in the *China Post*, January 30, 1976.
[2] When 10 primary infrastructure projects are completed in 1978, Republic of China should join the ranks of developed nations.

Taiwan, its shape likened to a tobacco leaf, is 240 miles long and 85 miles wide at its broadest, a total of 13,885 sq. miles. Hills and mountains cover two-thirds of the island; there are 62 peaks more than 10,000 ft. high. Additionally there's the archipelago in the Formosa Strait between Taiwan and the mainland known as the Pescadores but officially Penghu, one of the 16 provinces comprising the country.

Since December 7, 1949, Taipei (literally North Taiwan) has been the provisional capital of the Republic of China. In July, 1967, it became a special municipality with the same status as a province, thus upping its area to 105 sq. miles by adding six satellite districts (which include Peitou and Yangminshan). It is, of course, the country's largest city, followed by Kaohsiung (1,000,000), Tainan (515,000), Taichung (510,000) and Keelung (350,000).

QUICK REFERENCE GUIDE TO TAIWAN

There are six very valid reasons for visiting one of the world's few remaining travel bargains:

1) National Palace Museum in Taipei, one of the greats of the world, an experience so exhilarating — possibly more profound than any other in the Far East — as to alone provide the incentive to come here. But don't make the mistake of including it as part and parcel of a city tour: *it alone deserves the equivalent of one day*. Those who truly appreciate art and history should allot two days or more — one on arrival, other before departure; you'll be amazed how much you didn't see first time around. And then there's the National Historical Museum. . . .

2) Taipei's Chinese cuisines. There are, probably, more top restaurants here serving exquisite Chinese specialties than anywhere else, mainly because most of the masters of mainland cooking left there in 1948 and have handed down their recipes and expertise. Our own experiences indicate that, with the exception of some Hong Kong restaurants, the farther from Taiwan you go the less rapturous are the cuisines.

3) Spectacular Taroko Gorge drive.

4) Beautiful Sun Moon Lake trip.

5) Chance to see rural China as it's always been — an unlikely opportunity on mainland China in the immediate future for all but a comparative handful of foreign visitors.

6) Best shopping and hotel bargains in the Far East.

Taipei and vicinity, Taroko Gorge, Sun Moon Lake are the highlights. Other places mentioned in this section are, if time is limited, unessential.

TRIP PLANNING

Two Days — Spend both in Taipei enjoying the Museum, restaurants, opera and other top sights.

Three Days — Add day trip to Hualien for Taroko Gorge drive.

Four Days — Two days in Taipei and day trips to Toroko Gorge and Sun Moon Lake out of Taipei. Preferable, however, is

Five Days — This way you can take the three-day, two-night tour that crosses the East-West Highway from Hualien thru Taroka Gorge to Taichung after overnight in Lishan, then on to Sun Moon Lake for overnight; sightseeing and return to Taipei on third day.

Six Days — Add an extra day and night in Kaohsiung after seeing Tainan. Actually, though, if we had six days in Taiwan, we'd spend a minimum of three days in Taipei, assuming you want to thoroughly see the National Palace Museum and National Museum of History.

Local tour operators present a variety of combinations involving the above, definitely the basic highlights of a trip here.

GENERAL INFORMATION

Airport Departure Tax — NT$175.

. Beauty Shops — Not to be missed. A wonderful massage precedes the wash and set. And the prices (even in the best hotels) are a delight: about $4 for shampoo/set or haircut and shampoo, a permanent for under $12. Barber Shop prices correspondingly low. Tip 10%-15%.

Currency — 36 New Taiwan Dollars (NT$) equals $1 US, so NT$10 equals 28 cents, NT$100 is $2.80. Notes come in NT$5, 10, 50 and 100 denominations; coins in NT$1 and 5 (silver alloy), NT$0.50 (copper), 1¢ and 2¢ (aluminum alloy). Keep official exchange receipts when purchasing NT$; on departure, maximum of NT$8000 may be reconverted at airport's Bank of Taiwan, providing you have purchase receipts for same. Cash (not travel checks) must be declared on entry in order to leave with same; otherwise, only equivalent of $1,000 US in foreign currencies may be exported. Up to 4000 NT Dollars may be brought in but maximum of NT$2000 taken out.

Customs — Radios, tape recorders, TVs must be declared; no duty if taken with you on departure.

Climate and Clothing — Subtropical. Taipei is cooler than central areas, which are mild to warm, so a topcoat, sweater are handy in the city during winter. Otherwise no need for coats (except rainwear) or warm clothing. Extreme south may get quite hot. Spring and fall best seasons; October particularly great because of many festivals. Rainy seasons; winter, summer; July to Oct. is typhoon time (but rarely hit here).

Dental & Medical Care — Excellent and so cheap it's worth being sick; in fact, Japanese come here for their dental care (big tourist attraction). Some hospital charges (approx.); 2-room suite, $30; special class room, $23; specialist's (doctor) fee, $10; nurse, $3.00; resident doctor's fee, $3.00. Rooms come with color TV, refrig. A 2-night, 3-day complete physical costs $250. Foregoing applies to privately owned, U.S.-West Germany equipped *Central Hospital* in Taipei (looks like plush hotel).

Electric Current — 110v, 60 cycles, AC.

Language — Mandarin, Taiwanese; English widely spoken.

Postage — Airmail to US, NT$10 for letters, NT$6 for postcards.

Population — 17,000,000 with better than 2,-225,000 in Taipei.

Radio — Dial 100 for American Armed Forces.

Shopping Hours — 'Til 10 p.m. daily; many stores open on Sundays.

Telephones — NT$1 coin for public phones.

Time — 8 hours ahead of GMT. An hour behind Tokyo.

Tipping — 10% service added to room rates, restaurant checks. NT$20 per bag for porters. Tip cab drivers only if they provide an extra service.

Tourist Information — Tourism Bureau, Republic of China, 210 Post St., San Francisco 94108; 3660 Wilshire Blvd., Los Angeles 90010; 1 World Trade Center (Suite 86155), New York 10048. Offices in Taipei: At Airport and 280 Chunghsiao E. Rd. Sec. 4 (P.O. Box 1490).

Water — Don't drink from taps. Hotels, restaurants service distilled or boiled. Bottled available.

NATIONAL HOLIDAYS

Jan. 1 — Founding of Republic of China.

Mar. 29 — Youth Day.

Apr. 5 — Tomb-Sweeping Day.

Sept. 28 — Birthday of Confucius (Teachers' Day).

Oct. 10 — Double Tenth National Day.

Oct. 25 — Taiwan Retrocession Day.

Oct. 31 — Birth in 1887 of President Chiang Kai-shek.

Nov. 12 — Dr. Sun Yat-sen's Birthday.

Dec. 25 — Constitution Day.

OTHER MEMORABLE ANNIVERSARIES

Mar. 12 — Death of Dr. Sun Yat-sen (1925), observed as Arbor Day.

Apr. 8 — Buddha Bathing Festival.

Apr. 29 — Landing in Taiwan in 1661 of the Ming Dynasty loyalist, Cheng Cheng-kung (Koxinga), who ousted the Dutch colonists.

Oct. 21 — Overseas Chinese Day.

OTHER EVENTS

Observed according to Lunar Calendar; 1st moon generally in February.

Chinese New Year's Day (1st day, 1st moon). Businessmen celebrate with feast for employees. If chicken head is pointed at you, you're fired!

Lantern Festival (15th day, 1st moon). In Taipei, temples hold lantern competitions; don't miss this at Lung Shan Temple. Fireworks, lavish feasts.

Birthday of Kuan Yin, Goddess of Mercy (19th day, 2nd moon).

Birthday of Matsu, Goddess of the Sea (23rd day, 3rd moon). Celebrated in 300 temples, particularly in Peikang and Tainan.

Dragon Boat Festival (5th day, 5th moon).

Birthday of Cheng Huang, City God of Taipei (13th day, 5th moon).

Month of the Ghosts begins 1st day, 7th moon.

Mid-Autumn (Moon) Festival (15th day, 8th moon; Sept.).

ENTRY REQUIREMENTS

Passport, visa (no charge for U.S. citizens, $2.50 for others or $1.25 for groups of 15 or more), vaccination certificate. Visa obtainable from any Republic of China consular office, embassy. Transit visas are valid for three months from date of issue for 2-week stay (not extendible); tourist visas valid for six months from issue for month's stay (extendible for another month w/o charge). Group permits are good for two weeks maximum (not extendible); group must enter/leave together.

HOW TO GET HERE

From U.S. — China Air has non-stop 747s from SFO (12:10) and LAX (13:05) NW has 1-stop from SEA, 2-stop from CHI. CI and NW also jet in from Honolulu.

From Japan — It's a 2-hr., 10-min. flight from Tokyo, 1:35 from Osaka (CX, KE, NW, TG), 1:15 from Okinawa (NW, PA), all non-stop.

From Bangkok, Hong Kong — 3 hrs., 20 min. non-stop from former (KE), 1:20 non-stop from latter.

Often overlooked is the possibility of entering/leaving Taiwan from/for Hong Kong by way of Kaohsiung on southwest coast below Taipei. This eliminates return to Taipei when excursioning south to Kaohsiung.

ARRIVAL BY SEA

At Keelung, 18 miles north of Taipei, a 30-minute drive over scenic MacArthur Thruway. Pier No. 2, the passenger terminal, is one of the best facilities in Far East.

DOMESTIC AIR SERVICE

From TPE, Hualien (HUN) is a 25-min. flight, Kaohsiung (KHH) 40 min., Makung (MZG) 45 min., as is Tainan (TNN). Taichung is 35. Frequent, non-stop service to all by China Airlines (CAL) and Far Eastern Air Transport (FAT), mostly by jets. *Always carry your passport;* needed for check-ins.

BUS & RAIL SERVICES

Comfortable, well-maintained buses go everywhere inexpensively. There are excellent, air-conditioned express trains from Keelung and Taipei to Taichung and Kaohsiung.

TAIWAN'S ECONOMY

The impressive growth of its economy is reflected in its soaring foreign trade, i.e., from US $1.52 billion in 1967 to $17.77 billions in 1977 (expected to reach $20.8 billions in '78), as well as the rising living standards of its people which increased from $616 in 1967 to $1,079 in '77, thus ranking Taiwan as the world's 18th middle-income country.

A number of major construction projects have led to this growth, notably the world's second largest shipyard and an integrated steel mill at Kaohsiung, electrification of major rail lines; three nuclear power plants are under construction.

Textiles (yard goods and garments) are the leading export, then sugar which, until 1960, had been the traditional leader; others are electrical machinery, metals and metal products, plywood, processed and unprocessed food, fish and seafood. Leading imports are farm products (wheat, corn, soybeans, cotton), machinery, raw materials — and oil.

Due to the mountainous terrain, only about 25% of the land — about 2.3 million acres — can be farmed. Rice, sugarcane and sweet potatoes are the biggest and most important crops; others are bananas, summer vegetables, pineapples and citrus fruits. Tea is one of the better exports. Fisheries production is substantial, supports 250,000 people.

As of 1974, less than 38% of the population lived on farms.

INSTANT TAXIS

At any hour in any weather, no problem in hailing a cab — instantly. And metered fares may be the lowest in the world — NT$12 for the first kilometer, NT$4 for each additional 500 meters — plus NT$11 for luggage. You go anywhere in Taipei for NT$25 to $60 per ride (60¢ to $1.75). *But have destinations written in Chinese characters;* carry your hotel's card to be sure to get back okay.

Taipei's new Taoyuan airport is a short NT$54 cab ride from DT, about NT$34 to/from uptown hotels.

TAIPEI

In this era of soaring metropolitan prices, Taipei (2,250,000 pop.) is a pleasant discovery and oasis. Though prices have risen considerably in the past few years, the city remains comparatively inexpensive; its people are pleasant, efficient, charming (in all social classes), smiling and eager to serve, its restaurants have the finest regional Chinese cuisines in all of the Far East, and the after-dark attractions are both attractive[1] and reasonable.

But the color, fun and excitement of Taipei is seen to better advantage in the streets than thru the windows of a sightseeing bus. Which is why a two- or three-day visit is totally inadequate. We spent hours and hours ambling up one street, down another, poking into alleys and lanes and covered rows of food stalls — completely enthralled by the colorful sights and sounds and pleasing odors, impressed by the overall cleanliness and industriousness, amused by the many signs (Kentucky Fried Chicken Delight; Wan Yu Shan Ham & Tea Co.; Dear Donut) and desperately loved the pudding-cheeked, amber-eyed infants, extremely well-behaved, adorable children.

To savor old Taipei to the full, spend time strolling around the downtown sections, particularly the area bounded by the Railway Station[2] to the north, Chungsan South Road to the east, Tamsui River on the west and the south end of New Park. Heart of the shopping area — jammed with shops, department stores, food stalls, markets and street vendors — is around Chengtu Rd. (east-west) and Chungwa Rd. (north-south), once famous as Haggle Alley.[3]

Uptown (north), where most of the hotels are, the streets paralleling and intersecting Chungsan North Rd. are nearly as interesting, though they lack the variety and mass action. Particularly fascinating is Chyng Cuang Market, block and a half south of the President Hotel between Chungsan N. Rd. and Linsen N. Rd. — you'll pinch yourself to make sure you're really seeing a vendor in coolie hat carrying live chickens in wicker baskets slung on either end of a pole carried across his shoulders.

When downtown, don't miss Taipei New Park with its pagoda, pavilions, Chinese and Japanese gardens — particularly early in the morning (before nine) when hundreds of Kung Fu[4] enthusiasts and other physical culturists assemble to exercise in full view of Buddha, Confucius, God and fellow countrymen — truly an unusual happening.

For seeing Taipei on your own, the Tourist Bureau's *Taiwan Tourist Map* is essential. Get one before you leave the U.S. or upon arrival at the airport. In both English and Chinese characters, it's invaluable not only to locate streets and places but also to show taxi drivers where you wish to go; best to circle the desired destination in pencil to eliminate any misinterpretation.

---

[1] Hotel-departing females often create early a.m. traffic jams.
[2] If time permits, go inside and watch all of China stream in and out.
[3] Still a fascinating melange of food shops and inexpensive merchandise but no longer the mecca of those seeking antiques and bargains in better merchandise. In fact, it's almost impossible to find any Chinese antiques of value at any price, anywhere.
[4] A philosophic-physical body conditioning requiring intelligence, perseverance, patience, coordination and full development of one's potential thru the "marital art spirit." Possession of these qualities leads to an inner harmony, external calmness and tranquility.

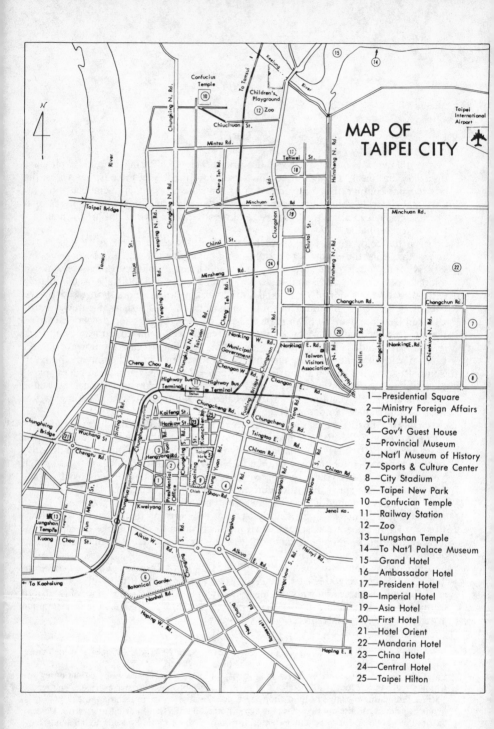

MAP OF TAIPEI CITY

1—Presidential Square
2—Ministry Foreign Affairs
3—City Hall
4—Gov't Guest House
5—Provincial Museum
6—Nat'l Museum of History
7—Sports & Culture Center
8—City Stadium
9—Taipei New Park
10—Confucian Temple
11—Railway Station
12—Zoo
13—Lungshan Temple
14—To Nat'l Palace Museum
15—Grand Hotel
16—Ambassador Hotel
17—President Hotel
18—Imperial Hotel
19—Asia Hotel
20—First Hotel
21—Hotel Orient
22—Mandarin Hotel
23—China Hotel
24—Central Hotel
25—Taipei Hilton

NATIONAL PALACE MUSEUM

There are simply not enough superlatives to describe the fabulous collections housed here, nor, if there were, would they adequately do justice to one of the world's most superb treasure houses. In fact, it is so completely unique there is no other to which it can be compared. So, for a cultural thrill unequalled except for a few of the greatest art museums, come to Taiwan.

The largest collection of Chinese art and history the world has ever known, one that has taken over a thousand years to assemble, beginning with the Ch'ing Dynasty court, is a consolidation of the Palace Museum of Peiping and Central Museum of Nanking collections flown from the mainland in 1948. Inaugurated November 12, 1965, specifically to house over 600,000 art treasures (if all displays were changed every three months, it would take 15 years to show them in their entirety), the National Palace Museum is a handsome, four-storied, air-conditioned building of classical Chinese style surrounded by the 110-acre Botanical Garden in northern Taipei, a 20-minute drive from downtown. Including two subsequent additions, total area is 4,761 *p'ing* (a p'ing equals 6 ft. by 6 ft. or 36 sq. ft.), of which 2,770 *p'ing* are for display. The Museum attracts over a million visitors each year, of which about 25% are foreign.

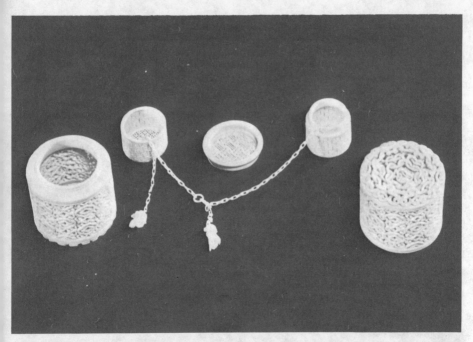

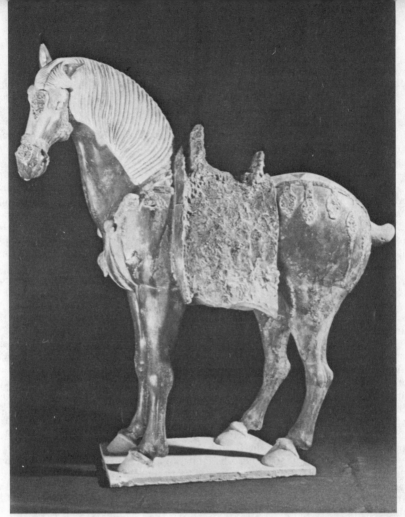

TANG DYNASTY HORSE National Museum of History

POTTERY-MAKING IN TAIWAN
"The Chinese," it's been well said, "are the greatest race of potters the world has ever seen."
Nowhere is this truer than in Taiwan today where the ancient craft is flourishing by producing fine
replicas of priceless originals housed in the National Palace Museum and the National Museum of
History. Outstandingly popular are replicas of pottery horses produced in rich reddish-browns
during the Tang Dynasty (618-907 AD). So, when you visit Taipei, you can place an order for the
next best thing to the originals — replicas by Chao Jun-po, a master potter specializing in horses
and two-humped, Bactrian camels. Orders can be placed with Fine Pottery Arts Co., No. 8, Lane
6, Hsienyen Rd., Chinmei, in Taipei; prices range from $20 to $150 — and you may have to wait
for delivery.

CH'ING DYNASTY IVORY CARVINGS,
NATIONAL PALACE MUSEUM (Opposite Page)
A sample of the exquisite workmanship and artistry that awaits you. Upper left is a small box (lid
is to the right) within which fits another box. Below is a dragon boat; sometimes you see miniature
human figures in the cabin. These and similar pieces are carved as a single unit from solid ivory,
never joined together; a single piece may be the work of two generations, father handing down
an unfinished piece to his son.

The displays begin on the second floor with five rooms for showing oracle bones,[1] bronzes and ancient objects; five rooms for porcelain (we saw an indescribably gorgeous exhibition of Ch'ing Porcelains dating from 1654 AD and reaching their zenith in 1736-1795); a hall dedicated to Dr. Sun Yat-sen and two corridors for paintings. On the third floor, 10 rooms display jade (you lose your mind), enamelware, snuff bottles, handscrolls and albums, embroidery, calligraphy, documents, rare books, ancient Chinese currency and other items, while three corridors show paintings. The top floor has three large rooms for special exhibits, such as fascinatingly carved ivory.[2] The ground floor is used for administrative offices, storage, workshops — and visitors' cloakroom *where you must leave your cameras.* To the rear is a huge storage tunnel where undisplayed treasure is kept in rows and rows of metal boxes and racks, many stacked atop another.[3]

Each major exhibit has an excellent one- or two-page printed commentary (in English and other foreign languages) that gives essential background information; a collection of these would form a textbook on Chinese art. Thus, visitors learn all sorts of interesting lore, history and tidbits:

During the reign of Huang Ti, the Yellow Emperor who ascended the Dragon Throne in 2697 BC, the Chinese had a well-developed system of writing, a good knowledge of astronomy, math and music — and they built boats, vehicles and weapons. Huang Ti invented the compass and his empress, Lo Tsu, was the first to make silk.

Many of the items were unearthed in archeological excavations and led to scientists discovering that as far back as Peking Man, half a million years ago, Chinese were making utensils of stone and animal bone; that about 25,000 years ago they made clothing from animal skins and hides, ornaments and carvings of stone, bone, shells and other materials; that 4,000 to 7,000 years back, pottery was invented and farm implements were fashioned from stone.

Among the many exhibits that attract special attention are bronzeware of the Shang-Yin Dynasty (1766-1122 BC) and the succeeding Chou Dynasty (to 255 BC) which Chinese historians call the Bronze Age.

Among numerous items of absorbing interest are a miniature nine-story pagoda on which 1,332 images of Buddha are carved (Northern Wei Dynasty, 386-535 AD); a huge, ancient, metal drum unearthed during the construction of the Burma Road in World War II; sculptures of the Goddess of Mercy, Goddess of Lightning, God of Thunder.

Personally, we'll never forget the special exhibition of snuff bottles, nor that concerned with so-called miniature treasures (which they were[4]).

All this, and more, for only NT$15 (about 40¢); NT$4 for children, servicemen. Open 9 a.m. to 5 p.m. daily. English lecture tour: 10 a.m., 3 p.m.

[1] Represent earliest extant forms of writing in China, the study of which has become an important branch of scholarship in the last 75 years. Ancient tortoise shells and animal bones have been unearthed bearing oracular lines with carved inscriptions recording events for which these divinations were sought.

[2] First time here, we were spellbound by this exhibit — balls within a ball within another ball within another, etc.; mini-scale junks with people seated, eating, within the cabin; items as delicately etched as cobwebby lace — all carved, painstakingly, out of solid ivory. Often a single piece might be handed from father to son before being finished. We were bitterly disappointed, several years later, not to find a similar exhibit. Except that the porcelain and snuff bottles beautifully filled the void.

[3] By special advance solicitation, you may rate an invitation to visit the caves, particularly if you're a teacher, professor or graduate student of Chinese arts, history, etc.

[4] Most of these valuable mini-objects were gifts to Ch'ing Emperor Kao-tsung (1736-1795) who amused himself by placing them in his Tuo Pao Ke treasure Chest of ingenious design. Countless compartments within the chest had numbers of concealed drawers which made locating a particular object hidden somewhehwere in the chest a fascinating, mysterious puzzle.

FORMAL SIGHTSEEING

As previously stated, the National Palace Museum, shopping and Chinese food are sufficient reasons for coming here. Another is Lungshan (Dragon Mountain) Temple,[5] the first highly ornate Buddhist temple you've seen (if coming here by way of Japan); we couldn't stop snapping photos of all those rooftop dragons. And if you can steal the time, stroll thru the surrounding market stalls — extremely colorful.

Usual half-day City Tours spend too much time in handcraft factories (so tourists can spend dollars, tour operators collect commissions), not enough seeing Taipei. We'd advise both groups and individuals to plan their tours — whether by charter bus, rental car with English-speaking driver[6] or taxi[7] — as follows:

North Taipei And Beyond

Starting with the Grand Hotel, an unusual sight, even though we prefer not staying there, and nearby Martyrs Shrine, your full day's drive should include the Chinese Culture and Movie Center, National Palace Museum, Yangmingshan Park, hot springs resort of Peitou (*BAY-toe*), favorite of Japanese males, the fantastic rock formations of coastal Yehliu Park (utterly fascinating, extremely photogenic). This delightful drive returns by way of Chinsan (Golden Mountain) Beach on the East China Sea and Tamsui, site of "The Shady Lady" (for the profusion of leafy trees), Taiwan Golf & Country Club. The half-day North Coast Tour, offered by local operators, is the only one we recommend; it covers the area north of the National Palace Museum.

Here's a complete rundown on everything of importance in the northern sector:

Confucian Temple (see enroute to Grand Hotel) — Of classical Chinese design, it's the largest here. On Sept. 28, Confucius' birthday, memorial services are held; people burn incense and small boys perform the plumage dance in traditional costume.

Chinese Culture & Movie Center — Excellent Wax Museum (8:30 a.m.-5:30 p.m.; NT$20 — NT$16 group rate) displaying robes, military uniforms, clothing as early as Han Dynasty; also aboriginals of Taiwan. Nearby (NT$10) is interesting replica of ancient walled city. Stop off for an hour enroute to nearby National Palace Museum.

Martyrs Shrine — Huge, colorful and imposing complex resembling the Ming Dynasty Tai Ho Tien (Hall of Supreme Harmony) in Peking where emperors received their court on ceremonial occasions. Shrine commemorates those who died for the Republic from the 1911 Revolution thru the struggle against communism. Interesting military memorabilia. Hourly Changing of the Guard (on the hour) is impressive, photogenic. (*Note:* here, as in most public exhibits and museums, displays are explained in English as well as by Chinese characters.) National memorial services held here on March 29, Sept. 3.

Postal Museum, 51 Shih Tou Rd., Hsintien. One of the few such in the world. Displays illustrate postal system of ancient China, evolution of written communications and postal systems, plus collection of world stamps.

Shuang Hsi Park, patterned after an ancient Chinese garden, has pavilions, fountains, arched bridges and 6,500 varieties of flowers, plants. Beautiful. So, too, is *Experimental Ornamental Gardens* in Shilin; splendid collections of orchids, chrysanthemums, cacti — plus special exhibits.

Yangmingshan Park, north of Palace Museum, has been planted hillside to ensure flowers in bloom at all times. Miles of winding walks thru carefully tended gardens. If here in March, don't miss the cherry blossoms.

---

[5] Dedicated in 1783 to Kuan Yin, Goddess of Mercy, and Ma Tsu, Goddess of the Sea, its architecture, stone sculptures and spectacular roofs of colored tile and pieces of glass are excellent.

[6] Large American cars rent for NT$325 an hour, NT$2400 per day thru hotel travel desks. Two couples sharing a car is a far better deal than taking individual City Tours.

[7] Most economical way to go — from NT$24 to NT$60 per ride. We probably took a hundred taxis, never had the slightest difficulty in getting one and only once or twice any problem in getting where we wanted to go.

Central Taipei

This, as already noted, is for walking. Aside from the always exhilarating street scenes, be sure to visit the Railway Station, New Park and Presidential Square. Latter is the political heart where thousands gather on Double Ten and other major holidays to celebrate with giant parades and rallies. Fronting it is the massive, imposing Presidential Building and Taipei Guest House (built by Japanese to resemble samurai armor).

Eastern Taipei

Cross town, due east of Presidential Square, is where "New Taipei" is a-building — government, apartment and

Classical Chinese paintings are attractively copied on tapestry

condominium hi-rises. Here, south of International Airport, are Chunghwa Sports & Culture Center, Municipal Stadium and Sun Yat Sen Memorial Hall. Latter, a stunning dedication to the father of the Republic, has 2,800-seat hall, library and exhibit rooms that host changing displays of national interest, art showings, etc. Don't miss the majestic grandeur of this building.

South Taipei And Beyond

On our latest trip, we "discovered" the National Museum of History. Were there not a National Palace Museum, this would be it. Stunning pottery horses, camels, warriors and demons from 200 A.D.; Chinese bronzes from 1122 B.C.; ancient coins, jade, lacquerware; exquisite, old ivory carvings — one series depicting the eight Chinese immortals. Rooms filled with imperial robes and costumes. On each floor, verandas overlook landscaped grounds, part of the Botanical Garden where every type of tropical, semi-tropical trees and plants abound. Costs only NT$5 to visit Museum — a steal! Nearby, on Nanhai Rd., is the National Art Gallery, National Central Library and, beyond, the National Science Hall, styled after the Temple of Heaven in Peking.

If not going to Taroko Gorge and/or Sun Moon Lake, the 4-hour afternoon tour south to Wulai Aboriginal Village is worthwhile. The drive past Pitan (Green Lake) is scenic and charming, the aboriginal girls and the ride in the Wulai push-cars entertaining. If doing this by car, stop off enroute to see the 100-year-old Chihnan Temple and adjoining Hsien Kung Miao, Temple of Immortals, both Taoist.

However, a somewhat longer drive (30 miles SW of Taipei), thru rural countryside reminiscent of mainland China, to Shimen Dam recreational area is even more attractive. In this delightful mountain setting is Taiwan's first international resort hotel complex (see Hotel Directory). Nearby, at Tze Hu, is the former and lovely summer and weekend residence of Chiang Kai-shek, now his temporary but impressive resting place.

Though developed primarily as an irrigation project for agricultural development, Shimen Dam Lake is a great area for land and water sports. Behind it are rice paddies, vegetable gardens and typical red brick farm houses with green shutters, tile roofs. Truly charming.

DINING IN TAIPEI
(13% tax, 10% service added
when bill exceeds NT$200)

As we've said, it's superb — with a choice of 735 licensed restaurants serving every type of traditional cooking, plus another 2,500 food stalls and shops (immaculate, too).

All hotels have coffee shops, dining rooms serving Western food, but many have some of the outstanding restaurants specializing in one or more Chinese cuisines. Chances are you'll do most of your dining there — you really can't go wrong; local American residents claim they're best overall for atmosphere, service and food — at least for American tastes. However, you'll dine reasonably early, for by 9 p.m. restaurants begin to empty.

Outside the hotels, we can personally attest to the excellence and popularity of *Ruby's* — from dim sum breakfast to Cantonese dinner; it's opposite the Central Hotel.[1] Don't leave without enjoying a Mongolian Barbecue (or its relative, Genghis Khan); we had a good one at *Great Wall.* Also noted for its Mongolian is the First Hotel. Had a marvelous Szechwanese dinner in the dining room of New Asia Hotel. *Kowloon* and *Fung Lum* are known for their Cantonese specialties.

Don't attempt to pre-judge Chinese restaurants by their decor — or lack of it

Because of former Japanese occupation and current resumption of large-scale tourism, there are numerous good Japanese restaurants. We enjoyed several nights of excellent dining in the President Hotel's Japanese steak house.

Not a bad idea to combine dining and entertainment in one of the hotel theater-restaurants, which are quite lavish and provide excellent entertainment (usually traditional), Chinese dining. *First, Golden Dragon* and *Hoover* are considered very good for both dining, floor shows.

Favorite native food, so-called Taiwanese dishes, include deep-fried small oysters mixed with bean sprouts; large prawns, crab and lobster as well as raw fish; cooked chicken and duck. Although there are many Taiwanese restaurants, center of local cuisine is Yuan Huan, known to tourists as The Circle, in the old downtown sector. Even if you don't eat here (though no reason why you shouldn't as it's perfectly sanitary), it's one of the great sights. Hundreds of food stalls, open and glass-enclosed, surround The Circle and its adjoining streets, for it's here that the average citizen convenes to dine en masse — amidst honking traffic, gesticulating and shouting people, vendors hawking their wares and stereos blaring from nearby shops.

SPORTS

No Asian golf tour can overlook Taiwan and, particularly, Taipei where there are four championship layouts. Kaohsiung has an 18-hole, par-72 layout.

If you're a baseball fan, you'll probably want to see what makes Taiwan's Little Leaguers and Pony Leaguers tick. Well, the season is May thru August, though most schools have teams playing year 'round. For on-the-spot game information, contact Taiwan Visitors Association, 69 Nanking Rd. East or Republic of China Athletic Association, 153-3 Chang-An East Rd.

There's skin diving among the coral reefs of southern Taiwan, mountain climbing at Yu Shan and skiing at Hohuanshan in the central mountains.

the short, happy life of a Peiping duck . . .

Here is a creature whose nature and origins are shrouded in mystery. And here are a few of the legends you may (or may not) have heard about. True or false?

1. A Peiping duck accompanied Marco Polo on his travels and served as his faithful interpreter in the Court of the Great Khan.

2. The mythological phoenix, a sacred emblem of ancient China, was actually a fast-flying Peiping duck seen crashing into the Forbidden City by a half-blind poet.

3. Donald Duck is a fourth-generation descendent of an illustrious line of Peiping ducks. He conceals his pigtail beneath his sailor hat.

4. Peiping Man was actually a Peiping duck with its bill broken off.

5. Backbone of General Chennault's Flying Tigers was an elite flock of Peiping ducks who flew supplies over the Hump.

6. Peiping ducks were the inspiration for Southern Fried Chicken. After the Civil War, Colonel Billy-Joe Hamfat, Confederate ambassador to the Court in Peiping, returned to Alabama and franchised the whole bit.

7. The American bald eagle descended from Peiping ducks stranded in Alaska while attempting a prehistoric 'round-the-world polar flight. Changes in the bird, as well as its baldness, were caused by the radical change in diet — from rice to hot dogs and hamburgers.

Unfortunately, all are untrue. But here are some true facts:

Peiping duck originated in Shantung Province during the Ch'ing Dynasty. The whole process of raising, preparing, cooking and serving duck is somewhat different on Taiwan than it was in North China. Here is the Taiwanese method:

K'ao ya (roast duck) is also called *t'ien ya* (stuffed duck) because the duck is force-fed for a week before being killed. When it weighs about three pounds, sorghun, cornmeal and millet are mixed with water to form a thick dough, then rolled into finger-size strips. The duck's mouth is held open, and the strips are forced down its throat. Since the dough is too thick for a duck to swallow by itself, the duck handler "milks" the neck above the lump of dough so as to squeeze it down by degrees into the stomach.

A supplementary measure insures the duck doesn't lose newly gained weight. Drinking lots of water, as ducks normally do, makes them excrete before the food is fully digested. So Peiping ducks are fenced in, kept away from water, so they won't lose the effects of force feeding, which is administered five times daily. So stuffed they can't even waddle, they sit there without water until nightfall, by which time the food has been digested and turned into fat.

After a week of force feeding, when the duck weighs five or more pounds, he is killed, dunked in near-boiling water and plucked naked. Then comes the autopsy:

1. A slit is made under the right wing thru which his innards are extracted.

2. Air is pumped thru an opening in the neck into the space between skin and meat, causing him to swell like a football.

3. Boiling water is poured over the skin to tighten it.

4. Skin is basted evenly with a paste made of malt candy mixed with water giving it a shiny, golden sheen that contributes largely to its later crispness.

5. Our duck is hung up to dry, after which boiling water is poured into the carcass (the rear end was previously plugged). The duck is now ready to be immortalized.

Ten ducks at a time can be hung inside a big, iron oven that looks like a giant beer keg. Roasting over a glowing charcoal fire takes 25 minutes; the water inside the duck turns to steam and makes the skin crisper, easy to cut. It is now ready for a dramatic presentation to the diners by the waiter, after which the duck is intrusted to a carver whose dexterity with a long, thin cleaver is marvelous to behold.

There are many ways to cut a duck, but most popular is to start at the neck and work down the other. First to come off, of course, is the skin, in pieces roughly the size of a potato chip — golden, shiny, crisp and juicy. Once all the skin has been removed and delivered to the table, the carver removes the meat just under the skin, in long, thick slices. (True gourmets eat only the skin; they don't touch the meat.) Finally, as the *piece de resistance,* the head is cut off and split in half lengthwise, so that you can savor the taste of the brain.

Prior to the triumphal entrance of our duck, three vital elements have appeared on the table: small plates of scallions, tortillas and a dark-brown paste. The tortillas are extremely thin and soft; the paste, called *t'ien-mien-chiang* (sweet dough paste), is thick and sweetish, and has to be tasted to be described.

When the first plates of duck-skin slices arrive, you proceed as follows: (1) Take a tortilla, place one or two pieces of skin on it. (2) Add scallions and brown sauce as desired. (4) Wrap up and eat it like a sandwich.

Leave out the scallions and/or brown sauce if desired, but they add a matchless flavor. Or dispense with the whole operation and simply eat unadorned skin — a practice generally regarded as barbaric.

Usually when you eat Peiping duck, you will get what is known as *k'ao ya san chih* (roast duck eaten three ways). The three additional dishes, brought in *after* the duck has been devoured, are: (1) Fried beansprouts mixed with slices of duck meat *(ya szu ch'ao ch'a ts'ai,* which translates, remarkably enough, as "duck slices with fried beansprouts"). (2) An egg dish, steamed, containing beaten eggs, pieces of scallion and ham, and duck oil. This dish is called *huang ts'ai* (yellow vegetables). (3) Soup made from the remainder of the duck (neck, bones, etc.) in a clear broth with vermicelli and vegetables, usually Chinese cabbage, called *ya chai t'ang* (duck frame soup).

All this — duck, scallions, brown sauce, tortillas, and the three additional dishes — serves four or five people quite comfortably. In fact, you probably won't be able to finish the soup. But that doesn't matter; you can always carry the soup home in a waterproof doggie bag. The important thing, the ultimate in gastronomic ecstasy, is the skin. The skin is the rage of every gourmet from Paris to Ulan Bator; and once having sampled it, you will on your deathbed be able to murmur, "I have not lived in vain."

Written by William Page and condensed from *Echo Magazine,* Taiwan.

CHINESE OPERA

It is said that the emperor of China once journeyed to the moon and watched a magnificent theatrical performance in the Palace of Jade. Inspired by this spectacle, he determined to enjoy similar entertainment in his earthly palace, and on his return he set up establishments where young men and women trained as vocalists, musicians and dancers. The drama schools flourished in the Pear Garden of the Imperial Palace, and Chinese opera actors are still called "Children of the Pear Garden."

In Taipei today, tourists are able to see several troupes performing classical Chinese opera — a unique form of entertainment which has no counterpart in the West. It is an amalgam of mime, ballet, opera and theater which has been frozen into a stylized pattern over the centuries. To the local audiences who crowd the theaters, the plots and characters, the costumes and heavily painted faces are all familiar. But to the Westerner an evening at the opera can be bewildering. For a start there is a dearth of scenery and props. The stage may be bare except for a small table and two chairs. But if you are familiar with the traditions of the opera, you will know that these few items can represent a multitude of things, depending on how they are placed: the table may be a court, or a mountain, and with a chair placed on top it becomes a throne. A piece of black cloth tied to two bamboo poles, and painted with white lines, represents a city wall; two flags with wheels painted on them clearly indicate that the lady between them is riding on a chariot; while four soldiers striding back and forth across the stage carrying banners may represent no less than an entire army traversing hundreds of miles of territory.

After discovering what the various props represent, you must then learn the meaning of the symbolic gestures used by the actors. A warrior will dismount from his horse by casting his riding whip on the floor; doors are opened and closed simply by bringing the hands together or spreading them apart; a character falls asleep simply by resting his head on his arm.

The audience knows what sort of character an actor is playing by the way he walks, the costume he wears and his makeup. A scholar will pace thoughtfully, while an official will stride out forcefully. If a warrior's face is black, he is honest and strong; if it is painted white, he is treacherous and powerful. A general who boasts a red face is brave and honest, while one with a blue face will prove himself to be cruel before the play ends. The more complicated a character is, the more vivid and intricate will be the lines and colors that cover his face. Face-painting is an art that must be acquired by the actor, for a false move with the brush can distort the entire characterization.

There are civil (wen) plays and military (wu) plays, though the two forms may be combined to achieve dramatic effect. Civil plays center 'round the ordinary people or the scholars and are either fictitious or drawn from current events. Comedy and satire fall within this category. Military plays portray the battles of the past where heroic warriors planned the overthrow of treacherous villains. A typical Chinese opera is *The Story of Su San the Courtesan.* A scholar falls in love with a pretty sing-song girl called Su San, and they are happy together. But he spends all his money, and the proprietress turns him out of her establishment. Taking refuge in a temple he sends a messenger to Su San who gives him enough money to make the journey to Peking and compete in the Imperial Examinations. Eventually he rises through the ranks of officials to become a judge. Meanwhile, Su San, who cannot forget her former love and thus loses her popularity, is sold to a rich merchant. The merchant's wife is jealous of the attractive young girl and tries to poison her, but it is the merchant who eats the poisoned food and dies. Su San is accused of murder and sentenced to death. But the climax can be guessed: her former lover is one of the examining magistrates. He discovers the truth and reveals the treachery of the jealous wife. There is a great trial scene in which Su San must sing of her past life for an hour while kneeling before the judges. The drama ends with the lovers happily united.

There are four main divisions of *Ching Hsi* acting; the *Sheng,* play the roles of scholars, statesmen, warriors and the like, and wear no makeup. They are all bearded, except for young men. *Tan,* or women's roles were, until recently, filled by female impersonators, and even today actresses must display a technique of femininity that was invented and brought to perfection by male performers. *Ching* roles portray warriors, bandits, evil ministers, righteous judges, statesmen, gods and other supernatural entities. Finally, *Ch'ou* roles comprise clowns and comics; the actors can improvise and must be mimics as well as acrobats.

No character in the opera speaks in his natural voice. An actor introduces himself to the audience with a *pai* — an account of himself, his situation and family background, which will help the audience to understand the action they are about to see. The *pai* is chanted, each line responding to a set of rules for rhyme and meter. The actor must find his own rhythmic tone, pitch and tempo depending on the character he is enacting, and the dramatic situation in which he finds himself. The art of chanting *pai* is extremely difficult and requires years of study. Besides this, the actor must also learn to sing.

The orchestra consists of 24 kinds of musical instruments, but some are rarely used. The drummer sets the tempo for both musicians and actors.

A full-length performance of Chinese opera can last three or four hours, but a night at the opera doesn't mean big money or dressing up. Seats are inexpensive, people come and go as they please during the performance.

There are daily performances of Chinese opera at the Armed Forces Cultural Activity Center, 69 Chunghwa Rd.; also Sat., Sun. at Sun Yat-sen Memorial Hall. Opera is frequently seen on local TV.

OPERA SCHOOLS

Most famous troupe in Taiwan is Ta Peng, founded by the Chinese Air Force in 1949 and now consisting of more than 100 actors and musicians.

There are also three opera training schools; leading one is the National Foo Hsing Opera School in Taipei in which the ratio of girls to boys in about 13 to seven. The training course lasts eight years and students taking it have to pursue the same educational studies as in regular schools.

Opera training usually begins from the ages of seven to 12. Students learn dancing, singing, acrobatics and fencing, not to mention countless other things that go toward making an accomplished opera star.

Preponderance of girl students over boys at Foo Hsing is of exceptional interest. Not until the turn of the century did women first begin to appear on the Chinese opera stage. Before, for about 900 years, all female parts were played by men impersonating women. After the establishment of the Republic of China on New Year's Day, 1912, this ancient practice began to fade, but it was not until Taiwan was restored to Chinese rule in 1945, after half a century of Japanese occupation, that it disappeared altogether.

This produced an interesting test for women playing the roles of their own sex: they had to act like men impersonating women to preserve the true, unadulterated flavor of Chinese opera.

NIGHT LIFE
(11 p.m. to Midnight Closing)

Number of nightclubs in Taipei has declined as the government has increased license fees, raised entertainment taxes, levied a food tax — all to combat vice. Total tax added to drink/food tabs is 39%, plus 10% service. When not dining, there's a cover charge of NT$135 to NT$275; drinks average NT$75 and up.

Theater-restaurant shows (1½-2 hrs.) are about 60% Chinese (usually good, interesting), balance foreign acts. Open nightly, the 9 o'clock shows are less costly than the earlier dinner show; latter in the NT$350 to NT$650 range (including tax, service). Aside from those in hotels (excellent and the most expensive), best are: *First Theater Restaurant,* 41 Chung Hua Rd.; Cantonese cuisine, three shows daily. *Golden Dragon, Hoover,* 21 Fushun St. (7:30 and 10:30). *World,* 15 Cheng Tu Rd.; shows at 12-2 p.m., 7-9 p.m.

Taiwan's local opera *(ko-tsai-hsi)* is less refined than Peiping opera. It is performed in the streets, lots, outside of temples on bare stages; costumes ornate but makeup simple. Accompanying music is distinctive with many Western adaptations. There are two types of puppet theaters: bag puppet *(pu tai shih)* and shadow puppet *(pi yin shih).*

In the Clubs, where you can drink alone or enjoy the company of a charming girl, beer costs about US$1.50, scotch from US$1.75. For the unattached male, there's still a few dance halls to be found, such as *Singapore,* 287 Chang An W. Rd. A real night on the town costs far less than in Hong Kong.

SHOPPING

Today, this is one of the world's most fascinating and reasonable shopping marts; in fact, it's replacing Hong Kong as a bargain emporium. From Art and Antiques to sleek Yachts (we didn't see any Zebras so we can't say A to Z), there's so much merchandise and such varied assortments you're literally swamped and almost surfeited. Only things you can't buy are all those hi-style, inexpensive Made in Taiwan items you snap up at home — they're for export only.

No wonder the people, from children to grandparents, look so happy, healthy and well dressed — shops, restaurants and food stalls are jammed with hordes of them at all times of the day until late at night. You'll enjoy watching them, particularly in the department stores,[1] even if you don't buy a thing. Their sheer exuberance is exhilarating.

Aside from traditional handcrafts and artifacts — scrolls, prints, carved ivory and jade,[2] dolls, jewelry, etc. — there are outstanding buys in coral jewelry (deeper shades best, most expensive), cloissonne, grandfather clocks (stunning and cheap), furniture (particularly small to large chests), screens, porcelain, reading glasses (both frames and lenses much cheaper than in States), custom-made clothing (less expensive than Hong Kong). And boats, both sail and power — usually all fiberglass with beautiful interiors of teak — delivered at comparatively low prices; Taiwanese boat builders boast they "make anything that floats."

If here for a short time, you'll probably do most of your shopping in hotel shops where you'll pay a bit more, but assortments are honed to Western tastes. Stores in the Hilton, President and Grand are, for most part, excellent. Uptown, Chungshan N. Rd., is a happy and convenient hunting ground with every type of shop, including those specializing in marine fixtures/equipment.

Whatever else you don't do, don't leave without shopping the Taiwan Handicraft Promotion Center (also known as Chinese Handicraft Mart; government-sponsored) at 1 Hsu-Chow Rd., 3 blocks south of Taipei Hilton and 2 blocks east. Display and sale of everything good in every type of handcraft, furniture, jewelry. Good source of information for importers and retail store buyers as displays on second floor list manufacturing sources. Worth a climb to third floor to see the International Doll Museum. Open 9 to 5:30.

Haggle Alley — blocks and blocks of small shops.

All better shops, department stores are one-price; elsewhere bargain away. Be particularly careful that you get maximum "discounts" when you buy in places to which tour buses take you, such as *China Arts Co.* and *Chinese Cultural City*[3] in Peitou, both huge factories with extensive stocks. The former's Museum has much finer items than those in the retail showrooms; many are antiques, some are for sale.

Buying antiques is very chancy for all but the experts; chances of stumbling on a genuine bargain are infinitesimal — and if it is a genuinely fine piece, you have to be prepared to pay a good price. Best to buy only in better antique shops. *Yang Lun Tien Antique Center,* 5th floor of 609 Sinsen N. Rd. (across from Imperial) has a beautiful and extensive selection of antique artifacts/paintings. *Kuo Hwa Tang Galleries,* 108 Hankow (3 blocks S of China Hotel), also has an outstanding collection for the serious collector. *Unicorn Handicraft Co.,* a block up from the President, has some good-looking pieces, but we'd want to carefully authenticate them before buying.

Two other stores near the President deserve special mention: *Asia Furniture,* corner of Chungshan N. Rd. and Te-Whei St., has a wonderful assortment of good-looking grandfather clocks that are well worth shipping home if grandfather needs a clock; *Kuen Fu Co.,* 12-3 Lou-An St. east of Chungshan N. Rd., has well-priced, colorful and large ceramic elephants, camels, dragons — also excellent selection of chinaware. By the way, when stores quote a shipping cost, *make sure that includes packing as well.*

Export Items

Purchasing agents, importers, retail buyers should shop at the Formosa Plastics Bldg., 201 Tunhwa North Rd., established by CETDC (China External Trade Development Council), a non-profit organization that promotes foreign trade. Ninth and tenth floors have booths of 371 leading manufacturers that produce everything from sporting goods, electronics, machine tools and building materials to plastics, textiles, hardware and motorcycles.

Other commercial exhibit centers: Chinese Products Display Center, 62 Sining South Rd.; Exhibition Center of International Trade, 215 Nanking East Rd., 7th floor; Exhibition Center of Exports, 65 Nanking East Rd., 2nd floor.

Best, most active is *Far East*; downtown on Chengtu Rd. just east of Chunghwa Rd. (Haggle Alley). Uptown, on Sinsheng N. Rd. near Ambassador and Gloria Hotel, is *Shin-Shin.*

Taiwan jade which is the most prevalent kind here, is a dark green not to be confused with more expensive jades mined elsewhere; latter is also handcarved here.

[3] Popular Oriental Arts, Jade & Wood Works Mfg. Co., 100, Sec. 2, Central S. Rd., Peitou. Has small shop at 181 Chungshan N. Rd.

Chinese Medicine — Ancient Remedies For A Modern World

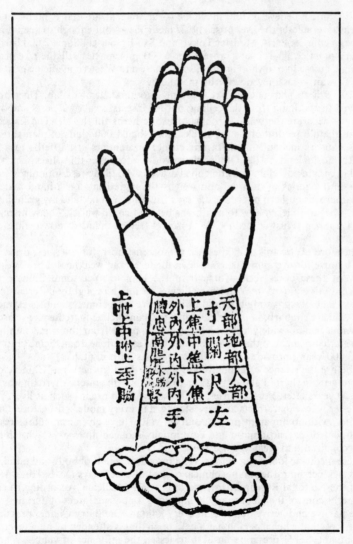

This ancient drawing of a wrist was used by Chinese doctors to teach their students anatomy. Traditional Chinese doctors are expected to diagnose an illness by taking the pulse of a patient at the wrist.

If your family doctor ever gave you a prescription for *toad's sweat*, you'd think he'd suddenly gone off his rocker and start looking for another doctor — or a shrink for him.

Not so if you were Chinese. Because your parents, grandparents and countless generations before them may have received the same exotic treatment. And it worked. Even scientists now know that the glandular secretions of toads contain a powerful heart stimulant like adrenalin which Chinese have been using as a medicine for centuries.

Not all Chinese believe in folk medicine — an ancient art that contains in embryonic form several later theories of scientific medicine — but enough to keep it alive in such foreign cities as Paris, Madrid, Tokyo and San Francisco. Some 2,000 licensed herb doctors practice in Taiwan, more than 6,000 pharmacies sell their remedies. Many young Chinese like to shop around, so Chinese and Western medicine exist side by side in Taiwan — as they do on the mainland.

A visit to a herb pharmacy is like stepping into an alchemist's lab. Tiger bones and preserved turtles hang from the ceiling; bottled insects, swallows' nests and dried animal organs decorate the walls. Aromas of exotic herbs fill the air. The Liu Shen pharmacy in the old section of Taipei stocks more than 1,000 kinds of plants, twigs, bark, roots, mushrooms and fungi. In one corner apprentices grind herbs to a fine powder with mortar and pestle. Others shave roots into paper-thin slices which are then stored in ornate porcelain jars and coded drawers. To fill a prescription, the pharmacist dips into a series of drawers and weighs the ingredients on a hand scale.

"My father was an herb pharmacist," says Liu Shen Yuon, "and my grandfather before him. I began to learn how to mix herbs before I could walk." Today he makes Almighty Lu Shen Pills according to a secret recipe handed down thru five generations.

Among more exotic folk remedies are rhinoceros horn for allergies, dried gall bladder of a horse for eye ailments, goat horn for fever and weakness. Thru Western eyes, many of these cures seem worse than the ailment. Yet some Chinese folk remedies are routinely used in Western medicine, although in slightly different form. From the *ma huang* twig, a time-honored Chinese cure for asthma, scientists extracted ephedrine. Chinese rhubarb, *ta huang,* contains the same active ingredients as cascara root and senna leaves, widely used as laxatives. A plant from the same family as *Rhemannia glutinosa,* an herb that's supplied the Chinese with heart medicine (and hair tonic) for 3,000 years, provides modern cardiologists with digitalis.

Long before the science of endocrinology was known to the West, Chinese doctors were prescribing thyroid glands of goats to patients with goiters; thyroxin was discovered 1,200 years later. For centuries, Chinese have used organs such as liver, pancreas and testes whose extratracts are now standard in every modern drugstore. Other herb remedies, with no apparent pharmaceutical value, have given miraculous results in the treatment of psychosomatic and emotionally induced illnesses which Chinese medicine recognized and treated since the Chou Dynasty.

"Chinese medicine looks at a person as an inseparable unit of body and mind, the patient as a sick person rather than a clinical case of disease," says Dr. Li Huan-Hsin, Director of the National Research Institute of Chinese Medicine. According to early teachings, herbs control the balance of yin and yang, opposing forces of darkness and light — the passive and active qualities in every human. Dr. Barry Chang, practicing herb doctor, says that when a person has a cold or an illness attended by high fever, the yang is dominant. "So I prescribe an herb to lessen the influence of yang." When a person is sluggish or suffers from low blood pressure, the yin is dominant.

Confusing? So think modern Chinese doctors who have little patience with such unscientific theories. "Chinese medicine was greatly influenced by Taoism, and yin and yang were used to explain phenomena not clearly understood," says Western-trained Dr. Li.

Traditional Chinese medicine teaches that the body is composed of five elements — wood, fire, metal, earth, water — part of the heritage of strict laws against human dissection that thwarted the development of anatomy and surgery in China. Since each element has its yin and yang, the herb doctor selects herbs to restore harmony among the unbalanced elements. Even today, these doctors shun Western diagnostic tools such as X-rays, electrocardiograms and blood tests, rely on observation, asking questions of the patient, taking 24 pulse readings as described in a book written by Wang-Shu-ho around 280 AD.

Only one school in Taiwan teaches this traditional medicine. Since 1956, the Ministry of Education has given priority to research rather than training more herb doctors. But advocates of Chinese culture claim that the 5,000-year practice deserves to be maintained. That view is strongly supported by the National Research Institute which has retained the special characteristics of the ancient art while unraveling some of its mysteries for the enrichment of modern medicine. Institute scholars have collected, classified and conducted chemical tests on 6,000 of Taiwan's plants.

"Our ancestors knew what herbs to prescribe for certain illnesses," says Dr. Li, and he taps a volume of the first Chinese Pharmacopeia, a classic he has completely modernized. "Chinese medicine is like a huge mine in which precious stones are buried. On the surface it seems unworthy to even glance at. If you are farsighted, however, its exploration proves a worthwhile investment."

Large drug companies agree. Bristol Myers supports a modern research institute on Tunhwa North Road where 20 chemists and technicians extract active ingredients from established herbal remedies. Chief chemist Dr. Hong-Yen Hsu reports that of better than 4,000 extracts tested, more than 800 have shown biological activity. "We have found several worthwhile extracts, including an analgesic, a muscle relaxant that could aid delivery, and an anti-depressant."

Work is sometimes painfully slow. For one thing, most prescriptions consist of five to ten ingredients that are traditionally brewed in water or soaked in wine and the liquid drunk like tea. "What happens during preparation when the herbs react with each other, not to mention the chemical reactions in the stomach, is still a big mystery," laments Dr. Hsu. "It's like trying to determine the nature of an egg by analyzing an omelet." Experts say it will take more than 20 years to analyze all Taiwan's plant species that might yield useful pharmaceutical products.

Dr. Wen-Yah Koo, an independent researcher at the National Taiwan University Hospital, has analyzed extracts from 5,000 species of plants, completed a book on 300 Chinese drugs. Of the 207 extracts she has submitted to the U.S. National Institutes of Health for special tests, several have shown certain anti-cancer properties.

In the search for drugs to combat cancer, one is the exploration of plant extracts. An obscure Chinese tree called *Camptotheca acuminata* attracted interest among drug researchers when the U.S. National Cancer Institute announced that a drug from this tree may be used against advanced cancer of the intestine and rectum. 50,000 seedlings of this now-famous tree have been planted in California, and an attempt to synthesize camptothecin was undertaken in several labs.

But other remedies are obtained by less scientific methods, have more imaginative origins. In the Liu Shen pharmacy, you can buy "five-colored dragon bone" guaranteed to cure hysteria and dispel the fear of fire-breathing monsters. Presumably then, you can venture forth on the Chinese New Year without a care in the world. But in any event, you'll enjoy nosing around these pharmacies, found by the dozens in any Chinese district, and talking to the pharmacists — secure in the knowledge that what he prescribes is not necessarily a collection of old wives' tales.

Condensed from an article in *Echo Magazine* by Dave Milne.

EAST-WEST (TAROKO GORGE) HIGHWAY

It came as a surprise to us, even though we'd known of it, that one of the most dramatic drives we'd ever taken was on an island with a topography quite unlike any other in Asia. Hills and mountains cover two-thirds of its 13,885 sq. miles; there are 62 peaks over 10,000 ft., including Yushan (Jade Mt.) which towers 13,114 ft.

But to get back to this drive over "The Rainbow of Treasure Island" (Chinese are masters of the felicitous phrase), Asia's most beautiful. Taiwanese describe it "as a highway of surpassing magnificence, sublime loveliness and awesome grandeur." It's all of that and one that any world traveler worthy of the name should not miss. By the way, try to sit on the right-hand side of the bus or car on the Taroko-Tienhsiang stretch.

This is an engineering marvel that took 10,000 workers 46 months to complete (1960) at a cost of $11,000,000 and 450 lives. It runs thru and over mountains and along the sparkling, bright green Liwu (Foggy) River that, over the ages, has cut its sinuous way thru 3,000 ft. marble corridors; in some places, the cliffs are so close together that the sun never penetrates unless directly overhead. Thus, the drive is along the bottom of the gorge, not around the rim, so that you gaze up in wonderment at the towering palisades of varying lines and striations, stopping enroute at Eternal Springs Shrine, Swallows Grotto (caves in the rocky cliffs), the Tunnel of Nine Turns and the lovely Bridge of Motherly Devotion before reaching Tienhsiang (Heavenly Fortune). This eastern 12-mile stretch with 38 tunnels comprises Taroko (near Hualien — *washleen* — on the Pacific) and ends at Tungshih to the west from where one can (and should) drive south to Taichung. Actually, there are two branches, but these are of little value at present to tourists as they are unpaved and very rough.

Tienhsiang *(tee-en-SHAN)* is a lovely spot nestled at 1,476 ft. at the foot of encircling green mountains and, even though a prime tourist attraction, idyllic at the end of day when quiet descends and the soft, tropical air lulls one to sleep

You'll want time to walk across the swaying suspension foot bridge that spans the gorge, to climb to aptly named Tien Feng (Heaven Peak) Pagoda and the Buddhist Temple beyond. Great photography from any angle. Tien Hsiang was named after Wen Tien Hsiang (1236-1283), a scholar-warrior who refused to pledge allegiance to his Mongol captors and was executed. His statue is another landmark (and climb).

HOW TO SEE TAROKO GORGE

Those with limited time should take a day trip out of Taipei with an early a.m. flight (25-35 min.) to Hualein over rural countryside, beautifully and lushly colored, picturesque with natives in coolie hats planting or cultivating rice. Per person, including lunch, RT air, is about US$52 (5-7 persons), $65 for 1-4, as low as $37 for large groups.

Tour buses traverse the gorge, stop for lunch at Tien Hsiang Lodge, leave at 2 p.m. for Hualien with stop enroute at South Sea Gardens to witness an Ami (aboriginal) dance performance; costumes are beautiful, dances fascinating to those who haven't seen such before, and there's audience participation that provides a fun finish. By the way, the return drive thru the Gorge is, somehow, even more spectacular. If faint of heart, close your eyes — bus drivers negotiate the downhill hairpin turns like race drivers.

Visiting a marble factory is the final item. Extremely interesting to see how huge slabs of marble are cut into strips, then fashioned, cut, decorated and polished. Finished products, which are for sale, range from architectural forms to tabletops, vases, sculptures, etc. Plane departs for Taipei at 4 p.m.

Individuals can hire a cab in Hualien to do all of the foregoing. Meter rate should come to about NT$125 *each way,* plus waiting time in Tien Hsiang. Or board one of the deluxe buses w/reclining seats; about NT$125 each way.

Instead of flying, take an inexpensive Express bus from Taipei — if you have the time (takes 7 hours). Fast rail service to Hualien should commence in 1979.

VISITING CENTRAL & SOUTHERN TAIWAN

Those with extra time, particularly if going to Hong Kong from Taiwan, should plan a journey south . . . not only to Sun Moon Lake but on to southernmost Taiwan, even over to the Pescadores.

Plan on using one of the excellent, air-conditioned express trains on the north-south trunk line linking Keelung to the north with Kaohsiung on the southwest coast. Fares are astonishingly moderate. Great way to see rural China. Seat reservations can be made two days before departure — but return reservations must be made at final destination (that applies to planes, too).

A North-South Freeway, also linking Keelung-Kaohsiung, is now operational. There is once daily express bus service from Kaohsiung to Oluanpi at the southernmost tip (3 hrs.) and Kenting Park (4 hrs.). Return at 3 p.m. RT fare is only NT$126.50 (M-Sat.), NT$131.50 on Sun., holidays.

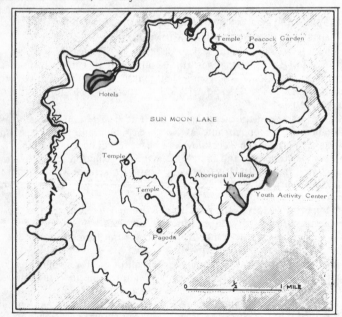

CONTINUING OVER EAST-WEST HIGHWAY

Those with more time should stay overnight at the Lodge, then continue over the East-West Hwy to Taichung. From there, drive to Sun Moon Lake before returning to Taipei.

Beyond Tien Hsiang, the East West Hwy climbs sharply out of the Gorge; from there on, there's more typical mountain scenery and driving. Occasionally you may ride above the clouds that envelope the valley below. Tayuling (Yu the Great Pass, after Emperor Tayu, who devised China's first flood control system) is the high point of your trip; Chinese compare the panorama here at 8,415 ft. to a perfect poem immortalized by a master painter.

To the south are many lofty mountains; particularly dramatic are craggy Mt. Chilai and the Mountain of Harmonious Happiness, Hohuan, 11,207 ft. high and a top summer, winter ski resort — known, predictably, as the Switzerland of Taiwan.

Before reaching Tayuling, at Pilu, there's a 2,000-year-old fir tree with a diameter of almost ten feet. Midway, at 6,381 ft., is Lishan (Pear Mt.) House, a temple-style resort. The regular two-day tour stays here overnight; there's a heated pool and bowling alley. To the north are more lofty peaks, including Snow Mountain, Taiwan's second tallest (12,740 ft.).

Highway then follows the Tachia River west past Tehchi where a giant (590 ft. high) hydroelectric power dam is situated. It has resulted in formation of a 12½-mile-long lake extending back to Lishan. Kukuan, 22 miles before Tungshih is a hot springs resort.

The Hualien-Taroko Gorge-Lishan-Taichung drive standard tour is incomplete without including an overnight stay at Sun Moon Lake.

Those not on a tour can take a Golden Dragon bus from Hualien to Taichung with stopovers at Tien Hsiang and/or Linshan — a most economical way to go.

Another way is to hire a metered cab (driver probably won't speak English) — you pay the meter rate RT, plus meals for driver, no extra charge for overnight. Air-conditioned sedan with driver will cost about $45 US per day.

ALISHAN FOREST RECREATION AREA

If you have the time and are looking for a change of pace, there's a narrow-gauge train trip (4 hours) out of Chiayi in central Taiwan (reached by train from Taipei) that's a pleasant experience. Train departs Chiayi at 8 a.m. and 2 p.m. daily for Alishan station, highest in Far East (7,392 ft.). Passengers are in a festive mood as train chugs past magnificent, varying scenery, thru tunnels and across hundreds of bridges. At country stations, natives rush to train windows to offer food.

Accommodations at Alishan House, 57 rooms (some w/bath, some Japanese style; about US$3-$18), are plain but clean. Arise at 4 a.m. for hike or bus ride (it's cold then, but coats are furnished) to Sunrise House on Mt. Chu to watch the Sea of Clouds (sunrise) over Yushan some 25 miles east; latter is a favorite of skiers, mountain climbers. Balance of day spent hiking, inspecting the fauna and flora at the museum, shopping and strolling in the village, playing tennis.

SUN MOON LAKE

Surrounded by hump-shaped mountains, it's as beautiful as any we've seen in our travels. When misty, as the weather often is, the effect is mystically oriental, almost ethereal, the silence hypnotic. The view from your hotel room balcony is alone worth the trip.

From Taipei to Taichung, it's a 2- to 3-hour trip (depending on class of train) by rail, 35 min. by air. If being taken as a day excursion, fly both ways — leave at 8 a.m., return at 4:40 p.m. But it's more enjoyable as an overnight excursion, particularly since it's possible to take the train at least one way.

Actually, the whole trip starts with the train ride because this is how you see beautiful, rural Taiwan as it streams by. Too, you have ample opportunity to observe Chinese and Taiwanese close up, and with the ambulatory tea service (a little man constantly patrols the aisle with a kettle of tea) and all, you know that at last you're in China.

Trains are clean, comfortable with reclining seats (get the reserved ones). A stewardess is in constant attention; cool towels supplied for keeping clean — and there's a litter bag in the pocket of the seat ahead. You can tell by indicators in the front of the car if Ladies and Gents are occupied; red for former, white for latter. Good dining service, too. All for about NT$225 OW.

From Taichung, the 50-mile drive (1-1½ hrs.) is a perfect gem and so photogenic you want to stop frequently to get closeups of toiling water buffalo and natives in the terraced fields of rice, banana, cane and fruit trees, of tiny villages attached to the road by swaying suspension foot bridges — again so much like what you imagined China to be you want to pinch yourself. All too soon, after a climb over a mountain range, the road drops down to Sun Moon Lake. Here, at 2,500 ft., Sun Moon Island is the geographic center of Taiwan. Evergreens and flowers surround the lake, one end moon-shaped, the other like the sun. Legend insists this happened because, once upon a time, dragons held the sun and moon here as captives.

The drive to the Pagoda at the head of the lake is definitely worthwhile. Stop enrouteat the several Temples (Wen Wu, though new, is exceedingly colorful and attractive) and Peacock Garden; latter's assortment of exotic fowl and birds, including peacocks, is an eye-popper to westerners. From Hsuan Kuang Temple, you can take a 15-min. climb to the seven-story Pagoda (empty but beautifully lit at night). Return by car or by one of the asthmatic launches to the village (lots of handcraft shops) or your hotel.

There's a good 3-hr. motorboat cruise from hotel docks if you don't want to go by car. Stops are made at all attractions, but each is a fairly stiff climb from the lake. If that isn't your thing, take a cab and do it in two hours or so.

If not taking a tour, cabs are available from Taichung. Golden Dragon and Golden Horse buses (deluxe) have six daily departures to/from Taichung, the provincial capital of Taiwan and a clean, interesting, small city with thousands of shops, many lovely parks. Trip takes 2 hours, costs NT$45 OW. Another way to go: by scheduled or chartered helicopter (Lishan and Sun Moon Lake). Contact Great China Airlines, 171 Nanking East Rd., Sec. 4, 12th floor, Taipei; phone 771-0911.

When driving to the Lake, don't fail to stop at the modern, four-story Handicraft Exhibition Hall at Tsaotun, 12 miles south of Taichung, which displays over 1,-600 craft items that run the complete gamut of cottage industry production, probably Taiwan's most extensive exhibit.

Continuing the trip south from Taichung *(TIE-choong)* to Tainan and Kaohsiung *(COW-shoong)* makes a lot of sense for those with the time to do so. From Kaohsiung, you can fly non-stop to Hong Kong (China Airlines) or return to Taipei via Taitung on the east coast. Another possibility is to fly from Taichung to the offshore Pescadores, then by plane or ferry to Kaohsiung.

TAINAN

Oldest city on the island, it was a political and economic center from the time of the Dutch thru the Ch'ing Dynasty. Fort Zeelandia, a classic Dutch fortress beside the sea at Anping, was the point thru which all of Taiwan's early contacts with the world were made. Here, too, is a famous shrine in honor of Taiwan's greatest hero, Prince Yen-p'ing (Koxinga), who drove out the Dutch in 1661. Kai Yuan Temple, with its three lofty pagodas, is a Chinese Buddhist landmark and also well worth viewing. An hour's drive brings a great oddity — the World of the Moon, a barren ridge of pure limestone, eroded by centuries of rain into multifaceted patterns, upon which nothing grows.

KAOHSIUNG

Though the industrial heart of southern Taiwan and the country's largest and busiest port, the city itself is of slight touristic interest — but nearby Cheng Ching Lake, according to all we've heard (and seen thru pictures), is. So, too, is Lotus Lake, famous for its Spring and Autumn Pavilion, the lotus blossoms that fill the lake during the summer. Both are great beauty spots.

Cheng Ching (Clear Bright) Lake is a large, artificial reservoir around which a beautiful recreational area has grown, including an 18-hole golf course and an imperial palace-type Grand Hotel. Attrac-

tions include a long Bridge of Nine Bends that zigzags across the surface (ideal for those who've always considered themselves good enough to walk on water), an inspiringly beautiful, seven-story Chung Hsing (Restoration) Pagoda, fresh- and salt-water aquariums, a lovers' bridge, an avenue of orchids and many classical-style pavilions from which to view this magnificent lake.

One of the most pleasant drives in all Taiwan is from Kaohsiung to Oluanpi, at the southernmost tip, a distance of 81 miles.

Situated 6.2 miles north of Oluanpi is Kenting Tropical Botanical Garden, set in rolling hills fronting the Formosa Strait and containing hundreds of varieties of trees, identified in Chinese, English and Latin. One of many interesting features is the Hsientung or Fairy Cave which extends for 135 meters and has a side arm 30 meters long. The cave is equipped with electric lights.

The Garden has a three-story hotel and a seven-story observation tower with elevator and circular restaurant. The hotel operates a branch and bungalows on the beach below the Garden.

ORCHID ISLAND

Lanyu, 42 ½ miles east of the southernmost tip of Taiwan, is the home of the Yami, smallest and most primitive tribe of aborigines in the country. They're of interest because they prefer to live in the simple manner of their ancestors, farming and fishing, rather than to acquire the rudiments of modern civilization, apparently because to do so would complicate their existence, eventually deprive them of their identity as a tribe with its own distinctive manners, customs and traditions.

It's a picturesque spot surrounded by deep blue waters upon which the Yamis paddle their brightly painted boats, carved from tree trunks, with upturned, pointed bow and stern. Colorful butterflies flutter across the wild blossoms that cover the volcanic mountainsides. However, since there's no hotel here, it must be seen on a day trip by plane out of Taitung.

THE PESCADORES

Back in the '50s, this area was very much in the headlines with the Communists shelling the fortified Amoy and Quemoy islands from which, it was feared, an invasion of the mainland was to be launched. Today, Penghu — the official name of 64 tiny islands with a total area of only 50 square miles — is peaceful, has a population of 120,000, 85% of which live in Makung, the capital, and three nearby islands which are linked by two causeways and the longest inter-island bridge (2,150 meters) in the Far East. The archipelago is second only to the Great Barrier Reef of Australia in the extensiveness of its coral fields. Consequently, shopping for coral ornaments and jewelry is big.

A visit here of a day appeals to those who collect offbeat destinations — but don't come during October-March when the Windy Isles are lashed by monsoon winds and rains. There are three air-conditioned, non-luxury but clean and inexpensive hotels — and more imaginatively named than most luxury places: Veined Stone, Four Seas and Ocean Palace.

During the season, April thru July, the 2,000-ton ferry, *Tai Peng,* leaves Kaohsiung daily at 7:30 a.m., returns at 2 p.m. (4½ hours each way for the 76-mile trip). There are multiple daily flights (30 min.) to/from Kaohsiung, once daily from Taichung and Chiayi (35 min.) and Tainan (30 min.), twice daily from Taipei (50 min.).

CHINESE LANGUAGE

What we know as Chinese[1] is actually the romanized, phonetic version of the spoken language based on the array of written symbols. Like French, it's spoken with highly nasal inflections impossible to indicate here. These are a few words and phrases that will help if you get completely off the beaten path; except for the small street shops and villages, you'll always find some English spoken — widely so in Taipei.

Good morning	*Tsao an*
Good evening	*Wan an*
How do you do?	*Ni hao ma?*
Please	*Ching*
Thank you	*Hsieh-hsieh ni*
Hello	*Ni hao*

Baggage	*Shing li*
Cigarettes	*Shyang yen*
Drugstore	*Yao fang*
Film	*Di bein*
Post Office	*You ju*
Stamps	*You pyao*
Taxi	*Chi cheng che*

One	*Yi*
Two	*Er*
Three	*San*
Four	*Sze*
Five	*Wu*
Six	*Liu*
Seven	*Chi*
Eight	*Pa*
Nine	*Chiu*
Ten	*Shih*

Twenty	*Er shih*
Thirty	*San shih*
Forty	*Sze shih*
Fifty	*Wu shih*
Sixty	*Liu shih*
Seventy	*Chi shih*
Eighty	*Pa shih*
Ninety	*Chiu shih*
100	*Yi pai*
1,000	*Yi chien*

Go; Stop	*Tso; Ting yiting*
Straight ahead	*Yi chih tso*
Turn left	*Tsopien chuan*
Turn right	*Yupien chuan*
How much?	*Dwo shau chyan*
Expensive	*Hen kuei*
Cheap	*Pien yi*
I want	*Wo yao*
I want to go	*Wo yao chu*
to the airport	*fei chi chang*
Goodbye	*Dzai jyan*

I—*Wo;* You—*Ni;* He, She—*Ta*
We—*Wo men;* You—*Ni men;* They—*Ta men*
Mine—*Wo te;* Yours—*Ni te;* His—*Ta te*

[1] Mandarin is the official language of China, is most widely spoken in Taiwan. Cantonese is the popular dialect of Hong Kong.

Hotel Directory

Compared to worldwide hotel rates, Taipei's hotels are great bargains; top-grade deluxe and first-class rooms are available at lower rates than almost anywhere else. Many hotels provide free airport transfers (let them know flight arrival). With service desks on each floor, service is quick and cheerful, room maintenance usually very good. Rooms generally small, mattresses firm, wardrobes inadequate, decor bland but inoffensive. *Advance reservations essential;* occupancy rates are extremely high, but a number of hotels are now under construction.

Hotel ratings are locally comparative, though DL and FC categories would be so rated anywhere else. Approximate rates, as of 1978, are quoted in U.S. dollars, double occupancy; 10% service charge is added to same. In restaurants, 13% tax and 10% service are usually added to checks.

TAIPEI
(All inspected by Jacobs)
DOWNTOWN

CENTURY PLAZA (FC-) — 250 AC, small R, SU w/rfg (150 R new wing in '79), TV. 4 dining rooms, bars, sometime nightclub. If maintenance were as good as service, would be FC. Out-of-way location overlooking river but within walking distance of Haggle Alley. Overpriced at $36-$39.

CHINA (FC-) — Great location opposite Hilton; ideal for economy-minded. 170 AC R, SU furnished Western or Oriental style. Attractive bar, coffee shop; also Chinese, Western rsts. $25.

TAIPEI HILTON (DL) — Great location near RR station, walking distance of New Park, Presidential Square, old shopping area. 520 AC R, SU in 22-story hi-rise. Plenty of action in coffee shop, rsts, bars, shops and nightclub; big with businessmen, groups. $40-$48. Conv. facilities.

UPTOWN (NORTH)

AMBASSADOR (FC) — Good central location on Chungshan N. Rd. 300 commercial-type R, SU. Exc. service. 5 rsts, 3 bars, nightclub, pool, shops. Conv: 1,500. $40-$52.

ANGEL (FC-) — Unattractive surroundings on Nanking E. Rd. but exc. for price ($20). 160 AC, small R. Attractive lobby, lounge. Dining room, bar.

CENTRAL (FC) — 300 AC R, SU w/TV, rfg, balconies; pool. Modern interior, lots of shops; coffee shop, several rsts and revolving rooftop rst. Good location: 122 Chungshan N. Rd. $37-$42.

EMPIRE — For economy-minded who want good location between President Hotel-Chungshan N. Rd. (in the girlie bar district). Commercial type. Dining room, bar. $20-$22.

EMPEROR — 120 R, SU w/TV, rfg are slightly larger than most. Rst and lobby have ornate Chinese motif. Commercial. $31. At 118 Nanking E. Rd. near banking district.

FIRST — 63 Nanking E. Rd. 164 large, plain R, good beds. Hillman rst considered good, nightclub well recommended. $23-$25. Same management as China Hotel.

GLORIA (FC) — Very attractive. 245 AC R, SU are bright, clean w/rfg. Rooftop dining, ground-floor coffee shop; Szechwan and Western food served in three other rsts. Behind Ambassador on Linsen N. Rd.; street stalls block away. $39 up.

GRAND (DL) — Huge, neo-Chinese Palace hi-rise looks like Imperial Grand Central Station. Luxuriously lavish but completely impersonal and lacking the charm of the old Grand — which, by the way, still reposes quietly behind the flossy hi-rise, overlooks huge pool (with only temple-style bathhouse in captivity) and four clay tennis courts. Original 250 rooms are large, have terrace and are cheaper ($34) than new 451 R, SU (some w/rfg) up to $50. For utmost charm, ask for rooms in main bldg. of old Grand (Chi-lin Pavilion), while at $27 the old annex is a bargain. Ornate and imposing lobby, many good shops; varied

131

Entrance to Lungshan Temple, Taipei

dining from Cantonese dim sum to elegant Ming Grill (one of the best), Shanghai-style teahouse and other Chinese and Western rooms. Isolated on hill overlooking city and airport.

IMPERIAL (FC) — 450 well-maintained R, SU (140 are in new wing). All w/TV, rfg, balcony; SU w/kitchenette. Pink Lady Bar and Steak House; rooftop Mabuhay Nightclub has dancing, panoramic views. In same nightclub-girlie district as President. A with-it hotel. $39-$42, SU $50.

MAJESTIC (FC) — Good, conservative hotel with 240 nice size R w/rfg, TV. Rooftop rsts serve Shanghai, Western cuisines. Coffee shop, shops. Good location at corner of Chungshan N. Rd. and Minchuan E. Rd. $36.

PRESIDENT (DL) — Spent a week here and loved it; gets our vote for best all-around hotel in town. 400 AC R, SU (adding 80 more in new wing), are good size, most attractive. Superb, friendly service — ice arrived in room almost before we hung up the phone. Coffee shop, Western style and Japanese rsts are good; Mandarin serves superb Chinese food w/traditional Chinese music, entertainment; elegant nightclub dining rooftop. $40-$46 — and well worth it.

MANDARIN (FC) — Overly elaborate Oriental style but just few blocks from airport and near many government agencies. 350 AC R, SU w/Oriental decor. Cantonese and Western dining rooms. Large conv. facilities, many shops. Chinese garden w/waterfall; pool, tennis. $39 up.

SESAME (FC) — Taipei's newest, on Hsin Yi Rd, near Sun Yat Sen Memorial Hall. 210 R, rst, nightclub, cocktail lounge. $37-$42.

Those staying several weeks or longer might want to rent a condominium apartment. *Lincoln Center* is a circular hi-rise at 121 Szu Wei Rd. in eastern sector (phone 751-4331). 1- and 2-bedroom AC apts. rent from $485 and up per month; weekly and daily rates, too. Coffee shop, restaurant and pool.

Economy rooms available at YMCA Hostel (19 Hsih Chang St.) and YWCA Hostel (7 Chintao W. Rd.); International House (18 Hsinyi Rd.) is very inexpensive.

HUALIEN

ASTAR — Attractive, unusual lobby, gardens, pool. 178 rooms overlook Pacific. Not many hotels where guests can see the ocean and watch peanuts and sugarcane being planted. Japanese, Chinese. Western-style dining, bars. $28-$38.

MARSHAL (FC) — Beautifully situated on Park Rd. 350 R with TV. Chinese, Int'l Rst, coffee shop, nightclub, pool. *Rsv:* Angel Hotel, 199 Sung Chiang Rd, Taipei. $28-$37.

KAOHSIUNG

GRAND (FC) — Chinese architecture — lobby, rst, rooms all done in the grand style. 120 R overlook Cheng Ching Lake in residential area. Golf club privileges. $23-$25.

HOLIDAY INN (FC) — 20 min. from airport, DT. Beautifully decorated in Chinese motif. In efficiency and maintenance, it's 100% Western. 120 AC R; pool and garden area attractive. Chinese and Western dining. Country Club privileges (girl caddies). $28-$49.

LISHAN (Pear Mt.)

LISHAN GUEST HOUSE — On Cross Island Hwy. Advance rsv. a must for this attractive, Palace-style resort between Taroko Gorge and Taichung. 67 simple, small rooms in annex and motel set in park-like setting. Superb mountain views. Tennis court, bowling alley, pool. $13-$21. 10% service.

SHIH-MEN

SHIH-MEN SESAME (DL) — Opened late '77, 65 km from Taipei in beautiful, hilly Shihmen (Stone Gate) recreational area. 250 AC R with tiled, flowered balconies, are individually, beautifully furnished; all have TV, rfg, large wardrobes and overlook large pool, garden area. 2 tennis courts. Hotel is built semi-circular with spacious lobby on top floor, rooms below. 7 rsts, nightclub (French cuisine) atop, sumptuous cocktail lounge. Twice daily bus service to/from Taipei. Airport transportation $8.25 OW. *Conv:* 300. A truly beautiful, elegant resort hotel. Loved it. $37-$50. SU (2 baths) $83-$240. *Rsv:* Shih-men Sesame, Lincoln Center, 121 Szu-Wei Rd, Taipei.

VILLA — Hillside above Fairyland boat docks. 16 family SU with bath, rfg built Chinese pavilion style. Chinese, Int'l cuisine. $15-$45.

SUN-MOON LAKE

2 hrs. (80 km) by car from Taichung. 3% local tax in addition to regular taxes.

EVERGREEN — Magnificent setting overlooking water, island and Pagoda. Within walking distance of town. 20 R in modern new wing at top best. Maintenance reported poor. All 72 R are simple, some w/terrace. Chinese/Western food. Sky Lounge bar. Pool, boat landing. $11-$19.

SUN MOON LAKE TOURIST HOTEL — Very attractive, unusual Pagoda-type hotel. Chinese decor in lobby, rst. 116 (some new) simple R overlook lake and Wen Wu Temple (ones on top levels best). Panoramic, hillside view of lake; great for honeymooners and those who like isolation. Friendly, good service. Own boat landing. Pool, water-skiing. Golf. $22-$26.

TAICHUNG

APOLLO — Second best. 145 AC simple R. Chinese/Western rsts. Nightclub, bowling alley. $17-$20.

TAICHUNG GRAND (FC+) — Very modern. Lavish use of marble. 115 AC R, SU w/color TV. Rooftop rsts, coffee shop, bar. Conv. facilities. $23-$29.

TAROKO GORGE

TIEN HSIANG LODGE — Pagoda style. 16 R (22 more in '78) are utterly charming w/private terrace, a lovely pool set below a church rising on the hilltop. Pleasant gardens, great spot to relax; birds, roosters and the flowing blue water are the only noises. Attractive small bar in dining room. Good food. Jammed at noon with day tours. Rsv. a must. $15-$18.

TAINAN

TAINAN — Available it is! Best we can say it's across from RR station, has a pool, large lobby. 3 rsts, nightly entertainment. 152 R need refurbishing. Overpriced at $20.

This is what awaits you from Victoria Peak. In the foreground is the Central District that runs (right) into the Wanchai and Causeway Bay districts. Across the Harbour (left) is downtown Kowloon.

HONG KONG

Let's put it this way: if there's one place that can't be left out of *any* Far East itinerary, it's Hong Kong.

It's a fascinating melting pot of people and races, great for walking and rubbernecking. It's a city that caters to the senses, a city of odors, sweet and enchanting. It's the rich of the Mandarin Hotel, the poor of the narrow streets leading from Queen's Road; stalls of fruits, fish, basketry. It's rows of laundry strung across the streets from apartment to apartment. It's men and women, with loads on their backs, in Chinese blouse and pants; earnest young men, with attache cases, in sedate western-style suits. It's the ferrys scurrying forever between Kowloon and Victoria, the wharfs with their sampans, junks; a harbor dotted with oceangoing freighters being loaded, unloaded. It's wizened vendors with rock and string weighing potatoes, women with kids on their backs, grandparents caring for grandchildren (who are *never* left alone). It has such an exciting aerial approach you're caught up in the anticipation of its wonders before even landing.

All this is Hong Kong — and more.

Make no mistake about it, though — Hong Kong is commercial. Commerce is her life, culture a by-product. Here the definition of a queer is a man who likes women more than money. You come here to buy, to enjoy the bustling throngs, the restaurants, bars, nightclubs, the ever-changing beauty of the harbor and, in general, a way of life that can't be found in any other port in the world.

Get a harbor view room and, from on high, watch ships edge in, sampans unload freighters, ferrys plying their diligent routes and, at night, neon lights in exotic, reflected patterns, warships festooned with gala lights.

But as fascinating and colorful as it is, Hong Kong is no longer the bargain emporium it once was. Domestic inflation and devaluation of the U.S. dollar coupled with increasing affluence (thousands and thousands here made killings in the stock market) have driven prices way up, reduced savings for tourists on consumer items to a pittance — if any. Hotel rates are high and service, though still good, is no longer eager.

The last paragraph is not meant to discourage, merely to forewarn. For us, just to spend a Sunday here watching families on their outings is to enjoy a not easily matched experience.

PLANNING THE HONG KONG VISIT

Except for a trip to Macau, there's no need for advance planning. This is a city where it's fun to do what comes naturally when you feel like doing it — walking, shopping, ferrying, dining, drinking, nightclubbing. Little need for tours except, possibly, one to the New Territories (also easily done by train or bus from Kowloon). You can see everything by ferry, bus and train — most economically and with an exhilarating sense of adventure.

Since Hong Kong is a major gateway to Red China, a visit to the New Territories, which borders People's Republic of China's Kwantung Province, has great impact on first-time visitors. You see only vague outlines of Red China, but rural New Territories and its people definitely look the way you expected Old China to be. A half-day tour is about right.

One bit of advance planning is necessary — hotel accommodations; or rather, where to stay. Victoria, on Hong Kong Island, is Wall Street and upper Fifth Ave., more sophisticated. Kowloon is Broadway with more colorful, noisy street scenes. Causeway Bay is like staying on the Manhattan side of Tri-Borough Bridge — near the airport with fascinating local street scenes. See Hotel Directory for all the details.

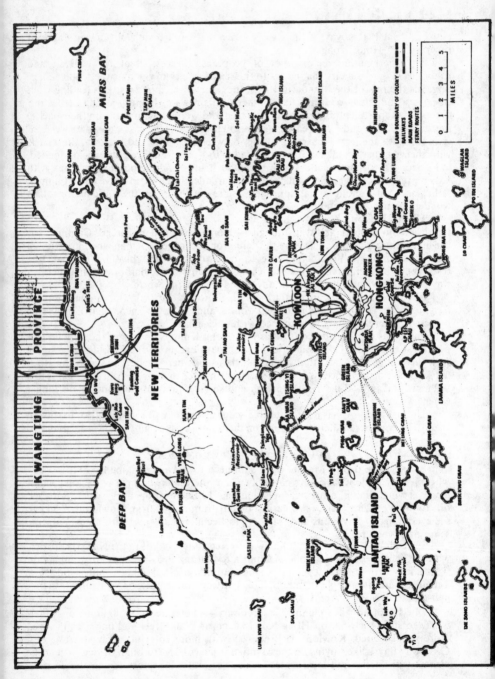

ENTRY REQUIREMENTS

U.S. tourists need only a valid passport, no visa for visits up to 30 days. Canadians need passport but no visa (for stays up to 3 months).

EXCHANGE RATE

HK$4.75=$1 US, or each HK$1 is 21¢. Divide Hong Kong prices by 5 to arrive at approximate US prices. *All prices herein, unless stated otherwise, are in HK dollars.*

Paper currency comes in denominations of HK$5, $10, $50, $100 and $500. Coins are 5¢, 10¢, 20¢, 50¢, $1, $2 and $5. Hotels, banks, money changers all give official rate of exchange, which can fluctuate.

TRANSPORTATION
AIRPORT TRANSFERS

Pre-arranged transfers a good bet unless your hotel has limousine service (many do; inquire when making rsv); some are free, in which case take advantage. There's a public limo service (almost hidden from view across the road from airport exit) that charges HK$4.50 for first mile to Kowloon, descending scale per mile thereafter; about HK$45 to Victoria hotels, less to Causeway Bay. Regular taxis may try to take you for a double ride — charge meter rate in US dollars instead of HK dollars.

Cheapest transfer: Airport Coach Service connecting Kai Tak Airport with major hotels in Kowloon (HK$1.50 per person) and Victoria (HK$2.50).

HIRE CARS

Rates for chauffeured cars vary, depending on make and size; a Rolls rolls for US$20 an hour, Avis charges that a day (plus mileage, gas) to drive yourself (though why any tourist would want to is beyond us). Two couples sightseeing by chauffeured car, on the other hand, makes sense. If alone, hotels can pair you with another couple.

TAXIS

Hong Kong and Kowloon taxi meters start (be sure they do) at HK$2, then 20¢ each additional 1/5 mile (or HK$1 per mile). $10 surcharge by ferry or tunnel from one side to the other. Baggage handling is another $2 charge. New Territories meters start at $1. Taxis usually available in streets, front of hotels; if not, phone 5-747311 (Hong Kong), 3-234141 (Kowloon).

BUSES

No problem going anywhere in one (from 6 a.m. to midnight). Get a list of which numbers go where (from HK Tourist Assoc.) and go. Buses clearly marked. Cost from 30¢ in the city to $1.50 for outlying trips. Besides the big ones, there are minibuses (yellow w/red band) that cost 50¢ to $3 per ride; pick you up when hailed, let you off anywhere on their route. There are also maxi-cabs running every 10 minutes from the Central District to Victoria Peak ($1) via Magazine Gap Rd.

FERRY SERVICE

From 6 a.m. to 2 a.m., Star Ferry is in continuous action between Kowloon and Central District. 40¢ for first class (upper deck) each way, 30¢ for lower deck. If you miss the last ferry, take a Walla Walla (motorized sampan) for $2, providing there are 6 to 10 other late souls — or $15 to ride in solitary splendor.

VICTORIA PEAK TRAM

Station near Hilton. Carries 72 passengers from 7 a.m. to midnight; $1.50. Other trams run between Kennedy Town and Shaukiwan on the north shore of Hong Kong island.

KOWLOON-CANTON RAILWAY

Visitors traveling within Hong Kong can ride to the next to last station before the Chinese border, Sheung Shui, for HK$7.40 RT first class, starting from the new station in Hunghom near the Cross Harbour Tunnel entrance on the mainland. *Avoid* on Sundays, holidays.

TOURIST INFORMATION

Hong Kong Tourist Association, a well-run organization with a wealth of information for travel agents and tourists, maintains U.S. offices at: 160 Sansome St., Suite 1102, San Francisco 94104 (phone 415-989-5005); 548 Fifth Ave., New York 10036 (212-947-5008).

In Hong Kong, headquarters is on the 35th floor, Connaught Centre. But tourists can dial 3-671111 for advice, information. Or visit one of these Tourist Offices for maps, guide folders (food, shopping, walking and ferry tours, etc.): Kai Tak Airport; Star Ferry Concourse, Kowloon; Government Publications Centre, General Post Office Bldg., and Connaught Centre, both in Hong Kong.

Hong Kong, city of a million lights, during annual Mid-Autumn Festival in September.

Hong Kong Facts:

Airport Departure Tax — HK$15 payable in Hong Kong dollars only at Kai Tak Airport.

Bank Hours — 10 a.m. to 3 p.m.; 10-Noon Sat.

Business Hours — 9 to 5 (lunch break 1-2 p.m.); 9-1 Sat. Many Chinese firms are open 10 a.m.-8 p.m. Dept. Stores open 9 to 6:30 Mon. thru Sat.

Climate — Nov.-Feb. best, coolest (as low as 50⁰) season. Clear, sunny days from Oct.-Mar. Some rain in April, May; annual rainfall is 85", mostly during typhoon season (May to Oct.).

Clothing — During winter, light knits, overcoat, suits; heavy clothing unnecessary. For spring, summer bring lightweight things, including raincoat and boots.

Consulates — Canadian at 14-15 F, Asian House (5-282222). U.S. at 26 Garden Rd. (5-239011).

Current — 200v, 50 cycle — but most hotels have 110v converters.

Phones — Local calls free from private phones, 50¢ from public (red) phones. Dial 3 first if calling Kowloon from Hong Kong, 5 from Kowloon to the Island, 12 for New Territories.

Population — 4,500,000, mostly Chinese.

Postage — Airmail letter to North America, HK$2; $1 for postcard.

Tipping — Figure on 10% unless service has been added to hotel, restaurant bills. HK$1 or 2 for handling luggage.

Water — Okay in better restaurants and in hotel rooms that announce purified water. Otherwise stick with bottled kind.

IT HAPPENED IN HONG KONG

It's fitting that Hong Kong was conceived as the result of commerce between China and England, for in 1699 an East Indian Company ship was the first to trade peaceably with Canton where, in 1715, a factory (trading compound) was established by the Company, although foreigners could stay there (without European women) only during the winter trading seasons (August to March). Over the years, opium from India became the leading import. In 1839, concerned by the growing Chinese addiction, Peking attempted to stamp out the drug; this led to the Opium War between Britain and China which, after invasion by the British, led to the 1841 occupation of Hong Kong Island by the Crown which was ceded in perpetuity by the August 1842 Treaty of Nanking; when ratified by both countries in 1843, the settlement was named Victoria and the main street Queen's Road. Thus did Hong Kong become a free port and British Crown Colony, which it is today, and Victoria a city of 29 square miles. Also, interestingly enough, by 1841 proclamation, citizens of Hong Kong of Chinese descent would continue to enjoy the traditional laws of China as applied to social and family life but would be protected by English economic and criminal laws. Thus, Hong Kong is the only place in the world where Tai Ching Laws (in effect in 1841) still apply in cases of Chinese marriage and divorce.

Kowloon (just a small section) and Stonecutters' Island were similarly ceded by the October 1860 Convention of Peking. In 1898, Kowloon beyond Boundary Street, the mainland district called New Territories, the large island of Lantau and many small islands were *leased* from China for 99 years, bringing the Colony's total land area to 365 square miles.[1]

Until British occupation, this "barren island with hardly a house upon it" was

[1] There must be about 400 square miles now. Much of Hong Kong's and Kowloon's present shorelines are reclaimed land for which fill was provided by leveling many of the surrounding hills which, in turn, provided additional building areas.

thinly populated by some 4,000 fishermen and maybe 2,000 living aboard flimsy boats. The fishing ports of Shau Kei Wan and Shek Pai Wan had been pirate lairs from Mongol Dynasty times. By June of 1845, there were 23,817 living here, 595 of them Europeans. The first influx of Chinese refugees began in 1850 during the Tai Ping Rebellion, and by 1861 the Colony numbered 119,321, all but 3,000 of them Chinese. After World War II, Hong Kong grew at the rate of 100,000 a month, and even more refugees crowded in during 1948 and 1950 when the population was estimated at 2,360,000. Today, it's around 4,500,000 — most Cantonese.

Majority of Chinese residents are Buddhists or Taoists, though some are Christians, a few Moslems. Church of England is the largest Christian church, but there are other Protestant faiths as well as Catholic. Hindu and Muslim religions are well represented. All of these without religious friction for the people of Hong Kong have learned that to survive, they must work hard and let live. Which they do.

You can see these two worlds, Western and Chinese, as a series of tours, from which you watch the passing parade thru bus or car windows, or as a sequence of do-it-yourself sorties that permit you to mingle. Whichever — or a combination of both — it's an exciting experience, but one that requires careful planning. The details which follow far exceed what most tourists can do in the average time allotted for Hong Kong. Nevertheless, they'll enable you to pick and choose which elements are most appealing — and should you come here on one of the growing number of one-stop charters that stay a week or more, you won't be at a loss for things to do.

The varied worlds of Hong Kong exist in five areas: 1) Hong Kong Island, separated by Victoria Harbour from 2) Kowloon Peninsula which leads to 3) New Territories, on the mainland adjoining China. 4) The other, lesser known, but fascinating islands reached by ferry. 5) The third-world of the *Tankas* (boat people).

Diners being "taxied" to one of Aberdeen's famed Floating Restaurants.

Each should be seen as an entity, not necessarily in the above order, to save time and money. One can waste a lot of both without knowing what's what. Here's what:

HONG KONG ISLAND

Referred to as the Central District, Victoria and Hong Kong, the terminology can be confusing until explained.

Hong Kong, whose length and main urban sectors run east to west along a narrow strip of land between Victoria Harbour and the mountains, contains the city of Victoria, or the Central District, the financial and economic heart of the Territory; the Wanchai district of Suzy Wong fame; the Causeway Bay Area with its sampan Typhoon Shelter, World Trade Centre, Art Centre, hi-rise hotels and office buildings. The Island (*Chau* in Chinese) also has such tourist attractions as Cat Street, the floating restaurants of Aberdeen, Ocean Park amusement complex, Happy Valley racetrack, Repulse Bay, Tiger Balm Gardens and, to top them all, Victoria Peak with its Peak Tram . . . all easily reached by car, taxi and bus, alone or on guided tours.

ABERDEEN, A FLOATING TOWN

A visit here, preferably with lunch on a Floating Restaurant, ranks in importance with riding the Star Ferry, shopping, dining and visiting New Territories. In other words, you can't leave without seeing it.

Named for a Foreign Secretary during the early days, Lord Aberdeen, Heung Kong Tsai (Fragrant Small Harbor) was the Chinese name, and still is, of this tiny village which gave Hong Kong its name. Historians differ as to whether the fragrance was due to incense makers who plied their trade here or to the fact that ships called to stock up on fresh water. Today, the fragrance of Aberdeen is that of fresh fish and seafood — which diners can choose from saltwater tanks alongside the floating restaurants.

Around 25,000 people live (and die) on the 3,500 boats that claim Heung Kong Tsai as a permanent home, although they sail out to sea to fish with their nets and lights (including kids, grandma and grandpa, pets), then return to the boardwalks that run between one cluster of boats to another; to the roadside stalls piled high with colorful mounds of fruits and vegetables, rice and other staples; to mend their sails and dry their nets; to the safety of the shelter and the chatter of their friends.

If you can spare the time, a short sampan ride[1] south to Aplichau will give you a glimpse of unsophisticated Chinese life few tourists see, for this island has most of the Colony's shipyards. You'll see men building a variety of craft, cargo vessels to dinghies; you'll see more of the boat people, people living on land in corrugated shacks, little alleys where "factories" turn out costume jewelry, toys, plastic flowers.

The ride out, between Harbour and hills, is very scenic and interesting. If you come by way of Victoria's old Chinese section, return from Aberdeen via the beaches of Deep Water Bay, Repulse Bay and South Bay. But for the most beautiful beach of all, and a look at Old China as it's still lived, detour to Shek-O beach and village. Cheek to jowl buildings on narrow streets in which ducks and chickens idle, shopkeepers tea, street vendors crying their wares — that's Shek-O village, though not the beach, already a victim of progress. No. 9 bus comes here.

Stanley, southeast of Repulse Bay, has become a very plush hi-rise residential area, but its market and village still remain charming and interesting.

TIGER BALM GARDENS

You'll love or hate it, maybe laugh at its grotesqueness, but you should see it — particularly the Haw Par Mansion, the former home of Aw Boon Haw who built this eight-acre monstrosity at a cost of HK$16,000,000 out of a fortune made on Tiger Balm patent medicine. Ask your guide to get the caretaker to admit you to the Mansion — its antiques and fabulous jade collection, oddly at variance with the grotesque statues in the Gardens, are more than worth a small tip. No. 11 bus from Wanchai comes here.

Like Aberdeen, the Typhoon Shelter at

[1] Best to have a guide for this jaunt. There's also a ferry.

Nathan Road's "signboard jungle."

Causeway Bay is home for thousands of fishermen. You can arrange for a ride in one of the sampans if you wish.

VICTORIA PEAK

Hotel rooftop rooms have splendid views, but only here can you get the complete 360⁰ panorama that is utterly indescribable. Reached by taxi, Peak Tram, bus and sightseeing tour. For the most fun, take the bus (No. 15 from Central District) up, tram down. Or grab one of the maxi-taxis. Or take a taxi to Aberdeen and Shek-O.

Not too many visitors realize there's a splendid circle walk — Harlech-Lugard Roads — of about 45 minutes (frequent resting places) from which you view the green hills of the South China Sea islands, stretching to Macau, as well as the Harbour, the skyscrapers of Hong Kong and Kowloon — without hearing a sound. Many of the Peak homes are the epitome of British colonialism. You can also climb Mt. Austin Rd. even further — from 1,350 ft. to 1,809.

There are three restaurants here (see Dining).

WALKS INTO OLD CHINA

There's much to see and do west of the sophisticated Central District. Every night, in the parking lot of the Macau Ferry Pier, the so-called Poor Man's Night Club comes to life with a blast of sound and a surge of activity that lasts 'til one or two a.m. You're unlikely to buy in this after-dark Thieves Market, but you'll surely enjoy.

As a matter of fact, the entire western district is intensely interesting. We made a habit of getting off a bus within reasonable walking distance of Central District in order to amble back, poking our noses into this side street, that little alley, gawking at the herb shops and their exotic remedies, food shops, tray shops, rope shops — every type of tiny shop, including those displaying coffins. See Shopping for more details.

Those interested in astrology, palmistry and the occult can visit a fortune-telling area near Possession Point. However, despite clairvoyancy being universal, speech is definitely limited to Chinese — so bring a guide.

But such fascinating sights and sounds are not limited to the western side — in Causeway Bay, to the east, you'll find a similar collection. Good way to get there is by tram from the Central District.

Get Hong Kong Tourist Association's folder, "Six Walks," an excellent, mapped guide to the most fascinating districts of Hong Kong Island and Kowloon; provides hours of good, inexpensive discovery.

A final suggestion: don't fail to take in the Art Centre (opened late '77) on the Wanchai waterfront, between Central District and Causeway Bay, and the stunning City Hall Museum, a few steps east of Star Ferry, Central District. Former has two theaters and two split-level floors of art galleries. Latter has displays of art, Chinese jade and other artifacts.

EXPLORING KOWLOON
& NEW TERRITORIES

Originally an old walled City of Nine Dragons, Kowloon was the last refuge of the last Emperor of the Sung Dynasty during the Mongol invasion. Today it's one of the world's most densely populated areas bursting with all types of activity.

No need for formal sightseeing — just roam up, and off, Nathan Road, the "Golden Mile," from Tsimshatsui, the tourist area around Star Ferry, Ocean Terminal and Star House, with their hundreds of shops, north to the typically Chinese shopping district of Mongkok.

Yet less than an hour's drive or train ride into Hong Kong's New Territories takes you back hundreds of years into a land where, to the casual observer, the clock has stopped on peasants toiling in the rice paddies, tilling the soil with buffalo, isolating their ducks for fattening. Here are villages with protective walls against enemy attack, villagers following traditional life styles, dressing as they did in the days when windjammers and pirate ships sailed the China Seas. Here live the Hakkas whose women are celebrated as laborers, the Tanka and Hoklo boat people (many now live on land) and of course, the Cantonese who comprise the majority.

Frankly, we think the observance of all the foregoing is far more interesting than the principal objective of all tours, Lok Ma Chau (Look, Ma — China), tourists' closest approach to Red China. Besides Kam Tin, the walled village, there are several monasteries of interest. Tsing Shan (Green Mountain) was established in 428 AD, present ones in 1918, including the Sea Moon Pavilion where, at night, visitors watch the moonlight on the sea below. A small cave higher up on the hill has the remains of whale that, supposedly, crashed at one time against the mountain. Ling Tou, established 1,500 years ago, is on the northern slope of Castle Peak. For groups of 20 or more (by appointment), privately owned Dragon Garden on Castle Peak Road is worth seeing.

Further details are given under Bus and Water Sightseeing.

HONG KONG-CANTON TOURS

These four-day packages into Red China are less restrictive now for U.S. citizens. Apply at Thomas Cook offices in U.S. or HK. Also Arrow Travel and China Travel Services in HK.

FORMAL SIGHTSEEING TOURS

We thoroughly agree with a Tourist Association statement that "Hong Kong offers the tourist more sights and sounds and happenings per square mile than anywhere else in the world." And when they say, "Plus a variety of ways in which to discover them," they're actually understating — there are too many tours.

Considering time available to the average tourist, the basics are a 3- to 4-hr. Hong Kong Island Tour,[1] 3- to 4-hr. New Territories Tour[2] and a Water Tour (from 2 to 4½ hrs.).

A time-saving package (6½ hrs.) is a combined Land-Water Tour of Hong Kong Island[3] covering Victoria Harbour-Yaumati Typhoon Shelter-Aberdeen by water, then by coach to principal points on the Island. There is also a combined Train, Junk and Coach Tour of New Territories[4] that adds a cruise around Tolo Harbour by junk to the usual land package.

For Night Tours, see "Always Every Night."

SCHEDULING A SHORT VISIT

Assuming a minimum of three days (following day of arrival) and maximum of five (before departure), here's what we suggest for broadest, quickest coverage of Hong Kong's varied aspects and pleasures:

1st Day — Browse and shop, ride the Star Ferry in the a.m. Lunch at *Jimmy's Kitchen*, Central District, then take a two-hour Harbor Cruise[5], followed by tea in the Peninsula lobby. After cocktails, dine at one of the rooftop restaurants to enjoy the bedazzling, after-dark splendor of the Harbour.

2nd Day — Tour Hong Kong Island; lunch at an Aberdeen floating restaurant. If kids are along, you may wish to visit Ocean Park. If not, spend afternoon shopping Cat Street and vicinity. For a different kind of dinner, try Food Street (near Patterson St., Causeway Bay), where 28 restaurants offer a wide variety of Chinese and Western food. Wind up the evening at the nearby *Palace* nightclub in Convention Centre.

3rd Day — New Territories Tour in a.m. After a *dim sum* lunch in the Central District, shop here or take a ferry ride to Peng Chau and Lantau. Select any of the restaurants listed under "All About Dining" — or perhaps the Miramar Hotel's lavishly costumed Chinese Opera dinner show.

4th and 5th days give visitors more time to enjoy many of the fringe benefits. Like spending more time in Harbour Village (see Shopping) and enjoying a good Chinese meal at *Jade Garden,* taking the Tolo Harbour excursion, riding the

---

[1] Range from HK$40 per person for AC coach to HK$180 for AC private car w/guide. Daily a.m. and p.m. tours.
[2] Rates about same as above for a.m. and p.m. tours.
[3] About HK$95 w/lunch. Daily at 11:30 a.m. (Blake Pier, HK), 11:15 from Ocean Terminal.
[4] Daily at 9:20 a.m. (HK) and 9:30 (Kowloon). About HK$100 w/lunch.
[5] At 3 p.m.; HK$40. 4½-hr. morning cruises cost HK$50, 3-hr. lunch cruise HK$75. A 4-hr. Sunset Cruise costs HK$70 w/drinks.

double-decker buses and the ferries, attending a concert, browsing thru an art exhibit, riding the Tram for lunch or dinner atop the Peak. We can't emphasize too much that formal sightseeing should not take up more than half your time, if that, since the enjoyment of doing nothing but what your feet and fancy lead you to is more than half the fun of Hong Kong.

SIGHTSEEING BY FERRY

There are 235 islands clustered in and around Hong Kong's waters, many deserted but some presenting a true glimpse of old China, of a life style long gone from Kowloon and Victoria. Islands nearest the Central District are serviced from the Outlying Districts Pier at frequent intervals, often by triple-decker airconditioned ferries. All fares are under HK$3 except on AC ferry to Silvermine Bay (HK$3 weekdays, HK$5 on weekends). Utterly delightful and relaxing way to see much that otherwise would go unseen.

TO THE WESTWARD ISLANDS

Lantau Island, twice the size of Hong Kong Island, is mountainous, has a variety of scenic walks,[6] beaches, temples, monasteries and old fishing villages but a population of under 20,000.

Most popular destination is Po Lin (Golden Lotus) Monastery, an hour's minibus run (HK$6) from the Silvermine Bay ferry pier, itself an hour's run from the Central District. On the Ngong Ping plateau (2,460 ft.), the main temple has three bronze Buddhas in the lotus position. On the birthday of Lord Buddha, thousands of the devout come to participate in religious ceremonies that include washing the statues with holy water.

Simple overnight accommodations are available here and at Sea House in Silvermine. A vegetarian meal at the Monastery costs HK$10. Or enjoy, of all things, an Australian barbecue at *Ned Kelly's Last*

[6] Get HKTA's "Lantau Island Walks" folder that maps 6 walks of two to four and a half hours each, a total of 15 hours.

Stand on Silvermine Bay Beach while you watch the junks, sampans and smiling Chinese kids.

Just behind the Golden Lotus Monastery is a tea plantation where different teas may be tasted, tea-picking watched. Horses and bicycles for rent. Guided trips thru Monastery and plantation can be arranged for groups. Ned Kelly's also has a variety of trips for individuals.

Tung Chung, north coast of Lantau, and Tai-O on the far west have less frequent ferry service from Hong Kong. Though a longer trip than to Silvermine, there's the interesting Tung Chung Fort built by the Chinese in 1817 to repel the barbarians (Europeans); has walls 200 ft. long and 300 ft. high. There's infrequent minibus service from Silvermine Bay to both Tung Chung and Tai-O; latter is a busy market town, fishing port and salt panning center of 12,000 with many monasteries and temples, principally a 1699 Taoist temple, Hou Wong.

A huge resort complex is planned for Lantau, at Discovery Bay. In five years, the island should be one of the Far East's finest resorts, will include a golf course reached by cable car.

Peng Chau is noted for its cottage industries (especially hand-painted porcelain) and the 1792 temple, Tin Hau (protector of fishermen), which plays an important part in local life. Most ferries for Lantau call first at Peng Chau (45 min.; $1). From here, you can take a sampan to reach a beach on Lantau below the Trappist Monastery (Haven of Our Lady of Liesse), one of the most austere Roman Catholic orders; monks run a dairy farm (mostly in silence), sell milk to a Hong Kong hotel. From Peng Chau, it's only a 15-minute ferry run to Silvermine.

Cheung Chau (Long Island) lies south of Peng Chau to the east of Lantau, an hour's run (HK$2.00) from Hong Kong. Without motor vehicles, the island preserves a charming, old-style way of life with hundreds of seagoing fishing junks, narrow streets crammed with workshops, small factories, retail shops and stalls.

There are a few good seafood restaurants — and many temples. Best known and most accessible is that of Pak Tai, a sea divinity and patron deity of fishermen. Legend has it that when a 1777 plague broke out in Cheung Chau, fishermen brought the Pak Tai image from China to suppress the plague; since then, the island has been prosperous. So, Pak Tai, Spirit of the North, is enthroned in his temple guarded by two martial gods, Thousand-Li Eye and Favorable Wind Ear. On request, you can see a Sung Dynasty sword raised from the sea over a hundred years ago and presented to Pak Tai as a symbol of good luck. It's five feet long, of iron with a dragon-shaped handle and still in good condition.

You can easily spend a day (and more) ferrying from Victoria to Peng Chau, Silvermine Bay, Cheung Chau and back to Hong Kong Island.

SIGHTSEEING BY PUBLIC BUS

If you have the time, this is the way to go. Take the double deckers, sit on top deck (preferably in the very front seats) and watch China roll by. Sometimes you're practically looking into apartments, inspecting the laundry hanging out of the windows on bamboo poles (some of those bras are much larger than you'd expect for such small women).

Don't take buses or trams during rush hours — like New York subways. All other times they're real fun things.

AROUND HONG KONG ISLAND

There are two routes. One is from City Hall in Central District to Shaukiwan terminal at Causeway Bay (No. 2 bus), then by another to Stanley Village (No. 14); change to 73 for Repulse Bay, Deep Water Bay and Aberdeen, finally No. 7 to Yaumati terminal, a few minutes' walk west of Star Ferry. Complete circuit costs HK$3.25 (paid by the segment); travel time is about 2 hrs. You can, of course, do any of the segments in reverse — and you don't have to go around the Island.

The second routing cuts across the Island to Stanley Village (No. 6 from City Hall), returns via Aberdeen on Nos. 73

TOLO HARBOR

Trip departs from Kowloon Railway Station at 1:08 p.m., returns by rail at 4:46. After train arrival at Tai Po Kau Ferry Pier, there's a delightful 1½-hr. cruise aboard an air-conditioned water taxi. Tickets (HK$20) can be purchased up to a week in advance at Kowloon Railway Station or Yaumati Ferry in Central Harbour Services Pier.

From Tolo Harbour, a large inlet on the eastern shore of New Territories, one gets glimpses of rarely glimpsed beaches, lagoons, fishing villages of the virtually unspoiled Sai Kung Peninsula to the east. A very popular, enjoyable outing.

FERRY TOUR OF HONG KONG ISLAND

Every Saturday June-September only. This circular tour takes 2½ hours, costs HK$15 for top deck, only $5 for other decks.

and 7. Time is 1 hr., 40 min.; cost is HK$3.00.

Between Aberdeen and Deep Water Bay is Ocean Park, the latest (1976) and possibly the most ambitious marineland in the world. The park's 252 cable cars (6 passengers each) can carry 5,000 passengers per hour in each direction over the mile-long stretch of peninsula between the lowland and headland sites; the 7-minute ride offers breathtaking views of countryside and outlying islands. On the headland, the Atoll Reef has four viewing levels, to a depth of 20 feet, is home to 30,-000 colorful and exotic forms of sea life. Then, of course, there's an Ocean Theatre for 3,500 to view the performing dolphins, whales and sea lions — who understand only Chinese (match that, Sea World). Plus, as they say, much, much more. Admission HK$20, children $9. Open 9 to 7 M-F; 9-9 Sat, Sun, holidays. On the latter days, No. 71A from Central Bus Terminal goes directly to Ocean Park; HK$1.50.

ROUND THE NEW TERRITORIES

Again there are two routings, one that goes almost all the way north to the border and then around, the other that cuts

Newest "floating" restaurant — but not as romantic as the ones requiring a sampan.

across inland before returning. Both start and end at Jordon Road Ferry terminal (not to be confused with the Tsimshat-shui terminal between Star Ferry and the rail station.

By Nos. 50, 76 and 70 buses, the first routing takes you past Yaumati and Mongkok shopping areas, resettlement and low-cost housing projects, Castle Peak industrial area; change to No. 76 at Un Long, a fishing center and ride past the Royal Hong Kong Golf Club to Lokmachau. Tourists get off here to walk to the border lookout point (about 15 minutes), then back to resume the trip to Sheung Shui where No. 70 is boarded; interesting segment as you pass Taipo Market, Chinese University, 10,000 Buddha Monastery, Shatin, Amah Rock and Shanhawai walled village and thru Lion Rock Tunnel to Kowloon. Travel time (not including walk to the lookout) is 3 hrs.; fares total HK$4.

Second routing starts out on No. 50. At Un Long, change to No. 74 and ride for 20 minutes to Kam Tin walled village; stop to see this, then take 74 again to Taipo Market (15 min.). 70 returns you to Kowloon. Fares total HK$3.80; bus time is 2 hrs., 30 min.

TO LAUFAUSHAN

This is an appetizing variation of the above routings — if you're an oyster lover; Laufaushan restaurants are famed for their Deep Bay oysters. You change at Un Long for a 17-minute ride (No. 55) to Laufaushan, passing Ping Shan pagoda on the way. RT fare from Un Long is HK$0.90. You can then continue around or across New Territories.

Dried oysters and oyster sauce (from Deep Bay oysters) are exported around the world. But never eat these oysters raw — always cooked.

GROUP FUN-SEEING BY TRAM

Special double-decker, private trams can be hired by the hour (HK$200 per hour, $300 w/trailer) for your own tours the length of Hong Kong Island at any time except 8-9:30 a.m., 4:30-6:30 p.m. Food/drinks can be catered (extra), or you can furnish your own. It'll be a cocktail party no one will ever forget. Seating capacity: 28 in upper deck, 24 below; a one-level trailer seats 34 more. Contact Hong Kong Tramways, Sharp St. East, H.K. (5-764321).

SPECIAL INTEREST TOURS

Local tour operators can arrange almost anything, from acupuncture and bird watching (over 370 species recorded, some very rare) to electronics, textiles, toys and other industry tours as well as social welfare; in fact, regular Welfare Centre Tours operate Tues. and Fri. from the YMCA, Salisbury Rd., Kowloon, covering a combination of special projects — vocational training, student aid, mentally handicapped children, etc.

You can play golf at the Royal H.K. Golf Club in Fanling, New Territories, one of Asia's most famous layouts. Packages, by private car, train or AC coach (latter for groups), include transfers, greens and caddy fees, club hire; Mon.-Fri. only.

ALL ABOUT DINING

Let's put it simply: you can dine on any type of cuisine, in any kind of restaurant — elegant to plain, expensive to inexpensive — and do it in delightful fashion.

There are, we feel, some standout performances and places that are uniquely Hong Kongese. Aberdeen's three floating restaurants are certainly unique, not for the Chinese food (only passable) but, for two of them, the unusual experience of being sculled in a sampan by a Chinese woman or girl to the anchored ships and by the exotic sights and sounds of nearby sampans on which families of water people live.

There's Food Street in the Causeway Bay district and, on another plane, the Christmas Day reception (for guests) at the Peninsula, so rightly and graciously 1890-ish — or, for that matter, any night at the Peninsula's *Gaddi's*, as much an institution as a restaurant. Then there's lunch in the Hilton Grill (men only M-F) — perfection. And Sunday brunch at the old Repulse Bay Hotel — nostalgia. For exquisite Chinese service, tableware and delicate specialties, nothing quite like the Mandarin's *Man Wah*, lunch or dinner.

In our opinion, no after-dark maritime view equals Hong Kong's, so dining rooftop at one or more of the hotel restaurants, or at *Peak Tower* atop Victoria Peak, is so electrifying and beautiful you may do more gazing than eating, particularly since all have music and entertainment. They include *La Ronda* atop the Furama Inter-Continental, *Harbour Room* (Mandarin), *Talk of the Town* (Excelsior), *Chinese Theatre Restaurant* (Miramar), *Eagle's Nest* (Hilton), Hyatt's *Polaris,* Sheraton's *Chinese Restaurant* and *Juno Revolving Restaurant* on Nathan Rd.

Below rooftop level, following are particularly recommended: *Hugo's,* Hyatt Regency (exquisite decor, food display); *Pavilion,* Lee Gardens; *Rotisserie*, Furama; *Victoria Grill*, Excelsior.

Jimmy's Kitchen, Wyndham St., HK, has been a medium-priced favorite of foreigners for years; small, personal and invariably good at lunch or dinner. *Swiss Inn,* on the waterfront, falls into same category. *Gaylords,* 43 Chatham Rd., Kowloon, specializes in Indian food. For those in a hurry or wanting a snack, you can't go wrong at any of the various *Maxim's* tearooms, coffee and fast food shops.

We understand that *Sherokie* on Nathan Road near the Miramar caters to gourmands with such delicacies as Sydney rock oysters, Russian beluga caviar, English strawberries, Tientsin cabbage, Peking duck[2] and other expensive exotica.

Since Hong Kong is a Chinese city, Chinese cuisines are rated tops, the variety of dishes and restaurants inexhaustible. By the way, don't judge most Chinese restaurants by their appearance since they're usually of very plain decor. One of the more elaborate is traditionally styled *Lo Fung* on Victoria Peak; if you're up there around noon, stop in for a delicious *dim sum*. For a 10-course meal in a private dining room[3] (order Beggar's Chicken a day in advance), *Jade Garden* in Harbour Village, Star House, is considered excellent and moderately priced for such an extravaganza[4]

Besides the foregoing, any list of better Chinese restaurants must include: *Luk Kwok,* 67 Gloucester Rd., HK; *Shanghai Lao Cheng Hsing,* 9 Stanley St., HK (Heung So Duck); *Yaik Sang,* 456 Lockhart Rd., HK (fried beef w/sliced doughnut).

Distinctively Chinese is the *dim sum* lunch served in many of the Central District restaurants from 11 to 2. These "little hearts" (meaning small bites) are also called *yum cha* (drink tea) because green tea is served while you're eating. Steamed in traditional bamboo containers, the dishes of each specialty are carried around the restaurant on large trays by girls who call their wares by

[2] In Chinese restaurants, it's unwise to order other duck dishes — they may contain less popular parts of the duck.

[3] It's customary for a party host to reserve a private room in the restaurant of his choice, order the complete meal in advance.

[4] Has six other locations including *Peking Garden* in Excelsior Shopping Arcade.

Sampan dining in Causeway Bay typhoon shelter.

name, serve you when beckoned. A waiter adds up the tab by counting the dishes; most cost around 45¢ (US), some more. Here's a list of specialties, courtesy Hong Kong Tourist Association:

Har Kau — Shrimp dumpling
Shiu Mai — Meat dumpling
Pai Kwat — Steamed spareribs
Ngau Yuk Mai — Steamed beef ball
Tsing Fun Kuen — Steamed shredded chicken
Kai Bao Tsai — Steamed Chicken bun
Cha Siu Bau — Barbecued pork bun
Tsing Ngau Yuk — Steamed beef ball in lotus leaf
Cha Chun Kuen — Fried spring roll
Woo Kok — Fried taro puff
Ham Sui Kok — Fried dumpling
Fun Gwor — Steamed dumpling filled with vegetables and shrimps
Daan Tat — Custard tart
Ma Tai Goe — Fried water chestnut sticks
Ma Lai Goe — Steamed sponge cake
Ma Yung Bau — Steamed sesame bun
Yeh Chup Goe — Coconut pudding
Shui Tsing Gou — White fungus sweet dumpling
Chien Tsang Goe — Thousand layer sweet cake with egg-yolk filling
Tse Chup Goe — Sugarcane juice roll

If really adventurous, you'll get away from the hi-rise area into the side lanes off Queen's Road where elderly Chinese meet in little teahouses to sip and chat, often with their birds in bamboo cages hung near them; it's considered important to take these pets for daily walks. *Lok Yu,* one of the oldest teahouses, is said to serve the very best *dim sum*; it's on 24-26 Stanley St., Hong Kong.

An even more adventurous, and distinctively Hong Kong, experience is eating aboard a Causeway Bay sampan — no, not the Yacht Club but in the Typhoon Shelter where all those *tankas* live; probably best to have an interpreter along. A boat girl sculls you to the eating sampan, outfitted with tables, chairs and tableware. Bar sampan paddles up for your orders. Band sampan floats nearby. Then up bob the food boats with their specialties — prawns, crabs, steamed fish, noodle soup and such, said to be great (by those who told us of this) at about one-fourth to one-third the cost of comparable restaurant meals.

If you think that's a little much, then hop a ferry at the end of Hoi Ning St., Shaukiwan, for Lei Yue Mun on the mainland (southeast of Kai Tak Airport) for a Cantonese seafood meal in one of the waterfront restaurants where you point to the live fish you want cooked. Take a No. 2 bus or tram from City Hall or Causeway Bay to the Shaukiwan; tram stop is close to Hoi Ning St., bus stops at Golden Star Theater. Waterfront restaurants are a 10-minute walk (right) from the Lei Yue Mun ferry pier.

These are all things you should do to know and love Hong Kong better. But one thing you *should not do,* if avoidable, is take local tours that includes lunches or dinners; the food is normally much less than the best.

HONG KONG'S NIGHT SCENE

With a vast array of establishments, it runs the gamut from elegant supper clubs, live-otheques and dance halls thru the rip-off bars of Wanchai, from professional escort services[1] to sleazy brothels. Not to mention Japanese-type "Clubs" featuring international (and good-looking) hostesses and aimed primarily at Japanese male tour groups.

Though not as expensive as counterparts in the Ginza, female companionship in Japanese clubs costs $9-$12 US an hour, *plus* drinks ($2.50-$3.50 U.S.), *plus* cover, *plus* (get this) a hostess nomination charge. And she's nowhere near the door. You'll know such clubs by their Japanese names, find most on Peking Road in Tsimshatshui, Kowloon, within inebriated walking distance of major hotels.

The Wanchai bars of nostalgic Suzie Wong days are, we're told, dead and buried, replaced by topless bars, bottomless bars, bars with bands, bars without bands — all with two things in common, Chinese girls and the Rip-Off. Even Pussy Pussy, of infamous fame, which has been in The Wanch for years. A beer costs HK$7, "rum cokes" for the girls H$24, a heart attack if you're rash enough to order scotch.

The drinking scene is safest in the array of stunning hotel bars (drinks about US $2.50) and their supper clubs or live band/entertainment rooms (expensive but good), the in-places to go for late dining or after dinner: Hilton's *Eagle's Nest* and *Den,* Mandarin's *Harbour Room,* Furama's *La Ronda* and *The Club,* Excelsior's *Talk of the Town,* Hyatt's *Polaris, Sheraton's Good Earth,* Peninsula's *Scene Discotheque.*

Miramar Hotel's *Chinese Theatre Restaurant* has long been noted for its lavishly costumed Chinese Opera shows.

[1] Male as well as female. Charge about US$7 an hour with three-hour minimum; agencies advertise in all tourist handouts.

Outside of the hotels, here are some reputable spots recommended by residents:

Bottom's Up is one of the top topless clubs — actually four inter-connected bars each with performer and topless barman (clad in sequined bikini). Drinks are $2.50 with happy hour from 6 to 9 (half price). Similar are *Kismet* and *Club Spot.*

For companionable drinking and chance to meet amateur talent, try English-style pub bars. For old-fashion, man-talk, elbow-bending, try *Ship Inn, Waltzing Matilda* and *Joe's Bar* (best pizza in Hong Kong). Before and after Wednesday night racing (Oct. thru May) at Happy Valley, *the* place is *Elbow Bar* of the Caravelle Hotel across from the track. Incidentally, get a guest badge for the Royal Jockey Club (HK$45 each) from Hong Kong Tourist Association.

There's nightly jazz at Ned Kelley's *Last Stand* (another Aussie bar) and *Speakeasy. The Den* at the Hilton has Sunday afternoon jam sessions. *Godown Bistro* (not the restaurant but the pizza place) and Montmartre Cafe & Bistro are for folk music; if you're that kind of singer or musician, go and join in.

Up Club is a swinging singles club (there may be others, too) that operates on weekends; check the entertainment ads in local English-language newspapers. That, by the way, is good advice for what's going on in the theatres, concert and music halls; tickets available thru your hotel.

An unusual evening can be spent aboard a Floating Nightclub — converted, air-conditioned ferries that ply the length of the Harbour while serving a basic Chinese dinner to the accompaniment of a live band — all for a bargain HK$35 a head (plus 10% service). These daily 1½-hr. cruises leave at 6:30 and 8:30 p.m. from Outlying Islands Ferry Pier, Central District, and 7:15 and 9 p.m. from Kowloon City Ferry Pier. Hilton Hotel has an authentic brigantine, *Wan Fu,* for day and evening cruises around the islands and beaches.

Against this spectacular backdrop of towers made of buns (rolls), residents of Cheung Chau make incense offerings to the gods during the annual Bun Festival. The papier mache demon figure is Dai Shu Wong. Festival is held to placate the spirits of those who suffered at the hands of pirates centuries ago.

Spectators at Hong Kong's annual Dragon Boat Races have a perfect view of this exciting festival event to which teams from other parts of Asia are invited.

There are guided Night Tours for those who prefer togetherness. Ranging in price from HK$100 per person (4-5-hr. coach tour to Victoria Peak, dinner on an Aberdeen floating rst, nightclub visit) to HK$I80 (combination cruise and land tour with dinner show at a nightclub), they offer a number of attractive, if sterile, options.

A YEAR OF FESTIVALS

Hong Kong people live two lives, one according to the Western calendar, the other by the Lunar calendar. Latter involves them in a series of year-long, family get-togethers with visits to temples and ancestral graves to make offerings to gods and forefathers. Thus, it's a happy mixture as people take part with equal fervor in preparations for Christmas as they do for the Mid-Autumn Festival. So, visitors find that a festival is never far off (get HKTA's *Chinese Festivals in Hong Kong*); if it's a Chinese event, it gives them an unique insight into traditions of a world of yesterday.

Public holidays (indicated by*) and outstanding events (1978 dates) are:

January — New Year's and day following.* 23-31 — Arts Festival. Horse racing season continues.

February — Arts Festival continues to 18th. 7-9 — Chinese New Year.* 21 — Lantern Festival.

March — Easter Holidays* (24-27).

April — Shing Ming Festival* (5th). 21 — Queen's Birthday.*

May — Birthday of Lord Buddha, Tam Kung Festival (both on 14th). Bun Festival. Soccer, Horse racing seasons end (30th).

June — Dragon Boat Festival* (10th).

July — Bank Holiday* (1).

August — Bank Holiday* (7th). Maiden Festival (10). Yue Lan Festival (17). Liberation Day* (28).

September — Mid-Autumn Festival (16th; 18th a public holiday). Lantern Carnival. Birthday of Confucius (18). Autumn Dog Show. Soccer season starts.

October — Chung Yeung Festival* (10). Cross Harbour Swimming Race, Waterski Marathon. Horse racing season starts.

November — Many sports events.

December — Chinese Winter Festival (22). Christmas Day* and Boxing Day* (26).

SHOPPING EXCITEMENT . . . LIKE NOWHERE ELSE!

Though no longer a bargain-hunter's paradise, shops are exciting, the hunting fascinating. Without question, this is the world's most lavish Oriental Bazaar.

European and Asian imports are best buys for North Americans since duties have been eliminated. Like on Swiss watches, French and Italian shoes/leather goods, English china and porcelain, Irish and French crystal, Scandinavian flatware. Japanese cameras, lenses, tape recorders, etc., can be good buys — usually cheaper than in Japan or U.S. But U.S. calculators are better buys at home than Japanese ones here. Incidentally, name brand cameras and accessories are usually sold thruout Hong Kong at pegged prices. Agfa color film is less expensive here than at home.

If you've dreamed of paying for your trip thru a buying orgy of handmade clothing at bargain prices, forget it; sweat shop Chinese no longer sweat inexpensively. In our opinion, Hong Kong cannot equal the range, quality of materials nor the smart styling of high fashion stores in the U.S. — yet prices are comparable. If you must have clothing made, be sure you get current American styling, deal only with better tailors in or near hotel arcades.

Genuine antiques of any type are hard to find, *very expensive*. Again, shop only the better dealers. In Kowloon's Ocean Terminal Shopping Center, a huge affair housing every class and type of shop, *Charlotte Horstmann* has outstanding antiques — at prices to match. *Yuan Feng & Co.,* 9 Hankow Rd., and *Y. K. Ma,* also on Hankow 1 ½ blocks up, have fine selections. For exquisite crystal and silver, shop *Town House* in Ocean Terminal. *Harbour Village,* in adjoining Star House, should not be missed as artisans make (and sell) their handcrafts while you watch. Foregoing are on Kowloon side. So is the latest complex — Ocean Centre.

In the Central district, there are fabulous antique shops in the Lane Crawford Building — swank shopping, in fact, all around the Mandarin Hotel, particularly in its arcade and the Prince's Building across the arcade bridge. In the latter, the *Tih Gallery* (to pick an outstanding example) has every conceivable objet d'art from all over China; expensive, yes, but so beautiful. *Craigs Ltd.,* across from the Mandarin on Ice House St. (love that name), has magnificent Royal Crown Derby bone china; if price is no object, this is it. That last statement applies to all luxury goods, particularly to the booming antique business in which demand has created a seller's market. A double strand jade necklace can easily sell for $25,000 US, while vases and plates start at HK$2,500.

The foregoing applies to the westernized areas surrounding the better hotels. To shop in China, one need not stroll far. On the Kowloon side, the further one goes along Nathan Road, the more apt he is to bargain for less. Streets jammed with shops intersect on both sides, and even though you don't buy, it's fun to stop, look and savor the flavor of the Orient. *Don't be afraid to bargain anywhere,* except in the finest stores — you'll be turned down quickly if it's one-price only. But beware of touts — if you fall for their lines, it it'll cost you their commissions; we *never* buy in a store to which we're taken by a guide.

Of course, you must browse along famed Cat Street (officially Upper Lascar Row) and down Ladder Street which descends from Hollywood Road, at the corner of which is Man Mo Temple. Hollywood has the best of the area's antique shops, but the action is on the side streets jammed with Chinese buying and selling, some in stalls, others in shops with substantial inventories, many just sitting on the haunches wheeling-dealing in stones, coins and curios. Unless you know Chinese, stick to the stores — most speak English. Here you can spend hours, particularly if a first-time visitor, strolling, browsing, gawking, enjoying. This is the real hustle and bustle of old China. You're in another world. Don't worry about getting lost — eventually you'll wander onto Queen's Road or back up to Man Mo Temple (where you can always get a cab bringing other tourists). Who knows, you might even find things to buy? First time here, we picked up a few fabulous bargains in antique jade and snuff bottles, but last time around, intending to really splurge, we found neither antiques nor bargains. Instead, an avalanche of sorry imitations from Red China at ten times (and more) what we paid previously for lovely carvings.

In the same area, off the intersection of Possession St. and Queen's Road West, is Fat Hing St., an alley known as Baby Lane because here is where traditional Chinese baby clothes and ornaments (red capes, padded coats, vests, jade bracelets and such) are sold. This section is also good for Chinese porcelain. Further east, between Queen's Road Central and Des Voeux is Cloth Alley (Wing On St.) which, in turn, is sandwiched between Li Yuen East and West Streets. Good bargains if you bargain sharply.

Today, anywhere in the world, much of the Chinese merchandise seen in stores comes, freshly minted, from the People's Republic — loads of jade and ivory looking  like they rolled out of the same machine. Yet there are savings here versus buying at home; we brought back some jade trees considerably under U.S. store prices. Largest assortments are in the *Chinese Arts and Crafts* stores (Communist) in Star House (Kowloon) and Shell House (Hong Kong). But before you buy from Red China, shop *Taiwan Man Sang Products,* 100 Nathan Road (near Miramar Hotel); excellent, extensive range of Chinese art goods, screens and handicrafts from Taiwan; has branches in Wanchai, North Point and Mong Kok.

Good idea, when shopping for anything of value, to buy only from stores display this red Junk emblem — signifies membership in the Hong Kong Tourist Association.

ARTS AND CRAFTS

Every street seems to have one or more workshops or "factories" of one kind or another, ranging from baking, brewery and carpet (those have organized, free tours) to the small shops where one can watch many things being handmade and carved, even junks being built — with the possibility, of course, of buying at factory prices. Harbour Village, Star House, is the comprehensive way to view them all quickly — but it lacks authentic flavor since it's set up for the convenience of tourists.

Newest crafts village, Yee Tung (Carefree East), is on the second floor of the Excelsior Hotel Shopping Arcade. Craftsmen's (and dining) stalls line the streets with variety, fascination and color. At a tea stall, for instance, you buy a catty (about 1.3 lbs.) of tea packed in hand-painted, wooden boxes. And all sorts of wondrous concoctions await you at the herb stall, like deer's tail (HK$500 per oz.)

for your back ailment or, if needed, as an aphrodisiac (like aspirin, we're always baffled as to how it knows where to go). Or perhaps you'd like to pick up a modest amount of a rare Chinese ginseng at HK$28,000 per oz.? Remember, though the price is steep, it's reputed to prolong life at the deathbed stage. Yee Tung is open daily from 11 a.m. to 8:30 p.m.

There's a good, half-day Arts & Crafts Tour that takes in porcelain, jewelry and ivory carving factories, plus Harbour Village. Or, on your own, you can visit a number of varied workshops, mostly by prior appointment, where explanations of what's being done are given. Get HKTA's *Arts and Crafts* leaflet that lists crafts (from Amahs' wigs to wooden bird models and bowls) by area, address, phone number and who to contact.

As previously noted, cottage industries flourish in the Outlying Islands, particularly Cheung Chau and Peng Chau.

Typical Chinese family out for a stroll in Central District.

More specialized visits are arranged by the Trade Development Council for retail store buyers and industrial purchasing agents. Address is Connaught Centre, H.K. (phone 5-257151). The Hong Kong Ready To Wear Fashion Festival is held annually early in the year (Jan. 21-27, '78).

HOW TO JUDGE PEARLS AND JADE

In past centuries, pearls and jade, almost exclusively owned by noblemen, were revered and prized for qualities far beyond adornment. Pearls had medicinal purposes — 'twas said that eating ground pearls regularly would preserve beauty, increase sexual vigor, improve eyesight. Jade had magical powers, was used in religious rituals and ceremonies.

It is very difficult for the naked eye to tell the difference between a fine cultured pearl and a real one. Only sure way is to x-ray. Cultured pearls are produced under controlled conditions by inserting a fragment of mother-of-pearl into an oyster; after several years of incubation, the pearl is removed. Artificial pearls are imitations, usually of glass. To determine if a pearl is cultured or artificial, rub it against your teeth. If gritty, it's real; if completely smooth, a fake.

Shape, color, luster, matching, threading and clasp are deciding factors in cost and value. A perfectly round pearl with no imperfections is almost priceless. However, most pearls have spots, cracks, flaws and an uneven surface. Every single blemish may take 10% off the price, and even the least expensive necklace should have just a few flaws. Loose pearls can be easily tested for roundness by rolling them on a glass surface. Each should roll in a straight line, not waver or come to a sudden halt.

Pearls come in many shades: white to yellow, off-white, black, blue or very, very pale pink; all should have sheen and luster. A smaller pearl with no imperfections is more valuable than a larger one with an imperfection. Price is also determined by weight, a unit called a pearl grain. Four pearl grains equal one carat.

In a fine necklace, pearls should be the same size and color. To detect variations in size, roll them in your hand, not on the tray.

Jade is one of the most difficult gems to appraise. It is a crystalline stone harder than steel. True jade is pure white, but impurities produce an array of shades from blue to green, brown, red, pink, grey, yellow, even black.

Originally a ceremonial stone, it was used to issue imperial proclamations and in symbolic carvings to protect a person after death. It is still carried as a talisman against disease and accident, as charms for happiness, good fortune.

In buying jade, it is most important to distinguish real from imitation. Commonest substitutes are glass, plastic and green chalcedony (translucent quartz). Glass and plastic are smoother than jade, chalcedony a blue-grey stone often stained a beautiful rich green with smooth, highly polished texture. On the other hand, jade is greasy in texture and slightly uneven with mottled patches. A drop of water on jade will stand out like a bead, on an imitation it will spread. Hold the stone in a strong light; the reflected spot should show an unevenness much like a distorted mirror, giving a bad reflection.

The most prized color is a clear, vivid green; an ideal stone would be this shade all over, as transparent as glass, perfectly shaped and highly polished. A carat of jade is equivalent to a one-sixth of an inch cube; any given weight will be worth more if it displays a large surface than a more compact one. Thus, if the stone is cut thin and shows a large diameter, value increases 40% to 50%.

Most jade sold in Hong Kong comes from China and Burma. Buy only from reputable stores — finding bargains in obscure shops are remote possibilities. Bargaining, though, should be done in all but department stores. But remember, always, that good jade, no matter the color, should be free of cracks, flaws, black spots and other blemishes.

Jade vendor on Canton Road decks himself out in some of the bangles, pendants, rings and buckles he has for sale.

For fun sightseeing, but not for shopping, visit Canton Road in Kowloon some morning between 10 a.m. and noon where, on one side, an entire stretch of pavement has been transformed into a sea of green. On makeshift tables and yesterday's newspapers, in aluminum boxes and plastic basins, all manner of jade trinkets are on sale, at prices ranging from the sublime to the ridiculous. A holiday mood prevails as Chinese men, women and children stroll along the narrow pavement between the portable "stalls." This is the people's Jade Market.

There are goldfish and birds in flight, green-brown turtles and red-brown tigers and pastel butterflies . . . rings, bangles and strings of green, bean-shaped beads . . and variations on the theme of "Pi," a circular holed disk that stood for heaven in the mythology of China past. Experts may be able to spot an occasional piece of value, but the vast majority of items are far from collectors' pieces. Remember, there is jade and there is "jade." But you'll enjoy.

ALL ABOUT A GIRL'S BEST FRIENDS

As one of the world's largest diamond trading countries ($170 million US, a carat value of 786,745), Hong Kong claims to be at least 10% under world market prices, indicating worthwhile investments for buyers. For a list of reputable diamond dealers and shops, visit the Diamond Information Centre, 7/F Seabird House, 22-28 Wyndham St., Central District. For certification of your purchases, the Hong Kong Standards and Testing Centre provides gemmological testing to determine whether diamonds and other precious stones are genuine, synthetic or imitation, provides a written report (takes several days).

Gold, of course, is another precious commodity in which to invest. Prices of gold bullion and platinum are posted daily on boards in jewelry shops, at the Chinese Gold and Silver Exchange Society. All prices are quoted in taels, each tael being equivalent to 1.3 oz. Hong Kong law requires gold sold here to be clearly stamped with the carat content. 14K gold items bear a .585 marking to indicate 58% gold content; 18K items are branded .750, a 75% content. Retailers are liable to prosecution, imprisonment and fine if found to have sold falsely stamped merchandise.

A Consumer Council runs three Consumer Advice Centres where it is possible for you to obtain purchasing information about all types of consumer products. Locations: 2/F South China Bldg., 1 Wyndham St., Central District; City District Office, 201 Hennessy Rd., Wanchai; City District Office (Shamshuipo), 299 Laichikok Rd., Kowloon.

Jewelers generally recommend that for investment purposes, loose stones such as diamonds, emeralds and rubies be one carat or more. And since there are more jewelry shops per square mile in Hong Kong than anywhere else in the world, the range of stones and settings are extremely wide — too wide for those who aren't sure what to buy. So, decide first on how much you wish to spend for that will narrow the range. You might wish to buy a loose stone as an investment, have it set in a special, customized setting or pick out a "ready to wear" piece. Hong Kong claims that thru low labor costs, lack of tax or import duty, jewelry bought here is a girl's best friend.

Hotel Directory

There are three districts in which a multitude of good to splendid hotels are located:

1) Hong Kong Island Central (Victoria) is upper Fifth Ave. as well as the financial heart of the Colony — and our favorite.

2) Tsimshatsui-Kowloon, the mainland across the harbor from Hong Kong Island, is Broadway and the heart of tourism. Here is still turn-of-the-century Asia despite gleaming, modern hotels. Nathan Road is one of the world's famed shopping streets. In 1979, a spanking new Trade Center complex makes its bow with some 200 shops and 3,700 sq. meters of gardens. Fronting the Harbour between Star Ferry and Salisbury Road, it includes a 951-room economy hotel and, by mid-year the 650-room, deluxe Regent.

3) Causeway Bay (east Hong Kong Island) on the southern side of Cross Harbour Tunnel opposite Kai Tak Airport — the newest development. Has the Colony's first World Trade Centre; new office buildings are a-building, also a large department store. To many, the area is a bonus, retaining as it does much of the unsophisticated atmosphere of "old" Hong Kong; shopping in the hotels and surrounding neighborhoods is good and not as expensive as in more tourist-oriented areas. Good local restaurants of every type (well priced, too), street markets, street activity until late at night (Central is dead then). However, it is a long taxi ride from Victoria or Kowloon, though near Wanchai as well as Happy Valley race track.

Whichever area, pay a bit more for a room with harbor view. Fascinating.

Double room rates are quoted here in US dollars. 4% tax, 10% service added.

CONVENTION & MEETING FACILITIES

Hong Kong Convention Centre's Oriental Rooms have over 1,300 square meters of flexible meetings and exhibition space that can be converted into smaller areas for groups of 50 to 1,500. Palace Nightclub can be transformed by day to provide facilities for up to 1,200. Both fully equipped with audio-visual and simultaneous translation equipment, are linked by closed-circuit TV. Catering facilities available there as well as in two restaurants and private meeting rooms.

Hong Kong City Hall's Concert Hall can accommodate up to 1,488 persons, has all necessary equipment.

Leading hotels (Hilton, Furama, Holiday Inn) can take care of up to 1,200 delegates, the Sheraton up to 700, Mandarin, Peninsula, Hyatt Regency and others have facilities for smaller numbers. All hotels have secretarial, translation and, of course, catering services. For complete details, get a color-illustrated *Meeting Guide to Hong Kong* from any Hong Kong Tourist Association office.

KOWLOON

AUGUST MOON — 84 R; dining room with Malaysian and European cuisine, bar, music. For those on a budget. $20.

CARLTON — Beautifully situated hillside, 4½ miles from bustle of town. Pool, lush gardens and dazzling view of harbor. 40 R ($22), eight 2-3-bedroom SU ($39 up). Be sure to get a room off Tai Po Rd, or you'll wish you had stayed in town. Well managed.

EMPRESS — 17 Chatham Rd, few minutes from ferry. 189 R w/rfg; most overlook harbor. Food is reasonable and hotel a good buy. Redec. $21-$32.

GRAND — Good tourist class. 200 AC R w/TV, rfg, have been redecorated. Rst, cocktail lounge, coffee shop. Few blocks from harbor. $22-$39.

HOLIDAY INN (FC) — 50 Nathan Rd, center of entertainment area. 650 R, SU. Rst serves int'l cuisine, German specialties. Viennese coffee shop. Rooftop pool. *Conv:* 1000. $39-$44.

NEW WORLD (FC) — HK's newest, one of its largest (855 R). Chinese/Western rsts, six bars, health club, shops. $30-$49.

HONGKONG (FC-) — Huge 790 R, SU, commercial hotel in Star Ferry complex. Several rsts, bars, coffee shop, open-air pool. Fabulous views from upper floors. Conference rooms. $36-$52.

HYATT REGENCY (DL) — 788 AC R furnished in oriental motif w/rfg, TV, closed-circuit movies. Rooftop Polaris discotheque. Hugo's rst and bar has beautiful atmosphere. $37-$52.

MIRAMAR (DL) — 600 R addition, several rsts, convention facilities now linked by bridge to original 730 R in main bldg an Plaza (latter best). Fine nightclub with Chinese shows; cocktail lounges. $39-$50. Good choice.

PENINSULA (DL) — Lovely, gracious, continental hotel. Its English lobby is *the* place for afternoon tea, drinks. Gourmet rsts, bars, shopping arcades, art galleries. 335 R, SU are large, comfortably old fashion; many with harbor views. Hotel has been refurbished in the Peninsula way. A landmark! $50-$96.

SHERATON (DL) — Magnificent location (opposite Peninsula) overlooking harbor. Rsts, coffee shops, bars and pool; glass elevator to rooftop supper club. Splendid shopping arcades. 922 R, SU. $39-$59.

YMCA — Salisbury Rd has rst, pool, tennis ($8-$20D). YMCA, Waterloo Rd. w/rst ($15-$17). YWCA, 5 min. from airport, $10-$14 w/bath D.

Those desiring inexp. hostels, campsites, write Hong Kong Tourist Association, 160 Sansome, San Francisco 94111.

VICTORIA

HILTON (DL) — This 800-room, older hotel has been refurbished, is well managed, has an excellent location on Queen's Rd. just back of the Harbour. Six fine rsts; Grill (men only at lunch) is tops — best roast beef and martinis in HK. Nightclub; Sound & Light Show in Chinese Rst. Pool. *Conv:* 1200. $44-$55.

INTER-CONTINENTAL FURAMA (DL) — 32-story hi-rise with 600 small, AC R, SU — all w/rfg, color TV. Several rsts, including revolving one on top, five bars, cocktail lounges, discotheque. Near Star Ferry facing harbor. *Conv:* 1200. $40-$52. *Rsv:* ICH.

MANDARIN (DL) — Precision run, impeccable personal service, delightful Chinese-style rooms/suites (with magnificent, front row view of Star Ferry and harbor). In short, one of the world's truly great hotels patronized by the world's most distinguished. If you've been here before, you'll probably get the same room and house boy. Elegant lobby, rsts, bars, shops (in hotel and adjoining arcades). An experience all too rapidly fading from the hotel scene. $46-$76.

CAUSEWAY BAY

EXCELSIOR (DL) — Public areas very striking, 1003 AC, small rooms unimaginative, though front ones have fantastic harbor-mt. views. Icemakers on each floor. Pool. Japanese, English and int'l restaurants noted for fine menus. Top floor nightclub has panoramic view of harbor, racetrack; Dickens bar on second floor features amusing art. Nightly entertainment, dancing. *Conv:* 250. $39-$56.

LEE GARDENS (FC+) — Inland behind Excelsior. 900 AC, comfortable and good-size R, SU w/color TV; SU w/rfg. Good, attractive, top-floor Chinese rst; other rsts, bars. Large, spacious lobby; audio-visual equip. for conv. Popular with groups. $37-$44.

LUK KWOK — 67 Gloucester Rd. Very simple, comfortable hotel with 102 R, w/rfg, TV. Rst serves Chinese & Western cuisine. Nightclub w/floor show. In the Wanchai area. And the price is right. $16-$19.

PLAZA (FC) — 850 spacious, comfortable R in 30-story bldg. but hotel lacks friendliness. Coffee shop, Japanese rst, cocktail lounge, disco. $32-$44. *Rsv:* JAL.

REPULSE BAY (20 min. from HK)

REPULSE BAY (FC+) — Another old landmark for those wanting quiet elegance, fine cuisine, impeccable service. Colony's smallest top hotel has 32 AC suites: $54-$56.

Three-wheeled pedicabs vie with trucks and late model cars on the streets of Macau.

The MACAU Adventure

From reliable sources,[1] we gather it's a toss-up whether you should/shouldn't come to this Las Vegas of the Orient, this "crossroads for smuggling, spying and gambling, an anachronism, the decaying foundation of Europe's oldest Oriental outpost."[2] And, one wonders, how much longer will the foundation last?

This six-square-mile dot bordering China, almost directly south of Canton, was settled by the Portuguese in 1557 when two square miles were ceded by China as a trading post. Sailors called it A-Ma-Kao (Bay of A-Ma, Chinese goddess of sailors).

But to answer the question, should I or not? Yes — if you like gambling, pelota (jai-alai), a fast jetfoil run and/or a fun ferry boat ride (with French strippers). No if you don't, for this siesta-oriented city (300,000 pop.) is 98% Chinese, hence another slice of Chinese streets with some Portuguese facades, churches and names; shopping is considerably better in Kowloon and Central District, though prices of some merchandise may be lower. Macau's flea market *might* turn up some antiques from Red China. Stores open at 10:30 a.m.

Weekends and holidays, Macau is mobbed — as many as 50,000 people inundate the town (it has about 1,600 hotel rooms) over Chinese New Year. Only 3% of all visitors stay overnight. Nevertheless, getting here was a problem as Hong Kong travel agencies block book (thru Macau) a major number of seats on all boats. Now, with many more jetfoils and hydrofoils in operation, that may no longer be a problem.

[1] Never got to Macau as we didn't plan a trip in advance, couldn't get transportation on days we wanted to go.
[2] Jerry Hulse, Los Angeles Times' Travel Editor — one of the best.

For a *Guide To Macau,* write or phone Macau Tourist Information Bureau, 3133 Lake Hollywood Dr., Los Angeles 90068 (213-851-3400); or Pier 26-North, San Francisco 94106 (415-495-5022).

GETTING TO MACAU

From the Yaumati dock in HK's Central District, jetfoils skim at 50 mph to Macau Wharf in 45 minutes (40 miles), carry 280 passengers at HK$35 OW on weekdays, HK$40 weekends. Hydrofoils take 75 minutes, cost HK$35 weekdays, HK$30 weekends OW. Hydrofoils leave every half hour during the day, jetfoils less frequently. In 1979, there should be night service as well.

There are six ferries (2½-hr. trip) if you feel like having a more leisurely cruise; fares range from HK$20 (day) to HK$75 for the midnight cruise (includes FC cabin w/bath) which, we understand, has good, spicy entertainment.

All prices are subject to HK$8 embarkation tax.

Between 9 pm and 1 am, there's helicopter service between HK and Macau and return (HK$20 OW).

To enter Macau, you need a passport, smallpox and cholera certificates and a visa, obtainable from the Portuguese consul at 3 Peddar St., HK (HK$20) or upon arrival in Macau (HK$27). But there's additional paperwork involved while going over — a yellow departure card, a details stub, Macau disembarkation and embarkation cards.

It's no trick at all to see Macau on your own. Flag drop for taxi meters is Pacata[3] (P) 2.50, P 20¢ each additional 1/5 mile. Pedicabs cost P2 per trip, P10-15 per hour. Sightseeing tours by private car cost about $15 US per person for two or more. Take a jetfoil in the morning, return by ferry (preferable) or helicopter in the evening. Be sure to get tickets in advance — *both ways.*

On short notice, probably best to take one of the many days tours offered by Hong Kong tour operators. These range from six to 10 hours, provide coach or private car tours of Macau, visa fees, embarkation tax, hydrofoil or jetfoil tickets, transfers from/to Hong Kong hotels for HK$200 to $250. Overnight trips of 12 to 28 hours cost HK$310 to $370.

GAMBLING & ENTERTAINMENT

There are four no-limit casinos — including Hotel Lisboa and Macau Floating Palace ("resembling a sea-soaked dragon"[2]) — open 'round the clock for craps, roulette, baccarat, chemin de fer, 21, boule, keno, fan tan and *dai siu* (big, small), the slots.

There's greyhound racing at the Canidrome, Basque jai-alai at the 6,000-seat

[3] On a par with HK dollar. Latter may be used in Macau — but not vice versa.

Palaci de Pelota Basca, Chinese opera, Portuguese bullfighting and, in November, the Macau Grand Prix. Sports Arena complex has pool, skating rink, nightclub, bars. Harness racing at a new $12-million track.

Mandarin, a Chinese junk, departs daily 9 a.m. & 11:15 a.m. from Macau's Outer Harbor for a fascinating 1½-hr. view of Macau's water life. You'll cruise past Praia Grande, under the bridge to the outer islands of Taipa and Coloane and past the Chinese Temple A-Ma. You'll see the floating casino (you can always return) and the godowns (warehouses). Entertainment and wine available.

MACAU DINING

According to reports we've received, the cuisines here are excellent — at prices (low) that Hong Kong hasn't seen for years. Sole, crab and roast pigeon are outstanding, while one of the Hotel Lisboa's eight restaurants serves African Chicken (grilled with butter, garlic and onion rings), said to be terrific. Good Chinese and Portuguese dishes are to be had, particularly at *Diamond* (Chinese) and *Solmar* (Continental). Portuguese wines are both excellent and inexpensive.

MACAU HOTEL SCENE
(10% Service, 5% Tax Added to US Prices Quoted Below)

Largest is the 600-room *Lisboa* (FC+) with its casinos, Chinese, Japanese and Western restaurants, supper club, hostess club, a room in which to rock (on the floor, not in a chair), pool. US $21 to $37 EP. Of the non-Chinese guests, Japanese predominate, generally the case in Macau.

Newest is the 300-room *Sintra* (FC) overlooking Praia Grande Bay, a few minutes' walk to Casino Lisboa. Designed for those who want a quiet tempo. $19-$21!

Less expensive is the 89-room *Estorial* (FC) at $14-$21, the 48-room *Matsuya* (FC) at $17-$34. For continental Portuguese style, the *Caravela* and century-old, hilltop *Bela Vista;* from $11-$20.

Smallest is the 100-year-old, renovated Pousada de Macao. Only 12 rooms but one of the finest dining rooms in town. Rooms have AC, twin beds and balcony overlooking beach. $28.

On the nearby island of Taipa, a 600-R hotel, as well as a harness racetrack, is scheduled for opening in early '79. Island of Coloane should have a 250-R hotel and golf course by late '79. At present, there's the Pousada de Coloane with 12 AC rooms, private beach, dining room and bar — all for about $14 a night double. Both islands have been relatively undiscovered, are known for quaint fishing villages, beaches and lovely pine forests. Both are easily reached over a 14-mile causeway by taxi (15 minutes) or bus, by ferry from Inner Harbor.

People's Republic of CHINA

HOW MANY & WHO CAN VISIT RED CHINA?

It's becoming easier. In '78, 10,000 to 12,000 tourist visas will have been issued to Americans (versus about 5,000 in '77); that number may double in 1979.

Whether it be a tour operator's package or a club/association tour, individuals (except for VIPs) travel in groups. And rigorously, too. Sightseeing programs start early, end late and are scheduled each day without time out for R and R. English-speaking, cooperative, pleasant guides are provided by Luxingshe (China International Travel Service); in fact, the Chinese generally couldn't be more welcoming, do everything possible to make trips pleasant. However, don't expect Western amenities; if only the comforts of Hong Kong are for you, inspect China from there. In other words, a trip to Red China is an experience, not a luxury vacation. Nor inexpensive.

Best way to go is with a cultural club, professional organization (such as medical associations), teachers' organizations (NEA allows friends of members to join), museum members and university/college alumni groups. These get the lion's share of visas.

WHAT TO DO FIRST

Clubs/organizations/associations should apply to China International Travel Service. Hsitan Building, East Chang An St., Peking. State purpose of the proposed visit, how long a trip is desired and, if possible, exactly what cities are preferred. Group cultural exchange programs (between US and People's Republic of China) are initiated thru the Chinese People's Association for Friendship with Foreign Countries, Pekings. Overseas Chinese are handled by Overseas Chinese Travel Service (same address as CITS). Businessmen wishing an invitation to the Canton Trade Fair (mid-April to mid-May, mid-October to mid-November) must obtain same from the Ministry of Foreign Affairs, Peking. Journalists should direct their inquiries to the Press Information Dept. of the same Ministry.

If a favorable reply is received from one of the above, application for visas must be made to Liaison Office, People's Republic of China, 2300 Connecticut Ave., NW, Washington 20008. Canadians apply to Embassy of the People's Republic of China, 100 Bronson St., Ottawa. When application forms are received and filled out, return with required passport photos. A fee is charged for each entry, exit or transit visa. An exit visa must be obtained before leaving China, the rules printed on it *strictly followed.*

Individuals must also apply for a visa following acceptance by a tour group. If your visa request is turned down, no trip.

FINALIZING GROUP TRIPS

With the granting of visas, CITS will then proceed with final tour schedules, hotel accommodations (assigned, not chosen), sightseeing tours, transportation and transfers, guides, etc. — all of which is paid for *in advance* thru a tour operator or travel agent; it's wise for the latter to stay out of the picture until visitation rights are secured. Obviously, the foregoing requires months (a year is not inappropriate) of advance negotiating and planning.

Businessmen receiving entry okays must then write to the Chinese Export Commodity Fair, Exhibition Grounds, Canton, for receptive arrangements, at the same time applying for a visa in Washington.

If all else fails and you're in Hong Kong, you can apply for entry at the CITS office at 77 Queen's Road, Central, or 27-33 Nathan Road, Kowloon. However, the tours we've seen advertised from here seem rather blah; most don't get as far as Peking.

ENTRY REQUIREMENTS

Valid passport,[1] visa, smallpox and cholera (required even if intransit) certificates. Exit visa must be obtained before being allowed to leave the country.

You may bring in, duty free, one bottle of liquor and a bottle of wine, carton of cigarettes, still camera, watch and 50 yuan. On departure, you cannot take out antiques over 150 years old, rare curios or Chinese currency.

[1] If it shows prior entry into Taiwan or Israel, you won't be granted a visa for the People's Republic — and vice versa by Taiwan.

CURRENCY

Approximately 1.87 yuan (Y) equals $1 US. So figure 1Y as 50¢ — divide Chinese prices in half to approximate dollar equivalents. Most travel checks are accepted for exchange *except American Express* (it has a trade arrangement with Taiwan).

Bills come in 1, 2, 5, 10 yuan as well as 1 yi jiao (US 10¢), 2 and 5 jiao. Coins are 1, 2 and 5 fen (fun). These you'll find difficult to identify. But not to worry. Just pull out a handful of cash, and the seller will pick out what is required. Chinese honesty is out of this world — no one's ever lost a fen.

Important — Keep your Declaration of Foreign Currency given you at Customs and present it to Bank of China when exchanging dollars for yuan. Supposedly, only unused currency shown thereon can be reconverted into dollars (with receipts to prove it); in actual practice, that may not be required or even checked.

Exchange of money except at an authorized bank is forbidden, as are gifts of foreign exchange. Chinese currency is obtainable at the Shumchun Rail Station at the Hong Kong border, on the train from/to the border, in Friendship stores and at any Bank of China, including international airports.

INTERNATIONAL AIR SERVICE

CAAC, the government-operated airline that flies both international and domestic routes has commissioned China International Travel Service in Hong Kong to offer a booking service there for Canton-Shanghai and Canton-Peking flights in conjunction with international tickets. This means that carriers can deliver an international air ticket direct to Peking or Shanghai via Hong Kong (plus rail to Canton).

See Peking and Shanghai for direct international services.

Japan Airlines, the only carrier from North America flying to Peking (connections in Tokyo) and other lines flying into the People's Republic can assist passengers in preparing entry documentation.

RAIL TRAVEL

Comfortable with mostly air-conditioned trains drawn by diesel locomotives. Report on the Nanking-Peking run: "Berths and dining car very good."

Most popular route is the 1,200-mile run (via Wuhan) on the Canton-Peking Express (35 hours). First class, AC compartments seat four, have soft seats; 2nd class also takes four, but seats are hard. Service is efficient, trains immaculate, food good.

From Shanghai to Peking is a 24-hour run, to Nanking 4½ hours. The new Yangtze River Bridge has cut the Peking-Nanking run to 20 hours.

International trains on the Peking-Hanoi and Peking-Ulan Bator, Mongolia, runs offer deluxe accommodations, those to Moscow first class.

DOMESTIC AIR SERVICE

Flying an assortment of jets (Boeing 707, British Trident, Ilushin) and jet props, CAAC has about 85 domestic routes with a weekly total of 230 to 240 flights to every major provincial capital (except from Peking to Foochow and Lhasa). Peking, Canton and Shanghai are the most heavily trafficed routes; there's daily service between the three. A recent deal with Boeing will, when the planes are delivered, give the service a new look.

CAAC (Civil Aviation Administration

of China) is a special agency of the State Council, equivalent to a Cabinet post — a position Pan Am and TWA would like to have instead of being subservient to CAB.

GENERAL INFORMATION

Bank Hours — Bank of China, Peking: 11 Don An Men St, 17 Fan Ti Hsi Lou 9-12, 2-4 p.m.; 34 Fan Ti Rd, 8:30-12, 2-5 p.m.

Business Hours — 8-12, 2-6. Most offices closed Sundays.

Climate — Varies widely. Best time to visit is late spring or middle of fall. Rains during summer in north and south. Most rain in Yangtze River valley during June, July. Temperate and humid year 'round in Southeast (Canton). Drier and extremely cold during winter in Peking.

Clothing — Lightweight in spring/fall. In summer, short-sleeve shirts (no jacket required), slacks, wash-wear dresses. Rainwear needed, particularly during spring and summer; also tennis shoes for walking the Great Wall. During winter in the north (Peking), thermal underwear, lined all-weather coat, down vest or jacket, gloves, heavy boots or galoshes, work socks, a furlined hat (latter can be bought in Peking).

Credit Cards — None honored.

Consulates — Canada: 16 San Li Tun, Peking (521-648). U.S. Liaison Office: 17 Guanghua Rd, Peking (522-033).

Electric Current — 220V, 50c AC in Peking. Bring an adaptor.

Emergencies — Your guide knows where to contact doctor, pharmacist and hospital. Should you wind up in the latter, a guide stays in the same room with you to interpret.

Film — Bring your own as popular brands generally unavailable. Do not take photographs when flying over China. Never photograph a statue or picture of Chairman Mao in less than full size. On departure, film might be exposed at discretion of Customs Official.

Gambling — None.

Health — Hospitals of a standard prevailing in U.S. during the 1950s. For non-emergency care: Shou Du Hospital, near the Peking Hotel (553-731) from 8:30-12, 2:30-6 p.m. Excellent Chinese pharmacy is Chinese Medical Herb Shop, 69 Da Zha Lan, Peking. Many medicines can be purchased without prescription, but instructions are in Chinese; best to bring your own.

Language — Northern Mandarin most widely spoken. Many regional dialects.

Mail — Airmail postcards to N. America cost 42 fen, letters 53 fen. Allow a week. Regular mail, 22 fen.

Measures and Weights — Metric.

Newspapers, Magazines — Most unavailable for export: *Ren Min Ribao* (People's Daily) and *Kuang Min Ribao* are. Bring reading material with you (but no girlie magazines).

Population — 880 million.

Religion — Buddhism, Confucianism, Christianity, Islam and Taoism have been replaced by Maoism.

Telephones — 5 fen for local (dial) calls.

Telegrams — Urgent (US$1 per word to US); ordinary and letter telegrams are less.

Time — Same as Hong Kong.

Tipping — None.

Water — Drink boiled or hot tea.

CALENDAR OF EVENTS

January 1st — New Year's.

February — Chinese New Year. 3-day holiday. Families visit relatives, friends.

March 8th — International Woman's Day.

May 1st — Celebrated with fireworks, parades, entertainment. 4th — Youth Festival.

July 1st — Birthday of Chinese Communist Party.

August 1st — Birthday of People's Liberation Party.

September — Autumn Festival.

October 1st — Birthday of founding of Republic; 2-day holiday culminating in large parade and fireworks in Tien An Men Plaza, Peking.

WHO HAS PACKAGE TOURS TO CHINA?

Both Japan Airlines and Pan Am have year 'round programs from the U.S.; Pan Am does not fly to Peking/Shanghai, JAL does. Other lines from the U.S. that fly into China (via connections in Europe) are Air France, Iran and Pakistan Airlines, Swissair; Ethiopian Airlines flies from Europe. All cooperate with one or more U.S. operators in delivering tour groups to China.

Lindblad Travel, New York, has scheduled 21 groups for 1979, departures from January 7 thru December 23, for 27 or 29 days; tours spend 15 days in China, 4 or 6 in Mongolia. They are considerably more expensive than JAL's tours (which spend nine days in China); Pan Am's are $200 or so more than JAL's.

CRUISES TO CHINA

Most ambitious program is *Lindblad Explorer's* (2,500 tons, 250 ft. length) six 20- to 25-day Air/Sea visits from various ports in the Orient. 14 days are spent in Chinese cities. Five air departures from San Francisco in 1979 from April 19 to July 4, another on Sept. 27. Minimum Land/Cruise fares: $3800 to $4900, plus air.

Holland America's *Prinsendam* visits Shanghai for 2½ days on its Spring and Fall Trans-Pacific cruises. Three Round The World cruises also stop briefly in China: *Rotterdam, Sagafjord* and *QE-2*.

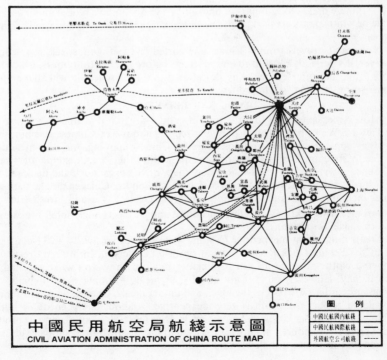

中國民用航空局航綫示意圖
CIVIL AVIATION ADMINISTRATION OF CHINA ROUTE MAP

CHINA IN BRIEF

Geographically, China is the one nation in the world that is completely isolated by mountains and sea, a country that has the highest mountains and one of the greatest deserts — the land between the Himalayas and the Gobi Desert is most forbidding. North China has a flat coastline and little regard for southerners; South China is mountainous, hilly, convoluted and with a rocky coast. "Of no country, could it be more absurd to separate the location from the essence of the nation."

This socialist state is divided into three groups: workers, peasants and soldiers. Workers stand for industrialization; modernizing China is their dream. Peasants symbolize the reality of China, which is 80% rural; producing enough food for the people is their great task. Three-quarters of the people spend time growing enough food. Soldiers stand for the international defense of the revolution; the People's Liberation Army is the bridge between the peasant and the modernizing task. It is a peasant army which best represents the political reality. It is Chairman Mao's weapon against revisionists who would leave the peasants behind. And, it's the intellectual who pays the price.

People cannot own homes, cars, TVs. Cars are government-owned and used as a means of transportation. You'll see jeeps, Fords, Toyotas and hundreds of thousands of bicycles (a luxury). Cyclists haul vegetables in from the farms; women wash vegetables on the sidewalks, sweep the streets, wash the gutters. You'll see no billboards, read or listen to any advertising.

Average family income for those living in communes is $600 a year; per person, $125. Thirty years ago, illiteracy was 70%-80% — today it's 10%.

You'll probably not get used to being stared at. Most Chinese have seen few foreigners, especially Americans. Our manners, clothes, ways we wear our hair are oddities. Chinese dress alike, a mass of blue and grey. A woman's blouse and man's shirt is blue or white, pants are dark, only the children wear colorful clothing and bright red scarves.

You can't travel around China unescorted even if you speak the language. However, it's perfectly okay to roam the streets before or after tour hours, which means before 7 am and after dinner. Any deviation from your schedule will shake up your guides, so be on time — and adhere.

DINING AND DRINKING

Most Americans agree that the food is good, though not as fine as in Hong Kong and Taiwan. We've had a few disparaging reports about Red Chinese cuisines, though these may come from those who don't care for Chinese cooking. A simple meal usually has five to six courses; if a guest, never inquire what they are. A sample of what you might encounter: cold dishes, swallow nest soup, dove's eggs, duck and duck soup, fish and fish roe, baked chicken, several vegetables, salmon fin. Chicken and fish are served whole, including head and, sometimes, innards. Dessert is usually fresh fruit. Only Western meal is breakfast — coffee, eggs, toast and jam — though hotels prepare other Western meals on request.

Meals range from inexpensive (Y3 and 4) to very expensive — an 11-course banquet at the Peking Duck Restaurant can run $40 per person. In ordinary restaurants, numbered clothespins are affixed to a center bowl to show you what you had, how much to pay. However, most if not all of your meals will have been prepaid.

Beer and cordials are part of the lunch and dinner meals. Chinese whiskeys are readily available, scotch isn't. Gin is very inexpensive — about 50¢ a bottle — but beer remains most popular drink. Most potent is *Mao-tai* (60% alcohol, or 120-proof) — always served at banquets, mainly for toasts, and tossed down from shot-size glasses; as it is impolite to refuse, sip slowly and wash down the medicinal taste with either red

wine (sweet) or dry white.

Most popular soft drinks are orange pop and, of course, tea — usually green with the leaves still in it. *Don't drink tap water* — only the boiled water left in the rooms in thermos bottles.

WHAT AND WHERE TO BUY

Friendship Stores, oriented to foreigners and with fixed prices, are government-owned and operated (as are all stores), in large cities and airports. Prices thruout the People's Republic are cheaper than in Hong Kong, including liquor and cigarettes. Here you find Chinese art, jade, hand-painted vases, pure silks (very low-priced; about $4 per meter), embroidered tablecloths, lacquerware, cloisonne (another bargain), carved ivory, snuff bottles, hand carvings. Also cashmere sweaters, fur caps.

All purchases must be paid for in Chinese currency. If buying antiques (less than 150 years old), keep your receipts and export document with its red wax seal to show to Customs on departure.

In Peking at *Tung Feng Commercial Center* (Eastern Wind Bazaar), you'll find over 600 shops and several restaurants. *Peking Municipality Department Store* is one of the country's best. *Yung Pao Zai* specializes in antiques.

Stores are open 8 a.m. to 7 p.m. (except on special holidays).

SPORTS

Physical fitness is both fashionable and the party line. Peking's Worker Stadium, a modern circular structure, has lighted artificial track, electronic scoreboard and 80,-000 seats. Admission is about 20 cents. Spectators arrive by foot, bicycle or bus. There are no vendors. The new stadium in Shanghai has 64 dressing rooms, a hotel, restaurant, 18,000 seats and is air-conditioned. Some events are televised, but as very few families have sets, fans watch on sets in public buildings. Thruout the country are many gymnasiums, some mediocre, and many sport clubs.

Track and field events, soccer, hockey, baseball, basketball, calisthenics are very popular. Chinese shadow boxing, fencing, archery, gymnastics, ice skating, skiing, table tennis and swimming are in vogue.

Tourists may swim, play tennis and ping-pong, bowl, shoot billiards daily (exc. Mon.) from 9 a.m.-10 p.m. at the *International Club,* 8 Tai Chi Chang, Peking. During winter, skate at the International Club, Beihai Lake or on the moat around the Imperial City from 4 p.m. During the summer, bathing is permitted at the Thirteen Ming Tombs Reservoir and Summer Palace Lake in Peking.

Athletes are not treated as celebrities, receive no special privileges except the chance to travel occasionally. When China picked up tab for our athletes, they received $3 a day, the Chinese even less.

Chinese are lean and healthy looking. They never seem to stop moving, always walking, running and exercising. Basketball courts are everywhere, women play badminton, joggers are out at dawn, schoolchildren exercise to martial music, workers exercise twice a day; there's no such a thing as a coffee break. If you're old or lame, you walk and shake your arms vigorously to keep the blood circulating.

There she winds — part of the Great Wall.

Road leading to the entrance of the Thirteen Ming Tombs.

PEKING

From the airport, it's an 18-mile drive into the city (35-45 minutes), during which you'll pass orchards, factories and workers. In the city (8,000,000 pop.) on tree-studded Chang An Avenue and Street of Heavenly Peace, you'll see many more bicycles than cars; at night, it's a traffic jam of bicycles.

Center of the city is famous Tien An Men Square, largest in China (98 acres), probably in the world. On its west is the Great Hall of the People, almost a quarter mile long, built in 1959 to hold state functions; atop is a huge statue of Mao, which is night-lighted, and inside are banquet halls, auditorium and many reception rooms. On the eastern side is a similar structure, also built in '59, housing two Museums — Chinese History and Chinese Revolution. Facing the Square from the south is Tien An Men, the huge, red Gate of Heavenly Peace, the main entrance to the Imperial City area (once walled) of former palaces but now comprising a network of museums and exhibition halls. From the balcony of Tien An Men, Mao Tse-tung proclaimed the People's Republic, and here, on May Day and National Day each year, the Chinese leaders review processions.

In the center of the Square stands the Monument to the People's Heroes, and to the north, thru a succession of courtyards, is the former walled Forbidden City containing the Imperial Palace. Completed in 1420, it was the home of emperors for over 500 years. Surrounded by a moat and once forbidden to most Chinese and all foreigners, the yellow tile-roofed buildings are now open to all. Imperial Palace Museum (open 8:30 to 4 p.m.) has beautiful sculptures and rare treasures of past Dynasties.

Other places of interest: National Library (rare manuscripts, prints); Colosseum (indoor sports stadium); Prospect Hill Park (panoramic views of Peking); Wo Fo Sze (Temple of Sleeping Buddha); Peking University; Tien Tan (Temple of Heaven); Summer Palace (acres of gardens, pagodas, lakes), seven miles NW; Evergreen People's Commune; Pei Hai Park (most famous); Peking Zoo (don't miss the pandas).

THE GREAT WALL

There were walls in China long before 22 centuries ago when Shih Huang Ti, emperor of China, ordered the Wall to be built at any cost, but none like this. For 2,500 miles, it traces a zigzag course over mountains and valleys across China, contains enough materials to build a barrier 8 ft. high and 3 ft. thick encircling the equator. It actually covers one-twentieth of the circumference of the earth — truly one of its great wonders.

Originally built to keep the barbarians out of agricultural China and to close the gap between the natural barriers of the Yellow Sea to the east and the Gobi desert to the west, it stands not only as a monument to the great builders of the past but also as the brick-and-stone realization of an idea, a summing up of China's concept of the relationship between itself and a hostile outer world.

To most tourists, the most exciting mo-ment in China is the trip northwest of Peking to the Great Wall, a two-hour (35-mile) bus trip thru the Nankou Pass to the Pata Ling mountains. Here the rebuilt wall is 30 ft. high, 25 ft. wide, with interspersed 40-ft.-high guard towers, while far in the distance "the ancient stones are crumbling and overgrown as the Wall stretches away."

About thirteen miles south of the Great Wall, in a ring of hills that form a horseshoe, are the underground palaces or monuments comprising the Thirteen Ming Tombs. Yung-lo, who died in 1424 and had chosen the site, was the first of the Ming Emperors to be bured here. The approach is along an impressive avenue lined with giant statues of men and beasts, two by two, in blue limestone: a pair of unicorns, a pair of marble camels, two lions, stone elephants and many more. During the late 1960s, a spectacular discovery was made — two jade death suits of a Han Dynasty prince and his wife who were buried in 113 BC.[1] The suits are made of oblong pieces of jade woven together with pure gold wires. These have been exhibited in San Francisco. During the Ming Dynasty (1368-1644), the Great Wall, which can be seen in the distance, was kept in constant repair.

For this trip be sure to wear warm clothing. Even in summer the underground palaces are cold. Try to avoid visiting on a Sunday (crowded).

LOCAL TRANSPORTATION

Cabs are metered; flag drop for larger taxis is 2Y, less for mini-cabs. As taxis never cruise, call 557-661 (in Chinese), and be prepared for an hour's wait. Most hotels have a few cabs available. If making several stops, arrange same beforehand so that cab will wait.

Be sure you have a pre-arranged transfer from the airport.

There's a recently completed subway but available only to Peking residents and by special invitation to foreigners.

HOW TO GET TO PEKING

There are direct non-stop flights from Tokyo by Air France (AF), CAAC, Iranian (IR), Japan (JL) and Pakistan (PK) lines. CA and JL fly from Osaka, AF from Fukuoka. From Europe, there's AF, CA, Rumanian and Swiss Air. From the Middle East, CA and IR non-stop from Teheran; PK from Karachi.

From Canton it's a 3¾-hour flight, 2:05 from Shanghai, one hour from Nanking, 1¼-hour from Hangchow.

Domestic fare from Shanghai is RMB 150, from Canton RMB 244.

[1] A much more fantastic archeological find was unearthed in 1974 in the northwestern province of Shensi of the tomb of Chin Shih Huang-ti, first Emperor of a unified China and founder of the Chin Dynasty (221 BC), and vast underground chambers containing possibly 6,000 life-size, pottery warriors, horses and chariots. Thus far, 314 helmeted, meticulously executed warriors almost 6 ft. tall and 24 horses have been removed; soldiers carry real bows and arrows, crossbows and spears, officers' swords (which were said to be still shiny and stainless). The Emperor's tomb is yet to be opened.

PEKING DINING & NIGHT LIFE

E Mei — Hsi Tan St. Szechwanese dishes.

Feng Tsu Uan — 67 Mei Shih Chieh. Seafood is the thing here.

Hung Qing Lou Fan Zhung — 80 Hsi Chang An Jie. Barbecued beef, chicken and cakes.

Peking Kaoya Dien (Peking Roast Duck). Peking duck has been served here for over 100 years. Don't miss. If you wish to order ahead, phone 751-648.

Ting Li Guan (Summer Palace) — Overlooks lake. Nice at lunch time. Orders hors d'oeuvres, rou-se mien, tang swan yu (sweet and sour fish).

Night life as we know it isn't. There are some bars but only in hotels. Principal entertainment are Chinese operas, ballets, theatrical performances, movies and sports programs — all very big in patriotic fervor and indoctrination. Peking opera has two forms, one with string instruments *(Jing Ju)* and other with wind *(Kun Ju)*. Ballet, such as the Red Lantern, Red Detachment of Women and White-Haired Girl are revolutionary in theme, usually anti-Western — but the acting, singing and dancing are excellent. Be sure to attend at least one performance.

For the best in Chinese music, attend a China Central Philharmonic concert.

International Club (San Li Tun district) is open to all foreigners for a Western or Chinese meal, ping-pong, bowling; has a good library. Some Embassies show foreign films from time to time.

PRACTICAL DO'S & DON'T'S

Don't get lost! There are no cruising cabs, few people who speak English. Carry your hotel letterhead with you.

Do bring an Instamatic or Polaroid camera. Since Chinese idolize their children, pictures of them will do more to bring West and East together than anything else you can do.

Carry ear plugs if you don't want to be driven crazy by horn-honking vehicles. Everyone, but *everyone*, has a bicycle so trucks/buses clear a path only by sitting on the horn. In your downtown hotel, the continuous cacophony drives you mad. Out of town you escape the noise but become frustrated by lack of transport. And, of course, you have no choice — you stay where Luxingshe puts you.

Walk the streets as much as possible — in perfect safety. There are no drunks, no beggars, no crawling insects. People you see are hard working, reserved but very polite.

Ask questions of your guides. You'll get answers — up to a point. And, of course, liberal doses of propaganda praising the present regime and condemning the Gang of Four.

Don't try to bargain — stores are one-price.

KWANGCHOW (CANTON)

A Tropical Garden City

If using Hong Kong as your gateway to China, you'll travel by rail from Hong Kong, walk across the border at Shumchun Station. Train departs Kowloon at 8:38 a.m., arrives Canton at 3:15 p.m. (times subject to change). First Class fare from Hong Kong to Shumchun is HK $3.50, from Shumchun to Canton 4.75 Y. From Canton you take a plane or train to Peking or Shanghai.

In October 1978, air service from Hong Kong was resumed, while in November a thrice-daily RT hovercraft ferry service was inaugurated (75 miles, 2 ½ hrs. OW).

For businessmen, the important place is the Chinese Export Commodities Fair open 8:30-11:30 daily (except Sun.); 2-5 p.m. (except Sat., Sun.), from mid-April to mid-May, again mid-Oct. to mid-Nov.

You'll want to see Lu Yung Temple (Buddhist), Hwa Tower, Huai Sheng Mosque (built in 627 AD), Chen Family Shrine (now a folk museum), the pandas at the zoo. To see Chinese at play, walk thru Kwangchow Cultural Park in the evening. Yueh Siu Park surrounds the Sun Yat-sen Monument, Chen Hai Tower (14th century) and Yueh Siu Shan Stadium. At the base of Yuet Siu Mountain is Sun Yat-sen Memorial Hall. You'll view the Memorial Garden to the Martyrs of the Canton Commune Uprising and the Mausoleum of the Seventy-two Martyrs of Hunghuakang.

At Fushan, 16 km from Canton, you can visit communes, ceramic factories, arts and crafts studios.

Canton can be hot and humid so dress accordingly.

CANTONESE DINING

Ideally situated in Pearl River delta, restaurants serve a wide variety of fish, crabs, shrimps and birds. Canton, as a gateway into China, also serves the best in foreign foods. Here are a few of the better eating places:

Friendship — Hsiangyang Rd. Dine in beautiful gardens or on an elegant balcony overlooking Li-wan Lake. Gourmet dishes, such as shrimp, and over 100 varieties of small cakes and cookies do full justice to the surroundings. Exquisite, skilled service. A must!

Economic — Shamian Island. Known for continental food.

Shamian Floating Rst — Shamian Island. Seafood here. Don't miss the deep-fried ice-cream balls (Chinese version of Baked Alaska).

Ta Tung — Hsihao Kou, Chang Ti. Dine simply on fried chicken or roast pork.

KWEILIN

A beautiful city, founded in 214 B.C., it's an exciting tourist destination. Located on the Likiang River in southeast China, the area is a natural wonderland. Within the city are famed limestone caves with intriguing names such as Reed Flute Cave, Sleeping Old Man. Rocks are shaped like animals, grottos are within grottos, carvings from the Sung and Tang dynasties decorate the walls of Pearl Cave, while the colored lighting in Seven Star Cave holds you spellbound. Allow three days here so you can take the spectacular nine-hour river trip (50 miles) by romantic-looking, diesel- and sail-powered junk, said to be a highlight of everyone's trip, down the Li River to Yang-shuo.

Kweilin, northwest of Canton, is reached by air.

For a quickie glimpse of Red China (week or so), a trip from Hong Kong to Canton and Kweilin is ideal.

Some cruise ships (QE2, Rotterdam, Marco Polo) offer 3-day side trips to Canton from Hong Kong in groups of 25 or so. It's reported that the Chinese offered free medical attention (if required), laundry service and even haircuts. This is most painless way to get to China.

SHANGHAI

This air gateway lies just 12 miles south of the mouth of the Yangtze River, is China's largest seaport and industrial city. Over 11 million live in China's most western city. Here you'll find shipbuilding, iron/steel factories, electrical plants, machinery, etc. Tall buildings line Bund Avenue facing the river, one of Shanghai's most impressive. Nanking Road is the main shopping street with several department stores and smaller shops. Downtown is People's Square, where rallies and celebrations take place. Other places of interest: Lu Hsun Memorial Park and Futan University.

To see old China, visit Lung Hua with its temples and pagodas set amidst peach trees; Temple of the Jade Buddha, where the six-foot image of Sakyamuni is carved from jade; Yu Yuan Garden and Shanghai Museum. You can watch children being taught Chinese folk art at Handicraft Research Institute. The newest techniques in brain surgery are developed at Hun Shan Hospital.

GETTING TO SHANGHAI

CAAC and JL fly direct from Tokyo and Osaka. It's an 1:40 flight (656 miles) to Peking or a 24-hour rail trip. Canton is a 2:05 non-stop flight, Nanking one hour.

HANGCHOW

This leading vacation resort lies 100 miles S of Shanghai. Ideally situated along the Chientang River near the Bay of Hangchow with mountains as a backdrop and blessed with the ancient, beautiful Hsi Hu (West Lake), it is truly a city to tarry in. Picturesque arched bridges and weeping willows overhang canals, beautiful botanical gardens have rare Chinese plants. There's the walk along Yun Chi (The Path Where Clouds Linger) amongst rows of bamboo trees, a relaxing boat ride to view pagodas, temples, gardens as you drift by. Or climb the 200 steps of the 13-tier Pagoda of Six Harmonies (built in 970) for a panorama of the lake below.

Hsi Hu is three-sectioned, divided by two ancient, tree-covered dykes. Its four islands are joined by causeways and bridges. Woodlands and gardens line the nine-mile shoreline. So many delightful places to visit you'll be breathless. To name a few: The Pavilion of the Autumn Moon and Chekiang Provincial Museum on Ku Shan Island; the lovely natural spring fountain in Ching Liang Temple; exquisite Chao Ching Sze Temple on the north shore; Ling Yin Temple, first built in 326, with its huge statue of Buddha; Yellow Dragon Cave whose waters empty into a pond; Mei Chia Wu, where Lun Chin green tea is grown (visit must be prearranged), and Tu Chin Sheng Silk Factory. Hangchow's silks are as famous as its beauty.

Hangchow is a 40-minute non-stop flight from Shanghai, 1 ¾-hour from Peking (700 miles).

Hotel Directory

All reservations are handled and assigned, without choice, by Luxingshe. You'll be in hotels catering to foreigners, not Chinese-style inns which don't accept foreigners.

Many of the hotels were built by the Russians during the 1950s, hence the rooms are big and drab but usually clean, though one visitor observed he never saw a single vacuum cleaner in the entire country. Furnishings are shabby, look like they belong in a 1930 movie. Most rooms are not airconditioned so are hot in the summer, can be very cold in the winter if there's no heat, which is likely. Ice is almost a nonthing. There's no TV in the rooms — just in the lobbies. However, best viewing is the street activity so you won't miss your favorite commercials.

Rooms do have private baths (there may be no shower curtains) — and if you want large bath towels, bring your own. But the service (24 hours of it) is great — employees are anxious to please, so much so they retrieve empty cartons from the wastebasket. Extra conveniences not usually found elsewhere: slippers, cold cream, shaving cream, toothbrush and paste thermos of boiled water for making tea (bring your own instant brand if you want coffee), a *Tung chi* to mend your clothes, do your laundry and dry cleaning — remember, though, not to tip him (or her).

Doors are never locked — nothing's stolen.

There may be a bar; if not, beer and cordials can be obtained from your floor waiter. Most hotels have shopping arcades, barber shop and beauty salon.

177

Here's probably the most important item of all: public rest rooms, both in and out of hotels, are designated by these two Chinese characters:
男 for Men (pronounced *nan*) and
女 for Women (pronounced *nu*).

So that you may know what to expect, here's a brief digest of hotels for foreigners:

CANTON
Ai-qun — Centrally located. 220 R.

Tung Fang Guest House — People's Rd. North — 220 R w/bath. Popular with businessmen.

New Tung Fang (Oriental Guest House) — 1000 AC R, near airport. New 12-story annex has R, SU, lounge, library, rst, bar. Overlooks Lake of Drifting Blossoms. Rooms said to be comfortable but dreary.

Kwangchow Guest House — Hai Chu Square. 27-story hi-rise with all amenities.

HANGCHOW
Hangchow — Nice vacation spot overlooking West Lake. Large rooms and terraces, lovely gardens.

KWEILIN
Banyan Tree Lake — 4-story low-rise with 100 R. 600 R hi-rise being constructed.

PEKING
Chien Men — Built within last few years. 9-story.

Hsin Chiao (New Overseas) — In old Legation district. Functional rooms with/without baths. Top floor Western rst, main floor Chinese rst. Bar open 9-12 p.m. Roof garden. Popular for journalists, businessmen, tourists. 9-14Y.

Peace Guest House — If you're a guest of the government, this is where you might stay.

Peking — 800 R, 17-story hotel opened late '74 on Ave. of Permanent Peace. This all-Chinese production is AC, modern, luxurious. Great views of the streets. Original 7-story hotel also has good accommodations. Most rooms are reserved for official and semi-official visitors.

Nationalities — Chang An Blvd, west of Imperial Palace. Widely used for government guests. $19 D.

SHANGHAI
Ching Chiang — Popular, commercial hotel. Reasonably priced.

Peace — Still one of the world's best; immense, unusual rooms. Marvelous views of Bund. Top-floor rst. Long-time favorite of businessmen.

International — Popular for foreigners. 18-story hi-rise. Restaurant reported good.

TIENTSIN
Grand Tientsin — Older, continental style.

178

TIPS FOR BUSINESSMEN
Best to arrange for an interpreter in advance, either thru your Chinese business contact (State Trading Organizations) or the China International Travel Service. If paying for services of an interpreter or guide, payment is made directly to Luxingshe. Unless you can speak the language, keep your guide with you during business hours.

Secretarial services are unavailable so if you need one, bring her with you (good reason for a trip to China) — also typewriter, tape recorder, stationery, carbon paper, etc.

Be punctual — and listen to what your Chinese counterpart has to say. Try and learn a few Chinese phrases. Have your business card printed in Chinese characters and phonetic script. Don't make jokes. Their sense of humour is not ours. Always refer to China as the People's Republic of China — never by any other name.

As a race, the Chinese are courteous, friendly, polite and honest. Most of the police you see are directing traffic, not chasing criminals. Don't worry about walking the streets, day or night — you're perfectly safe. Your only problem is getting lost. Don't leave your hotel without its name and address written in Chinese.

When attending a banquet or function, be sure to return the applause. If a toast is made (usually a dozen), sip your drink and return the toast. *Never* address a waiter or bellboy by any other name than *Tung chih* (comrade). Remember, in China, everyone is equal. And *never, never* tip — that is the extreme insult.

For information on foreign trade and exhibitions write or contact *China Committee for the Promotion of International Trade*, Hsi Chang An Chieh, Peking. They will put you in contact with firms dealing in your particular product. To arrange for custom clearance, deliveries, etc., contact the *China National Foreign Trade Transportation Corp*, Erh Li Kou, Hsi Chiao, Peking.

Authors' Note: All material in this section has been compiled from sources considered reliable, but we cannot vouch for all information being 100% correct.

BURMA

Known as the Land of Pagodas, Burma, one of the world's least traveled and developed countries, is visited for history, culture, majestic sights and to witness a very elementary form of communism — certainly not for good accommodations and living. As one friend put it, "Compared to Burma, Communist China has got to be paradise." Yet thanks to its great art and architecture, archeological sites, mountain scenery and beautiful beaches — plus its wealth of pearls, rubies, opals and jade — fascination abounds. The people, mostly unspoiled and pleasant, make up for most of the discomforts one encounters, such as touring by jeep or other open vehicles (regular cars are few), the barely adequate domestic planes.

RANGOON

This capital has one of the most sacred shrines in Asia, the hilltop, 2,500-year-old Shwedagon Pagoda covered with gold and diamonds; smaller pagodas cluster about. Visit before 10 a.m. or after 5 p.m.[1] Four stairways, 360 steps each, lead upward and are lined with fascinating shops on either side. On the south side there's an elevator — easiest to ride up and walk down. Try and see again at night.

Almost as interesting are the Sule Pagoda and Bo-ta-taung Pagoda (2,200 years old) situated in the heart of the city; the Great Sacred Cave and the National Museum where the Throne of Burmese Kings is displayed.

Burmese classical dancing can be seen at the School of Fine Arts, and a Burmese boxing show is not to be missed — nor is the zoo for a spine-chilling snake charmer act (complete with a kiss from a poisonous cobra).

At Pegu, 50 miles from Rangoon, is the rebuilt (1954) 374-ft. Shwe-maw-daw Pagoda which enshrines the sacred hair and tooth of Buddha. The Shwe-tha-lyaung houses the reclining Buddha. Drive is over the famous road to Mandalay.

PAGAN (Nyaung-U)

Center of a desolate stretch of parched desert that runs north and south thru the center of Burma between the northern grasslands and southern rice padis. In April, padis are dry and cracked, and heat is almost unbearable. But Pagan is one of the richest archeological sites in Asia; here are remains of 5,000 pagodas sacked by Kublai Khan. Most prominent are the Ananda Temple built in 1091 AD and crowned with a tapering tower; the Bupaya Pagoda dedicated to the God of Storms; the Thatbyinnyu, standing over 200 ft. Additional monuments are decorated with elaborate carvings, ornamental friezes, stucco figures. Minimum stay here is one day but best to stay overnight.

MANDALAY

Mandalay is rich in ancient monasteries and pagodas, famous for its Palace grounds within which moats sprawl in all directions — all in the shadow of the Shan Plateau to the east. Formerly the capital, it's still the center of Burmese social, political and educational life, still renowned for Burmese wood carving and architecture (such as the Shwe-Nan-Daw Monastery), the Mahamyatmuni Pagoda with its hundreds of handicraft shops.

JETTING TO BURMA

Burmese visa specifies that you must arrive by air and only in Rangoon, the only international airport. Gateways are Bangkok (1:35 via Thai International, Burma Airways), Singapore (Burma), Kathmandu and Calcutta (Burma, Thai).

Best ingress is thru Bangkok as there are organized tours[2] (4 and 6 days) from there. Shorter one takes in Rangoon, Pagan, Mandalay and back to Rangoon before flying back. Longer tour gives more time in Pagan and Mandalay, continues on to Heho, Taunggyi, Lake Inle before returning to Rangoon for two days.

Beautiful Lake Inle, noted for its unique floating islands, is hidden in the mountains and surrounded by evergreen trees, flowers and

Since shoes must be removed when entering any pagoda, marble pavements can be too hot at other hours for tender feet.

[2] By Diethelm Travel, 544 Ploenchit Rd., Bangkok, principal operator from Thailand. 4-day tour departs every Sat., 6-day tour on Thurs.; both return to Bangkok on Tues.

winding roads; outboard motors power the vendors from village to village, island to island with their wares. Here, too, is woven fabrics akin to Thai silk. Climate is temperate.

Arrangements can be made (at least 3 weeks in advance) with Burma Airways, 104 Strand Rd., Rangoon, for individual or group tours directly out of Rangoon for the above as well as Pegu and the Sandoway beaches.

DOMESTIC FLIGHTS

Today's Road To Mandalay (and most everywhere else in Burma) is by air. From Rangoon, it's an hour and a half by F27 to Nyaung-U, 55 min. more to Mandalay; 50 min. non-stop by DC-3 to Heho.

BURMESE HOTELS

Burma's colonial past and her current Road to Socialism has produced a strange array of hotels. None is truly first class, though those mentioned below have clean, air-conditioned rooms with bland, but probably wholesome, food. Lighting generally poor, beds hard. 10% service, 10% tax added to quoted double rates.

RANGOON

INYA LAKE — Resort type, six miles from town on way to airport. Built as a gift from Russia in early '60s, now quite dilapidated. Nonetheless, it's where all visiting dignitaries, most businessmen stay (except the Chinese). Has 222 R, 3 rst, pool, tennis court and Rangoon's only nightclub. About $20.

PRESIDENT — Simple but clean. DT. $7 double, a bargain.

STRAND — Once a grand colonial hotel (same era as Raffles), it has fallen on hard times; needs renovating, public areas large, smoky and dirty. But location, on the waterfront, can't be beat. About $7.

MANDALAY

MANDALAY — Modern but simple. Opposite palace grounds. Tourist Burma has offices here so sightseeing can be arranged on the spot. $27 AP.

PAGAN

THIRPYITSAYA — Modern (1971) and best in country. Each of the 40 cabins have four AC doubles w/large private patio; try to get one overlooking Irawaddy River. Reasonably good food, bar. Tourist Burma offices here. $28 AP.

GENERAL INFORMATION

Airport Tax — Kyats 2 for male passengers purchasing tickets locally and embarking in Rangoon. Payable at airport or carrier's office. Holders of diplomatic passport, personnel of United Nations, transit passengers are exempt.

Climate — Best season is Nov.-April when it's cool, dry; Nov. and Dec. are coolest. Dusty most of the time. April to Nov. is very hot (100°-115°).

Clothing — Lightweight summer clothes. Bring insect repellant.

Currency — Official exchange rate about K7 (Kyat) equals $1 US; the black market will get you 20. Full declaration of foreign currency, travel checks required on arrival. Amounts entered on your customs form for endorsement whenever money is exchanged.

Customs — Officials carefully scrutinize incoming luggage, note all valuable items (cameras, radios, jewelry, etc.) on customs form which you must present on departure, together with listed items. If any are lost or stolen, obtain a police certificate covering same. One bottle of liquor, a carton of cigarettes may be brought in. These are commonly, but illegally, sold to taxi drivers and others at three times cash value. Amusing to see every young tourist arriving with a bottle of Johnny Walker and a carton or more of cigarettes. Lipsticks are in demand by young girls. On departure, arrive at airport two hours in advance as you're subject to an intensive body and luggage search.

Entry Requirements — Passport, visa (obtainable in Thailand; $7.50) good only for 7 days; also re-entry visa to Thailand if returning there, smallpox, cholera certificate.

Government — Communist. Everything government-owned.

Language — English widely spoken.

Religion — Buddhist.

Shopping — Carved ivory best buy; gemstones conspicuous by their absence (presumably all exported). Good woodcarvings, lacquerware. Articles requiring export permit, such as jewelry, must be bought in gov't shops or hotels (require foreign currencies); shops at Strand, Inya Lake and airport open to tourists (bargaining in order). Domestic handcrafts sold by souvenir shops.

Time — GMT + 6½.

Tipping — Porters, waiters, drivers: K1 to 5.

Water — Drink bottled only.

THAILAND

Wat Bencha, the Marble Temple, is surrounded by these stylistic marble lions.

Nowhere in the Orient does Oriental pomp and splendor continue to exist as lavishly as in the soaring, many faceted and gleaming architecture of the palaces, Wats and Chedis of Thailand. Lose yourself in the grounds of the Grand Palace, the summer palace of Bang Pa-In, the Winter Palace in Chiang Mai, the noble ruins of Ayutthaya, the breathtaking sumptuousness of Wat Phra Keo, and you feel that *you* are living in a richly decorated dream world of, perhaps, the eighteenth century.

To us, Siam, like Persia, has always symbolized the nadir of ancient romanticism. We're happy to report that despite modern dress and problems, the trappings if not the essence still remain. Like Hong Kong, though for completely different reasons, we rank Bangkok as an essential destination in every Far East itinerary.

Thailand has evolved from Buddhists of the east coasts of India and Thais who descended south from Yunnan Province in China during the 13th century. By the start of the 15th century, a new dynasty was founded in Ayutthaya which controlled all of Siam until 1767 when the capital was destroyed by the Burmese. Incidentally, Siam came by its name from the place, Sayam, where the Thais wrested control from the Khmers around 1238. Renamed Sukhothai, Dawn of Happiness, it became the capital of the new Kingdom of Sukhothai. Rama IV, in 1856, was the first to officially use Siam, though the popular name Muang Thai, Land of the Free, had been used since early days and still is today.

When the Burmese were driven off, the successful general Tak-Sin became king and established a new capital at Thon Buri, twin of today's Bangkok. He was succeeded by Chao Phraya Chakri, founder of the present Chakri Dynasty, who as Rama I established the capital at Bangkok in 1782. An absolute though benign monarchy reigned until 1932 when, thru a military coup and the establishment of a constitution, the monarchy became largely ceremonial.

King Mongkut (Rama IV), who ruled from 1851 to 1868, was largely responsible for modernizing the country along western lines. Mongkut is the king of *The King and I*, a book more myth than fact according to historians — so much so that the movie was banned in Thailand. His son, Chulalongkorn, came to the throne at the age of 15, ruled for 42 years and was the first Thai king to travel to Europe and Southeast Asia. He brought in Westerners to continue modernizing the country, insisted the poorest children should have the same opportunities as his own (all 76 of them) and freed the serfs. King Rama VI, his son, established compulsory education, abolished gambling and developed the current *Tri-rong* (three color) national flag. His brother, Rama VII, last absolute monarch, abdicated in 1935 and was succeeded by his nephew, Ananda Madidol, who reigned until 1946 when the present monarch, King Bhumibol Adulyadej, Rama IX, ascended the throne.

In November of 1971, Field Marshal Thanom Kittikachorn, the Prime Minister, and the Army took over direct control, dissolving both Houses of Parliament and the entire government, with a National Executive Council, headed by the Prime Minister, taking control. But vigorous student demonstrations in October of 1973, 1976 and again in 1977 have resulted in successive dismissals of civilian Prime Ministers and consequent tightening of military control. The Army is firmly anti-Communist and decidedly pro-American. Other than along the Cambodian border, the country remains peaceful

It's interesting to note that since 1768, the country has remained independent, gotten along successfully with its neighbors and remains the only country in Southeast Asia never to have come under Western colonial rule.

About the size of France (approx. 321,000 sq. miles), Thailand stretches 1,000 miles, at its longest, from north to south, has a maximum east-west spread of 500 miles. Central Thailand, where Bangkok is located, is the most fertile and heavily populated area, a low alluvial plain watered by the Chao Phraya River and crisscrossed by vast network of *klongs* (canals). Northern Thailand is hilly and mountainous, forested and cooler. Parts of the country have heavy jungles teeming with game, while bougainvillea, flame of the forest, frangipani, roses and orchids are found in abundance everywhere.

There are 71 Changwad (provinces) headed by governors appointed by the Ministry of Interior. Each Changwad is divided into Amphurs, Tambols and Mubans (districts, sub-districts, villages).

80% of the 44,000,000 population (of which about 94% are Thais) are in agriculture, forestry and fishing. Rice, principal food and crop, is the leading export, followed by rubber, tin and teakwood; 70% of the land is forested. Water buffalo have widespread use in farming, while wild elephants are still rounded up to be domesticated and trained in forestry work. Both are picturesque additions to the tourist scene.

INTERNATIONAL TRANSPORT

BANGKOK ARRIVAL BY AIR

Although the processing thru Immigration is quick and efficient, we understand (last time we were here we were met) that from here until you get to your hotel can be a bit wearing. The porter with "No Tipping" embroidered across his shirt expects a tip, and the Transport Counter, at which you pay for an "air-conditioned limousine" to your hotel, seems to pull numbers out of a hat, all of them high. Here, too, you can pay much less for a seat in a bus, but it's very slow. We'd suggest a pre-arranged transfer with English-speaking guide so you can tell him to tell the driver not to drive like all the other maniacs on the road. Don Muang International Airport is 15 miles from downtown, a sufficient distance to reduce strong men to nervous wrecks. Which is silly — they should close their eyes and keep them shut until arrival which, miraculously, always happens.

It's okay to take a hotel taxi back (see Local Transportation).

ARRIVAL BY SEA

Thai Commercial Navigation Company has bought a former French liner (2,000 passengers), now named *Phithakseri,* for service in a regularly scheduled Bangkok-Hong Kong-Taiwan run.

ARRIVAL BY TRAIN

Singapore-Kuala Lumpur-Butterworth (Penang)-Bangkok is a two-day run, leaving Singapore around 8 a.m., KL 7½ hrs. later. Key, however, is the *International Express* between Butterworth, Malaysia (departs M, W, F at 7:50 a.m.), and Bangkok (ars. T, Th, Sat) at 7:50 a.m. FC fare is about US$30, AC single berth roomette about $9.50. Train leaves Bangkok M, W, Sat at 4:10 p.m., arrives Butterworth 4:20 p.m. next day with connections to KL and Singapore. Butterworth to KL, FC fare is $19, to Singapore $36. There are three daily express services connecting Singapore, KL and Butterworth. Singapore to Bangkok is 1,192 miles, 945 miles from Kuala Lumpur.

Since reservations cannot be made on the *International Express* until 10 days prior to departure, and then in person, the services of a local travel agent or tour operator is needed in the city from which passengers will be departing.

ARRIVAL BY BUS

Tour Royale[1] offers an excellent service from Singapore. 40-passenger, air-conditioned super-bus leaves every Monday for 7-day trip to Bangkok; includes one night in Kuala Lumpur, two in Penang, one in Haad Yi and two at little-visited Phuket Island. $330 per person, including meals, first-class accommodations and sightseeing.

The reverse trip leaves Bangkok on Saturdays.

[1] 392-27-28 Siam Sq. Soi 5, Rama 1 Road, Bangkok.

ENTRY REQUIREMENTS

Passport, smallpox vaccination certificate. U.S. and Canadian citizens do not need a visa for stays of 15 days or less. Visa, valid for 90 days from date of issue and for 30 days within Thailand, costs $4.

CUSTOMS REGULATIONS

On entry, one still and one movie camera with 5 rolls/3 rolls film, respectively; additional film is subject to duty totaling 40% of cost. One liter of liquor allowed.

On departure, there is no duty on purchases of precious stones, gold and platinum jewelry, other items valued at less than Baht 10,000. An-

'tique Buddha and Deity images cannot be exported; new ones require export permit from Dept. of Fine Arts, Dept. of External Trade.

For export of items over Baht 10,000 in value, obtain from a bank a Certificate of Exportation (issued by Bank of Thailand).

CURRENCY

Official rate has been almost constant for years at 20 Baht to US dollar, thus each baht equals 5¢. To translate Thai prices into dollars, divide by 20 or multiply by 5.

Bills come in denominations of 10 (brown), 20 (green) and 100 (red) baht. There are 100 satang to the baht. Coins are 25 and 50 satang, 1 and 5 baht.

Not more than 500 Baht may be brought in, or taken out of, the country.

DOMESTIC TRANSPORTATION
AIR

Thai Airways, not to be confused with Thai International, has frequent jet flights to all parts of the country as well as to Penang, Malaysia, and Vientiane in Laos. *Reservations must be made well in advance.* Distances are short, fares reasonable. Chiang Mai, the most likely destination for visitors, is 788 km (489 miles); fare is about $59 RT.

BUS & RAIL

Both go to all parts of the country, are extremely reasonable. Buses are air-conditioned, are the only way (other than by car) to Pattaya, a 3-hour trip (at 8, 10, 12 a.m., 3 p.m.) for 100 Baht RT. Several lines operate multi-daily 9- to 10-hour service to Chiang Mai for (hold your hat) about $18 *round trip* — it's 434 miles by road each way, and fare includes meals, drinks enroute.

The express train to Chiang Mai leaves daily at 5:05 p.m., arrives next morning at 9:40. OW fare is $14, RT $24 — plus B20 for express service, B150 and 225 for berths (each way) in air-conditioned cars.

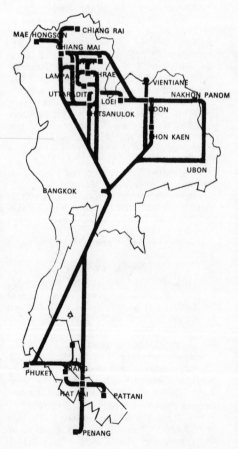

Thailand Facts

Airport Departure Tax — Baht 60.

Bank Hours — 8:30-3:30; 8:30-12 Sat.

Business Hours — 8:30-4:30 Mon-Fri. Stores open 8 to 8.

Current — 220v AC. Better hotels have 110v converters.

Climate — Hot year 'round except in north. November-March best tourist season; Jan., Feb. the coolest, May-Aug. hottest. Monsoon season is May-Sept. All tourist hotels, rsts air-conditioned.

Clothing — Lightweight summer things. Tie, jacket needed for dinner.

Embassies — Canada, 185 Rajdamari Rd. (57650); U.S., 95 Wireless (59800).

Language — Thai. English spoken in hotels, better restaurants and shops.

Museums — Outside Bangkok, usually closed Mon, Tues. (check).

Population — 44,000,000 with 4,000,000 in Bangkok.

Postage — Airmail is B6 for first five grams, B3 for each additional five. If mailing purchases home, pay store to do it as merchandise must be inspected by Customs, then wrapped in presence of inspector.

Religion — Buddhist.

Time — An hour behind Hong Kong.

Tipping — 10% usually added to hotel, rst bills. B3 per bag at airport; on departure, pay at desk as you enter building. Never tip 1 Baht — considered insulting.

Tourist Information — Tourist Organization of Thailand: 510 W. 6th St., Los Angeles 90014 (213 627-0386); 20 E. 82 St., New York 10028 (212 628-7902). In Bangkok, Mansion 2, Ratchadamnoen Ave. (218151); open 8:30 to 4:30, Mon-Fri. In Chiang Mai, 135 Praisani Rd. (35334).

Water — Drink bottled or distilled only; hotels, rsts serve latter.

NATIONAL HOLIDAYS & FESTIVALS
(Festivals based on Buddhist lunar calendar)

Jan. 1 — New Year's.

Feb.-April — Kite Flying Season. Also Dance & Music Festival (p.m. at Music Pavilion on National Museum grounds).

Early Feb. — Magha Puja, Buddhist Saint's Day.

April 6 — Chakri Day, celebrating start of Chakri Dynasty in 1782.

April 13 — Songkran Festival, the Thai New Year; lasts for several days.

May 5 — Coronation Day Anniversary. Also in May are Ploughing Ceremony (religious rite blessing the rice seeds) and Visakha Puja, one of the most important festivals with candle processions around monastery grounds.

July — Asalha Puja (First Sermon Festival) and Khao Parnsa (Buddhist Lent).

Aug. 12 — Birthday of Queen Sirikit.

Oct. — Tod Kathin. Important festival celebrating last month of rainy season and annual offering of new yellow robes to monks. Features a Royal Barges procession in Bangkok; elsewhere, long processions of people sing and dance their way to monasteries with gifts.

Oct. 23 — Chulalongkorn Day, commemorating death of King Rama V. Thousands place floral wreaths and incense at foot of his equestrian statue fronting the National Assembly Hall.

Nov. — Golden Mount Festival (worship of Buddha's relics). Also Festival of Lights (Loy Krathong) which may come end of Oct. In mid-Nov., Elephant Roundup at Surin featuring elephant demonstrations, races, tug-of-war (100 men against one elephant). On third Sunday, Trooping of the Colors takes place in front of National Assembly. On Dec. 3 a similar parade of Royal Guards.

Dec. 5 — King's Birthday & National Day. Celebrated everywhere with colorful pageantry; buildings spectacularly lighted.

Dec. 31 — New Year's Celebration.

Partial aerial view of Bangkok's Choa Phraya River; Temple of the Dawn is at the left.

BANGKOK

Were it not for its Wats, Palaces and Klongs, there would be little reason to visit this sprawling city. But the Big Three are more than sufficient to provide days of exciting sightseeing. No city, with the possible exception of Kyoto, more typifies the magic aura of the Far East than Bangkok. Overlook the traffic jams, honking horns, demonic drivers and decrepit cars, the minor rip-offs by cab drivers and vendors and concentrate on the many splendored edifices, fascinating street and canal scenes, fine hotels and satisfying eating places. You'll be enchanted.

Possibly the best testimonial for Bangkok, and for Thailand as a whole, is that it's been "discovered" by Europeans, particularly thrifty French and West Germans who like luxury living at (comparative) bargain prices, which is the exact formula the Thais have to offer. Their products are extremely attractive and reasonable, hotels offer facilities, accommodations and food not easily matched in price, and sightseeing is both fascinating and comparatively inexpensive. We saw nothing in Japan, Hong Kong and Singapore to match all these factors; Taiwan lags a bit in less sophisticated restaurants and hotels.

This is *not* a walking city, and most of the attractions are widely spaced, so tours and/or car and guide are essential.

Dusit Maha Prasart Hall in the Royal Grand Palace

SIGHTSEEING — HOW TO GO ABOUT IT

There are a multiplicity of tours, many quite innocuous of which the City Tour is a prime example — you'll see all you want of the city while shopping and traveling back and forth between the prime attractions, which are (more or less in this order):
1) Grand Palace, Wat Phra Kaeo and Wat Po, an exciting and almost overwhelming introduction to Thailand.
2) Visiting the other Wats, list of which follows.
3) Life on the Klongs. If time's limited, then the nearby Floating Market, otherwise the Rural Floating Market near Nakhon Pathom, 56 km (35 miles) from Bangkok.
4) Half- or full-day trip to Ayutthaya and Bang Pa-In, preferably via the *Oriental Queen.*
5) Half-day tour to Rose Garden for the Thai Village Show. Can be combined with the Rural Floating Market as an enjoyable full day.
6) If available, set aside a few hours to see the re-created Ancient City, the weekend Market and, without fail, a Thai Classical Dance Show.
7) Full day (or longer) for the Bridge on the River Kwai.
8, 9, 10) Shopping, shopping, shopping.

THE GRAND PALACE

Men must wear jackets, women dresses — but that's a small sacrifice, even in hot weather, for the grand spectacle this square mile complex affords, presenting as it does a spectacularly colorful combination of Siamese and Western architectural styles.

You'll enter thru the handsome Gate of Supreme Victory and continue thru the inner palace Gate of the Abode of Victory (Pratu Piman Chiasri); as you do, imagine richly caparisoned elephants doing the same during state processions. Next you'll see the Dusit Maha Prasad, built by Rama I in 1782 (he was the one that started the whole thing) as a ceremonial hall; when Rama I died, he lay in state here, and since then it's become the world's most elaborate funeral parlor. Then comes the Chakri Palace, Italian Rennaissance style with an unadulterated Thai roof by a British architect; on the top floor, golden urns hold the ashes of the Chakri kings. Eastward is the Amerinda Throne Hall (after Amerinda Vinichai, audience hall of the god Indra) where Thai kings in full regalia are presented after their coronation.

This walled city within a city also contains a magnificent Royal Chapel, that of the Emerald Buddha. See Wat Phra Keo that follows.

Only still cameras allowed here (but not in the Chapel). Admission 15 Baht (Sundays, Buddhist holidays free). Open daily 7 a.m.-6 p.m. Note: the Royal Family does not live here; the Palace Residence, on imposing, park-like grounds, can be seen to/from the airport (no visiting rights).

BANGKOK'S MUSEUMS

These are well worth visiting:

NATIONAL MUSEUM, the largest in Southeast Asia, contains splendid collections which are of significant value to visitors wanting to know the historical background and cultural growth of the country. With sufficient imagination, one can ride on elephants in magnificent howdahs, watch battles with soldiers in colorful uniforms bearing ancient weapons, hear strange music on exotic instruments, admire artisans at work on lovely pottery. There are many archeological exhibits, particularly the stunning stone figures and heads of Khmer and Thai workmanship. Open daily (except M, F) from 9 to noon, 1-4 p.m. Admission 5 Baht except Sat., Sun. when it's free. Not open on National Holidays.

JIM THOMPSON'S HOUSE, a composite of six, rebuilt Thai homes (one was 150 years old) housing the unique personal collections of the American responsible for commercial success of the Thai silk industry. Jim Thompson disappeared mysteriously in Malaysia in 1967, has not been heard from since, but his fine assortments of ceramics, bronzes, stone sculpture (all old), Thai paintings remain. Of unusual interest is the *bencharong* (five colors) porcelain ware made in China from 1600 to .1800 to Thai specifications. Open 9-12 M, Th only. Admission 30 Baht (for charity). At 6 Soi Kaseman II near Grand Hotel.

SUAN PAKKAD PALACE is a fine example of Thai architecture, a group of wooden houses assembled by Prince and Princess Chumbhot of Nagara Svarge to promote fine arts. There's something of everything here so that one gets an excellent feel of Thailand, plus learning a lot about the cultures of China, Cambodia and Burma. Open T, Th, Sat, Sun. 9 to 12, 2 to 4 p.m. Admission: 30 Baht.

Giant Reclining Buddha at Wat Po, Bangkok's most extensive monastery.

WHAT'S A WAT?

It's a monastery compound, usually with monks *(bikkus)* in attendance. Although referred to as a temple, Wat actually covers the entire complex; generally a *bot* is the temple or shrine hall where ceremonies are held, offerings to Buddha made. The most sacred of buildings (we'd call them chapels), *bots* usually face east and are identifiable by a boundary stone *(baisema)* area within which women are not permitted. *Viharns,* similar to *bots* but without *semas,* house images of Buddha used for public devotions; a Wat may have several *viharns.* Other terms:

Stupa (pagoda) is a mound or rounded structure topped by a spire. Phra Chedi, the most revered spire, is tapered; Phra Prang is elliptical.

MonMondop (library) houses the Holy Scriptures and also, perhaps, a sacred Buddha object. *Sala,* a dormitory for pilgrims, is a roofed pavilion. Those serpents you see on roofs and railing of temples are *naga* (pronounced *nak*), a demigod of rain.

Wats usually charge no admission (signs may ask for donations), but reverence is expected. Shoes are removed before entering temples, and it's preferable, even when not requested, for men to wear jackets, ties and women dresses.

THE WATS OF BANGKOK

Wat Phra Keo, or Monastery of the Emerald Buddha, is within the Grand Palace enclosure and contains much of the finest in Thai art of the Bangkok period — for example, splendid mother-of-pearl inlaid doors. The Chapel of the Emerald Buddha (no cameras) houses the famous image which is actually green jasper believed to have been carved around 1450; thrice a year, it is magnificently arrayed with ornaments of gold and precious stones. You'll be impressed by the Pantheon of Kings containing the mondop and awed by the superlative golden Chedi. Together with the Grand Palace area, a whole morning is none too long, particularly since shutter bugs go insane here.

Wat Po, the Monastery of the Reclining Buddha, an image 160 ft. long and 39 ft. high commemorating Buddha's passing and attaining *Nirvana* (heaven). Covered with gold leaf, the soles of the feet are inlaid with 108 mother-of-pearl signs symbolizing the marks and qualities by which a true Buddha may be recognized. Wat Po is the most extensive in Bangkok with four large and 91 small Chedis, the largest collection of Buddha images (the *bot* alone contains 394 images of the seated Buddha). For us, though, Wat Po's most intriguing sights were the marvelous collection of stone statues in the courtyard: grand, old Chinese warriors snarling at invisible foes, funny-faced animals and a dozen or so Yogis with twisted faces, arms and legs giving eternal lessons in curing body aches and pains. Open daily; 5B admission. It's near the Grand Palace so see it at the same time. Many of the better temple rubbings are done here.

Wat Arun, Temple of the Dawn, is multicolored with Chinese porcelain and glass inlay. The central tower is 217¾ ft. high. Usually seen as part of the Floating Market tour. Open daily; 3 Baht.

Wat Benchamabopitr, the Marble Temple (1899), is considered a fine example of modern Thai architecture demonstrating both East and West influences. Stylized lions *(rajasih)* guard the main entrance; interior is beautifully rich and elegant. In the cloisters is an outstanding collection of bronze Buddhas. An eastern gable shows Vishnu, the Hindu god, mounted on a Garuda, a legendary bird; on the northern gable is Erawan, the three-headed elephant. All in all a great show — and free (daily).

There are, of course, many more but for the average westerner, those are the most inspiring, beautiful and interesting. For those who still haven't had enough, add Wat Trimitr, built about 1238, containing the 10-ft.-high, 5½-ton Golden Buddha, one of the biggest, oldest. Wat Sraket, the Golden Mount, houses relics of Lord Buddha.

A "sleeper" is San Jow Paw Lak Muang Temple. This is where Buddhists of modest means pay girl dancers to perform for the gods in thanks for having answered the prayers of the believers. Here, too, the devout pay 5 Baht for the privilege of releasing a bird from its cage in the belief that this act will change the liberator's luck. Few tourists come here, but you're perfectly free to do so and enjoy some fine performances. Here's how to get there: From the main gate of the Temple of the Emerald Buddha, walk east to a gas station at the intersection of the Weekend Market area, Temple of the Emerald Buddha and the Ministry of Defense; an undistinguished-looking building behind the station is the temple you're looking for.

Part of the early morning traffic jam prior to departure for the Floating Market.

Thai-style dining in one of the entertainment restaurants.

TOURS & EXCURSIONS

Aside from the foregoing major attractions, there are such minor ones as the Zoo, Snake Farm (see venom extracted from cobras) and Crocodile Farm. We see no particular reason to view those when there's so much of the unusual elsewhere. Matter of fact, this is one of the few cities where we don't recommend a City Tour as such — you'll see enough of it while getting to and from the main attractions.

Major local tours are: Grand Palace and Wat Phra Kaeo; Floating Market; Temple Tours (morning and afternoon to cover all major ones); Museum Tours.

Because of its importance, whether by tour or on your own, herewith a description of Bangkok's Floating Market. It should be emphasized, however, that the Rural Floating Market (see Nakhon Pathom) is more authentic, less touristy.

INSTANT KLONG

Bangkok's Floating Market trip is on everyone's agenda, so plan to get to the Oriental Landing *early* for the 8 a.m. departure as it's always jammed. Traffic is so bad that policemen stand on boats to direct outbound traffic, which heads across the river into the klongs, where the waters are badly contaminated. In fact, the Floating Market has deteriorated into a tourist thing — yet still very much an eye-opener to meticulous Occidentals. You'll see Mom washing the kids, Pa brushing his teeth (and someone else taking a drink), Grandma fishing for breakfast, dogs and cats scrounging for food, small craft selling Coca-Cola, flowers, vegetables. Jungle-sheathed stilt houses line the banks while hordes of small boats weave in and out in a cacophony of activity.

A 30-minute stop is made at a store (Thai Home Industries) where just about anything Thai can be purchased. Boat returns by another route to the Chao Phraya River to see the Temple of Dawn.

This is a 2- to 4-hour trip that tour operators offer at varying prices (about $6, including transfers); you can get a seat-in-boat for 15B, or hire your own for 100-125B (they'll ask more) for 1½-2 hrs.

BARGE TOUR

An AC bus picks you up at 3 p.m., takes you to Soi 73 on outskirts of City. Board a fast craft for a trip thru large and small canals and past paddy fields to view country life. Stop made at a country house where you can ride a buffalo, watch a cockfight. Return to Bangkok is on a large, converted rice barge pulled by a tug. All you want to drink, fruit and hors d'oeuvres are included at $8.50.

ANCIENT CITY

This is a 200-acre outdoor museum where Thailand's most beautiful temples and historical monuments have been re-created (somewhat miniaturized though very imposing). In a way, this is old Thailand in miniature, for there are waterfalls, klongs, rural village and even a man-made mountain. Interesting data on the palaces and temples is posted in English. Elephants to ride, too. A tremendous, visionary project by a wealthy man, apparently out of love for his country as it's difficult to see how he'll recoup the huge expenditure.

When we wrote the above, admission was 50 Baht — now it's 200 ($10). So, he realizes now what we did then. Frankly, we wouldn't pay $10 to see it — plus extra fee for car or taxi to drive thru, take you from Bangkok and back. Best bet: an Ancient City Tour if you're two couples or a group. From $8 to $11 each, including transportation.

EVENING CRUISES

For groups, a Candlelight Cruise with supper around Bangkok can be arranged aboard the *Oriental Queen.*

For individuals, a converted 60-ft. teak barge, *Tahsaneeya,* departs from the Oriental Hotel at 6 and 8 p.m. for a cruise on the Chao Phya River past famous landmark Temples. Bar and food serviced by President Hotel. Carries 40 passengers, has a 12-man crew.

Best excursions outside Bangkok are these:

AYUTTHAYA & BANG PA-IN

If you go nowhere else outside Bangkok, be sure to visit the magnificent ruins (some restored) of this former capital and, enroute, the lovely grounds and buildings of the old Summer Palace.

55 miles from Bangkok, the ancient site is both imposing and stunning; with a little imagination, one conjures up the magnificence and pomp that was Siam. Here is the Chedi Sri Suriyothai, a memorial to the brave Queen Sri Suriyothai, who risked her life to save her beloved husband during elephant-back combat in 1563. Poo Khao Thong Monastery has a 260-ft.-high Chedi built in Mon style in 1569 and remodeled in Thai style in 1745. The Royal Palace consisted of five main buildings; one, Trimukh, was rebuilt by King Rama V in 1907. In the former Royal Chapel, a Buddha image 60 feet tall once stood — covered with 579 lbs. of gold (figure that out at $165 an ounce); the Chapel was burned by the Burmese to peel off the gold.

But the Phra Monkol Borpitr, one of the biggest seated Buddha images in bronze, does survive. Completed in 1620, it remains seated serenely before the Wat Phra Sri Sarnpet. In-

Babette Jacobs before one of the many treasures of Ancient City, a classical four-sided Buddha.

cidentally, possibly even more imposing is the tremendously long Reclining Buddha reposing roadside between (as we recall) Ayutthaya and Bang Pa-In — a great photographic prize.

At the entrance to the ruins is Chao Sam National Museum (closed M, T) which, among other things, houses various bronze images of Buddha 500 to 1,000 years old. Nearby are scores of restaurants (local specialty is shrimp) and shops selling all types of items (mostly junk).

Bang Pa-In (literally where king met girl named In) is a thoroughly delightful change of pace thing where one strolls thru the beautiful Palace grounds feeling every bit a king or queen. There are stunning Thai roofs featuring graceful serpents, a replica of a Peking Palace and Gothic Church, two buildings of Grecian lines and a Royal Pavilion in the center of a lagoon where the King received the homage of nobles from their barges.

The Palace itself is off limits, but the other buildings are visited and admired.

This delightful day's outing (also done in a half day) can be taken by tour bus, private car, seat in car or, preferably, by the *Oriental Queen* excursion.

"ORIENTAL QUEEN" TRIP

Best way to see Ayutthaya — one way by ship, other by bus. Tour 1 departs Bangkok daily (except M, F) from Oriental Landing at 8 a.m., returns by bus at 5 p.m. On Tour 2, bus departs Oriental Hotel and Siam Inter-Continental (8, 8:15) for Ayutthaya and then Bang Pan-In where boat is boarded for down-river trip. $23 includes coffee/tea and croissant, nice lunch aboard ship — a great day's outing.

The 146-ft. ship is very comfortable and un-crowded (as long as there aren't 200 aboard), completely air-conditioned with picture windows, outer decks and a dining salon below — and a good running commentary over the PA system. Great photography of klong life, strings of barges, water taxis, outboard canoes. Beautiful view of the Grand Palace and several Wats. You pass sampan villages similar to Hong Kong's though not as extensive, see teakwood carrying barges and teakwood houseboats (large sampans). As Bangkok is left astern, the country becomes more open and rural with small temples amidst stilt houses lining the banks.

Those taking this cruise need not take a Floating Market trip to see native life. And it's a far less commercial type of sightseeing; very relaxing, too, and a good change of pace for those who've been constantly on the go. One can even sunbathe — or sleep.

Before reaching Bang Pa-In, where the bus ride begins, a stop is made (20 min.) at Bird Sanctuary. The natives who sell simple but not unattractive ceramics (very cheap) are interesting, but the birds (open bill storks) are not — and they smell.

The return from Ayutthaya is over a good highway past fields being plowed with water buffalo, ditches where men and women fish; this is very flat land occasionally punctuated by dugout runabouts racing down a muddy klong. But the village roadside litter is appalling, ecology obviously unheard of; the boat trip is much more appealing and photogenic.

BY SPEEDBOAT TO BANG-PA

60- or 70-passenger speedboats depart hourly from 6 a.m. (last trip 3 p.m.) for the 3-hour trip (10B). Can then go by long-tail motorboat in 40 minutes to Ayuthaya (7B).

ROSE GARDEN TOUR

This might well be called Thai Roundup as the Thai Village Show (3 p.m. daily) presents a wedding ceremony, boxing, sword fighting, bull fighting, traditional dances, cock fighting, umbrella making and elephants at work. This should be included in every itinerary, especially if not going elsewhere in Thailand. Pickups at hotels around 1:15 with return trip (25 miles) after show.

Not a bad idea to stay overnight or longer here, particularly in one of the hotel's seven antique-style (but aircondition) Thai houses overlooking a lake, magnificent rose gardens, 300 species of tropical birds. There's boating on the canal, golf (18 holes) and tennis, Chinese and Thai food is served in the Riverside Restaurant, and Thai silk is woven here.

NAKORN PATHOM

The oldest city in Thailand was here when Buddhism was first introduced, became the prosperous capital of the country during the Dvaravati Empire (900 to 1400 A.D.), then was abandoned until 1853 when King Rama IV restored it.

Main attraction is the famed, 380-ft.-high Phra Pathom Chedi, oldest, largest and tallest in Thailand; its golden-tiled, bell-shaped dome topped by the graceful Chedi can be seen from miles away. During the last two days of October and first two of November, thousands of pilgrims flock to the Phra Pathom Chedi Fair, an especially colorful time for tourists to visit. Reconstruction of this ancient pagoda was begun by Rama IV, completed by his son.

56 km from Bangkok via a good highway, it also affords the opportunity of enjoying the so-

This is the famed Bridge on the River Kwai.

called Rural Floating Market, at nearby Damnoen Saduak village, with its colorful and lively (but touristy) atmosphere. Just beyond are some interesting caves at Ratchaburi.

Nakorn Pathom and the Floating Market are usually added to the Rose Garden Tour to make a full day's outing.

BRIDGE ON THE RIVER KWAI

In Kanchanaburi Province, about 80 miles west of Bangkok, a picturesque area of wild jungles and rugged hills, stands the bridge made famous by the movie. It is here in the Allied Soldiers' Cemetery that some 9,000 prisoners are buried, including many Americans and English who lost their lives while constructing the bridge and railway into Burma for the Japanese.

Kanchanaburi landing (Muang Kan for short), where the Big and Little Rivers meet, looks like a combination of old New Orleans (overhanging wooden balconies) and frontier shanty town. From here it's about 2½ miles to the foot of the Bridge on the River Kwai — a Hollywoodism that translates Bridge on the River River since Kwae (not Kwai) in Thai means River; actually, the bridge spans the Big River. Here you can enjoy a nice meal at the River Kwai Restaurant (who are the Thais to quibble with a good thing?), either walk or ride an engine across the bridge, take a boat to the Cemetery or up to some of the lower rapids of the Big River. Those wishing more than a day trip can find inexpensive lodgings at Wang Thong Bungalow or Floatel Hotel.

Kanchanaburi Tours operates regular AC bus service six times daily from Royal Hotel, Bangkok, to Kanchanaburi and return; OW fare is 30B. A special tourist train leaves Bangkok at 6 a.m. on Saturdays, Sundays, arrives back at 7 p.m. Visits made to the Great Pagoda, Bridge, Allied Cemetery and Sai Yok Waterfalls. Tour operators offer various day packages. If arranging your own tour by car, good idea to stop overnight at Rose Garden on way back to Bangkok.

Diethelm Travel, 544 Ploenchit Rd., Bangkok, a top operator, offers 2-, 3- and 4-day bus trips to River Kwai Village (see Hotel Directory) that include, besides the Bridge and Cemetery, such things as a boat trip, Death Railway tour, etc., plus swimming, fishing and elephant rides.

However taken, this is an enjoyable outing to spots not usually seen by tourists. Also to verify that the Bridge on the Big River was not, after all, destroyed by Bill Holden, Alex Guinness and Jack Hawkins.

ELEPHANT ROUNDUP

If planning a mid-November visit to Bangkok, take advantage of a very unusual happening — an Elephant Roundup of more than 200 of the behemoths with a dozen exciting events lasting three hours. Leave Friday evening, Nov. 16, 1979, on special sleeping cars, arrive in Surin in time to witness the next morning's events. After lunch a trip to the Khmer ruins of Phanom Rung Hill, time for shopping before returning. Arrive Bangkok 6 a.m. on 18th. Cost is $70 (Baht 1400) thru Tourist Organization of Thailand; advance rsv. necessary.

GETTING AROUND BANGKOK

Cabs are metered, but that doesn't mean a thing — so bargain (if you can be understood) and keep your cool. Else take a hotel taxi; it'll cost you more but usually is air-conditioned and insured (there are many times you're sure you're going to collect), and drivers speak some English, have been instructed to drive slowly. Many hotels have posted rates from one point to another; buy a chit at the porter's desk to give to the driver. We've had some hilarious experiences with regular cabs; once we passed the same point three times while, supposedly, being taken direct.

Samiors (3-wheeled scooter taxis) are numerous, fares low (but, again, determine them in advance).

THAI-STYLE DINING

If you like highly spiced food liberally laced with red chilis, you'll go for Thai dishes. Otherwise, except for many Chinese and some Japanese restaurants, stay with some of the very good restaurants specializing in various international cuisines.

However, you're almost sure to find Thai dishes served in the hotels to be a more bland "Thai food for foreigners" that goes well with Western stomachs. Same applies to restaurants specializing in Thai classical dancing — you'll enjoy the food and style of dining quite as much as the superb entertainment.

Rice is the staple of a Thai meal which usually consists of four or five dishes: soups of fish and meat, curries of beef, chicken or shrimp, then roast beef, pork or chicken — topped off with fruits or a very sweet dessert whose basic ingredient is coconut milk.

ENTERTAINMENT RESTAURANTS

Most have a set price that includes a table d'hote Thai meal (served around 7 p.m.) and entertainment (9:15 p.m.). Reserve in advance.
Baan Thai — Sukhumvit Rd Soi 32 (913013). Stately Thai house.
Maneeya Lotus Room — 518/4 Ploenchit Rd (opposite President Hotel). Splendid decor, delicious food. Phone: 56412.
Pinman — 46 Soi 49, Sukhumvit Rd (918017). Sukothai period with antiques, carved doors, elegant atmosphere; food served by traditionally costumed girls.
Sala Thai — Indra Regent Hotel. Authentic replica of 15th-century Thai resthouse luxuriously appointed. A top dance group is accompanied by a Thai orchestra (instead of usual taped music).
Sbaithong — Rajprasong Shopping Center. Table d'hote meals said to be superb; nostalgic, old Siamese setting.
Sukothai Room, Dusit Thani Hotel — Beautiful, traditional decor. Classical and folk dances nightly (except Sun.).
For Thai food without entertainment:
Preeda Room, Soi 8, Sukhumvit Rd — Upperclass Thai cuisine that Westerners like.

Royal Kitchen, Soi 30 Sukhumvit Rd — Upstairs in private house; genuine Thai atmosphere, good service, moderate.
Tahsaneenya Nava — Boat-restaurant cruises Chao Phya River every night for two hours. Departures at 6 and 8 p.m. Make reservations (38478).

INTERNATIONAL RESTAURANTS

All of the better hotels have good restaurants, with and without entertainment. However, even if you're not venturesome, at least try *Nick's No. 1* (1 Sathorn Rd), Bangkok's most famous dining spot that specializes in Kobe steaks, Hungarian dishes (like goulash, chicken paprika, schnitzel). Another famous restaurant *Normandie,* atop the old Oriental, is tres francais and romantic with an intriguing view of the Chao Phya lights, and the food is definitely superior, though a tourist may get less than attentive attention.

Jimmy's Kitchen, in New Imperial Hotel, is a favorite of locals as it's open 24 hours with any style food — Chinese, Japanese, Thai, Western. We had a very good Chinese dinner with marvelous, continuous entertainment (all-Chinese girl musicians, dancers, singers) at Indra Regent's *Ming Palace.* In Siam Square, *Neil's Tavern* is renowned for stuffed Phuket lobster, Kobe steaks, beef stroganoff and Vienna chocolate cake. *Chokchai Steak House,* atop a tall building on Sukhumvit Rd, has spectacular view of Bangkok At Night and equally fine steaks.

BANGKOK AT NIGHT

It's claimed to be the most varied in the Far East, from lavish on down, and not nearly as expensive as elsewhere.

Most nightclubs have hostesses, all are air-conditioned and have an admission of 80 Baht and up; open from 9 p.m. to 12 (1 a.m. on weekends). They're to be found by the score on Gaysorn and Ploenchit Roads. *Sani Chateau* on Gaysorn has glamorous hostesses, good floor show — but costly. At *Three Sisters,* also on Gaysorn, no trouble in going in for a drink, coming out with a gal. *Honey Club,* Suriwongse Rd, next to Manohra Hotel, is the biggest.

Patpong Road is a solid mass of bars, a happy hunting ground for the unattached. *Grand Prix* is busiest, oldest bar in town. Here, too, are *Don The Beachcomber* (unrelated to the original Don) and his go-go dancers, *Honey Club, Moulin Rouge, Rofeno, Roma* and *Joker Club,* to name a few of the more renowned.

On the refined side, you might enjoy mingling

THAI DANCING

with Bangkok's swinging youth at *Safari* (Siam Inter-Continental), the psychedelic cellar *An-An* (Montien Hotel), *Tropicana* (Hyatt Rama), *Cat's Eye (President)* and *Ali Baba* (Dusit Thani). In the elegant supper club class is the *Tiara* atop the Dusit Thani, *Tropicana* (Hyatt Rama), *The Den* (Indra Regent).

For top Thai singers, there's *Suzie Wong* (also unrelated) and *The Sida,* both on Rajdamnern Ave.

DRINKS

Imported liquor costs about the same as it does elsewhere in the world. However, hotels are very innovative when it comes to exotic drinks. Here are some of the Dusit Thani's concoctions: *Bangkok Blessing,* served in a hollowed-out pineapple; *Singing Bamboo* (ditto in bamboo); *Surin Special* (this time in a coconut) and *Bimbo,* out of an elephant (carved).

Don't leave without enjoying it, particularly the classical style which evolved, in ancient times, from the Indian epic, The Ramayana, but has since been given Thai interpretations so that today the various dances present the Thai personality and character.

Easiest way to see this lovely art form (along with Thai boxing, sword fighting, etc.) is at the Siam Inter-Continental at 11 a.m. on W, Sat. or at the Oriental Hotel every T, Th, Sun. at 10:30 a.m. But the best is to combine the classical dancing with a Thai dinner at one of the restaurants specializing in same (see previous list); we spent a wonderful New Year's Eve with friends doing just that. All presentations feature lavish, gorgeous costumes and the traditional, spiral headgear; meanings of the dances and their movements are explained in English, as is the menu and dining customs.

Folk dances are primarily agricultural in motif, costumes are plain and a dance team may be all female.

BANGKOK SHOPPING

Thai products are extremely reasonable and attractive. Famed Thai silks are exquisite, cotton prints stunning, silver and gold jewelry exotic, lacquerware and bronzeware unusual. Teak salad bowls are cheaper than anywhere else. Here's a quick rundown on the best of Thailand's offerings:

Good antiques are, as elsewhere, difficult to find and usually expensive, but they are to be found, either in the hotel arcades or, less expensively, in Chinatown off Yawarad Road, where you may find ancient Thai work in wood, gilt and bronze, also paintings and porcelain — even such exotic items as Shan war drums, Burmese elephant bells, Chinese antiques are expensive. Incidentally, there are many skilled craftsmen turning out excellent antique imitations so make sure you're not paying old antique prices for new ones.

Thai bronze is a rich copper shade, takes a steel-hard knife edge, is fruit acid-resistant and can be washed in warm water, polished with silver polish. Flatware place settings, usually with black buffalo horn or ivory handles and packed attractively in wood cases, make distinctive and practical gifts. Many other bronze items, including delightful sets of Thai temple (wind) bells.

Buddha and deity images are reproduced in large numbers; these are the only ones that can be exported, but a permit must be obtained from Dept. of Fine Arts (for deity images) and from it and the Dept. of External Trade for Buddha images.

Some really good hand- and machine-made Tai-ping carpets are sold by some rug stores on Ploenchit Rd.

Celadon is high-fired stoneware which, in its ancient Chinese form, is priceless. It's said that the formula for making it was lost for 300 years but has now been recreated in Chiang Mai. Modern Thai version retains the beautiful color and luster of the ancient ware but is quite cheap.

Thai dolls are truly beautiful and amazingly life-like. There are classical dancers in various poses, hill-tribe folk in colorful native dress, farmers, fishermen and street vendors. You can see them made at Bangkok Dolls, 85 Soi Rachataphan, Makkasan.

Thai silk needs little introduction except that besides the lightweight fabrics used in garments there's a heavier version much in demand by interior decorators worldwide. Incidentally, it takes a weaver a minimum of three hours to produce a yard of silk. Although this cottage industry was centuries old, it took an American, Jim Thompson, to make it an industry. Today, Thai Silk Co., which he started, alone employs better than 3,000 weavers.

Not so well known is Thai cotton, but it's most attractive and colorful and very well priced. A 3½-yard length, used by Thai women to make their pha-sins (sarongs) is usually the right length for a Western dress.

JEWELRY & GEMS

Shopping for jewelry is a major hobby because many precious and semi-precious stones are mined here, are quite cheap. Princess rings, made up from nine varieties of gems, are great buys, as are Harem rings (usually with one color of gem though sometimes with two or three). Earrings are also big — combinations of small pearls and turquoise, ruby and turquoise, sapphire and turquoise and on and on.

Thais invest in gold jewelry the way you put money in a bank. Good gold shops post the day's gold price — you pay that, plus 10% or so for design and labor.

One of the better, less expensive buys comes in fun jewelry which is produced here in quantity and with real talent in a variety of exotic-looking shapes and types.

Here's a quick rundown on gems:

Rubies — Burmese Mogok rubies are considered purest; Thai rubies are equally red but have slight brownish tinge, while Ceylon rubies have much more sparkle but lack depth of color. The ruby is of the same family, corundum, as sapphire.

Sapphires — Pailin type, a deep clear blue with a tinge of green, is best, most expensive and well received on world markets. Most common sapphire is the Bang-Ka-Cha, a very deep blue sometimes with a tint of green (undesirable hence very cheap); often recognized by silky streaks running thru them. Sapphires also come in red, pink, yellow, sherry, greenish blue and white; latter extremely rare, very expensive. Incidentally, emeralds are not indigenous but are imported from India (not as good as Colombian emeralds); often green sapphire is presented as emerald.

Star Sapphire — Very common and come in black, grey and blue. The better the star the higher the price. By the way, the star can always be seen even when the gem is cut into several pieces (also true of a star ruby). Best buy is a well-proportioned stone that's not too thick.

Zircon — Mostly from Thailand and Ceylon, it's goldish-brown but when placed under intense heat becomes blue, later a pure white. Because of its high sparkle, it's often called a Siam or Ceylon diamond — which means, beware of diamond claims in Thailand as they're not mined here. But white zircons are very common, very cheap. Blue zircons are more expensive as their heat treatment is chancy.

Recently, the art of lacquerware was given a boost by government subsidies to spur its revival; the Thai product is unlike that of Chinese or Japanese design, similar to that of Burma except the finish is said to be much better.

You'll see a lot of Nielloware, an essentially Thai product that looks like enamelware, but is actually a black amalgam of several metals, used in cuff links, bracelets, cigarette boxes, cocktail sets and similar ornaments and items. Quite interesting to see craftsmen engraving intricate designs (usually Hindu) on beaten silver, then filling in with black niello, after which it is heated until the black fuses with the silver, later polished. One of the places this is done is the backyard factory of Thai Nakon Co., 276 Chaprapetch Rd.

WHERE TO SHOP

Although prices of pure silk blouses have gone way up and jewelry about doubled, there's still much attractive merchandise at comparatively reasonable prices. For example, *Phorn Pen Thai Silk Co.,* 330 Silan Rd, makes custom blouses, dresses, etc., at half the price of Star of Siam; ask for owner Arunee Sukayamun.

The four-story *Siam Shopping Center,* opposite Siam Inter-Continental, had fine jewelry and fashion shops whose prices were

slightly lower than in the hotel arcades. Center has cocktail lounge and restaurant on the top floor.

Adjacent to the Oriental Hotel is *Thai Home Industries,* great for everything Thai; only stainless steel flatware we saw was here.

For local color, Weekend Market on Phramane Ground can't be beat. Open Saturdays, Sundays from sunrise to sunset, there's a vast assortment of flowers, foodstuffs and all types of Thai-manufactured products — including $4 watches that run. All in clean, neat stalls. Either take a cab, book one of the many Klong tours that come here or hire your own boat — but be sure to go in the early a.m. to see men, women and children, shaded by enormous straw hats, paddling their sampans to market. Avoid the Sunday afternoon crowds.

Best shopping advice: Bargain for everything, even in better shops. Remember, many English-speaking clerks are difficult to understand — have same *r* and *l* difficulties (Rand Lovel) as Japanese — so if down to critical bargaining, get them to write their quotes in numerals.

SPORTS

Thai boxing is a regulated form of mayhem in which boxers lash out with feet, knees, head, elbows and fists — and no below the belt rule. It's shown on TV (usually weekends), but it's more fun live with the fans and the music adding extra excitement. Two boxing stadiums present cards year 'round. Exhibitions of Thai boxing are given at Timland and Rose Garden, but again the real thing is better entertainment.

A fight card of eight bouts (last one usually regular boxing) lasts for about four hours; usually the fifth bout is the main event. Bouts are scheduled for five rounds of three minutes with two minutes between rounds.

A fight begins, after a short praying ritual, to the accompaniment of music which continues thruout to the tempo of the fight and adds to the excitement; during each round it increases in volume and pace. Audience participation keeps pace so that even a lousy fight is an entertaining production.

Bowling — Sukhontha has 24 lanes.

Cock and Fish Fighting — Rose Garden.

Horse Racing — Sat. at Royal Bangkok Sports Club, Sun. at Royal Turf Club from noon to 5 (12 races).

Golf — At above Clubs.

Thai Boxing — Lumpini Stadium on T, F, Sat at 6 p.m., Sat 1:30 p.m. Ringside costs Baht 165. Ratchadamnoen Stadium stages cards on M, W, Th at 6 p.m., Sun. at 5 and 8 p.m. 140 Baht for ringside seats.

CHIANG MAI

As fascinating as Bangkok is, it can no longer offer the provincial charm nor the close contact with Thais one gets in Chiang Mai *(Chang My)*. This lovely city, Thailand's second largest, with beautiful flowers, attractive klongs, good hotels, lies in a valley within a semi-circle of mountains. It has a more prosperous air than rural areas around Bangkok, homes are more substantial, many most attractive. Wandering thru small side streets is delightful, though hot (it's cooler in the mountains), the people are charming, many of the girls beautifully featured, its Cultural Center is excellent, and the Zoo has many gorgeous birds.

However, the trip north from Bangkok is not of prime importance and should be taken only by those who would not have to eliminate, because of timing, a place of major importance elsewhere in the Far East. But it's a great change of pace — we thoroughly enjoyed it — and a grand opportunity to pick up some real shopping bargains.

THINGS YOU SHOULD SEE & DO

Besides the shopping, which can take a major portion of your time, you'll want to see the Royal Family's Bhubing Palace grounds (open on Fridays, Saturdays, Sundays and holidays) for its gorgeously landscaped vistas and the riotously colored flowers (roses so huge they're hard to believe). This is 26 km from the city, 6 km beyond (and usually included in the tour) is what's booked as a visit to exotic Meo tribesmen (over a very rough road); acutally, this village is very poor, its scraggly inhabitants pathetic. They have a rather striking black costume, but that's reserved for appearances elsewhere when they get paid for being photographed. A primitive race that still believes in spirits.

The best tour (half day) is called Sutep Mountain and takes in Wat Phra Dhat Doy, a sacred temple and a stiff 200-step climb (we found the magnificent rose garden easier to take); Wat Chedi Jed Yod, a seven-spired structure; Wat Suan Dork, site of the important Songkran mid-April Festival, contains relics of Lord Buddha while many of the small pagodas house ancestors of Royal Family; Wat Chiang Man, oldest monastery here (1300) which contains Chiang Mai's most valuable Buddha images, one of which is made of precious stones. On weekends, Bhubing Palace is included. Usually taken from 9 a.m. to 12.

The afternoon Handcrafts Village Tour was, except for the Umbrella Village, a waste of time and money in our opinion. The villages are merely rows of shops with merchandise more easily purchased in Chiang Mai. But watching umbrellas being made was something else. You see men pound the pulp, dry it in the sun. Others make and sew the finished paper into umbrellas, then small boys paint them — a family project. Families live upstairs in teakwood stilt houses, the lower part enclosed for shop or factory. A stop at the Celador kilns was enjoyable, not only to see the pottery being fired but also the beauty of trees and flowers surrounding the kilns.

Another tour is to the White Karen Hill Tribe, of Tibeto-Burmese stock and an agricultural people. This is a 9 to 1 trip — but after our experience with Meos, the idea of seeing Karens was not intriguing. It does, however, take you further out into the countryside past the villages of Lampoon and Pasang. By the way, anyone interested in the six hill tribes of northern Thailand should visit the Tribal Research Center at the University here.

WHAT TO BUY — AND WHERE

You really can have a field day here as this area is famous for its lacquerware, woodenware and wood carvings, silks and cottons, silverware, jewelry and antiques. Because of increasing tourism, conditions might have changed since we were here a year and a half ago, but merchandise bought here represented huge savings for comparable things in the States, even 20% or so less than in Bangkok. We're ashamed to say what we paid for a huge and stunning teak salad bowl, eight small salad bowls and large serving fork and spoon — so we won't.

There are so many shops here there's no need of a list. Except for *Chiangmai Carving* at 144 Rajah Rd. (where we bought our salad bowl set) and *Chiangmai Antiques,* a branch of the former at 21 Wualai Rd., for Thai silks and cottons (very reasonable), silverware and jewelry.

Under no circumstances fail to visit *Old Chiang Mai Cultural Center* at 185/3 Wualai Road — those who like the unusual in antiques and replicas of same, like Temple Lions, Victory Drums, handcarved wood panel screens, will go crazy.

You'll save a lot of time and energy — and still get the best — by using the above named for most of your purchases. And you can bargain, too. These and other of the better stores can be relied upon to ship purchases for you; ours arrived in about two months.

DON'T LEAVE WITHOUT ENJOYING A KANTOKE

This is a northern Thai-style banquet, featuring Thai specialties, where guests are served while sitting shoeless and cross-legged on matting or carpeting and reclining against a back cushion. Very Oriental, very delicious. We were told that the best *Kantoke* and folk entertainment were those put on at the *Cultural Center* — and they were standouts. Dinner is from 7 to 9 p.m. (come earlier to shop), followed by the one-hour Hill Tribe Show. The folk music and traditional dancing (different from what you see in Bangkok) was most entertaining, the finger and candle dances particularly delightful, the girls beautiful, and the sword dance simply great. Cost of this double feature is around $10-$11 per person.

Some hotels also have a weekly *Kantoke* as well as serving western-style food. Too, there's excellent and inexpensive Thai dining in the gardens of *Chitr Pochana*.

Almost forgot — before you leave, be sure to smoke at least one *Chalyo* — a long cigarette wrapped in a banana leaf.

All in all, you'll enjoy your Chiang Mai safari.

THE WEATHER

Cooler than down south with Oct.-Jan. a moderate 70⁰ (but can get chilly at nights). Balance of year is warmer (as high as 90⁰) with monsoon rains in summer.

Leave your heavy luggage in Bangkok, bring only informal clothes. Men don't need jackets.

FESTIVE EVENTS

Great time to be here is in late Oct. or early Nov. for *Loy Krathong,* Festival of Lights. Thousands of *krathongs,* lotus-shaped banana leaf boats, with an offering of betel nut, flowers or a small coin, are lighted with candles and floated down the Mai Ping River, which winds thru the city. During *Songkran,* the Thai New Year, hotels are sold out months in advance for this exuberant affair.

LOCAL TRANSPORTATION

Although there are the usual cars and buses for sightseeing, if you really want a fun adventure, take one of the many mini buses (small pickups with homemade superstructure) into the country — to Wat Phra Dhat Doy, even

beyond to the Meo village. Sitting hunched over as you must (the roof is *very* low), it'll be one of the most uncomfortable rides you've ever had, but also one of the most hilarious, with all your Thai busmates laughing along with you. Costs a pittance, of course.

WAYS TO GET HERE

Most Bangkok tour operators offer two- and three-day packages by bus, air, train — or a combination of two. We'd say that two full days, preferably on a weekend to see the Palace grounds, are sufficient.

FITs can leave at 7:30 a.m. on Thai Air (9:10 arrival), leave late the next afternoon or at 9:30 following morning. But air reservations must be made well in advance, *including return flight which should be reconfirmed upon arrival;* bookings are very solid.

Night train leaves Bangkok at 5:05 p.m., arrives 9:40 a.m. Fly back or take the train at 4:10 p.m. Buses are available both ways (9-10 hours) morning and night; latter is very popular (airplane-type reclining seats) as it saves a night's lodging.

No, this is not Pattaya Beach — but on the way down, and on all drives out of Bangkok, this is the type of rural scene you'll be seeing.

PATTAYA BEACH RESORTS

Very popular with Asian and European groups due to the many good hotels with comparatively low rates — in fact the only international-class beach resort in Asia — we don't see many North Americans becoming enthused over it since better and more congenial resorts are much closer to home.

Pattaya *(pah-TAH-yah)* lies along a narrow stretch of beach on the Gulf of Thailand 154 km (95 miles) southeast of Bangkok, connected by a good highway that runs thru some picturesque countryside. Reached in three hours by air-conditioned buses (about $6 RT); stop is usually made first at Bangsaen Resort.(closer to Bangkok but definitely not for Americans). You can hire air-conditioned cars for about $30 OW. Taxis from Pattaya charge about $20 to Bangkok. Some hotels pick up guests at the airport in Bangkok (for a fee), return them there if desired.

There's something of everything here: sailing, water-skiing, scuba diving, deep-sea angling, water scooters, moonlight cruises, speedboats, para-sailing, jungle tours, horseback riding, tennis, wind surfing, excellent golfing. And Thai dances.

OTHER PLACES, OTHER THINGS

A number of other resorts, nice as they are, are not yet of international class, though Phuket Island, 921 km south of Bangkok enroute to Malaysia, is being carefully planned for that type of development. Presently there's two small but nice beach hotels. Coastline is said to be magnificent, has many lovely beaches.

Further south, and on the bus route to Penang, Kuala Lumpur and Singapore, is Haadyai, one of the country's richest cities. It has shops, shops, shops. Great for buying silks, cottons and batiks as they specialize in cloth.

A final place worth noting is Saraburi, 108 km north of Bangkok. Its Phra Buddha Badh Shrine (Shrine with the Holy Footprint of Buddha) is an exquisite thing and is surrounded by a number of enormous bells. Wonderful time to come here is during the Shrine's Festival (usually early Feb.) when Buddhists gather with candles, incense and flowers to pay homage. Take it as a full-day drive out of Bangkok.

Indra's attractive pool area. In the background is Sala Thai, a replica of a 15th-century resthouse, where Thai dances are presented.

Hotel Directory

10% service, 8¼% government tax added to room rates, *quoted here* (double) *in US dollars.* Most hotels add 5½% food-beverage tax — 11% with entertainment.

BANGKOK

There are many good hotels, several superb ones, and a few that are real bargains (you'll recognize them by their rates). All have air-conditioning (or air cooling), most have pools, shopping arcades, good restaurants and bars. All inspected by the Jacobs.

AMARIN — Near Embassy section. Thai decor in 220 R. Chinese, Japanese, Western dining, nightclub. Pool. *Conv:* 300. $19.

CHAVALIT (FC) — 247 R; 530 R new wing is great. A real jumping hotel with coffee shop, Chinese, Japanese and Royal Grill. Nightclub on 7th floor; Oscar Club is true go-go. Pool. Good service and well priced. Popular with Japanese/European tours. *Conv:* 1200. At Sukhumvit Rd. From $20.

DUSIT THANI (DL) — Huge, elegant, pagoda shape hi-rise. Lobbies and pool area w/waterfalls stunning. 525 small R can be noisy. 5 rsts, rooftop nightclub; pool. When service and employees are gracious, the place is sensational. *Conv:* 1600. *Rsv:* Western. $35-$42.

ERAWAN (FC) — Thai atmosphere prevails; public rooms beautifully furnished, teakwood walls. Good food in 6 rsts; Chelsea bar (exp) has English club atmosphere, Ambassador nightclub is staid. Charming pool and tropical gardens. 210 AC R are old-fashioned, high ceilings. Popular with Europeans. *Conv:* 300. $38-$45.

HYATT RAMA (FC+) — Well located DT. 516 AC R have been remodeled. New pool, closed-circuit movies, lounging area; tennis courts. Seafood rst, coffee shop, grill, Tropicana nightclub. Attentive service. *Conv:* 800. $31-$39.

INDRA (DL) — Luxurious — even to teak elevators. Exquisite pool area, garden bar; Ming Palace Chinese Rst serves Chinese food. Sala Thai rst features Thai dancing, garden room serves buffet luncheons. Den nightclub has good mod music. 500 AC R are beautifully decorated, Thai furniture; SU are huge with colored TV, rfg, finest appointments, 2 tiled baths. *Conv:* 1500. $36 and up.

MANDARIN — 210 AC R on Rama 4 Rd, center of city but not main business section. Modern decor; hotel being refurbished. Rst overlooks pool. Coffee shop, bar. Conference rooms, shopping arcade. Popular w/Japanese, Chinese. $23.

MONTIEN (FC+) — Great for those wanting to be in center of business area. Not as commercial as Sheraton. Attractive courtyard entrance; beautiful garden and pool area. Reasonable dining. 400 AC R w/rfg in new wing, 200 AC R w/rfg, balcony in old. An-An Room (psychedelic cellar) is a non-stop blast. *Conv:* 700. $34-$39.

NARAI — Well located — popular with Japanese groups. Revolving rst, German beer cellar, Carousel Bar is it for hard drinking amongst soft lights. Pool. 519 AC R, modern hi-rise. *Conv:* 1400. $25 up.

ORIENTAL (DL) — Beautiful gardens and pool area overlook Chao Phya River (only hotel that does). All the excitement of waterfront (watching the sampans, barges) with interior refinements. No other hotel here quite like it — definitely for the discriminating. Former lobby (in original section, w/120 quaint R) is now a salon, European style with special menu and music. Lovely rooftop Normandie Rst. New riverview wing has 285 large, tastefully furnished, luxury R. $39-$63.

PRESIDENT (FC) — Very attractive Chinese decor in lobby and 420 AC R w/tremendous closet space, soft beds. Thai food and service is good. Cat's Eye Room with entertainment is "in." A modern hotel with oriental feeling. Pool. Shopping arcade. *Conv:* 1000. $35-$37.

ROSE GARDEN (FC) — New resort complex 38 km S on Nakorn Chaisri River. 80 R, SU w/rfg, balcony. $16-$35. Antique Thai houses, $28. 2 rsts serve Thai, Chinese, Western cuisine. On lovely grounds with orchards, boats. 18-hole golf course, tennis, Thai Cultural Show daily.

SHERATON (FC) — Center of business district. Popular with businessmen, groups. 254 AC commercial R. Tawana coffee shop. Rsts, bars. Swinging music in the Cavern. Pool. *Conv:* 1200. $28-$35.

SIAM INTER-CONTINENTAL (DL) — 411 AC R low-rise built in several sections. Magnificent pool and garden area within 26 acres. Several rsts, bars; top service in coffee shop. Thai entertainment, dancing in main dining room. Jumping hotel makes up for unimaginative rooms. AC taxi service (also at Oriental); tell doorman where you want to go and pay in advance (no haggling). Across from Siam Shopping Center (don't miss). $41-$50.

VIENGTAI — Close to central market in Banglumpoo. Good economy hotel. 110 AC simple rooms in newest section are recommended (40 others are not). 2 rsts, bar, small pool. Attentive service. $10.

On weekends, book in advance; advise hotel time of arrival for complimentary transportation.

CHIANG INN (FC) — Opened late '74 with 175 R. Chinese rst, grill, nightclub. Pool. *Conv:* 200. $22 up.

CHANG PEUK — DT on Chotana Rd. Opened '74.

NOPPAKOA (FC+) — DT. 400 R opened in '78. Has excellent *Coq d'Or* rst.

RINCOME (FC) — In residential area, 15 min from airport/railway. 160 R, SU w/good beds, balconies. Thai-style decor. Exceedingly pleasant service. Attractive pool and dining area (food passable). Supper club. $20-$22.

SURIWONGSE — Good location for walking around town. 250 simple R. Dining room, bar, pool. $17.

PATTAYA BEACH

Because of its economy and a rash of new hotels, this has become an extremely popular destination for European and Japanese tour groups — Instant Group Tropics no less. But Americans and Canadians have superior beach resorts much closer to home — an Asian Puerto Vallarta it ain't despite more lavish hotels. We've been here, found it lacking in ambience. October-May double rates are higher than those quoted below (US dollars).

ASIA PATTAYA (FC) — Hilltop overlooking Gulf of Siam. 270 AC R, SU with ocean or mountain views. Several rsts, bars, a nightclub, 9-hole golf, tennis in 22-acre site; 4 pools, private beach, marina. Conv: 1200. $22-$25.

HOLIDAY INN (FC) — 360 R have ocean view/balcony. Rsts, grill, nightclub, bars. 2 tennis courts, pool. Airport transfer from Bangkok B650. $25-$30.

HYATT PATTAYA PALACE (FC+) — Across road from palm-studded (narrow) beach. 220 AC R, SU with refrig. Two pools, two tennis courts, mini-golf amidst gardens; sport center has para-sailing, scuba equip., ponies. Nightly dancing. Thai entertainment; several rsts. Conv: 350. $23-$28.

OCEAN VIEW — Our choice for small, quiet, tastefully decorated (Thai decor), informal hotel w/120 R. Across from broad beach, many rsts and shops nearby. Lush gardens, pool, tennis courts. Dining room, beer garden, bars. $19.

ORCHID LODGE (FC) — Extensive, beautiful grounds w/elephant. Very spacious with 2 lighted tennis courts, miniature golf, badminton. 2 pools (one very large), 250 yds of beach. Rst, nightclub, snack bar. 176 individually AC R, 14 have terrace, 6 loggias. $19-$25. AC coach service to Bangkok.

PATTAYA (FC) — Formerly Regent Pattaya. On beach. 300 R. Several rst, plus seafood floating rst. Rooftop nightclub, 4 cocktail lounges. Outdoor Thai dancing. Pool, tennis courts, miniature golf. All water sports. Conv: 160. $25-$28.

ROYAL CLIFF (DL) — Overlooks Royal Cliff Bay. Opened '75 with 650 AC R, SU w/balcony. Several rsts, bars, nightclub, bowling alley. All water facilities. Pool. Tennis; 2 golf courses nearby. Conv: 1200. $23-$31.

SIAM BAYSHORE (FC) — Opened '75 facing Gulf. 279 AC R, SU amidst 20 acres of tropical gardens. Several rsts, cocktail lounges. 2 pools, 4 tennis courts, all boating facilities. $23 up.

SIAM COUNTRY CLUB — 20 minutes inland from Gulf. Mountains/golf view R with private bath, music, some w/rfg. Rst, bar. Par 72 rolling, hilly golf course is well maintained; greens dry in 15 min. Pretty pool, tennis, riding.

TROPICANA (FC) — 120 R, 2 rst, coffee shop. Pool. Weekly barbecues, Thai dances. $23.

RIVER KWAI

RIVER KWAI VILLAGE — 125 miles from Bangkok by bus or by train/-boat. 5 single-story longhouses each w/12 R (economy class); separate longhouse w/rst and bar surrounds courtyard with waterfall pool; orchid house. $22 includes tax, service. Rsv: Diethelm Travel, 544 Ploenchit Rd, Bangkok. Best to take package tour with Diethelm.

PHUKET ISLAND

PEARL — 250 R and pool in tropical setting. Rooftop rst, nightclub, bowling alley. Beach Club. $18-$22.

PHUKET ISLAND RESORT — Beach resort with fishing, scuba diving, golf, tennis. Sea view rst specializes in seafood. Indoor/outdoor dining. 194 AC R and bungalows on 54 acres of tropical beauty. $20-$27.

Peninsular Malaysia *(Mah-LAY-see-ah)*, 456 miles long by about 200 miles wide, extends from southern Thailand in the north to the state of Johore Bahru, just across the straits from Singapore, in the south. Here is gentle, rolling, rural country accented by hills, palms, beaches (on both east and west coasts), bananas and trees, and centrally bisected north to south by a mountain range of greenery. A land where rubber trees thrive on 50,000,000 acres of land bearing some 360 trees to an acre — most extensive in Johore with some in the far north. It includes a sophisticated capital, Kuala Lumpur, the charming, northern beach resort island of Penang, the Genting Highlands gambling resort, fine hotels, good shopping and a variety of sports. It also includes, on its East Coast, one of the least publicized and most charming beach areas of the Orient where, from May to September, huge turtles swim in to make their multiple egg deposits.

That, briefly, is West Malaysia, about 130,000 sq. miles in all. Little known and far more remote is East Malaysia, an entirely separate entity, just below the typhoon belt, on the world's third largest island — Borneo. Here, along the northwestern coast, are the states of Sabah and Sarawak; the balance of Borneo belongs to Indonesia and Brunei. And here is a fascinating world, almost unexploited, that no doubt will be explored more thoroughly by tourists of the 1980s; even now there is a small trickle, by ship and plane, into a few cities. There are almost no roads. Three-fourths of Sarawak, about the size of England and Wales, is inaccessible rain forest. Sabah, about half the size, has Mt. Kinabalu (13,455 ft.), highest peak (which, usually, can only be seen at dawn) in southeast Asia; here, according to the natives, is the final resting place of the spirits of their ancestors.

A BRIEF HISTORY

The present Federation of Malaysia, reputed to be one of the most democratic nations in Asia (though with vicious in-fighting between the Muslim majority and the affluent Chinese minority), came into being on September 16, 1963. It incorporated the 11 states of the Federation of Malaya — which, as a Malayan Union, had emerged from British control in 1957 — the British Crown Colonies of North Bornea (Sabah) and Sarawak and the state (former Crown Colony) of Singapore; the latter seceded in August of 1965 but remains closely integrated.

For hundreds of years, these states were Sultanates — and still are under the federal government. However, the British had been firmly established in Malacca, Penang and the Borneo states since the 1800s. On December 7, 1941, Japan landed on the east coast at Kota Bharu and by the end of January of 1942 controlled the whole peninsula. But on September 13, 1945, Kuala Lumpur was the scene of the surrender. The British then established their Crown Colonies while the Federated and Unfederated States became a Malayan Union. From 1948, the country had to contend

This is Penang where trishaws are part of the ambience and autos seem out of place. In the background is the Clocktower built in 1897, in commemoration of Queen Victoria's Diamond Jubilee, by a private citizen, Mr. Chia Chen Eok.

with attempted Communist domination, but, by 1960, democracy was and continues to be firmly in control.

This is the only country where the Royal Head of State (Yang di-Pertuan Agong) and his deputy (Timbalan Yang di-Pertuan) are elected by secret ballot of the Rulers of the 13 states; both hold office for five years. The Cabinet is appointed by Head of State from members of the House of Parliament, composed of a 58-member Senate and 154-member House of Representatives. 32 of the Senate are appointed by Head of State, 26 (two from each state) are elected by the state legislatures and serve six years. House of Representatives is elective for five years; 114 are from Peninsular Malaysia, 24 from Sarawak and 16 from Sabah.

As in all nations with British origins, the Prime Minister wields executive power and, in fact, advises the Head of State who to appoint to the Cabinet.

Two of the 11 Peninsular states have Governors, others Rulers; each has its own state government. The Borneo states have a Chief Minister and, since they're a long way from Kuala Lumpur, possibly more self-determination (Sabah is establishing its own airline). The capital, Kuala Lumpur, has a similar status to Washington, D.C.; administered by a Commissioner and his Advisory Board.

Malaysia has been built on tin and rubber; the latter, introduced in 1876-77 from Brazil by way of London, accounts for 32% of its export earnings while supplying 44% of the world's requirements for natural rubber. As a consequence, the country is flourishing, its currency and economy very stable.

Peninsular or West Malaysia has about 4,450,000 Islamic Malays, 3,300,000 Chinese, maybe 1,000,000 Indians and around 150,000 others, of whom 15,000 or so are Westerners. On the other hand, 64% of the urban citizens are Chinese, only 23% Malays.

Islam is the official state religion and is headed by the Yang di-Pertuan Agong. However, there is complete religious freedom, thus providing the visitor with a host of colorful religious festivities to view.

That, in a general way, is Malaysia. But before passing along to specifics, let us say quite firmly that the country deserves far better treatment from North American tour operators than it has been receiving, viz: at best a day or so in Kuala Lumpur, at worst a blithe disregard as groups hop from Singapore to Bangkok or Hong Kong. Frankly, we much prefer Malaysia's East Coast, for example, to Singapore. Nothing wrong with the latter, understand, except it's far from unique and can be easily duplicated elsewhere — whereas the East Coast is and can't.

ENTRY REQUIREMENTS

Passport and smallpox certificate. No visa required for up to 90 days. As in all countries, yellow fever immunization necessary only if coming from infected areas.

CURRENCY

M$2.36 = $1 US, or each Malaysian dollar is approximately 42¢; multiply Malaysian prices by .4 to get approximate US dollar price. Malaysian and Singapore dollars are interchangeable. Notes come in denominations of M$1, 5, 10, 50, 100 and 1,000.

MALAYSIAN TRIP PLANNING

A stopover in Kuala Lumpur is better than not seeing Malaysia at all — but try to do more than that.

When coming this far, we'd settle for nothing less than Penang, East Coast of Peninsular Malaysia and KL, particularly since it's done in logical sequence. Coming from Bangkok, stop off in Penang, fly to Kota Bahru, travel down the East Coast and across to KL by road. Admittedly the road segment is not inexpensive as car or bus must be sent to Kota Bahru from KL but worth it. Reverse the routing when coming from the south.

Seeing little-visited East Malaysia is surprisingly easy. Fly from Hong Kong or Manila to Kota Kinabalu, thence to

Brunei, Kuching and on to Singapore or direct to Kuala Lumpur.

West coast of West Malaysia can be seen by bus or train. Unlimited train passes (two weeks of travel) cost $62.50. Masmara Tours has bus tours to east and west coasts from KL, Singapore, Penang and Bangkok.

MALAYSIAN FACTS

Airport Service Charge — M$7 for Int'l flights (passengers arriving/departing within 72 hrs. exempt). M$4 to Singapore, M$2 for domestic flights.

Climate — Tropical, except in Highlands, with generally cool nights. Rains almost daily (afternoons, evenings) with Sept.-Nov. heaviest on west coast, Oct.-March on east coast (Dec. monsoon season the wettest). Annual rainfall: 80 to 100 inches

Clothing — Lightweight, informal. Rainwear essential.

Convention Facilities — Excellent, both public and hotels; all audio-visual aids. Negara Stadium has facilities for 8,500.

Current — 230v, 50c; better hotels have 110v adapters.

Customs — Reasonable personal effects; 1 bottle liquor.

Economy — Prosperous, stable; even in rural areas, people are well dressed, contented, happy. Rubber, tin, timber and rice are the basics.

Language — Bahasa Malay, Chinese, Hindi and English.

Mail — Letters to North America, M$1.10; postcards, M$0.55.

Population — 10,450,000. Kuala Lumpur has 910,000.

Time — Half hour behind Hong Kong; same as Singapore.

Tipping — Hotels add 10% service, 5% tax. Restaurants, nightclubs usually add 10%.

Tourist Information — Malaysian Tourist Information Centre, 600 Montgomery St., San Francisco 94111 (415 788-3344). In Kuala Lumpur, P.O. Box 329; phone 89837 or 80507

Transportation — Taxis still inexpensive. In KL, most drivers speak some English. Rate is M50¢ for first mile, M20¢ each half mile thereafter. About M$5 per hour. M10¢ added for each passenger over two. From airport to hotels, about M$8; allow an hour during rush hours.

Water — Okay, even from taps.

HOW TO GET HERE

There are non-stop jets from Bangkok, Hong Kong, Jakarta, Manila and Singapore; one-stop from Tokyo.

For direct rail and bus connections with Singapore and Thailand, see schedules under Bangkok and Penang.

FESTIVALS & HOLIDAYS*

An * indicates Public Holiday. Dates are for 1978.

January — New Year's Day. Thaipusam (24th) — Hindu devotees pierce their bodies with skewers, walk on fire as fulfillment of a vow or act of repentence; holiday in Penang. Mandi Safar — Malays bathe in certain rivers to rid selves of mishaps/sickness.

February — Federal Territory Day (1st). Chinese New Year (7-8). Birthday of Jade Emperor (God of Heaven) — Food offerings placed outside Chinese houses. Ban Hood Huat Huay — Buddhists throng Kek Lok Si Temple in Penang for 12-Day Observance.

March — Chingay Procession in Johore State (10th). Birthday of Prophet Mohammed* (13th) — Rallies, processions; especially large, colorful in Kuala Lumpur.

April — Palm Sunday Procession (3rd), St. Peter's Church, Malacca.

May — Wesak Day* (2nd) — Buddhist celebration highlighted by impressive Lantern procession. Kandazan Harvest Festival, Sabah State (13-15). Kota Belud Tamu Besar, an annual market day for Kota Belud (48 miles from Kota Kinabalu) that's sensationally colorful. Bachok Festival — 2-week cultural event in Bachok, State of Kelantan (kite flying, giant top spinning, dances, etc.).

June — Birthday of Supreme Head of State* (1). Dragon Boat Festival (21). Feast of St. Peter (29) in Malacca.

August — Festival of the Hungry Ghost (28) — Lavish Chinese food offerings to the ancestral spirits; opera and puppet shows. National Day of Malaysia* (31) — Commemorates formation of Malaysia, celebrated with much much pomp/ceremony.

October — Festival of Nine Emperor Gods; firewalking on the ninth day.

November — Deepavali* (10), joyous Hindu commemoration of the killing of the demon by Lord Krishna.

December — Christmas.* Month-long carnival in Penang.

WEST MALAYSIA

KEY

Main Roads
Railways
National Parks
Beach Resorts
Hill Resorts

THAILAND

Pulau Langkawi
Kangar
Alor Star
Georgetown
Butterworth
Penang
Maxwell Hill
Taiping
Ipoh
Cameron Highlands
Pulau Pangkor
Lumut
Fraser's Hill
Templer Park
Genting Highlands
Port Klang
Kuala Lumpur
Port Dickson
Seremban
Malacca

Kota Bharu
Pulau Perhentian
Pulau Redang
Kuala Trengganu
Kuala Dungun
Taman Negara (National Park)
Kuala Lipis
Jerantut
Kemaman
Kuantan
Mentakab
Gemas
Pulau Tioman
Mersing
Kota Ti
Johore Bahru

SINGAPORE

213

KUALA LUMPUR

Commonly called KL, the capital of Malaysia is a beautiful, modern city with an exciting mixture of architectural styles, one of the most stunning airports in the world, a lovely, 16-mile drive along a winding river that brings you into the heart of a very with-it city. Don't let anyone talk you out of visiting Kuala Lumpur *(KWAH-lah LOOM-poor)*.

KL's tour operators have one of the fullest, most interesting day tours we've ever taken. Good values, too, either as two 3-hour tours (a.m. and p.m.) or combined 4½-hour tour; seat in coach or private car basis. Matter of fact, these are so well organized that one could, if time's a factor, see all of KL's most interesting facets in a single day: Chinatown, Railway Station (looks like a Moorish mosque, the most unusual RR architecture you'll ever see), many buildings of Chinese and Moorish design, beautiful Lake Gardens, stunning National Monument (to World War II Allied dead; wonder what Japanese think when they look at their prostrate warrior?) and Parliament House.

National Museum is extremely interesting, particularly the ground-floor Cultural History Displays of old Muslim and Chinese life styles, houses, furniture and costumes; fascinating shadow play exhibits. Natural History section has unusual displays (to an Occidental) of Giant Flying Squirrels, Flying Lemurs and a Malayan Scrow (wild goat) the size of a deer. Open 10 a.m. to 6:30 p.m. daily (closed 12-2 Fridays); free admission.

The tour continues along beautiful Ampang Road (Ambassador's Row), KL's finest residential area, and on into the countryside to a batik factory, rubber factory, Selangor Pewter factory and the unusual Batu Caves, a Hindu shrine to which one climbs 272 steps (there's also a small cable car). Not to be missed when Thaipusam Festival occurs (Jan. or Feb.). A Natural History Museum and Hindu Mythology Caves have been added.

A visit to the stunning National Mosque, largest in Southeast Asia, is also included. Harper's Tours is one of the better operators.

OTHER PLACES, OTHER TOURS

Mimaland — Malaysia in Miniature (11 miles from KL) features a Malaysian village, rubber plantation, botanical gardens, 30-acre lake, jungle treks, restaurants, handcrafts, orchid farm and more. In fact, you can live in a *bagan* (stilt house) over the lake if you wish (M$30 to $50). Admission is M$2.

Pineapple Hill, reached by bubble car from Jalan Weld or chair lift from Jalan Ampang, is a jungle area with aviary, orchid pavilions. Restaurant has a spectacular view.

Safari Park, at the National Zoo, has 44-passenger buses that traverse the area.

Everyone is taken on the tour to Malacca. *Try to resist it.* Although the latter part of the drive enroute to the city, founded by the Chinese and occupied by Portuguese and Dutch, is like one of our attractive Teng batiks — quaint Minangkabau stilt houses with peaked roofs seen thru lattices of rubber trees or against a framework of palms and bananas — it's not worth $15 US or more per person; you can see more attractive colonial cities closer to home (in South America, the Caribbean). If you still must go, take an express bus for the 90-mile drive; they depart Jalan Pudu in KL at 8 and 10 a.m., 1 and 3 p.m. (M$3 OW).

If going to Singapore by road, Malacca can be seen enroute. However, from what we've seen of Jahore, the state adjoining Singapore, it's the least scenic part of Malaysia — better to fly than be bored.

Other regularly scheduled tours: Night Tour (includes Malay Cultural Show), Cottage Industries & Handicrafts — both 3 hours. There are day packages to Mimaland, Genting Highlands, Fraser's Hill — longer ones to Cameron Highlands, Penang, the East Coast (latter 3 or 4 days).

DINING & DRINKING
Malay Style

Cuisine is spicy but not as hot as Indonesian; prepared with lots of coconut milk. Rice dishes with chicken curries, fish, prawns or beef predominate. *Nasi lemak*, rice cooked in coconut milk with fried eggs and cucumbers, is usually eaten in the mornings. Coffee shops sell *nasi padang*, a variety of specialties; *satay* (described in Singapore section) is not to be missed. Other goodies: *gado-gado* (green vegetables w/peanut sauce), *nasi kerabu* (rice w/oriental herbs), *serunding* (shredded beef w/spices), *korma ayam* (chicken, potatoes w/curry).

Top Malaysian specialty, however, is the Steamboat — a large, circular urn which has a hole in the center thru which live charcoal is dropped to heat the broth in the urn; diners then drop delicacies of their choice — fish, prawns, chicken, vegetables — into the broth to cook. A companionable, fun dinner.

Merlin and Regent hotels have regular nights on which they combine a Malaysian Cultural·Show with typical Malay dinner. Other hotels do the same on special occasions or for large groups. Many regularly feature the Malaysian Buffet at lunch and/or dinner.

For more information on Malaysian cuisine and restaurants (with addresses), get *Eating Out*, a well-researched folder published by the Tourist Development Corp. Here's a quick rundown on some of the best restaurants, number of which we've enjoyed.

Most typically Malaysian are the inexpensive night eating stalls serving Malay, Indian and/or Chinese food. Open from 6 or 7 p.m. to 1 a.m. at five different Jalan (Road) locations, at Benteng (River Embankment) and the Sunday Market (on Sat. night). Good Malay specialty restaurants: *Bintang, Budaya, Sri Yazmin* (has cultural show) and *Majid Satay House.*

Le Coq D'or, 121 Jalan Ampang, in a lovely old mansion filled with antiques, serves excellent French and int'l specialties. For Indian food, *Akhbar* and *Bilal*. Some of the top Chinese places: *Fatt Yow Yuen, Kum Leng, Hakka, Dragon Court* (Merlin Hotel), *Mandarin Palace* (Federal Hotel) and *Lee How Fook.*

For a light lunch, try the restaurant at Weld Supermarket and *Palong* in the Ampang Shopping Complex.

NIGHT DOINGS

Big hotels have splendid nightclubs with good bands, entertainment. Top discos are *Tomorrow, Tin Mines* and *Regent Club.* For the coldest, cheapest beer in town (and the most atmosphere), it's the Coliseum Cafe and Hotel. The joint is discouraging at first look, but when you see the mob of local Westerners shaking dice and drinking beer (M$3), you'll be quickhy reassured. Adjoining restaurant has fine, inexpensive steaks, shuffling Chinese waiters.

SHOPPING
(8:30 a.m. to 9:30 p.m.)

Traditional brocade, batiks (yard goods and paintings), sarongs *(kain songket)*, Kelantan silver (exquisite filigree) and, above all, stunning pewter of modern and traditional design are top buys — well worth spending at least a day to discover. Mara Arts & Crafts Centre has excellent assortments of fine workmanship at fixed prices slightly less than the hotel arcades but about the same as in smaller shops.

Selangor Pewter has a demonstration shop (craftsmen actually produce pewter items) in annex of E & O Hotel; don't miss. Kampng Batik Factory in Selayang Bharu has fine blockprints, paintings. For best batik paintings, see writeup on Teng under Penang. For some of better modern oil paintings, see those of Khoo Sui Hoe.

Along Jalan Raja Chulan are the shopping arcades of the Hilton, Merlin, Holiday Inn, Equatorial and Regent hotels, Weld Supermarket and Fitzpatrick Department Store. Further along, on the slopes of Pineapple Hill (Bukit Nanas) is the Tourist Development Corporation's Handicraft Centre, a complex of chalet-type shops selling simply everything made in Malaysia. Open 9 a.m. to 8 p.m. daily.

There's a duty-free shop in the Ampang Shopping Complex on Jalan Ampang. Purchases valid only for international flights (but not to Singapore).

216

Jalan Petaling in Chinatown is another important shopping street. Robinson's is the best department store (there's one in Singapore, too). Elsewhere on KL's streets you often seen pitchmen hawking everything from coins to grasshoppers, medicine cures, currency, orchids and much else.

By all means visit Kampong Bahru (Sunday Market — held on Saturday night) to see every conceivable type of product as well as all kinds of Malaysians. A huge variety of food and delicacies are on sale in the hundreds of stalls.

Outside of KL, top spot to buy silverware, gold cloth and batik yard goods is Kota Bharu, state of Kelantan in the north (see East Malaysia).

You cannot buy in duty-free shops on trips to Singapore or within Malaysia.

COOL HILL RESORTS

Everyone in Malaysia retreats to one of the top four whenever possible as they are 4,500 ft. or more above the sea, the temperature generally in the stimulating 60s to 70s (cooler at night) and the views spectacular. There are forest and jungle walks, gorgeous flowers and shrubs, great bird and butterfly watching.

Nearest to KL (32 miles) is Genting Highlands, 5,800 ft. up and the most go-go of the resorts with Malaysia's only gambling casino, a penthouse nightclub, two hotels, conference center, 18-hole golf course. If you don't want to drive, there's helicopter service (about $11 US) from Subang Airport.

Picturesque Fraser's Hill is 65 miles north of KL, provides great views of the Straits of Malacca, the states of Selangor and Pahang. Jeriau Waterfall dam provides a huge swim pool

Cameron Highlands, the most complete mountain resort, is closer to Penang than KL. There are large tea estates here, golf, tennis and other sports. A popular excursion is to the Perak Cave Temple, two hours away, near Ipoh on the main north-south highway. It's a 300-step climb to this beautiful cave whose walls are covered with paintings by artists from Burma, Taiwan, Hong Kong and India. There are 40 different statues of Buddha with one huge one towering above.

NATIONAL PARKS

It comes as a surprise to learn that Malaysian jungles are older than those of the Congo and Amazon — they remained untouched by nature (including the glaciers) and man for an estimated 100 million years. As a consequence, these magnificent gorges, rivers and towering hills provide outdoorsman and photographer with a full quota of thrills — boating thru rapids, stalking game with camera, flyfishing for giant carp, mountain climbing, exploring limestone caves, bird watching and camping.

Templar Park is the one most visitors are apt to visit as it is just an hour's drive from KL; possible to go from skyscrapers to jungle and rushing streams and back to city pavements in a single day. Flying lizards, monkeys and other harmless animals greet the visitor ambling along jungle paths into the interior. 1,500-foot Bukit Takun and Anak Takun (Son of Takun) escarpments are of great interest,

The 272 steps of Kuala Lumpur's Batu Caves.

particularly the latter with its network of caves.

Taman Negara National Park, near the center of Western Malaysia, offers considerably more. There are seven salt licks with observation blinds from which a wide variety of game — usually wild pigs, tapir, sambar and barking deer — can be photographed. At Jenut Kumbang, there's a high blind in which visitors stay overnight to observe elephant, tiger, black panther, seladang (wild ox) and lesser animals.

Fishing for native members of the carp family is superb (Feb.-Mar. and July-August). *Kelah* (the famed Mahseer of India) to 20 lbs., *serbarau,* a silver carp, and *kelasa,* a fighting jumper, are the big three. Artificial lures, light tackle are used.

Travel within the Park is mainly by river with wonderful stretches of rough water. There are lodges and rest houses which can be reserved, in advance, thru the Chief Game Warden, MABA Bldg., K.L. We'd suggest contacting a local tour operator for complete arrangements. There is a regular 3-day, 2-night River Safari out of KL.

EAST COAST (WEST MALAYSIA)

In our travels, we constantly research new, different, unspoiled places. Infrequently we come up with a gem — a San Agustin in Colombia, a Zihuatanejo in Mexico, a Tonga in the Pacific. The East Coast is just such a find, as beautiful, colorful, interesting and untouched an area as one could hope for — yet surprisingly accessible. Its people are so unspoiled they'll pose for pictures any time; they're warm and friendly, love entertainment and the many different racial groups — Hindus, Indians, Chinese, Malays — practice their respective traditions. There may be (and are) racial tensions (notably Muslims versus Chinese) in the more cosmopolitan areas of West Malaysia, but there were no evidences of it when we were here.

Thanks to the cooperation of the Tourist Development Corporation, we made a quick but thorough trip by car from Kuala Lumpur to Kuantan, Trengganu and Khota Bharu. It's an eye-opener with enough native color and excitement to titillate the most blase. We met a Boeing representative and his charming New Zealand wife who've traveled the world; they were in their glory snapping photos like mad, said they'd never had a more exhilarating day.

KUANTAN

From Kuala Lumpur, it's a comfortable 4-hour drive at 50 miles an hour (over that speed the unevenly paved road can shake a car badly). First hour and a half is a winding mountain drive past the entrance to Genting Highlands, after which you cross the rural flatlands to the east coast; at frequent intervals there are road markers to gauge flood levels — often as high as five feet.

Reaching bucolic Kuantan in time for a delicious shrimp lunch at the Hotel Merlin, we then were treated to as excitingly different and fun afternoon and evening, eight hours in all, as we've ever experienced anywhere, any time, any place. No reason why groups shouldn't follow the same pattern and schedule; individuals, too, should come here but only on an escorted tour basis which, of necessity, would be more expensive and could not include many of the special performances enjoyed by groups.

To say that the area surrounding Kuantan and its beaches is terrific is an understatement. The simple graciousness and unmitigated freshness of the people, particularly children, was overwhelming — as was the impact of the varied aspects of native life, dress and games. As a photographer, you'll be busier than a one-armed paper hanger. The kids alone are a treat — sometimes solemn, often grinning, always delighted to be your subjects, and so cute and handsome you want to keep shooting their pictures forever. Bring a Polaroid — nothing creates more excitement and pleasure. Everyone, in fact, is obliging and friendly, not a hint of commercialism (though for special performances — not visits — there are modest fees for the village treasury). Miss Yang, a former welfare worker and then head of the Pahang (state)

Tourist Bureau, was responsible for the excellent cottage industries of the region; her office sets up programs such as we saw. Ours was necessarily kaleidoscoped into one day — we'd suggest minimum of two days here.

Here's all we did in eight hours:

1) Watched Malaysian brocade (Songkit) being woven in a cottage "factory."

2) Saw a top spinning contest and learned to spin the big top (and bought one) at Besear village.

3) Visited nearby batik factory (Batik Rekaan Malayu, 132 Jalan Bukit Bintang, KL) where good-looking (and less expensive than KL) cottons, cotton voiles and jerseys are hand-blocked, dipped in steaming color vats, then set by throwing into the river. Far more interesting, colorful (prints more colorful, too) than silk screen process.

4) Something we'd never seen — a baboon climbing coconut tree, wrestling nuts from tree and dropping them to the ground.

5) Visit to shell cottage industry center at Karang Darat Village where 80 villagers turn out imaginative, unusual objects assembled entirely of various shells. We bought a cute little turtle for 70¢ (28¢ US). Wonderful example of proper use of otherwise worthless material — the ability of Miss Yang to inspire something from nothing.

6) At Balok Village, saw the fascinating ballet called Silat — the Malay Art of Self-Defense in pantomine and imitative sword play — set to an eastern Malay dirge of pipes and drums. All the while, men skillfully play Sepak Raga (ball game) with head and feet using a softball-size ball of palm.

7) Excellent dinner at Twin Islands Resort, then to a 10- or 12-man Rodat Dance (similar to Boria in Penang) at fishing village of Sungai Ular. Dance is a plea to the sea gods to bless their fishing with good luck. Traditional dances are usually connected with native activities.

8) Wayang Kulit at Cherating Village — intriguing and interesting to peek behind scenes to see how puppeteer and narrator manipulates the "actors" fashioned of bullock skin, see the large supporting cast of musicians.

9) At the turtle beach hut, women were weaving mats of pandanus leaves, pounding and measuring rice (padi) while young girls played a Malay-style backgammon called Chongkak.

Side trips from Kuantan can also include a visit to picturesque Lake Chini, the Panching Caves — or deep-sea fishing for blue marlin.

KUALA TRENGGANU (Treng-gah-noo)

If we hadn't been to Kuantan, Kuala Trengganu might have had its moments — but it didn't. The marketplace makes an interesting stop, and if you haven't seen local craftsmen at work, the numerous cottage industries at Marang, south of Kuala Trengganu, is interesting. Short boat trips can be made to nearby islands. Accommodations here are more primitive than at Kuantan. *Village Motel* is best but only adequate, though clean. You won't suffer, but you won't want to tarry. 20AC R, 10 chalets, dining room (food okay), bar and pool. Overlooks town and sea. Soon to open is a 66-room resort hotel at Rantau Abang, another turtle beach.

KOTA BHARU

By leaving Kuantan early, can reach Kota Bharu without staying overnight in Kuala Trengganu. This is a lovely drive along the coast. Kota Bharu is colorful, a melange of trishaws (never seen so many) with rattan seats, women in sarongs with red, orange and other bright colored tops, men in wrap-arounds and bright turbans, medicine men exhorting the fascinated ring of onlookers and at same time treating sufferers, pitchmen doing what comes naturally. You'll see more action in ten minutes around the Central Market than elsewhere in a day.

Hotel Murni is modern, FC. 38 AC R, SU w/rfg, TV are very nice. Chinese Rst,

SINGING & SOARING KITES

In the breezy months of April, May and June, people visiting Kelantan state, on the east coast of Peninsular Malaysia, are greeted by one of the most picturesque sights in the Far East. Huge, fantastically shaped kites dot the sky and add music to the wind. They flap and shudder, plunge and soar in the wind. Some are fashioned like owls or cats with enormous, demonic eyes; others are swallows with black wings, curved and graceful; some are dragons with monstrous green and gold paper tails streaming behind them in a crazy, wind-tossed dance. Other popular designs are the tern, quail and peacock. Wing span is about five feet. On the heads of many kites is an attachment that resembles a bow and arrow. The reed bow is made from bamboo, but the bow string is cut from a nipah leaf or thin rattan. It is the bow string that vibrates and quivers in the air making a musical, whirring sound.

These Waus (kites) always consist of two parts joined by sticks in the center. Usually attached to tough fishing lines, a Wau is designed to fly high and remain stable in varying winds. Some fly as high as 1,500 ft. In competition, the man whose kite reaches the greatest vertical height is the winner. Skill in maneuvering may gain points. It is usually the Waus with the reedy bow and arrow attachment that give off the humming sound in the breeze, fostering the legend that kites come alive once they are aloft. Without these attachments, the kites when carried by each gust of breeze make a faint and oddly disconcerting rattle, like the sound of rapid small arms fire. The rattling grows louder and more insistent if heard within an open square.

As the kites are large, two men are needed to launch. The launcher holds the central part of the frame in his right hand and the string, loosely joined to the two ends, in his left. The roll of string is held by the second man standing twenty yards away. Each roll may contain from 600 to 1,800 feet of string. The launcher stands facing the direction from which the wind is blowing and launches the kite by throwing it up into the wind. The second man steadily unrolls the string as the kite climbs. When it is in the air, the launcher either assumes control or takes turns with the second man. Great care and skill are required to land the kite without damage. Once again the two men work as a team — the launcher waits to catch the kite as the other man brings it slowly down.

---

nightclub and coffee shop. $12-$18. Beach of Passionate Love (how about that?), 6 miles from town, has a motel with 16 AC chalets w/bath. Rst, bar. $11.

From here, return to KL by plane or, if heading north, to Bangkok by way of Penang. Another way to return to KL is by the *Golden Blowpipe Express* of the East Coast Rail Line, a 327 mile ride diagonally across West Malaysia — grand way to see the interior.

EAST COAST TRIP PLANNING

Although Kuantan and Trengganu have plane/bus services, there are no sightseeing facilities on arrival. Hence, it's essential to rent an AC car in KL (about $20 day and up) or, preferably, one with driver. Groups can see the East Coast very economically by bus; this, without doubt, is one of the best group tours in the Far East.

Best to drive up and fly back, either from Trengganu or Kota Bharu (we suggest the latter), letting the driver return to KL — or, if economy's a factor, drive both ways.

Allow a minimum of three days with overnight stops at Kuantan and Trengganu or Kota Bharu.

However, the East Coast is ideal for both sightseeing and relaxation at one of the beach motels, so it would be most enjoyable to spend a week or more in the area. There are uninhabited, offshore islands easily reached by boat for a day's uninhibited sunning. Or, further south, there's Pulau Tioman, the Bali Hai of the *South Pacific* movie, with a comfortable Merlin Samudra Resort Hotel.

Instead of flying or driving back to KL, it's easy to drive down the East Coast from Kuantan to Mersing (120 miles), where one can take a short boat ride to Rawa Island (a small resort) or a longer one (about 3 hours) to Pulau Tioman (arrange in advance thru the Samudra Resort), then driving 83 miles to Johore Bahru and Singapore — in this way continuing your onward journey.

Pounding padi is just one of the fascinating exhibits of native life one sees in East Malaysia.

SEA TURTLE ADVENTURE

Giant leatherbacks — 8 feet in length, 7 feet between outstretched flippers and weighing up to 1,000 lbs. or more — visit the beaches between Kuantan and Trengganu (and especially at Rantau Abang) each year from late May thru August; these largest living Chelonians (even bigger than Galapagos tortoises) are most numerous in the latter part of August. Females only come ashore after dark (1 a.m. to 2 a.m. seems to be a choice egg-laying period), drag themselves over the high tide mark, dig a large, three-foot-deep hole into which they drop from 80 to 140 (usually about 120) flexible, ping-pong- to tennis ball-size eggs within 15 minutes. When the hole has been covered with sand and smoothed over (the eggs are removed by licensed collectors as dropped), the big girls lumber back into the ocean — and neither flashlights nor audience deter them from their appointed rounds, which take about two hours to complete. Some Mother Turtles return to the same beach 10 days or so later to lay more eggs. Research shows that these monsters, many known to be over a hundred years old, return to the same beaches — either annually or after a lapse of a year or two — from as far away as Japan.

Those of you aghast at the egg thefts mentioned before can be reassured. Rantau Abang has a Hatchery Conservation Area where more than 50,000 eggs annually are bought from licensed collectors to hatch under natural conditions (50 to 60 days); 40% to 60% of them are hatched and returned safely to sea.

We have enjoyed this experience on a very remote beach in Surinam, South America, where the same species is not quite as large nor are the eggs larger than ping-pong size. It's quite a spectacle (don't forget flash equipment), one which we can unqualifiedly recommend to anyone, particularly since here on the East Coast you can operate easily out of a comfortable motel, waiting for spotters to announce a sighting; in Surinam, we made our trip by dugout canoe (and in pouring rain). However, it must be noted that you're not guaranteed a sighting in any one night as the landing sites are many and far apart, so allow several nights or more.

Scheduled for completion in '79 are 20 chalets on a 20-acre lagoon site and another 100 R hotel five miles south of turtle beach.

East Coast children are most appealing, friendly.

MALAY DANCES

As in other Oriental countries, so in Malaysia — basic native entertainment far outclasses imported versions as far as interest to visitors is concerned.

There are traditional (based on Indian mythology) and folk dances. The former, such as the century-old dance drama, *Anak Raja Gondang* (Triton Shell Princess), is making a popular comeback after once having been performed only in royal courts. Most of the parts are performed by women; only the comedians are men.

Most popular folk dance, in several variations, is the *Ronggeng*. Danced by a couple, its catchy rhythm is produced by flute and drum; sometimes the couple sings impromptu verses to each other.

Other popular folk dances are *Tari Sapu Tangan* (Handkerchief Dance), dedicated to "sweet sorrow"; the Candle Dance *(Tari Lilin)* and Umbrella Dance *(Tari Payong); Tari Tudong Saja* (Food Cover Dance).

In ancient times, it was thought that death and sickness were brought on by evil spirits, so obviously there must be Exorcism Dances in which the medicine man drives away the spirits.

In the state of Sarawak, the various native dances are said to be the most colorful, exotic and entertaining to be seen in Malaysia.

INDIAN FIREWALKING

In early April, kavadi carriers converge on various Hindu Mariamman temples thruout Malaysia to carry out their vows to the goddess Sri Mariamman. The ritual, held the last month of the Hindu year, is a time for believers to cleanse their souls. Ceremonies commence with a large procession headed by a chariot and followed by devotees. That evening, at the temple, the kavadi bearers fulfill their vows by walking over pits of burning coals.

We have seen this mystic, eerie firewalk in Surinam — an experience you'll always remember for even when you see it, you don't believe that these men and boys — who appear to be in a self-induced hypnotic trance and not in any way doped — can walk repeatedly over red-hot coals without the slightest burn. If you have the opportunity, don't fail to attend.

Cheeks pierced with metal skewers, devotees, in a trance, walk barefooted across a pit of burning charcoal during the Nine Emperor Gods Festival (Chinese Taoist).

MUSLIM CEREMONIES

Every important stage in his life is commemorated. When a woman is seven months pregnant, the *leng-gang perut* ceremony is held for her first child — to facilitate birth thru magic. At birth, the prayer is whispered into the baby's ear. Seven days after birth the head-shaving and name-giving ceremony is held. At four, the child is taught to read the Koran, and when he has completed the Koran, the *Khatam Koran* ceremony takes place.

Ceremonies around marriage are quite involved. First is the investigation of a prospective bride's background to the introductions to in-laws. Then the boy's representative comes formally to ask for the girl's hand. When a favorable reply is given, the engagement ceremony is held. Length of the wedding ceremony depends on the wealth of the family.

Final ceremony — the funeral rites — consists of feasts, prayers for the soul of the dead on seventh, fortieth and hundredth day after death. For cremation ceremony, see Bali section.

SHADOW PLAY (Wayang Kulit)

Introduced to Malaysia from Java, originally each act told a story based on the Indian epic, Ramayana. But thruout the centuries, themes have changed to apply to various cultures and customs.

Wayang is Malay for drama, *Kulit* means skin. The method of producing shadows has been to cut a figure from a dried buffalo hide, then scrape it until it is a stiffish sheet. A figure is then traced or sketched on the sheet — to reveal the various characters taken from the Ramayana or, more recently, figures taken from literature or stories.

The stage is small and installed with a cloth screen. Figures (sometimes 20-30) are silhouetted on the screen with the aid of a hurricane lamp and manipulated, from behind, by a puppeteer. Characters are heroes, heroines, giants, monkeys, clowns, etc. The puppeteer must also be a storyteller, impersonator and singer. Before the performance, the puppeteer blesses each puppet and the audience joins him in prayer. Then the musicians — a five-piece orchestra of flute, Indian drum, gong, cymbal and violin — play traditional, accompanying music.

Kuala Lumpur's old Central Mosque

MAGNIFICENT MOSQUES

Most of the mosques in the country are built along traditional Moorish-style lines. Latest ones, however, reflect the influence of modern architecture. Whether it be a humble village mosque or an imposing one in a large town, all have a common feature — the minaret.

This is the tower, complete with spiral staircase, from where the call to prayers is hailed. In the past, the man engaged to do this job climbed the staircase to the top of the tower to make himself heard by as many people as possible. Today, thru microphones and speakers, he does this without climbing. But no mosque is complete without a symbolic minaret, even though its actual use is in the past.

On entering a mosque, one is gripped by its serenity. Devout Muslims walk barefooted into the spacious prayer hall which is usually carpeted or lined with mats. Inside is the mimbar, or pulpit, from where the Imam (priest) delivers his sermon.

Another interesting feature is the pools. Before prayers, Muslims take the ablution — washing of face, ears, neck, hands and feet. In the past, they washed at the pools, but today, these are only ornamental as a dozen or so taps in washrooms serve this purpose.

The mosque is not only a place of worship but also a community center where people come to discuss religious affairs, community problems. Before schools were built, children were taught to read the Koran as well as to write Jawi, the Arabic script, and the basics of Islam religion.

One of the oldest and most beautiful mosques is the Sultan Abu Bakar in Johore. Located in the sprawling grounds of the Sultan's palace, the interior with its high ceiling, beautiful chandeliers and two huge, Chinese brass incense-burners is magnificent. The floor is Italian marble, the carpet lining the big hall is from Britain.

On the East Coast of Peninsular Malaysia, there are a few old timber mosques splendidly adorned with flowered panels, pulpits carved in high relief.

Oldest mosque in Kuala Lumpur is Masjid Jame. Opened in 1909, it is traditional Moorish architecture; each of the two minarets, at the far end of courtyard, are 84 feet tall.

Malaysia's National Mosque in the heart of Kuala Lumpur is a beautiful building symbolizing the unity, faith and aspiration of the young nation. It took five years to build at a cost of M$10 million. Communities, state governments and federal government contributed the money. The 235-ft.-high minaret, in the shape of a folded umbrella, is accessible by elevator; from the top, you have a panoramic view of the city.

Fountains and pools enhance the mosque which has a gallery, a library, a lecture and prayer hall accommodating over 2,000 people. At one end of the mosque is the National Mausoleum where the late Deputy Prime Minister of Malaysia, Tun Datuk Dr. Ismail, is buried.

PENANG

Two miles off the west coast of the Malaysian Peninsula below the Thai border and at the top of the Straits of Malacca is this perfectly delightful, tropical island where palms, pineapple, betel nut and banana trees thrive, where rubber trees loom on the hilly, central spines and padi (rice) fields and spice plantations cover the rest of the lush, green 110 square miles.

Georgetown is as attractive a provincial city as one finds anywhere in the tropics — lovely tree-shaded residential areas, colorful shopping streets humming with people, trishaws and teksis (taxis). Weather is warm and on the humid side, though not drastically so when we were there (March), and there are breezes or showers to cool things off. All of Penang is practically insect-free (no mosquitos, generally true of all Malaysian cities, though not the rural areas).

The "Pearl of the Orient," as she is often called, has a romantic history. Once known as Pulau Pinang, Island of Betelnut Palms, and part of the Sultanate of Kedah, it was a hideout for pirates until 1786 when it became the first British settlement in the Straits of Malacca and a commercial center under the British East India Company. Thus, Fort Cornwallis, in honor of a governor of Bengal, was built with convict labor in the early 1800s, and even today there are survivors in the form of colonial buildings (Town Hall, Supreme Court, St. George's Church) and streets named after British towns and celebrities.

Today, the 350,000 population is divided amongst Malays, Chinese and Indians — each, of course, with their religious observances. Incidentally, learned while here that male Muslims (who may have four wives) will not marry a Chinese woman (or any other, for that matter) unless she's willing to convert to Islam. Yet the family is not as important to him as to the Chinese. By the way, if he's wearing a white hat (fez-type without fez), he's one of the chosen — been to Mecca.

December is carnival time — Pesta Pulau Pinang — featuring traditional events relating to a rich cultural heritage, such as Dragon Boat Races, the Chingay Procession of tall (up to 40 feet) flags which are balanced on foreheads and shoulders, Float Processions, International Film Festival, Trade Fair, folk dances and drama. Dec. 13th is the Governor of Penang's Birthday, a public holiday, and also the national holiday of Hari Raya Haji which honors Mecca pilgrims thruout Malaysia.

February is most eventful, too. Thaipusam, the Hindu festival, occurs then or in January. On the Birthday of Jade Emperor, Chinese visit Th'nee Temple near Hill Railway. During the 12-day Ban Hood Huat Hoay, thousands of Buddhists throng

GETTING TO PENANG

Bayan Lapas International Airport, Malaysia's newest and best equipped, handles Cathay Pacific jets from Bangkok, Hong Kong and Singapore; Malaysian from the foregoing, plus KL and Haadyai; Thai Int'l from Bangkok, Haadyai and Pattaya; Merpati from Medan.

Rail — Malayan Railway links Penang (Butterworth) to Bangkok (M, W, F at 7:50 am); train leaves Bangkok 4:10 pm M, W, Sat. FC fare: M$70 OW; AC berth is M$20. There are five daily departures for KL-Singapore and vice versa; 6 hrs., 10 min. to KL, 10:50 to Singapore by fastest express. FC fare to KL, M$45; to Singapore, M$85.

Bus — Mara Express (AC) has two daily runs (am, pm) between Butterworth and Singapore

(M$30) in 15 hrs., including a stop in KL (M$15 OW). Mismara Travel has AC, 45-passenger bus tours between Singapore-KL-Penang and vice versa with enroute sightseeing at Ipoh, Kuala Kangsar and Taiping, Lake Gardens (10 hrs. KL-Penang). See Thailand section for Butterworth-Bangkok service.

World Air Transportation Consultants, San Francisco, has 3- to 7-day coach tours from Singapore with stops at Malacca, KL, Ipoh and Butterworth.

Ferry — There's a little-known service from/to Belawan (Sumatra, Indonesia, port) by cargo vessel taking 57 deck passengers. Lvs. Belawan on M, Th for 16-hr. trip. Fare is M$45 OW. Penang agents: Soo Hup Seng Trading Co., Victoria St.

Kek Lok Si Temple; there are ceremonies from 8 a.m. to 9 p.m. (visitors may watch). On the 27th, Birthday of Chor Soo Kong, a deity, takes place at Snake Temple with performances of Chinese opera.

Although restaurants for gourmets are lacking, there's a great variety of good and interesting food, particularly in the many open-air stalls. Fresh crabs are marvelous; so is *Penang Laksa,* a fish curry with noodles and fresh vegetables. We had a delicious seafood lunch at the E & O Hotel. *Mandarin,* United Hotel, is always mobbed as it serves best Chinese food in town. Merlin's top-floor restaurant is popular.

As in Singapore, it's a fun thing to attend the night bazaar (Pasa Malam); since the site changes every two weeks, inquire at your hotel for directions.

And now, you may well inquire, why haven't we mentioned Penang as a beach resort? There's a simple answer: the beaches are narrow fringes of sand, the waters dull — they provide a very secondary reason for coming here. But the beauty of the surroundings, the fascination of the temples and pagodas, the interesting people (some very beautiful girls) and the pleasing ambience make Penang an essential stopover (for several days) between Kuala Lumpur and Bangkok.

May to October is the economy season — Penang's hotel rates are 20% to 30% lower then than during balance of year.

SHOPPING

Batiks are *the* thing — alone worth your coming here — and Teng, Malaysia's foremost batik painter, is the one you want to buy. He and his son, S. Teng, also a fine artist, have the Yahong Gallery at 31-B Leith St., a branch at 47 Leith. Chuah Thean Teng, born in 1914 in China, came to Malaya in 1932, had to work as a servant for the Japanese during the occupation. Since 1955, he has had exhibitions all over the world, including one in Palm Springs, Calif., where we first learned of him (and where his batiks sold for considerably more than in Penang). You can also see some of his paintings in the National Art Gallery in KL. One critic, who most nearly expresses our feelings about the Tengs we own, wrote, "He has a delicate vein of eroticism which Matisse might envy, and his combination of flat decorative design with perspective is so skilled that at times you marvel. The detail, richness and intricacy of his color patterning is almost staggering." Nothing in our modest collection is more satisfying, particularly since we've mounted the two batiks in fluorescent shadow boxes where they glow like richly stained glass.

Selangor Pewter, brand name for quality pewter made of 97% Malaysian refined tin blended with copper and individually handcrafted, is another quality buy — though no cheaper than in KL. The local handcrafts are exceptionally good.

OUTSTANDING SIGHTS

You may or may not like the Snake Temple, but it's an eerie sight that's gotta be seen if only to run off and say "ugh." You see hundreds of greenish, drugged (by the incense) snakes twined around everything, lying on the floor, a few moving sluggishly. You only hope they won't awaken while you're there.

Sure to please is Kek Lok Si, the Chinese Temple of Supreme Bliss, one of the largest in Asia, housing hundreds of Buddha statues. Built hillside on several levels, it's a long climb to the beautiful, gold-topped Ban Hood Pagoda of 10,000 Buddhas (in mosaics adorning the walls), seven stories, 100 feet high with a gold, marble or alabaster Buddha on each floor. Lower floors are of Burmese design, upper floors Thai. Overall there are 30 acres of gardens (with statues of fierce warrior gods), turtle pond, fish ponds — in a word, fascinating.

Khoo Clan Guild, a Chinese meeting-house, is intensely interesting; so is the Kuan Yin Tong (Goddess of Mercy) temple on Pitt St., 155 years old, whose interior, redolent with mystery, hums to priestly incantations. We remember with pleasure the lovely Kapitan Kling mosque where a Muslim guide took us in tow, was so enchanting we tipped him outrageously

(and he never even asked, just looked expectant).

You'll also want to see the lavish interior of the Penang Buddhist Association, the Siamese Temple with its huge reclining Buddha (third largest in Asia), Botanical Gardens[1] and Waterfalls, and, above all, Penang Hill for a spectacular view of city and bay (especially at night). You can climb it in three hours — but the usual method is the cable car that runs daily from 6:30 a.m. to 8:15 p.m. (midnight on W, Sat). It's a 30-minute ride; costs M$1.60 OW first class (M$2 on W, Sat, Sun). Lunch/dinner served at hotel.

SIGHTSEEING

Of the three regular tours, Island (M$16), Hill and Temple (M$26), City (M$16), the first two are the most important; city sights you can see on your own. Each tour is 3 or 4 hours, so you can see most everything in a day — also with car and guide. Of course, you need at least one extra day for city rambling and shopping.

[1] While here, don't fail to see (if, in fact, they can be coaxed into sight) the world's smallest hoofed animal, the pelandok or mousedeer, in the Pelandok Experimental Farm.

Hill and Temple Tour shows you Kek Lok Si Temple, Botanical Gardens and Penang Hill (by cable car). Round Island Tour is basically a 45-mile scenic drive (mostly along the coast) with stops at the Snake Temple, clove and nutmeg plantations, fishing village, batik factory and pewter center. The adventurous can cover the island for about M$2 using public Yellow, Green and Blue buses (leave from Prangin Rd. terminal).

In George Town, see Fort Cornwallis and other colonial relics and buildings (by trishaw is fun), Sri Mariamman and Goddess of Mercy temples, Kapitan Kling mosque, Khoo Clan Guild. Green bus takes you to the Reclining Buddha temple and Penang Buddhist Association. Twice daily, there's a 2½-hr. Harbour Cruise.

Taxis were inexpensive: M50¢ for first mile, 20¢ each half mile thereafter and M$5 per hour. Trishaws about the same, but determine price in advance. Taxis charge M$8 to airport.

There's an 18-hole golf course at Batu Gantong, part of the Penang Turf Club complex (M$15 weekdays, M$30 weekends), a putting green at Rasa Sayang Hotel. Beach hotels have tennis courts (so does E & O), boating, water-skiing, fishing boats.

OTHER ISLAND RESORTS

Those looking for unheralded paradises should know about Pulau (Island) Langkawi north of Penang just off the Malaysia-Thai border, Pulau Pangkor and Pulau Tioman, already mentioned in the East Coast drive. According to those who've been there, they have great charm, beauty and romantic pasts. Added to their isolated advantages are the comforts of modern resort hotels.

Langkawi is the largest of a group of 99 islands with marble outcrops, rich in legends and folklore, most famous of which involved a local beauty, Mahsuri, accused of adultery in a court intrigue. In those days, adultery was a serious offense so, without ado, the girl was tied to a tree and pierced with a spear. White blood gushed, and before she died, Mahsuri cast a curse on Langkawi — that it would not

prosper for seven generations because of the injustice. Her tomb has since become a shrine; if you say anything rash while enroute to it, prepare for a siege of bad luck.

Interesting to note that prosperity here lagged for years after the beauty's death. In fact, a scorched earth policy was necessary against attacking Siamese resulting in still visible areas of black (burned) rice.

There are other fascinating legends — plus fine, secluded beaches and waterfalls, an exotic atmosphere, the 120-room Langkawi Country Club complex. Access, though, is a problem — a 5-hr. ferry ride from Penang. 1½-hr. from Kuala Perlis. Much quicker to take Malaysia Air Charter flight from Penang ($20) or KL ($67; about 2 hrs.).

PULAU PANGKOR

185 miles northwest of KL by road or 40 minutes by air to Ipoh, thence by road (55 miles) to Lumut, a half-hour ferry ride brings one to this island surrounded by calm green waters renowned for possibly the best skin diving and fishing in Malaysian waters. In the 1700s, Pangkor was a Dutch stronghold; remains of forts can be seen as well as rock on which the Dutch East Indian Company's coat of arms was chiseled.

PULAU TIOMAN

This volcanic island was formed in a rather unconventional manner. A beautiful lady dragon was once on her way from Pahang to Sarawak to wed her betrothed but, unable to find a place to rest, transformed herself into an island so that other seafarers might find shelter in the ages to come. However, she forgot to equip herself with a resort hotel so that until very recently, when that oversight was corrected, Tioman was distinctly off the beaten path — even for dragons.

Besides the usual coral-hued waters and reefs that provide good swimming, snorkeling and beaches, Tioman provides a most uncommon sport for tropical paradises — mountain climbing on the island's tallest peak (there are several), Gunong Kajang, 3,999 feet above the sea.

Bajau horsemen of Kota Belud, 48 miles from Kota Kinabalu, are the cowboys of Malaysia.

EAST MALAYSIA & BRUNEI

As we've noted, Borneo is virtually undiscovered territory as far as any degree of large-scale tourism is concerned; a few tours include it as a segment between Singapore or Kuala Lumpur and Hong Kong and usually include the three capitals: Kuching, Bandar Seri Begawan and Kota Kinabalu; the latter is developing the fastest as a "last frontier" tourist attraction.

The climate is one factor limiting large-scale exploitation: tropical humidity is extremely high (72% to 98%), temperature averages 88° during the day and plunges to 72° at night, while the annual rainfall can be anything between 60 to 160 inches. Along the northwest coast, where the capitals are located, heaviest rains occur during May-August. However, similar conditions exist in Panama and haven't hindered traffic to and thru the Crossroads of the World.

It should be emphasized that Brunei is an autonomous country and not a part of Malaysia. However, since it will be visited at the same time as Sarawak and Sabah, if at all, it's included here.

TRIP PLANNING

On a circle trip out of Hong Kong, most sensible routing is Bangkok-Penang-Kuala Lumpur and then to Kuching (direct in 1½ hours, or from Singapore, an hour, 10-min. flight) and back to Hong Kong via Brunei and Sabah. Takes an hour to fly non-stop from Kuching to Bandar Seri Begawan, only 25 min. from there to Kota Kinabalu, from where it's 1¾ hours to Hong Kong. Borneo, except for the Indonesian sector, is in the same time zone as Hong Kong.

Malaysian Airline flies KUL and SIN to all points; Cathay Pacific and Royal Brunei Air fly certain segments between Hong Kong and Kuching.

Tours which do include the area devote about one day of sightseeing for each of the three capitals. Individuals who dote on the offbeat can easily spend considerably more, particularly if interested in climbing Mt. Kinabalu. They might also be interested in the Straits Steamship Company's sailings every two weeks from Singapore to Sarawak, Brunei and Sabah — either as a round trip (13 days) or one way. Very inexpensive; write Mansfield Travel, Box 398, Singapore. Or check Cathay Pacific for details re their air/sea packages (same ships) of six and eight days.

KUCHING, Sarawak

The capital (65,000 pop.) lies 19 miles upstream on the Sarawak River. Once the colonial seat of the British White Rajah, the river bustles with local and export activity; ferry boats ply to and from the town's bazaar quarters while rubber, timber, pepper, copra, bauxite and petroleum (also bird's nests, for that famous Chinese soup) are loaded for shipments abroad.

Principal attraction: Land Dayaks' longhouses — rambling villages on stilts housing hundreds of families represent a completely different life style. Natives are usually only too happy to oblige with an Iban, Kayan or Harvest dance. Usual trip is a 3-hour one by car, or a longer cruise along any of the rivers to some of the Sea Dayak longhouse villages. Another popular river safari (2 days) is to Bako National Park, where native animals roam freely.

Kuching (means "cat" in Malay) is one-third Malay, two-thirds Chinese, has a number of historical mosques and temples, the Astana Palace and the Sarawak Museum (archeological); adjoining the latter is the Art Council Shop that has the best in local handcrafts.

Sarawak is about the size of West Malaysia and almost the same length, has a population of 1,000,000.

For complete tour information: Sarawak Travel Agencies, P.O. Box 725, Kuching.

Unmetered cabs charge about M$3 from airport to hotels, but latter meet guests on request. Incidentally, there's a M$5 airport departure tax (also from Kuching).

Principal exports are timber, rubber, copra and palm oil, prawns (be sure to eat them while here) and hemp.

KOTA KINABALU, Sabah

This provincial city of 42,500 is noted for its splendid sunsets, a fine 3-mile long beach, Tanjong Aru, near the airport (Borneo Hotel close by) but, primarily, for the splendid Mt. Kinabalu National Park in which majestic Mt. Kinabalu is located. This 275-square-mile, forested domain is filled with beautiful flowers (including over 800 types of orchids, the world's largest flower, *Rafflesia,* with a diameter of up to three feet), 300 kinds of butterflies, 600 bird species (include such exotics as Argus Pheasant and Mountain Black Eye), Sambhar deer, bearded pig and the protected orangutan (from Malaysian *orang,* man; *hutan,* forest) ape. Some of the wild birds are so tame they can be induced to perch on arms and heads and pose for photos.

A normal ascent of the mountain is not unduly arduous — mostly a long, stiff climb requiring only good physical condition. The ascent is begun early in the morning; usually two or three days are allotted for ascent and descent (latter takes 6 hrs); there are shelters enroute. But if you don't wish to make the climb, a visit for two days is very much worthwhile to see some of the flora, fauna and interesting native villages; there are also hot springs at the foot of the mountain with several open-air baths. Arrangements for guide, porters and accommodations must be made well in advance thru Park Warden, Box 626, Kota Kinabalu. Lodgings range from inexpensive hostel to luxurious chalets (M$35); necessary to bring food. Charter landrovers in Kota Kinabalu (about M$50 for 6-passenger, M$70 for 12).

Good idea to be in KK on a Sunday for day trip to the colorful village of Kota Belud for the pony and buffalo races, the bustling *tamu* (marketplace). At Tuaran, only a half hour's drive, there's a smaller Sunday market.

Other prime trips are to Papar to visit the friendly Kadazans (particularly during May Harvest Festival) and to Sorob for a glimpse of brilliantly attired horsemen. Both reached by bus or taxi, but to Papar the train, with its frequent stops at small villages, is particularly recommended.

BRUNEI

In many ways an oddity, it's perhaps just that which makes the capital, Bandar Seri Begawan (Brunei town), an interesting stopover. For one thing, this oil-rich, Islamic sultanate looks like it belongs in the Middle East; for another, chronologically it should be in the 19th century when it became (1888) a British protectorate, which it still is. By a 1959 constitutional agreement, the United Kingdom appoints a British High Commissioner to advise on all matters except those relating to the Muslim religion and customs.

Oil is what brings most Westerners here. Nonetheless, there are tourist attractions, notably the Omar Ali Saifuddin mosque which dominates the town physically and spiritually. Constructed at a cost of $5 million (US), it has been compared favorably to the Taj Mahal in beauty and magnificence of architecture. Those who've seen it say it's a mystical experience which should be undertaken three times: at dawn when bathed in soft pink, at noon when the interior is cooly refreshing, and at night when it glows translucently in the moonlight.

It should be noted that Brunei has been Islamic for many centuries; during the 15th and 16th centuries, it sent out missionaries to spread the faith in surrounding countries. Hence the rightness of such a splendid mosque.

A large artificial lake reflects the mosque with mirrored faithfulness; in the center of it is a religious stone boat (Mahaligai) which is joined to the mosque, and spread out in front of the boat is one of the Kampongs Ayer — water villages whose houses are built on piers over the water. A boat can be hired (for about B$10 an hour) to visit them — and

Complete tour information: International Travel Service, 11 Beach St., Kota Kinabalu; particularly valuable for mountain trips. Also Harrison & Crossfield (branches in Kuching, Brunei).

If we were to come here (and we hope to soon), we'd not do it as a one- or two-day affair — sounds too fascinating.

Native-built suspension bridges, like this one in Sabah, are still the chief means of crossing rivers.

try to make the boatman understand you want to stop, too, at the landing steps of the Royal Tomb.

In the Churchill Memorial Building is the Hassanai Bolkiah Aquarium, said to be one of the most attractive and interesting in Asia. Then there are the Royal Ceremonial Hall with gold-crowned roof, the Cultural Centre and the Museum (a few miles out of town); latter has world's largest collection of brass cannon (famed and feared in Brunei during the 16th and 17th centuries).

Not to be missed is Borneo Discovery Tours' (Box 234) Long-house Tour (full day) by speedboat into the Borneo wilds and then 50 miles into the interior by road to visit the Ibans, headhunters not too long ago, who are delighted (a prospective meal?) to welcome you to their longhouse — in effect an entire village under one roof. Human skulls hang from the bamboo rafters; they still have a religious significance, thus occupy places of honor. Gongs are sounded, and the *ngajat* dance of goodwill is performed by girls and men in warrior outfits.

For the daring and hardy, there's a week's Jungle Tour into Central Borneo by longboat; overnight stops are made in longhouses.

Best hotel is *Ang's* — 84 AC rooms, suites; has restaurant, bar. About US$25 D, EP. Other hotels: *Brunei* (55 AC R; about $21 D) and *Puspa* (42 AC R; about $18 D). Best restaurant: *New Hoover.*

GENERAL INFORMATION

Banks — First National City Bank has four branches.

Currency — Brunei Dollar is about 40¢ US, on a par with Malaysian and Singapore currency. Notes in B$1, 5, 10, 50, 100 denominations. Coins are 1¢, 5¢, 10¢, 20¢ and 50¢.

Entry Requirements — Passport, smallpox and cholera certificates; no visa for Americans, Canadians.

Electricity — 240v AC.

Local Customs — Remove shoes when entering Muslim institutions, homes. Don't walk inside mosques on Friday, Muslim holy day.

Income Taxes — None for individuals, 30% for corporations.

Tipping — 10% service added to bills.

Taxis — Unmetered. Very inexpensive (about B$1 a mile).

GETTING HERE

Mostly by plane as previously described but also by Straits Steamship vessels and the *Rajah Brooke,* an old-time sailing ship. Cabins are large, airy and w/bath; food reputed good. Can be taken as an 8-day round trip (B$370 each) from Singapore with two days in port (sightseeing included) and three days sailing each way. Or take the trip one way by sea. Reservations: Discovery Tours, Box 234, Bandar Seri Begawan.

Many beach resorts look like typical Malay villages with nipa palm thatched buildings — plus all modern amenities.

Hotel Directory

There are any number of surprisingly good hotels — and in Kuala Lumpur several that are superb. In today's inflated market, they're all priced right, too — downright bargains compared to most world capitals. Most have Chinese- and Western-style restaurants and/or cuisines. Some rooms in older hotels may be inside ones.

Government-owned Rest Houses have slightly lower rates than lowest mentioned below.

To the rates quoted here (in US dollars, double occupancy), 10% service and 5% tax are added.

KUALA LUMPUR
(All hotels personally inspected.)

EQUATORIAL (FC) — Opened '74 with 300 AC R and all amenities. In City Center. $27-$31.

FEDERAL (FC) — 450 R modern hi-rise. Redecorated lobby, revolving bar, 3 rsts, two nightclubs. $24-$31.

FEDERAL PORT DICKSON — 200 R. Opens early '79. $18 up.

FORTUNA — 81 AC R furnished alike, same size. DL R have/rfg, TV. Coffee house, rst, bar, nightclub. Patronized mostly by Asians. $18-$20.

HOLIDAY INN (FC) — Near racetrack, 20 min. from airport. 200 AC R, SU. Malaysian rst, grill, 2 cocktail lounges. Pool. $26 up.

HILTON (DL+) — 585 AC R w/fabulous views of Turf Club and central highlands. Paddock rooftop rst/bar. Gazebo nightly barbecue, supper club, several bars, coffee shop. Pool, shopping arcade. Beautiful, well-run hotel. Tennis, squash courts. *Conv:* 1350. $38-$50.

JAYA PURI (FC) — Opened summer '75. In suburban industrial section. Chinese/Mandarin theater rst.

MALAYSIA (FC-) — 58 R older, well-maintained hotel with excellent service — employees anticipate every wish. If room facilities equaled service, this would be tops. Hot water heater must be turned on before you bathe. In Chinese area. 2 rsts, cocktail lounge. $20-$35 *including laundry, coffee.*

MERLIN (DL) — Magnificent pool area. Several rsts, a coffee shop, bars, entertainment. Excellent service. Leather-walled halls lead to 700 AC R w/rfg. Near embassy. $25-$29.

REGENT (DL) — Malay decor with beautiful batiks, teakwood carvings. Garden lounge, pool, nightclub. 400 AC R. Payang coffee shop looks like a fishing village. Cont'l and Chinese rsts. In posh int'l area. *Conv:* 400. $34-$42.

SHAHS MOTEL — 6 miles from airport. 44 AC typical R w/rfg (upper floors recommended). The Hut features 15 Malay delicacies ($7) and traditional dances at 8:30 & 9:30 p.m. Shadow boxing in inner courtyard. Nice way to pass an evening for transit passengers. $17.

SHIRAZ — Student class. ½ mile from center. Rst. 60 R at $10.

TRAVEL INN (FC) — Opened '77 DT in 15-story complex (main bus and taxi terminal). 200 R, 6 SU. Coffee house, bar, Chinese rst and discotheque. $15 up.

WISMA BELIA (YOUTH HOSTEL) — On Lornie Rd, 20 min from town. Operated by Malaysian Youth Council. Accommodates 200. Way to meet Malaysians and foreigners. 2 rsts, snack bar. $8 single w/bath.

CAMERON HIGHLANDS

FOSTERS LAKEHOUSE — Opened '77 with 16 R, dining room, cocktail lounge. Boating, fishing. $23.

COUNTRY INN — 20 R, dining room, bars, overlook golf course. Lovely area of rose gardens, tea plantations. $27.

MERLIN (FC) — Attractive 60 R, hillside resort. Rst, bar, lounge, conference rooms. Golf. *Conv:* 300. $23-$37.

FRASER HILL

MERLIN (FC) — Popular hillside resort with 18-hole golf course. Horseback riding. Rst, coffeehouse, game rooms. Great climate. $23 up.

GENTING HIGHLANDS

GENTING HIGHLANDS (FC) — 410 R, 3 rsts, coffeehouse (dinner inexp), 2 bars, cocktail lounge, entertainment. Big deal here is the casino; about M200 ($82) refundable deposit required to play. Riding, golf, pool. Helicopter service from airport about M25 ($11). 8,000-ft cable car system. Boating. $15-$29.

There are 3 other FC hotels in the complex — $10 up.

MALACA

SHAHS BEACH — Enlarged to 50 R and AC chalets overlooking Straits of Malaca or pool. Indoor-outdoor dining. Good luncheon spot. $16.

STRAITS TRAVEL INN — 6 AC R. Coffee house, rst, disco w/live entertainment. $13.

MALACAN — Opens late '79. 106 R.

PENANG — GEORGE TOWN

DOWNTOWN

AMBASSADOR (FC) — Very attractive Eastern motif decor in lobby and coffee shop. Excellent use of carvings, shells and batiks. 76 AC R furnished in Malaysian decor. Top-floor rst, bar. Chinese rst. Good service. Well maintained. $20.

E & O (FC) — Original section built in 18th century, newer wing in the 1960s. Beautifully situated on crescent-shaped bay. Attractive pool, tennis area landscaped with frangipani, palms; seawall walk separates hotel grounds from sea. At night, flickering lights of boats and town are breathtaking. English-style lobby, good rst (order lobster), 3 bars. Top service. 125 AC R (semi-suites w/rfg and sitting area are huge). *Conv:* 750. SU recommended at $32.

HOLIDAY INN — Opening in '79 w/162 R.

MALAYSIA — 81 AC R, commercial hi-rise on Penang Rd. Dining/dancing in 10th-floor Micado Rst. $15.

MANDARIN (FC) — ½ mile from center. 88 AC R w/rfg. 3 rsts, coffeehouse, Captain's Bar. Nightclub features Malayan dances. Teng batiks and sculptures decorate lobby and rst. Free airport transfer. *Conv:* 200. $24-$27.

MERLIN (FC+) — Modern hi-rise, block from bay. 150 nicely furnished AC R w/terrace and rfg. Revolving rooftop rst and bar. Jumpin' Cellar Bar. Dragon Palace serves good Chinese cuisine. Attractive coffee shop (food fair). Merlin Beach Club at Batu Ferring 11 miles from city. $25 up.

Youth Hostel, Farquhar St., offers dormitory R in wings for men/women.

BEACH RESORTS

Most on Batu Ferringhi Beach, 11 miles from town. Buses, taxis available.

CASUARINA BEACH (FC) — Named after trees that line the beach. 165 AC R w/balcony face the sea; TV, rfg. Dining room, coffee shop, two bars. Nice pool area, tennis cts, putting green, boating facilities. $22.

GOLDEN SANDS (DL) — Rebuilt 210-R resort opens Oct. '79. Same management as Rasa Sayang. $32-$48.

HOLIDAY INN (FC) — Opens in '79 with 162 R. Polynesian rst, cocktail lounge, pool.

MERLIN BEACH (DL) — Opens mid-'79 with 78 R and all amenities.

PALM BEACH — Economy; popular w/Europeans. 147 R; 60 in newer wing best. Dining, cocktail lounge, pool. $14-$18.

PENANG HYATT (DL) — Scheduled to open in late '79.

RASA SAYANG (DL) — Beautiful, charming resort w/300 AC R from standard to DL in separate wings. Three rsts, coffee shop, bars, cocktail lounge, disco. Tennis, pool, all water sports, squash cts. Sited on 11 acres, narrow beach. $29-$41.

SRI BANTAI MOTEL — On beach, 6 miles from city. 24 AC R w/tiled bath. Privileges of adjoining Chinese Beach Club (fee). Coffee shop. Good buy at $11 for those desiring beach life.

LANGKAWI ISLAND (Island of Legend)
West Coast, near Thailand border

LANGKAWI COUNTRY CLUB BEACH RESORT (FC) — 100 AC R, 2 chalets w/4 R each. Malaysian-style architecture. Several rsts, bars. All water sports, good fishing. Golf, tennis, riding. Jeep riding, mountain climbing in unspoiled wildlife sanctuary. A true paradise. $18 up.

PANGKOR ISLAND, Perak
West Coast

PANTAI PUTERI DEWI (Princess) — On bay with golden sand beaches. 55 R, some w/AC, private bath; Malay-style houses, chalets w/o AC. Rst (specialty: quail egg soup) serves European Chinese, Malaysian cuisines. Malaysian. Bar. Boating facilities. Good skin diving in crystal-clear waters — ages away from civilization. Sea Carnival held in Aug. $10-$23. Half-hour ferry ride from Lumut.

SEAVIEW — Pasir Bogak. 22 R in individual chalets w/baths and toilet. Dining room. $55 for cruiser to fishing grounds about 4 hrs. away. 1800-lb marlin, 60-lb barracuda, sails caught here. $10.

KUANTAN & EAST COAST

CLUB MED — North on Cherating beach. Opens May '79 w/600 beds in 15 bungalows. Pool, rst, bar, theater, dance floor, shops, beauty salon.

KUANTAN HYATT (DL) — Opens mid-'79 with 250 AC R, all amenities.

MERLIN (FC) — 124 family-style R; rst, bar. Freeform pool in attractive setting; boats. On crowded public beach three miles from airport. $23-$27.

JARA BEACH — Opened mid-'78 w/100 R at Tangjong.

TITIK INN — Near Twin Islands. Budget type. Rustic dining and lounge-bar. Extensive grounds facing beach. 16 Malay-style chalets plain but adequate. 4 dorms w/bath. $13 up.

TURTLE BEACH CHENDOR — Fabulous location for turtle watchers. 45 min from airport, 29 miles from Kuantan. 40 R, 7 chalets plain but comfortable. Large dining, bar area. Cultural dances. *Rsv:* necessary between May-Sept (turtle time). $12 up.

TWIN ISLANDS MOTEL — Magnificent broad beach over which you can drive for 23 miles. Up to 8-ft surf in monsoon season. Isolated, near fishing village, not far from Chendor (turtle) Beach. 14 nicely furnished, good-size rooms in Malay-style bldg. Attractive bar and dining room. Good food. Catch your own prawns, lobster in stream that runs past your porch (7 AC R w/porch). Still our No. 1 choice. $16 up.

GOVERNMENT REST HOUSES

RUMAH REHAT TELOK — Gov't Rest House, 3 miles from Kuantan. Terrific buy. Malay-style brick bungalow. 8 R w/2 comfortable beds, large bath, no AC but fan/mosquito netting for beds. Faces shallow bay and lovely stretch of breezy beach. Open-air rst. Adjacent to golf course (rough). Attractive, clean facility; quiet setting. $8.

BESERAH HALTING BUNGALOW — Like to live in a fishing village next to beach where boats unload their catch? A double R with foam rubber mattress, mosquito netting, bath w/shower (primitive but workable) in an old wooden Rest House complete w/porch. About $3.

PULAU TIOMAN ISLAND

This is Bali-Hai of *South Pacific* fame — but don't visit during monsoon season (April-Aug).

MERLIN SAMUDRA RESORT (FC) — In Kampong Lalang (island's west coast) amidst 750 beautiful, lush acres. 74 AC R, mini-casino, cocktail lounge, rst; tennis, boats for fishing, island trekking. Reached by light plane or helicopter — or by taxi from Johore Bahru (2½ hrs.), KL (6 hrs.) to Mersing, then 37 miles by speedboat (2½ hrs.). $19.

SABAH (Borneo)
KOTA KINABALU

CAPITAL (FC) — 15 min. from airport. 102 AC R, dining room, cocktail lounge, entertainment. Boating facilities. $31 up.

KINABALU INT'L (FC) — Opened '76 with 350 R facing China Sea. Chinese, Japanese, Malay, Continental rsts, bars. 24-hr. coffee shop, nitely entertainment. Pool; golf nearby. *Conv:* 500. $36-$45.

SARAWAK
KUCHING

AURORA — DT, 15 min. from airport. 86 large, remodeled and updated R. Dining room, coffee shop, bar, nightclub. $21-$31.

HOLIDAY INN (FC) — On Sarawak River, 20 min. from airport. 165 AC R. Several rsts, nightclub; cultural dances. Pool. Golf at Sarawak Country Club. Hour's boat ride to beach. Conv. facilities. $33-$38.

SINGAPORE

Few know that a songwriter's lament, "Bill Bailey, won't you please come home?" was written about an actual Bill Bailey who, many years ago, was so enamored of the dives of Singapore (which no longer exist) that he stayed on and on. That was when the Lion City (from the Sanskrit *singa* and *pura*) reigned as the Crossroads of the Seven Seas; incidentally, there were never any lions, though elephant and tiger were numerous — it's recorded that an average of one man per day fell victim to tigers. Today's tourists need only beware of shopkeepers' touts.

Singapore is still one of the world's busiest ports; on any given day, where the Singapore River meets the sea, up to 150 or more tramp steamers, cargo ships, cruise· liners, yachts and fishing boats can be counted at anchor. Too, it is an important air transit point between north and south, east and west. It's busy and very prosperous, it's clean and handsome, combines the most modern with elegant colonial — and though it's not our most favorite city, it deserves to be visited for its historical importance, fine hotels, excellent dining and shopping.

The island, connected by a causeway to the Malaysian state of Johore, still has large rubber and coconut plantations, national parks with original forests — and six types of venomous snakes. Streams and ponds hold unusual tropical fish, while butterfly collectors have, literally, a field day.

With a history dating back to the 1300s, known at one time as Tumasik, Malay for Seatown, this was an island of swamps and jungles when England's Sir Thomas Stamford Raffles arrived in 1819 to start Singapore's modern history. Its logo, today, is the Merlion — lion's head, mermaid body.

Just 70 miles north of the equator, the climate is humid and hot, yet the city is both healthful and exceedingly clean (fines for littering). Water is safe to drink from the faucet, food sold in the numerous street stalls also perfectly safe (some stalls are as immaculate as first-class restaurants).

Sampan-lined Singapore River cuts thru the very center of the city, the two halves connected by bridges, of which Anderson Bridge is a tourist landmark, connecting Raffles Place and Change Alley in the commercial sector to the south with the old English government buildings and lawns to the north. On the south side of the river are food stalls. This, for the tourist, is the heart of Singapore — a montage of color and sound and motion that's definitely one of *the* most attractive in the Orient. However, we must admit that on our last visit to Raffles Place, we were accosted, jostled, pestered and harangued — to such an extent that we fled in distress and anger. And crossing streets, anywhere in Singapore, is an adventure — even with stoplights; let the pedestrian beware is the rule. Still, in comparison with Bangkok, for example, Singapore is a rest cure.

Despite the hustle and bustle, there is tranquillity to be found in the beautiful, green residential areas, in the parks and Botanical Gardens. There you could be in the forests of Cambodia or Burma; thousands of monkeys swing from trailing vines to alight at your feet.

Local dress seen in the streets is as varied as the languages that go with it (Malay is official but a dozen others can be heard). For Raffles' liberal trade policies encouraged a vast tide of immigration: southern Chinese, both farmers and businessmen, responsible for much of the wealth both past and current; Sikhs, Pathans, Paks, Arab businessmen, Ceylonese gem cutters and merchants, Filipino entertainers and, of course, Westerners and Malays; latter comprised much of the police and military forces. This polyglot society of about two million persons, 75% Chinese, has made Singapore what it is — though not without some multi-racial problems.

By all means take the half-day City Tour[1] (pickup at hotels 9-9:30 a.m.; S$15), probably one to Sentosa Island and another to see the city from the water — but do spend time strolling across Anderson Bridge and along Elizabeth Walk into the turn of the 19th century. And, for sure, spend time in Chinatown which we found utterly fascinating and unlike any other we've been in. Good time to arrive is around 6 p.m. Tell the taxi driver to let you off at Shopping Market from where you can stroll (and eat) for hours; you won't get lost and you're perfectly safe. Walk up Temple Street, see the opium dens and death houses on Sage Lane, the innumerable coffin shops, pharmacies with (to us) incongruous collections of remedial herbs and concoctions. Later on dine and drink, if you wish, in one of plush hotels' lavish restaurants/nightclubs — like a transplant in time and space.

Those red/white Merlion signs signify historic or scenic attractions of particular interest.

GETTING TO SINGAPORE

For many Far East itineraries, this is the end of the line — the turn-around point for the return to North America, although an alternative routing is available thru Indonesia and/or the South Pacific.

Singapore has direct air connections from all major Far East cities.

Bangkok to Singapore by train (via Butterworth-Kuala Lumpur in Malaysia) offers an ideal change of pace for air travelers; see Thailand for details. Also by bus. From Butterworth and Kuala Lumpur, Mara Express Bus Service operates two daily runs, a.m. and p.m.; takes 15 hours from Butterworth. Fare on AC bus (a.m.) is $12.50 US. There's a similar return schedule from Singapore.

Masmara Travel (KL) has package deal by AC bus from KL to Singapore (and vice versa) that leaves at 8:30 a.m., arrives at 6:30 p.m. after sightseeing at Seremban, Malacca and Ayer Hitam. Rate (about $29 US) includes two-night accommodation (double basis).

ENTRY REQUIREMENTS

Passport, valid smallpox/cholera certificate. No visa required for stays up to 14 days. Hippies unwelcome.

CURRENCY

Approx. exchange is Singapore (S) $2.48 equals $1 US, or about 40¢ to each S$1. Declare currency on arrival. Licensed currency exchanges of Change Alley give best rates, so shop around before changing large number of dollars.

[1] Travel agencies handling inbound traffic are licensed by the Singapore Tourist Promotion Board; prices of standard conducted tours are fixed. STPB maintains tight control over all phases of the tourist industry, Singapore's fifth largest; even tour guides and shops catering to visitors are licensed. Any complaints? Contact the Board in Tudor Court, Tanglin Rd.

TOURIST INFORMATION

is provided by the Singapore Tourist Promotion Board — extremely well, too. *Singapore Guide Book* is available, on arrival, at its headquarters and information center at Tudor Court, Tanglin Road, Singapore 10. Open from 8 a.m. to 5 p.m., except Sundays, to assist visitors with information, free literature and arrange for services of an official guide. Phone 2356611.

Singapore Tourist Promotion Board office in the U.S. (251 Post St., San Francisco 94108; phone 414-391-8476) dispenses information and two illustrated booklets, *It All Starts In Singapore* and *Hotels of Singapore.*

Any number of maps are available on arrival.

SINGAPORE ATTRACTIONS

Jurong Bird Park — 50-acre landscaped park w/7,000 birds (350 species). Five-acre walk-in aviary. 9 a.m.-7 p.m. S$2 admission, plus S$1 for Jurong Falls (100 ft.).

Botanic Gardens — Attractions of this beautiful 80-acre garden in Tanglin area are: Lake, Sundial Garden, Plant House, Sun Rockery and Orchid Nursery (Singapore is one of world's leading orchid growers). First rubber plant was introduced from Brazil in 1877. Sunday band concerts. 6 a.m.-10 p.m. daily, Wed. 10-10. Floodlit at night.

Mandai Orchard Nurseries — Finest open-air collection in world. Over 300 varieties (half million plants); Black Orchid from Sumatra blooms in July, Tiger Orchid (with 5-ft. spikes of richly marked flowers) from Sept.-Oct. Orchids are planted hillside surrounded by tropical trees. Open 9 a.m. to 6 p.m. S$1.

House of Jade — Tanglin and Nassim Rd. Over a thousand priceless pieces. Etchings and Chinese paintings. 9-5:30. Pass must be obtained from Eng Aung Tong, 87 Neil Rd.

Chinatown is one of Singapore's most interesting sights — somehow distinctively different from similar districts elsewhere.

Singapore ranks as one of the most beautiful cities in the Orient with much of its charm due to the contrasting mixtures of British colonialism, modern architecture and Malay provincialism.

Instant Asia Cultural Show — Daily at 11 a.m. (S$4) at Pasir Panjang Paradise, near Tiger Balm. Oriental dances to exotic music. Show lasts 45 min.

Sentosa Island — Don't miss visiting this coralarium complex, open daily from 10-6 (S$2); has huge ¾-mile lagoon and swimming pool, 18-hole golf course, chalets and bungalows. Reached by cable car from Mt. Faber or by ferry from Jardine steps every 15 minutes.

Tennis — Singapore Tennis Centre, East Coast Park. 14 all-weather courts, 2 squash courts, rst. S$2.50 per hr, S$3.50 after 5:30.

CRUISING

Fairwind Junk (authentic sails) Cruises — Day/evening cruises to Malay fishing village and Chinese temples. Top deck is for dancing. Emerald Cruises at 10 a.m., 3 p.m. from Clifford Pier; 2½ hours, S$17. Starlit Cruise 6 p.m. for 3½ hrs. is S$35 w/buffet.

Sampans — Singapore has 54 of them. From Clifford Pier or Jardine steps for trips to offshore islands.

RENTING A CAR

Wouldn't bother with one just for driving around Singapore, but for those with time to take in Malaysia, it makes sense. Roads are fairly good and easy to follow.

From downtown Singapore, it's 17 miles to Johore Bahru in Malaysia and 230 miles more via Malacca, the most scenic routing, to Kuala Lumpur. However, as stated in the Malaysian section, we wouldn't miss going via the East Coast to Kuantan, a 200-mile, 5-hour drive. There are two ferry crossings (no charge; 24-hr. service). Kuantan to Kuala Lumpur is a 178-mile drive; see Malaysia for reasons for coming here as well as for a possible stopover at Tioman Island. Malaysian Tourist Development Corp. has an *East Coast Adventure* brochure that is helpful for motorists.

Asian Highway 2 continues to Butterworth (Penang), where, if you've rented the car for a week or more, it can be returned without extra charge, and you can go by air, bus or rail to Bangkok. KL to Butterworth is 238 miles.

Cars rent from $18 to $28 US a day (plus gas, mileage), $118 to $180 (496 free miles) by the week, $350 to $560 per month (1,488 free miles). Those are Avis and Hertz rates (approx.).

Singapore Facts

Airport Departure Tax — S$10 International, S$2 to Malaysia.

Business Hours — 9-5 Mon.-Fri.; Sat. to noon. Banks open 10-3, 9:30-11:30 Sat.

Current — 240-250v, 50 c. Adapters available in better hotels.

Climate — Warm, humid year 'round. Rainy and cooler Nov.-Feb.

Clothing — Lightweight. Jacket and tie, dresses for evenings.

Embassies — U.S. at 30 Hill (30251); Canada on Orchard Rd. (371322).

Language — Malay, English (widely spoken), Chinese.

Mail — S$0.55 to North America.

Population — 2,225,000 of which 1,100,000 are in Singapore.

Time — Half hour earlier than Hong Kong, same as Malaysia.

Tipping — Unnecessary as most hotels, restaurants add 10%. For luggage, S$0.20 to .50 per bag.

Tourist Information — Singapore Tourist Promotion Board, 251 Post St., San Francisco 94108 (415 391-8476). In Singapore at Tudor Ct./Tanglin Rd. (633611).

Water — Pure.

TRANSPORTATION

Airport Bus — S$3 per person to any hotel (9 a.m.-10 p.m.). By taxi about S$5-$7 (5 to 6 miles).

Taxis — S$0.80 first mile, 20¢ each additional half mile. About $9 per hour. 50% additional from 11 p.m.-6 a.m. Hotel taxis without meters charge more; determine rates before departure. Taxi drivers speak English, know their Singapore and are generally reliable.

Car Rental — Limousine and Car Rental service counters at airport. Perfectly feasible to drive yourself. Roads good. Rental firms have drive-away holidays to Singapore and Malaysia (no drop-off charges) with AC cars, 6 nights' accommodations, airport/-hotel transfers, sightseeing tours in Penang, Kuala Lumpur and Singapore.

Cruises — Launches depart 9:30 a.m., 4 p.m., Junks 10:30 a.m. and 3 p.m. from Clifford Pier. S$20 for 2-2½-hr. cruise. Sampans available by hour (S$20), full day S$80 per sampan.

Public Buses — S30¢ to most sections.

HOTELS○

1. Adelphi; 4. Cockpit; 5. Connaught; 6. Equatorial; 8. Goodwood Park; 9. Imperial; 10. Holiday Inn; 11. Ladyhill; 12. Malaysia; 13. Mandarin; 14. Marco Polo; 15. Merlin; 16. Ming Court; 17. Miramar; 18. New Hong Kong; 20. Orchid; 21. Peninsula; 22. Phoenix; 24. Raffles; 26. Royal Ramada; 28. Shangri-la; 29. Hilton; 30. Hyatt; 31. Summit.

TO WEDNESDAY
NIGHT PASAR
MALAM (3 miles
approx. from GPO.)

PLACES OF INTEREST

1. Albert Street (Chinese Restaurants); 2. Aquarium & National Theatre; 3. Buddha Gaya Temple; 4. Cathedral of the Good Shepherd (R.C.); 5. Cenotaph (Esplanade) Esplanade Open Air Restaurant; 6. Change Alley; 7. Chettiar Hindu Temple; 8. Chinese YMCA; 9. Cultural Centre; 10. Denmark House; 11. Empress Place — Government Building, Victoria Memorial Hall, etc.; 12. Fort Canning; 13. General Hospital; 14. General Post Office, Fullerton Building; 15. Hindu Siva Temple; 16. Immigration Depot; 17. Immigration Dept.; 18. Istana Negara; 19. Jade House; 20. Kallang Housing Estate; 21. Kallang Park; 22. Merdeka Bridge; 23. Mount Faber; 24. Multi-story Car Park; 25. Muslim Restaurants; 26. National Library and Museum; 27. Outram Park Shopping Centre; 28. Parliament House; 29. People's Park (Food Stalls & Shopping); 30. Railway Station; 31. Republic of Singapore Yacht Club; 32. Siang Lim Sian Si Temple; 33. Singapore Chinese Chamber of Commerce; 34. Singapore Cricket Club; 35. Singapore/K.L. Express, Singapore/Johore Express; 36. Singapore/Malacca Express; 37. Singapore Recreation Club; 38. Sri Mariamman Hindu Temple; 39. St. Andrew's Cathedral; 40. Sultan Mosque; 41. Supreme Court and City Hall Building; 42. Tanglin Club; 43. Telecoms External Services; 44. Thian Hock Keng (Chinese Temple); 45. Tin Hou Kong Temple (Kheng Chiu Building); 46. Tourist Promotion Board and Tudor Court Shopping Centre.

TO BOTANIC GARDENS
(3½ miles approx. from GPO.)

TO JOHORE BAHRU
(17 miles approx. from GPO.)

TO KRANJI WAR MEMORIAL
(14 miles approx. from GPO.)

TO JURONG (12 miles
approx. from GPO.)

TO BUKIT TIMAH
NATURAL RESERVES
(8 miles approx. from GPO.)

TO MANDAI ORCHID
GARDENS (13 miles
approx. from GPO.)

TO SINGAPORE TURF CLUB
(6 miles approx. from GPO.)

TO McRITCHIE RESERVOIR
(4½ miles approx. from GPO.)

TO SILETAR RESERVOIR
(9½ miles approx. from GPO.)

TO SINGAPORE ISLAND
COUNTRY CLUB (7 miles
approx. from GPO.)

TOA PAYOH
HOUSING ESTA'

ANDERSON — ROAD

BALMORAL ROAD

SCOTTS ROAD

SCOTTS ROAD

PATERSON ROAD

NEWTON ROAD

THOMSON ROAD

ORCHARD ROAD

BUKIT TIMAH ROAD

CLEMENCEAU AVENUE

AVENUE

BALESTIER ROAD

TO DARI LAUT
(12½ miles approx. from GPO.)

TO VILLA SALJANA
(13½ miles approx. from GPO.)

TO PASIR RIS
(12 miles approx. from GPO.)

TO CROCODILE FARM
(8 miles approx. from GPO.)

TO SINGAPORE AIRPORT
(7½ miles approx. from GPO.)

RACE COURSE ROAD

RANGOON ROAD

SELEGIE ROAD

JALAN BESAR

JALAN BESAR

BENCOOLEN STREET

Chinese
Restaurants
& Food Stalls

Sungei Road
(THIEVES'
MARKET)

VICTORIA STREET

VICTORIA STREET

KALLANG ROAD

Open Air
Food
Stalls

NORTH BRIDGE ROAD

BEACH ROAD

BEACH ROAD

BEACH ROAD

HILL STREET

NORTH BRIDGE ROAD

SINGAPORE RIVER

RIVER VALLEY ROAD

SINGAPORE RIVER

RIDGE ROAD

QUEEN ELIZABETH WALK

NICOLL

NICOLL HIGHWAY

NICOLL HIGHWAY

CLIFFORD PIER

GEYLANG ROAD

MOUNTBATTEN ROAD

MOUNTBATTEN ROAD

OLD KALLANG
AIRPORT
SPORTS
& YOUTH
CENTRE

TO SINGAPORE
AIRPORT
(7½ miles approx.
from GPO.)

STADIUM NEGARA

TO CHANGI BEACH
(15 miles approx. from GPO.)

TO SINGAPORE SWIMMING CLUB
TO CHINESE SWIMMING CLUB
(5 miles approx. from GPO.)

The famed Steamboat, one of Singapore's gourmet delights.

DINING & WINING

(10% service, 3% tax added)

Dining here is an experience. Excellent beef and seafood, spicy Malaysian and Indonesian curries are served at stand-up stalls or in elegant style at the hotels and better restaurants. As for attractive and exotic foods, think of anything you'd like to eat, and chances are that Singapore's hotels have it. Hotel coffee shops are a delight — and most of them beautiful — great for breakfast/lunch.

From 5 p.m. on, vendors move into Orchard Road Carpark with their portable kitchens. Never will you dine so well for so little. Popular, too, are the food stalls along Albert St. in Chinese quarter. All immaculately clean.

For a change of pace, start a "stall crawl" to the pubs all over the city. The Satay Club is housed in 28 units (each unit containing 4 stalls) located next to the port at Esplanade along Connaught Drive. Open from 6 p.m. Men in sarongs are perched on stools in front of a brazier brushing sticks of meat with oil, Indians sit before round pots; others make the Javanese soto (chicken). The Satay man makes satay — Malay barbecue of spiced beef, chicken or mutton marinated in saffron sauce, secret herbs, put on stick and dipped into a sauce of chili tomatoes, roasted peanuts (S$0.20).

As for restaurants, here are some of the best:

The rijstaffel lunch served on Sat, Sun. at *Cockpit Hotel* S$10 (also has good French Rst), with so many courses it takes all afternoon to eat, is out of this world.

Omar Khayyam, 55 Hill (Kashmir specialties) is considered *the* best. Lunch from S$7, dinner S$12.

For lovers of Chinese food, *Cathay,* in Cathay Bldg., serves sumptuous Cantonese cuisine, like delicious suckling pig, chicken in wine and baked garoupa with sweet/sour sauce. Elegant decor, good music. For Peking duck, it's the *Mandarin Court* (Mandarin Hotel); traditional music, too. For Szechuan dishes, *Phoenix Room* of the Equatorial Hotel; incidentally, when ordering Szechuan food, tell them to go light on the pepper if you don't

245

like it hot. If you'd like to eat where many of the residents do, try the *New Hong Kong* on the 15th floor of Hong Kong Hotel; considered tops for dim sum. For a dim sum lunch, it's Mayflower, DBS Bldg., Shenton Way.

For marvelous curry, there's *Shalimar,* Tanglin Shopping Center; expensive (S$19-$21 for dinner) but fun to watch the cooks at work. *Jade Room,* 290 Orchard Rd, is good for tearoom-style lunch.

Go western at pub-style *Beefeater,* 417 River Valley Rd; *Forster's Steak House,* 25A Amber Mansions off Orchard Rd.

Chalet, Ladyhill Hotel, is rated by some to have best European cuisine in Far East. For Italian food, it's *Gino,* 91 Tanglin (S$12 lunch/dinner).

Reached by launch from Kalong Park's waterfront, the *Palace Kalong* reeks of atmosphere. Lunch only but a nightclub after dark.

Want to catch and eat your own fish? Do so at *Tai Seng,* Block 17, Outram Park or at *Hung Kang,* 38 N Canal.

For seafood and glamor, dine atop Singapore's highest peak at *Mt. Faber Rst,* then hop on the new cable car to Sentosa Island for fabulous view of harbor and surrounding islands. Cars leave continuously 10 to 10 (S$3 RT) for 9-minute ride.

Do have a drink or tea at Raffles Hotel just to see how it used to be.

In good hotels, bar Scotch costs US $1.75-$2.25, small local beer US 90¢- or imported at US $2.75. Happy Hours discount as much as 50%.

RIJSTTAFEL

This Eastern specialty, pronounced *RYE-stah-fel,* was developed by the early Dutch settlers of Java who, because they loved good and unusual food, experimented with many spices and other native delicacies found there and added them to a basic dish of curried chicken and rice. Lo, the Rice Table — Rijsttafel.

In Singapore, every Saturday and Sunday lunch, this meal is served at The Cockpit Hotel in traditional style by teams of Malay boys, dressed in colorful batik sarongs and tanjaks (turban-like headdress), from wooden trays carved in Indonesia and decorated with flowers. First is the long, wild rice of Thailand, reputedly the world's best, presented, steaming, in a wooden bowl; then comes the chicken cooked in a rich curry sauce that's subtle rather than hot. For a bit of variety, there's also Udang Curry — prawns. From a succession of platters come the *sambals* (accompaniments) and special delicacies, including *satay* — lamb skewered on sticks and roasted over charcoal. Here's a list of the side orders:

Achar — Mixed vegetables in vinegar, spices. *Kropok* — Fried prawn crackers. *Telor Asin* — Salted duck eggs. *Seronding* — Grated coconut. *Pisang Goreng* — Fried bananas. *Kachang Tanah* — Buttered peanuts. *Ikan Goreng* — Fish fritters. *Kobis Koreng* — Fried cabbage. *Kachang Pandjang Goreng* — Fried long beans. *Timun Belanda* — Vegetable marrow. *Bendeh* — Ladies' fingers (?). Plus the *Sambals:* Spiced mutton, beef, prawns and small fish; shrimp paste; dried shrimp, whitebait, salted fish; finally mixed spices with hot chilis.

Finally? Not at all. Dessert is *Gula Malacca,* tapioca with sauces of coconut milk and molasses.

The cost is about S$10 now (about $4.30 US), but even so. . . .

Malay dances are part of a typical folklore show, one of the most interesting bits of Singapore entertainment.

NIGHT DOINGS

Singapore has become quite puritanical — the government looks down a patrician nose at the offbeat. Girlie bars do not exist, though there are a few cabarets, like *Pink Pussycat* and *Oasis* (9:30-1), where you find dance hostesses.

There's a Night Cultural Tour. Forget it, for you can go to the *Adelphi Hotel Roof Garden* (28101) on your own for Malay folk dances, wedding dance, snake charming. Dinner show nightly 8 p.m. exc. Sun (S$20). *Tropicana,* on Scotts Rd, features name acts and strip-tease (they introduced it).

Gala evenings can be enjoyed at the various hotel nightclubs. Currently in are the *Eye,* Connaught House, and *Pub,* Hotel Malaysia. *London House,* Marco Polo Hotel, is a small, underground bar with authentic street signs, gas lamps providing great atmosphere for dancing; closed Mon. Downtown at Overseas Union Shopping Center is the huge *Neptune* theater-restaurant with lavish Chinese show. 20 miles out over poor road is *Villa Saujana Jalan Loyang;* excellent Malay show and dinner in 2-acre garden setting. Rsv a must (93139). Very exp. Not recommended in rainy season.

SHOPPING

A free port. Best buys: antiques, scrolls, screens, porcelains, Persian carpets, batik, exotic silks, antique maps (Raffles Place), ivory chessmen, Malaysian silver; pewter. And, of course, the usual Japanese imports.

Most popular shopping areas: Raffles Place, High St, North Bridge Rd, Orchard Rd, Tanglin Rd. Largest shopping arcade is huge People's Park Complex, open 11 a.m.-10 p.m.; prices reasonable. If you like to haggle, sort thru the trash in Thieves Markets' many stalls and shops on Sungei (River) Rd. just a block from Rocher Canal; daytime only. Downtown Change Alley is where the action is — if you enjoy being touted (we didn't).

Check your hotel for the location of Night Market (Pasar Malam) as it changes nightly (Wed on Tanglin Rd). Begins at sunset, closes 10:30 p.m. Wear walking shoes, you'll literally walk a mile. Need them, too, on Orchard and Tanglin Roads (where better shops are). Everything is done to discourage walking; if it isn't the traffic, it's the lack of sidewalks in front of hotels.

SINGAPORE WORLD TRADE CENTER

Opened late '78, it has a 21,043-square-meter convention hall seating 4,000 delegates and two-story exhibition facilities of 8,364 sq. meters. It also contains a trade library, computer data bank, conference rooms, restaurants, clubs and secretarial services.

There are also other convention facilities. For complete details, contact Singapore Tourist Promotion Board's Convention Officer.

Hotel Directory

There are more reasonably priced Deluxe and First Class hotels here than, possibly (even probably) than anywhere else in the world — an assemblage, with varying, stunning decors, that's positively eye-popping. The following listing represents only the outstanding ones in their class; with the exception of Century Park Hotel, Holiday Inn and Peninsula, we have personally inspected them all.

Most hotels are in the residential area 3 ½ to 4 miles from the center of town, 15 to 25 minutes from the airport, either on or adjacent to Orchard Road. Cuscaden, Hilton, Holiday Inn, Hyatt, Mandarin and Ming Court are on Orchard; Goodwood Park, Marco Polo, Shangri La a few blocks off. Closer to town (1 ½-2 miles): Cockpit, Imperial, Phoenix. Center of town: Adelphi, Peninsula, Raffles.

All are air-conditioned, most boast of completely modern facilities thruout. In all, about 10,000 rooms are available. 10% service and 3% room tax are added to quoted double rates *(in US dollars)*.

DOWNTOWN

ADELPHI — A century-old, 2-story hotel across from Govt. buildings, parks. 90 recently refurnished, garden rooms w/terrace. Antiquated baths, halls, elevators. 4 rsts (Malay Cultural Show nightly), 4 bars. $24.

MERLIN (FC+) — DT on Beach Road at the harbor. 260 view rooms; rst, 2 bars. Pool. Conv. facilities. $26 to $37.

PENINSULA (FC) — Great DT location. 315 R. Chinese Theater Rst, Indonesian rst, coffee shop, piano bar, cocktail lounge. Pool. Popular with businessmen. $26 up.

RAFFLES — One-time famous DL hotel that was very, very British; still retains a diluted colonial atmosphere. Candlelight dining in Palm Court. Pool. Malaysian Cultural Show. 3 bars. 125 R (some inside). Luxury rooms furnished in "rattan colonial." Those who stay here love it. $27 up.

NEAR DOWNTOWN

COCKPIT (FC+) — Attractive chandelier in center of spiral staircase leading to superb rsts. Georgian-style hotel has 2 wings; new modern section (200 AC R) and older section w/60 R facing Japanese Garden with beautiful walks, fountains, rock gardens, charming pool area. Mandarin lobby decor w/painted glass murals. Famous for Sat, Sun rijstaffel buffet. Top French cuisine, too. Charming hotel with a lot going for it. $31-$47.

MIRAMAR (FC-) — Overlooks Singapore River in Chinese district. 214 R; Chinese, Japanese, Western cuisines. Cocktail lounge $26.

NEW HONG KONG (FC-) — 101 Victoria, 232 R. Chinese Rst, nightclub, bar. Pool. A mile from DT. $22-$28.

OBEROI IMPERIAL (DL+) — Hillside in gorgeous natural setting; magnificent view of city. Across from National Theater. Huge ground floor pool area. Elegant lobby, bar, beautiful use of wood with orange/gold decor. 600 plush R w/balcony. An elegant hotel; popular w/Australians. $39 up.

CENTURY PARK HOTEL (DL) — Tanglin Rd., opposite Singapore Handcraft Center. 464 AC R. Poolside bar and rst. $38-$48. *Rsv:* Sheraton.

EQUATORIAL (FC) — Near University, in residential area. Gorgeous grounds. Several rsts, bars, coffee house. Rijstaffel (Sat) in Laksamana Room. Pool. 225 R. Well priced at $26-$31.

GARDEN (FC-) — Designed in shape of courtyard with gardens and pool in center. 92 AC R with patio. Grill, cocktail and tea lounge. In residential area, 15 min. from airport. $26.

GOODWOOD PARK (FC+) — Quiet, beautifully situated amongst lovely grounds. Long-time favorite that's had a major facelift — you won't know the old gal. New supper club, conv. theater for 800. Original tower wing restored to turn-of-century look. Several pools, rsts, bars. Charming lobby area. Top service. 280 R w/terrace or patios. $40 up.

HOLIDAY INN (FC) — On Scotts Rd, off Orchard Rd. 2 specialty rsts, entertainment, bar, pool. 560 AC R. *Conv:* 400. $35 up.

HYATT (DL+) — Hillside. Chandelier ceiling with 50,000 blue/white pieces of glass (who counts?) covers mezzanine lounge. Exquisite Islander Rst, plus Hugo's for cont'l cuisine. Regency lounge for music/dancing, Pete's Place for snacks & pizza. 900 R have closed-circuit movies, 24-hr. electronic bar. 4th-floor pool. 16-lane bowling alley. *Conv:* 1200. A bargain at $41 up.

LADYHILL (FC-) — 180 R, older hotel that's been remodeled (same mgt. as Goodwood Park). *Le Chalet Rst* serves excellent international cuisine. Coffee shop, 2 bars, pool. $25-$30.

MANDARIN (DL+) — Luxurious marble lobby w/gold embossed mural. Chatterbox coffee shop exquisitely decorated in gold. Revolving rooftop rst, plus 5 others serving every type cuisine. 5 cocktail lounges, nightclub. Freeform pool. 700 R. 1,000 in staff to serve you. Shopping arcade. $43-$50.

MARCO POLO (FC+) — Tanglin Circus. Under Peninsula Hotel mgt. has been upgraded, refurbished. 310 attractive R (6 rooftop). Exclusive Marco Polo rst; new, very posh Disco Club (strict attire). Pool. Excellent service. $41-$45.

MING COURT (DL-) — On Tanglin Road near Tudor Court — great location. 350 R older hotel. Pagoda pool set in Ming Garden on 5th floor. Barbella Bar discotheque. Photogenic, costumed doormen. *Conv:* 500. $36.

ORCHARD — Pleasant, friendly service in 33 R economy hotel. Rst, bar. Top location for those not looking for all the extras. $22-$25.

PARK LANE (FC) — Formerly Summit. 21 Mt. Elizabeth Rd. 420 AC R, SU. Grill room, Japanese rst, coffee shop. Pool area. Upgraded in '78. $34-$44.

ROYAL RAMADA (FC) — 321 modern R w/view of city. On Newton Rd, eight minutes from Orchard. Tropical gardens, pool. Royal Palace supper club, several rsts, bars. *Conv:* 650. $26 and up.

SHANGRI-LA (DL) — Singapore's largest convention hotel. Large pool within 12 landscaped acres w/waterfalls. 3-hole pitch/putt, tennis, badminton; snack bar. Noisy and exp. coffee shop; quiet and exp. Golden Peacock Rst; Tiara Rooftop Rst, bar (closed Sun). 509 R with stocked rfg, balcony. 165 R garden wing opened in '78. *Rsv:* Western Int'l. $46 up.

SINGAPORE HILTON (DL) — Top location — and one of Orient's best hotels; marvelous service. 410 R, some w/balcony. Harbor Village Rst, ablaze with lighted lampposts, serves excellent filet, lobster thermador. Lobby completely remodeled with bronze mirrors, lovely woods; spacious and elegant. Second-floor lobby for group check-ins. $40-$46. Delightful open-air, rooftop rst. Coffee shop is a beauty with frontage of tropical planting, waterfall and birds behind a glass wall; quiet and fully carpeted, it serves a delicious breakfast. Pool.

INDONESIA

"Story of Radja Pala," by I. Made Djata, shows Radja Pala stealing the garment of a heavenly nymph.

If hordes of tourist buses shuttling back and forth between sightseeing attractions turn you off, we suggest turning on Indonesia. Here, for a variety of reasons, none related to the undeniable charms of its attractions, touristic growth lags. Except in Bali, one of the most fascinating, beautiful islands we've ever seen, though we've received some negative reports on treatment visitors receive in major hotels (due, mostly, to overbooking) and number of tour buses.

Let's face it. Luxury accommodations cannot be provided in glorious isolation. Where there are large numbers of tourists, there must be some problems. Notwithstanding, we urge seeing Bali now, even if you don't go elsewhere in Indonesia, while still *comparatively* unknown rather than later when all the world is beating a path — as it surely will.

So, buy Indonesia this year or next — it's still a bargain.

Indonesia consists of over 13,000 lush, tropical islands in a semi-circle straddling the equator — islands of unique sights, sounds and taste. Customs, dress, climate, ceremonies, arts and handcrafts are almost as varied as the landscape — starting with Jakarta, the capital, and extending to the enchantment of Bali, the archaeological parks in Central and East Java, Samosir Island in Lake Toba and on to Yogyakarta with its palaces and magnificent Borobudur, largest Buddhist sanctuary in the world.

The 135,000,000 people that make up the world's fifth largest country are basically of Malay and Polynesian ancestry, plus fusions of Chinese, Arabian, Southeast Asian and East Indian bloodlines, resulting in a population of infinite variations. More than 300 ethnic groups speak better than 200 distinct languages.

By 600-700 AD, there were Hindu and Buddhist kingdoms in Java and Sumatra of various dynasties that flourished for 700 to 800 years and presented to the world some of its most magnificent temples and monuments; their glories can still be seen in the architecture of Borobudur and Prambanan. In the early 1300s, the Mojopahit Kingdom, under Gajah Mada, unified a powerful Indonesian empire, from New Guinea to the Philippines, under one rule; this Hindu-Buddhist kingdom was the last of a united Indonesia until modern times. Islam, from an original base in Malacca on the Malay Peninsula, gradually became the predominant religion.

Meanwhile, as a result of Vasco da Gama's discovery of a sea route to the East, the Portuguese dominated these valuable "Spice Islands" until Portugal was annexed by Spain (1580), after which the Dutch East India Company took over (1596) the spice trade and gradually brought Java and other large islands under Dutch rule, though not until the latter part of the 19th century was the process completed. But in the early 1900s, Indonesian nationalism became so strong that the Dutch set up a Volksraad, People's Parliament, with limited powers. Agitation for reform continued; under the Japanese, the nationalists strengthened their organization so that on August 17, 1945, they were able to declare their independence. The Dutch attempted to restore its control and bloody confrontations resulted until, in 1949, actual independence was achieved; in 1950, Indonesia became a member of the United Nations.

In 1974, Indonesia introduced a new system of place name spelling. Here's how it works:

"The 'c' is now read like the English 'ch' in children. This was formerly written 'Tj' like in 'Tjirebon' which is now spelled 'Cirebon.' The letter 'j' is read like 'j' in 'joy.' Thus 'Djakarta' is now spelled 'Jakarta.' The letter 'y' is read like 'y' in 'you.' Thus 'Surabaja' is now spelled 'Surabaya.' 'Yogyakarta' is an exception. Although pronounced 'Jogjakarta,' it is written 'Yogyakarta.' This is because originally in Javanese this town is called 'Ngayogyakarta.' "

INDONESIAN TRIP PLANNING

At this stage of the nation's tourist development, we suggest Bali as your major destination, Yogyakarta as the next most important while using Jakarta mainly as a means of exit/entrance. In an effort to bolster the capital's importance, make it a longer stopover, the Government has canceled many flights to/from Bali; this, in effect, also favors the national carrier, Garuda, which handles Jakarta-Bali traffic. According to an international hotel chain executive, 75% of their Jakarta hotel's guests arrive from Singapore — and 75% of those are businessmen. Of the tourist 25%, very few are from North America or even outside Indonesia. Quite a contrast to neighboring countries which Asians of various nationalities are visiting en masse.

There are non-stop jet flights to Jakarta from Bangkok (GA, KL), Hong Kong (GA), Kuala Lumpur and Singapore. Tokyo is one-stop (at Denpasar) on Garuda.

To Denpasar, Bali, only Garuda flies non-stop from Hong Kong, Singapore and Tokyo; also Bangkok, as does Thai Int'l. Thus, it's feasible to schedule a Hong Kong-Bali-Singapore routing (and then on to the Australia for a return via the South Pacific) if desired, leaving out Jakarta — unless you wish to visit Yogyakarta (also spelled Jogyakarta), which is advisable, and some of the more adventurous islands.

A secondary (and, possibly, supplementary) recommendation is to take a cruise in Indonesian waters from Singapore; see Sea Travel for details. Only disadvantage: not long enough in Bali. Depending on space availability, embarking or disembarking there in order to spend more time in the Island Paradise might be arranged. Another possibility is to book a cruise from Australia.

For explorers who want to get further out, we're including a few thumbnail sketches of interesting possibilities. We hope, in years to come, to elaborate more fully as new territories and facilities open up.

ENTRY REQUIREMENTS

Passport, visa ($2.80; 2 photos) good for 30 days. No visa needed for intransit air/ship passengers. For tour groups, there's on-arrival visa issuance in Jakarta, Bali and Medan. International certificate for smallpox and cholera compulsory. Typhoid and paratyphoid vaccinations are not but strongly advised.

CUSTOMS

Custom declaration must be filled in on arrival. Foreign currency exceeding $500 must be declared. 2 liters of liquor allowed.

CURRENCY

Rp (Indonesian rupiah) 415-418 equals $1 U.S.; figure Rp 40 as 10¢. There are 100 sen to each rupiah. On departure, rupiahs equalling $50 U.S. can be converted into foreign currencies.

CLIMATE

Warm, humid in coastal areas all year. Cool to cold in higher regions. November-March is rainy season. Best time to come: April-October. Clothing is casual.

INDONESIAN FACTS

Airport Exit Tax — Rp 1000 for international flights, Rp 800 for domestic.

Banks — 8-4 (some open on Sat).

Business Hours — Most observe 12-2 p.m. siesta.

Current — 110v-130v, 50c. 220v in Jakarta.

Convention Facilities — Jakarta International Convention Hall in Senayan has finest equipment. Theater accommodates 3,850.

Gambling — Roulette, blackjack. Cockfights (Bali), bull races (East Java).

Horse Racing — Jakarta Canidrome Sports Club on Thurs, Sun. Admission Rp 1000. Minimum bet Rp 200. Greyhound races Wed, Sat. Hotels arrange for guest cards.

Language — Bahasa Indonesia, English.

Population — 135,000,000. Capital: Jakarta (3,250,000).

Sports — Pencak silat (art of self-defense), judo, karate, kite-fighting. Singing contests for perkututs, a local bird.

Time — Three zones: Western (Java, Bali, Sumatra, Madura), GMT + 7; Central (Kalimantan, Sulawesi, Nusa Tenggara), + 8; Eastern (Irian Maluku). + 9.

Tipping — Porters: 100-200 Rp per bag. Taxi drivers not tipped. Taxis charge extra for luggage.

Tourist Information — Indonesian Tourist Promotion Board, 323 Geary St., San Francisco 94102. (415-891-3585)

Water — Drink only purified or bottled.

CALENDAR OF EVENTS

Perhaps nowhere else in the world will you find so many festivals. Bali has the most since a temple festival is held for every occasion. Thruout the country are 10,000 temples, each with its own anniversary. Calendars differ, so dates are complex. Check on arrival what's going on, but see at least one.

January-February — Chinese New Year, Glodok (Chinatown) in Jakarta. *Grebeg Basar,* Yogyakarta. Sultan leads procession from his palace to Grand Mosque. Goats, water buffalos are slaughtered as offerings. Court dances are held at Paku Alam Kraton, Yogyakarta, monthly. In Bali, Galungan holidays (New Year) are celebrated with happy reunions with ancestral spirits. Gay music, dances, colorful village decorations.

March — Sacred golden carriage of the Sultan is bathed (Siraman Kreta Kraton), Yogyakarta.

April — *Kesada Festival,* East Java. Midnight offering at Mt. Bromo crater.

May — *Waicak Day* (Buddha's birthday) — Spectacular at Borobudur Temple, Central Java. Thousands of Buddhists assemble here; Buddhist priests and followers clad in yellow and white robes, carrying lighted candles, walk from Mendut Temple to Borobudur, climb the stairs and circle the temple.

June-October — Ramayana Ballet Festival, Yogyakarta. Hundreds of dancers, musicians perform on moonlight nights at Prambanan Temple. Anniversary of Jakarta is celebrated with month-long festivities — street dancing, parades, cultural events.

September-October — Bull races in East Java. Bulls trained on raw eggs and beer.

SUGGESTED READING

After researching the Indonesian tourist situation, there is little doubt in our mind that the archipelago offers an almost unlimited horizon to those looking for the unspoiled and offbeat. But it's virtually unknown, difficult to obtain accurate information. Fortunately, *Guide to Java* and a companion, *Guide to Bali,* both excellent, in-depth coverages of about 400 pages and beautifully illustrated in color (but, strangely, without a single map), are available at $8 per copy (includes surface mailing) from APA Production, Ltd., P.O. Box 219, Killiney Road Post Office, Singapore 9.

WHAT TO BUY

Carvings are utterly beautiful and still inexpensive, especially the primitive ones produced in West Irian. Exquisite silver filigree work from Sumatra and Central Java is exceptional. But Indonesia is probably best known for its fine batiks (by all means visit a batik factory during your stay in Jakarta). Fine handmade fabrics inlaid with gold and silver thread are woven in Bali and Sumatra. Probably the loveliest and most typical Indonesian art is Balinese watercolor.

Best buys are found in the villages of the various islands. Those not going to Denpasar in Bali will find local sarongs, masks, paintings, woodcarvings, tablecloths, leather, antique jewelry (so they say) in Jakarta's markets. Instead of patronizing beach vendors along Sanur Beach, visit Denpasar's curio shops. And those interested in seeing a fine art collection, a beautiful home and gardens, should ask their hotel to contact artist Jimmy Pandy (near Bali Beach hotel).

Shoppers wanting reliability, quality and well-priced merchandise (no bargaining) should take a ten-minute drive from Denpasar to visit the attractive Sanggraha Kriya Asta center. Attractive Balinese-style buildings house local arts and crafts as well as crafts from other parts of Indonesia; can watch craftsmen at work.

Antiques may not be exported.

DINING INDONESIAN STYLE

Indonesian cuisine differs from island to island. If you've tasted one, you haven't tasted them all. The basic staple is rice served with either meat, eggs, vegetables. As in China, all dishes are put in front of you, and you pay for what you eat. And, if you've always wanted to forget cutlery and use your fingers, do it — Indonesian style.

Best known menus are Javanese: spicy, sweet, sharp but not hot; Sumatran *(nasi padang)*: spicy with chili pepper. Satay (barbecued meat) varies with the sauces. And don't miss the krupuk (crackers) made with shrimp, fish or fruit.

Painting batik cloth takes hours of patience and skill.

BATIK

Earliest examples of batik that have been preserved are the seventh or eighth century Chinese silks still displayed at the Shoso in Nara, Japan.

Batik making by the traditional *tjanting* method was nurtured for centuries in Indonesia's villages. A *pengobeng* (woman batik maker) would take six months to complete an intricate sarong length — an arduous process of tracing fine wax patterns from the *tjanting* (wax holder) on both sides of the fabric, then mixing vegetable dyes, steeping, drying, boiling the fabric to remove the wax, then repeating the process several times.

Patterns were regional and reflected wildlife, mythology, vegetation and social customs. After Indonesians had been converted to Islam in the sixteenth century, it was forbidden to copy any living thing — especially the human body. Consequently man was shown as he would look in a puppet play.

Until recent years, the courts of Jogjakarta and Surakara used only traditional patterns. Members of the royal house reserved their own; these were forbidden to anyone else. But times have changed. Under the influence of the west, chemical dyes instead of vegetable made the standardization of colors possible, and the introduction of the *tjap* (engraved copper block) to stamp out wax patterns has changed the art of batik making.

Using high-quality cotton cloth instead of silk, the *tjanting* is able to glide smoothly across the fabric, resulting in intricate designs which could never be produced on silk. However, in Indonesia today, some batik makers are being encouraged to recreate traditional colors and designs and apply them to chiffon and silk shantung. Unfortunately, there's a cost factor involved.

The foregoing applies to yard goods. Picture quality batiks are being "painted" in wax, then individually dyed, by a number of skilled artists in Malaysia, Singapore and Indonesia. Often called the poor man's stained glass, batiks become gloriously hued when framed in a shadow box lighted by fluorescent tubes. Our purchases of batiks in Penang (Teng, dean of Malaysian artists, has galleries there) and Singapore rank among the most satisfying art buys we've made.

If interested in making your own batiks, there are several good books on the subject.

On Bali, *Jo-Jo* behind Bali Beach Hotel serves good food in delightful surroundings. *Puri Suling* near Ubud has excellent Indonesian specialties. For Chinese, try *Puri Salera,* Denpasar. Lovers of lobster, here's your chance — all hotels serve them.

In Jakarta, if you are hungry enough, indulge in the rijstafel at the *Oasis*; strolling musicians, too. Rijsttafel, the 64-dish Indonesian buffet, is widely served in a carefully balanced assortment of flavors and spices; the hotter the day and the hotter the food the better. Actually, you should eat it at noon; at private parties, hostess expects you to leave the table and go home to bed.

Art and Curio serves both Western and Indonesian food in a setting of antique Indonesian art. Open from 9-midnight. *Bamboo Den* (open day/night) is conveniently located in entertainment center. Its coffee shop, bar and Imperial Room serve European and Chinese food (good steaks); also has gambling. *Flamingo Restaurant* specializes in superb Chinese food; top dance band. *Grill House* is known for excellent regional cuisine.

BALI . . . Throne of the Gods

So unique is the Balinese way of life that the Indonesian government shifts uneasily from one horn of its dilemma to the other: authorizing new hotels to attract more tourists, then eliminating some jet flights from abroad to lessen tourist impact. Which comes first, culture or commerce?

The magic of Bali — the countryside, the people, the dance and temple spectacles — is such a rich and rare and beautiful phenomenon that it should be kept inviolate, yet because of this richness, beauty and infinite charm, Bali's allure is irresistible. It is:

> . . . the red eye of Gunung Batur glowing in the dark, the first light creeping down the ancient, scarred slopes of Gunung Agung, home of the gods.
>
> . . . the heady scent of incense and frangipani; the beguiling grace of a slender legong dancer and the untamed frenzy of a ketjak chorus, the extravagant beauty of a landscape patiently carved into symmetrical green terraces over unhurried centuries.
>
> . . . decorative, honey-skinned people who live in constant communion with the gods on the sacred crests of volcanos, with the spirits of the underworld in the unholy depths of the ocean.
>
> To the Balinese who believe in reincarnation, Nirvana is Bali "devoid of all trouble and illness." They cannot conceive of a better heaven than this.[1]

Neither can we. But can it survive the inevitable tourist multitudes? Is paradise lost, or by some miracle of the gods can it be retained? Today it is still there — but in the natural, uncommercialized pageantry of village and commercial life, not in the posh hotels.

BALI . . . WHAT IT WAS AND IS

One of 13,000 Indonesian islands, its volcanic peaks (there have been eruptions in 1917, 1926 and 1963, the last by mighty Agung) are part of the mountain range that forms the backbone of the archipelago. About 2,750,000 people live on and off the intensely fertile 2,000 square miles of terraced rice lands (there are two, sometimes three, crops annually), coconut and coffee plantations, colorful vegetable gardens which produce the principal exports: coffee, copra, cattle and pigs. The mountains split the island east to west where, because of that sector's dry desolation, an occasional tiger and other wild game roam. Overall, though, it is lushly green and, above all, beautiful.

Separated from the island of Java by a narrow strait, Bali has usually been influenced, if not dominated, by its big brother. In the 1300s, it was subjugated by

WEATHER WISE

It's mild, pleasant thruout the year. From April to September (dry season), sunny days, pleasingly cool evenings prevail. During the rainy season (Oct.-Mar.) it's claimed there's no such thing as a miserable day as showers are closely followed by sunshine. Average monthly temperatures range from $82°$ to $86°$ (Feb., Mar.) — but it's up to $10°$ cooler in the mountains.

Java's Mojopahit Kingdom and became Hinduized, but when the new faith of Islam swept Java, Bali resisted the tide; today it is a lone Hindu outpost in a Moslem sea.

Since early Indonesian civilization, mutual cooperation (gotong rojong) was essential for rice cultivation — irrigation of rice fields, one below another, requires a good neighbor policy. In Bali, the bandjar assistance organization supervises almost every village activity, from marriages and cremations and upkeep of

[1] Condensed from Sawasdee (Welcome), Thai International's bi-monthly publication — the best in-flight magazine we've ever read.

temples to irrigation and expenditure of communal funds. The *bandjar* also owns padi fields, worked communally to provide the village with funds. Membership is compulsory for married men; should one refuse to join, he is declared "dead" and ostracized by the village. In the 1965 Communist uprising in which 300,000 Indonesians were killed before the government prevailed, 40,000 Communists died in Bali alone — proving that though communal, the majority was not Communist.

UNDERSTANDING BALI

To do so, one must know its religion, the force that inspires everyone, from tiller of the soil to dancer, artist, musician. For here is a life style wherein the creation of beauty, whatever its nature — a food offering, a carving, a batik — is essential in pleasing the gods. Ceremonies designed to satisfy the divinities are relatively incidental.

Belief is that the mountains, with their lakes and rivers that feed the earth, symbolize all that is good and powerful, hence are the earthly palaces of the gods who, legend has it, created Gunung Agung and Gunung Batur (with a silent, blue lake twixt the two) for that purpose — the holiest place in the whole world. The ocean, on the other hand, became the dwelling of underworld spirits, of sharks and the Fanged Giant and lurking demons who emerge from the blue to haunt lonely beaches.

Thus, between the high and the low, the good and the evil, were human beings who kept up a steady dialogue with both supernatural powers. Consequently, religion became interwoven with the fabric of daily life. Each community is held responsible for harmonizing these opposing forces, thus the constant festivals; the spiritual life-force of any village can be depleted if not continuously regenerated by religious acts and protestations of faith. Should evil predominate, crops fail, calamities befall and the temple priest must communicate with the gods thru self-induced trances in order to discover what's gone wrong — a shrine allowed to deteriorate, an anniversary overlooked, a feast prepared without

suitable elaborateness. Whereupon amends to the gods must be lavishly made with gorgeous offerings, exquisite temple music and dances.

In the early centuries A.D., Hinduism was introduced by Indian traders, and Hindu gods were soon welcomed into the Indonesian pantheon.

Balinese-Hinduism is essentially a monotheistic religion with Sanghyang Widi the one supreme deity — though with hundreds of manifestations, principally the trinity of Vishnu, Brahma and Shiva. But the gods and goddesses of mountains, seas, rivers, villages, homes and crops remain. In fact, the island's religion, today, is a mixture of Hinduism, Buddhism and native animism. It's interesting to note that when neighboring Java came under the sway of Islam, Bali alone kept alive the old religious traditions and ceremonies.

BALI'S UMBILICAL

Temples *(Pura)* synthesize art, religion and living. Each village must have at least three temples: Pura Desa (main one where official religious celebrations are held), Pura Puseh (where ancestors are worshipped) and Pura Dalem (death and cremation). A *pemangku* (temple priest) attends to routine matters, a *pedanda* (high priest) is the medium between the gods and the people, presides over important rituals.

Though they have common features, temples are not alike. A low wall surrounds each. Entrance into the first courtyard is thru an elaborately carved, split gate; within are carved statues, several thatched pavilions for offerings, village meetings, the orchestras. The next ornamental gate, mirroring the design of the first but not split, is guarded by two huge, fierce statues; directly behind it a stone screen, festooned with demons, to ward off evil spirits. This gate leads to the second courtyard containing altars and shrines; latter are pagoda-like, thatched affairs *(merus)* with three to eleven receding roofs which serve as rest houses for the gods.

The most sacred temple, Pura Beskih, attracts worshippers from all over the

Legong dancer adjusts her ornate golden helmet crowned with yellow frangipani before her lovely performance begins.

island. It is the sanctuary of the holy spirit of the Great Mountain, Gunung Agung, on whose slopes it stands. This interesting complex, which you should visit, consists of three main temples representing the Hindu trinity; the central one, Pura Panataran Besakih, is flanked by the other two, of which the one to the northwest, Pura Panataran, was built in the 11th century. Certain buildings within the main temple are maintained by noble families.

Supposedly there are over 10,000 temples in Bali, and each celebrates the anniversary of its consecration with a temple festival *(odalan)* — which means it's nearly impossible to miss at least one of these feasts, major social events for local communities, that require elaborate preparations: temporary bamboo altars within the temple hold food offerings to the gods; demon statues are dressed up. Women are continually arriving bearing colorful offerings on their heads. You can watch in utter fascination for hours. Without fail, inquire at your hotel where the day's best festival is taking place.

Dusk is, perhaps, the most dramatic time for festival watching. By the flickering light of coconut oil lamps, a procession will be enroute to or from a temple to the chanting of women, handsomely clad in sarongs, the shrill clamor of the gamelan orchestra. Carved deities, shaded by ceremonial parasols, are carried in sedan chairs to a river for a symbolic bath. In the temple courtyard, after the religious ceremonies are over, dances and dramas begin; they may last until early morn.

Towards the end of the Balinese year, when evil spirits and *leyaks*[1] (vampire-like creatures) bring tropical fevers and the island is in a state of spiritual pollution *(sebel)*, exorcism ceremonies, in the form of Sanghyang trance dances, become necessary. There are many versions with one thing in common: while women chant,

They're not supposed to reveal themselves to foreigners, hence it's unlikely you'll see one. But if you're determined, you might be lucky. That is, if you follow these secret instructions: stand naked in a cemetery at night, bend *backward*, peer intently between your outstretched legs — and wait.

temple priests exercise their hypnotic powers on the girl dancers who, on emerging from the trance, have no recollection of what they did nor how they performed the movements. Sanghyang Deling has boys and/or priests dancing around and thru glowing fires of coconut husks.

THE CREMATION CEREMONY

This is an extravagant, festive feast and one of Bali's greatest attractions — which you may, with perfect impunity, enjoy.

A cremation ceremony has the sacred duty of liberating the soul of the dead from the body — a mere shell no longer of importance — so that the soul may journey to heaven to rejoin the Hindu cycle of reincarnation.

While members of the family purify themselves (and arrange to finance the steep costs, which may run a thousand dollars or more), the corpse remains at home in a temporary coffin decorated with flowers and ornaments. When the priest decides the cremation day, elaborately ornamented wood and bamboo towers are used to carry the body to the cremation grounds. Here the bodies (many are mass cremations in order to lessen the expense) are placed in coffins hewn from tree trunks and shaped like cows, the towers and coffins then set afire. While the bodies burn, families and villagers gather around to joke, sing and dance. After cremation, ashes are collected for a purification ceremony the next day, then scattered in the sea or nearest large river.

As with festivals, inquire at your hotel where you can attend a nearby ceremony. We passed one accidentally, were absolutely enchanted by such a colorful gathering.

BALI TRIP PLANNING

At the very minimum, three days — but that isn't enough. You need a week to cover just the major facets. Because of the hills and mountains, much of Bali is not interconnected making necessary a series of day trips out of the Denpasar area. Besides, roadside traffic, the beauty of the landscape, the fascination of local markets and festivals keep highway travel to a deliberately slow pace.

Although it's possible to circle the island in a rental car, stopping overnight in government rest houses, we'd advise against it unless you have a guide. Running commentaries are essential to understand what you see of Temple architecture and carvings, festivals, local customs; otherwise you get the color without the meaning. Thus, a series of escorted tours is the best answer. Here are the most important ones:

3-Hour — Museum at Ubud; Sangeh and Mengwi (very good); Ketchack Dance; Art Galleries at Sanur Beach; Kuta Beach.

5-Hour — Bedugul and Bratan Lake; Tjeluk, Mas, Ubud, Tampaksiring; Klungkung, Tangkas.

8-Hour — Tjeluk, Mas, Bedulu, Tampaksiring, Bangli, Kintamani; Bratan Lake, Singaradja (north Bali); Klungkung-Besakih (very good).

10-Hour — Klungkung, Besakih, Karangasem; Bedugul, Singaradja, Kintamani.

Thus, the minimum stay of three days should include an all-day tour (most important is to Kintamani), two shorter tours on another day, the third day for shopping and enjoying the beach. As we've said, all too short a time.

Important Note: Readers complain that Bali bus tour rush you around too fast, that heedless camera bugs amongst the passengers are indifferent to others' enjoyment. Solution: take a car or taxi with guide driver — not too much more than a conducted bus tour — and go at your own pace.

Despite the above, and the persistence of vendors and shopkeepers, Bali still fascinates thru its sculptures, crafts, artistry and dancing. It's still worth seeing.

GETTING TO BALI

Aside from previously mentioned plane and cruise ship arrivals, bus service between Java and Bali can be arranged for groups with advance notice; buses are air-conditioned. It is necessary to ferry between Ketapang, Java, and Gilimanuk, Bali. Great way to see rural people and countryside.

Garuda has frequent daily jets from Jakarta (1:35; 625 miles) one daily jet, three jet-props from Yogyakarta (1 hr; 345 miles). Incidentally, reports on Garuda's service, equipment and on-time percentage have not been flattering — but it's the only way you can go by air.

If arriving in Bali and continuing your trip thru Jakarta, then, if time permits, stop at Yogyakarta enroute to the capital. If arriving first in Jakarta, then a circle trip, Yogyakarta-Bali-Surabaya-Jakarta, would be ideal for those not in a hurry.

DENPASAR

The capital of Bali isn't much by cosmopolitan standards, but it (the name means "North of the Market") has some interesting facets: museum, market and dance school. Denpasar Museum houses within its temple-palace-style facade a display of Bali's artistic achievements from their very beginnings. Well worth visiting, as is the Kokar Conservatory of Instrumental Arts and Dance where diminutive dancers train and musicians learn the intricacies of the gamelan. Cultural Art Center has great handcrafts, good show.

A few of the specialties you should try: *Babi guling,* roast suckling pig; *Betutu bebek,* duckling roasted in banana leaves; *Gado Gado,* distinctively flavored, fresh salad; *Ikan asem manis,* sweet and sour fish; *Kare udang,* curried shrimp; *Opor ajam,* chicken cooked in coconut milk; *Nasi goreng,* spicy meat and shrimp fried with rice; and, of course, *satay* (barbecued beef, port, chicken, turtle) flavored with peanut sauce.

All hotels feature these and other Indonesian specialties as well as international cuisines. In Denpasar, there are many good Chinese restaurants; *Puri Selera* is said to have top Cantonese food.

UBUD, THE ART CENTER

Although this can be visited on a 3-hour tour, best to make it a day's excursion by stopping at Tjeluk (best Balinese filigree jewelry in gold and silver), Batuan (for Dwarawati handcrafts), Djody's handcraft center just before reaching Mas (batik and handweaving) and, of course, the famous wood carvings of Mas itself; for generations, the best carvings have been exported from here, and the best here are those of Ida Bagus Tilem (Adil and Siadja also considered excellent).

The quiet charm of Ubud has lured not only top Balinese painters but also celebrities and artists from all over. Art lovers who'd like more time in this delightful spot can stay at the *Hotel Puri,* an old, converted palace, or the *Hotel Tjampuhan,* nearby at the junction of two rivers, in a bungalow; green, terraced hillsides fall right into the riverbeds. Be sure to visit the Museum Puri Lukisan for a fine cross section of modern painting and sculpture.

There are two experiences you'll not want to miss on the return trip: Goa Gadja, the Elephant Cave, and *Puri Suling,* House of the Flute, both near Bedulu. Former was a Buddhist monastery, probably as far back as the 11th century, with a huge demon head and other carvings across the entrance, in front of which carved nymphs and goddesses hold water spouts. The latter is Bali's most famous restaurant; no one comes here without enjoying Bob Hargrove's souffles or other of his Indonesian and Western dishes. *Puri Suling* (has its own gamelan musicians) is also accessible on other day trips.

EXCURSION TO KINTAMANI

We found that anywhere one drove into the countryside was a beautiful experience, but there is little doubt that this excursion, in one form or another, is the best overall since the drive introduces some of the most beautiful temples. If on your own, be sure to stop at the following:

Batubulan, famed for its stone carvers, to see its Pura Puseh which has an exceptional gate carved with dieties of the Hindu pantheon, plus a meditating Buddha.

Blahbatuh's Pura Puseh boasts of a 14th-century stone head of Kbo Iwa, a mythical (and fearful) giant credited with creating many of the island's stone monuments.

As you drive up the slope to Bangli, stop at the town of Sidan to see the intricate relief carvings of the kulkul (drum) tower of the Pura Dalem; they show what fearful tortures await the wicked in the depths below.

Bangli has its Pura Kehen, the district's holiest; unfortunately, because of its popularity, it's become a tourist trap, and you have to fight off juvenile entrepreneurs. Whether the impressive structure, with Chinese porcelain inlaid courtyard, is worth it is questionable; this was the only spot where we were accosted and annoyed.

The climb continues past Pura Ulan Danu with its fine gateways, many priceless relics — like a solid gold bell given by a ruler of Singaradja in penance for having insulted the gods. When you pass the old town of Kintamani and continue to the mountain sanctuary of Penulisan, you've reached the highest temple in Bali (be sure to have sweater or light coat) — well, almost; a seemingly endless flight of worn steps climb upward to this unrestored, 11th-century temple complex and its amazing collection of Balinese kings staring sightlessly into the past. On a clear day, the view of half the island — terraced, green mountains stretching to ocean blue — is unforgettable.

Kintamani has an interesting market; some remains of pre-Hindu civilizations are to be seen in the nearby, picturesque villages of Abuan Sonyang and Trunjan.

VISIT TO KLUNGKUNG

Only 24 miles from Denpasar, the city is another in the "don't miss" category, primarily to see the Kerta Gosa Hall of Justice and the Bale Kambang pavilion.

Kerta Gosa is an excellent example of the art and architecture prevalent in the days of the powerful Rajas of Klungkung (1300s thru the 1600s). It must have proved a frightening experience for those standing trial for facing them, besides austere judges, were a series of terrifying paintings showing the reception the guilty might expect when he went to hell. On the pavilion's ceiling, however, are the beauties of heaven.

Nearby Bale Kambang also has a spectacular graphic display on its ceiling — illustrations of the Balinese calendar, religious and social customs and epics. One group deals with marriage by proposal, the conventional style. You should know, however, that in Bali there is another approved form — by elopement; the girl's family shows great surprise, even outrage (though greatly pleased) when a young man runs off with their daughter. Undoubtedly many Western fathers would like to see more elopement marriages.

Excellent shopping for silver and gold jewelry at the handcraft center.

Final stage of the journey to the temples of Kintamani.

SINGARADJA

Those with time and an adventurous spirit should "discover" the northern side. The round trip is done in a day, but an extra day is better as it gives time to stop and browse; stay overnight at a government rest house in Singaraja (but have a sweater as temperatures drop 10^0).

This is a gorgeous drive thru wildly beautiful mountain ranges. At Bedugul, the ancient crater of Mt. Bratan is now a lovely lake with a resthouse on its shores. Below Bedugul is an orchid market.

Many interesting temples near Singaradja of different design from those you've seen in the south; gates are taller and the soft, pink sandstone quarried here permits carvers even more fanciful, detailed works.

The capital of Buleleng district, this city of about 17,500 is a leading port, particularly for the export of coffee, and a fascinating melange of many ethnic and religious groups. It was a Dutch center during the colonial period.

BALINESE DANCES

The dance is a vital part of Balinese life: it appeases the gods and delights humans, binds the community together and may even exorcise spirits, and expresses a religion which lives as much in the present as in the past — the spiritual battle between the forces of good and evil.

This battle is dramatized by the *Barong Dance,* a mythical lion who protects mankind from the evil influence of Rangda, the hideous witch-queen. Barong is danced by two men, one of whom manipulates the mask of snapping jaws and bulging eyes, the other the body of golden scales and mirrors. The community is represented by male dancers brandishing kris daggers; when necessary, they come to the aid of Barong who, eventually, triumphs — but only temporarily since the basic battle between good and evil remains unresolved, as witnessed by Rangda being placated with the sacrificial blood of a chicken.

Actually, this is the finale of an infinite dance-drama, *Tjalonarang,* that lasts from midnight to dawn while relating the story of Rangda Tjalonarang, the wicked widow-witch who tries to destroy an idyllic kingdom. But *Barong* is easiest to present for special showings.

Legong is the enactment of allegorical legends in abstract pantomime. Common to any story are two identical dancers and a Cjondong (principal protagonist) dancer. With immobile, painted faces and tender bodies swathed in brocade, these little girls (they usually "retire" at 12, some to graduate to Oleg Tambulilingan) are utterly dazzling and unbelievable. Of all the dances, Legong is considered the finest; in it the formal gesture and movement of Balinese choreography reaches a unique perfection.

Oleg Tambulilingan, a modern (1952) dance, is a charming duet in which two dancers, male and female, portray a pair of bumblebees romancing in a summer garden. They tease, caress, retreat, make intricate gestures of bodies, arms and fingers — each expressing a new mood, a new degree of intimacy. Such a dance may last an hour, yet the dancers, pulsating to the gamelan, seem unconscious of fatigue.

In the *Kebyar Duduk,* a solo exhibition, the male dancer rarely raises himself from the ground; he concentrates on arm movements, a swaying of the torso, facial expressions. This dance combines the delicacy of Legong with the manly heroism of the *Baris,* a traditional, triumphant warrior dance.

Wonderful as these are, for astounding, electrifying impact, nothing approaches a performance of the *Kecak,* often called Monkey Dance. Its mad, frenzied magic may blow your mind, even terrify. It takes you on a trip into a savage world of sound in which the voices of one hundred men split the night into staccato choruses of wild chattering; without musical accompaniment, they imitate the sounds of instruments, plus the shrieks and jabberings of monkeys in the jungle. Naked torsos gleam in the light of flickering flares as they sit in concentric circles within which the principal dancers enact a chilling episode of the Hindu epic, *Ramayana.* A crescendo of chanting, hissing, sighing — which rises and falls with the swift writhing of arms and bodies — seems to cast a spell on the audience as well as the dancers.

Kecak (literal meaning, voice) originally was performed to invoke the gods in times of disaster, later became a Ramayana sequence. It is essentially a temple dance performed after sundown. As in other Balinese dances, the dedication of the performers and the responses, even participation, of audiences are integral parts of worship.

Sanghyang trance dances, in which young girls become possessed by divine spirits, is no longer permitted as entertainment. If you hear of one taking place in a temple, don't miss it.

The distinctive music which accompanies most Balinese dances is produced by gamelan musicians who sit cross-legged behind their instruments: iron-keyed metallophones (played by sharp taps of a mallet and the placing of fingers on keys to stop the sound), bronze gongs, chimes, bamboo flutes, cymbals and long drums which actually lead the others, control the tempo. As the introductory notes to a dance ripple forth, an almost magical hush falls over the temple courtyard. And you become part of ancient ritual.

JAKARTA, Capital of Indonesia

Considering the amount of time the majority of tourists spend in the Far East, and in comparison to its formidable competition (Hong Kong, Bangkok, Kuala Lumpur, Singapore, Manila to mention the nearest), one must inevitably decide that Jakarta is a destination one can live happily without. Not that it doesn't have its moments. And it's certainly important to businessmen — in fact, primarily so — but it lacks beauty and graciousness, which could be overlooked if it substituted charisma. It doesn't. It's also one of the most traffic-clogged cities in this part of the world, which is quite a tribute in reverse. Yet it has its moments.

Jakarta is a Moslem city where men wear black fez hats, women carry baskets on their heads. You can buy food from portable stalls or dine in elegance, listen to Javanese opera or watch a Balinese dance in one of the plush hotels. Modern skyscrapers loom over buildings of intricate Indonesian design. Downtown, an area, has been restored to what it looked like when the city, called Batavia, looked Dutch. Early in the morning, fish vendors shout their prices at Fisherman's Wharf in spirited auctions. Nearby stalls of merchandise, notably semi-precious gems, invite the tourist to bargain. On cobbled Fatahillah Square, antiques, spices, batiks and other exotica are sold in shops resembling those of the olden days; food and drink is served in taverns and 18th-century coffeehouses. Old City Hall (1710) is a museum with a large collection of historical mementos. Glotlok, the Chinese quarter, is also being restored.

One of the most interesting sectors is Pasar Ikan, the old harbor of Batavia, where sailing vessels from the outer islands, old warehouses, a welter of shops selling everything and anything relating to the sea are assembled. And if flea markets attract you, visit Jalan Surabaya where you can bargain for most anything, including Dutch oil lamps and antique Chinese ceramics.

Jakarta is noted for the monuments built during the Sukarno era. Most impressive is the National Monument, a 350-ft. tower topped by a flaming torch, Flame of Freedom, in Merdeka Square. Here in Freedom Park is the Presidential Palace, City Hall, Gambir Railway Station and Istiqlal Mosque. Museum Pusat, west side of Merdeka Square, is recognized by its huge, bronze elephant — often referred to as Elephant House; houses a superb exhibit of village and architectural styles in existence thruout the country. Here, too, is a fabulous collection of Chinese ceramics. Open 8 a.m. to 1 p.m. daily except Monday.

Near Halim Airport is Indonesia in Miniature, a 150-acre park in which the cultures and architectural styles of 26 regions have been assembled for a quick, overall view of the country. Each region has about three acres on which typical buildings, manned by men and women in local costumes, have been erected. Centrally located is a lake in which islands have been built to duplicate the Indonesian archipelago. Temples, mosques and a convention center complete the project, which can be viewed by aerial cable, train, pedicab or horse and buggy.

Morning and afternoon City Tours, together, show everything there is to see, including a batik factory, oceanarium, handcraft center — but not Indonesia in Miniature. Cost is about $9 US per tour.

JAKARTA EXCURSIONS
Bogor and Presidential Palace

The Botanical Gardens, 35 miles south at Bogor, West Java, extend over 275 acres, include more than 10,000 species of trees and the largest collection of orchids in the world. Here, too, is the Rafflesia, world's largest flower, some three feet in diameter, that blooms every five years. Obtain a special permit and visit the grounds of the summer palace. Coach tours available from Jakarta. Can continue on thru beautiful Puncak Pass to the resort area at Pelabuhan Ratu. Stay at the *Samudra Beach Hotel* on the edge of a palm-lined beach.

Pulaua Dua (Bird Island)

Three hours by car, plus a half-hour boat ride. Great for bird watchers and photographers. Some 70 different species of birds.

There are over 1,000 islands off the coast of Jakarta where you can see coral gardens, watch the birds. Skyvan Air Taxi lands at Pulau Putri (20 min) where bungalow accommodations are available.

TRANSPORTATION

Taxis — Some unmetered. Airport to hotel, US$5. Ratax Taxi has meter: Rp 200 first km, Rp 75 each additional km. Jakarta's Halim Int'l Airport, 10 miles SW of town, has minibus service to hotels.

By Road — Traffic is horrendous — don't even think of driving yourself in Jakarta, especially since SMCR hire cars (AC) with driver are still inexpensive. About Rp 1500 per hr, Rp 2000 out of town. Sari Express Bus Line has AC Mercedes-Benzes for land tours across Java and Bali; arranged for groups only.

JAVA BY BUS & RAIL

You could easily circle this island by public bus, either during the day or by night express (be sure you get an air-conditioned one). Best coach companies: Kembang Express from Jakarta to Surabaya (about 561 miles); Bhayangkara or Remaja Express, Jakarta-Yogya (383 miles via Semarang). Fares are reasonable (like about $7 US to Yogyakarta during day, $7.50 at night, plus 50¢ service, insurance).

Railways, abbreviated to PJKA, are state-controlled, provide service on Java and Sumatra. Best for tourists are: Bima Express between Jakarta-Yogya-Surabaya (AC coaches, sleepers; US $30 first class to Surabaya); Mutiara Express (AC coaches only) to Surabaya; Parahyangan Express from Jakarta to Bandung.

TIPS FOR BUSINESSMEN IN JAKARTA

Buy a large street map, even though it costs several US dollars. Before leaving hotel, have your destination marked on the map. Unless you're making a short trip, don't use a taxi. Hire car w/driver (Rp 1500-2000 per hr.); usual minimum is 2 hrs. Taxis charge meter rate, plus Rp10 for each 48 seconds waiting time, or Rp250 for each 20 minutes. If you do use a taxi and a hotel is not near, keep it waiting — you may never find another. Be sure you agree on waiting time rate — otherwise it can be very costly.

Don't plan on making business appointments by phone; telephone system is overworked, and operators or receptionists usually do not speak English. Best, cheaper and less trying on nerves just to arrive at your objective unannounced. Appointments in Indonesia mean nothing, anyway.

JAKARTA ENTERTAINMENT

This is a gay city after sundown with all types of entertainment that portray its blending of East and West. Cultural dance performances can be seen at leading hotels. Taman Ismail Marzuki Art Center has traditional Javanese, Indonesian and modern entertainment. Panca Murti Theater has nightly performances of Javanese *wayang wong* (shadow play).

There's local and foreign singers, plus international floor shows. Currently, top spot is *Nirwana Supper Club,* Hotel Indonesia. Dress is formal, reservations essential. *Flamingo* is a good restaurant featuring dance bands, entertainment. *LCC Nightclub,* under the shadow of the National Monument, serves exotic drinks in romantic atmosphere. Looking for hostesses? They're at the *Marcopolo* (topless show, dining) and *Paprika,* Jalan Ir. H. Djuanda 19.

There are three licensed casinos, usually open 24 hours: Copacabana, New International Amusement Center and Pix Amusement Center.

WILDLIFE PHOTOGRAPHY

Thruout the archipelago are 115 wildlife reserves. Udjung Kulon, on the Panaitan Peninsula in West Java, has the famed one-horned rhinoceros, buffalo and boar, deer and mousedeer, tigers and panthers, wild dogs, crocodile, snakes and a wide variety of birds. Observation towers command strategic spots.

On the western tip of Flores Island and on nearby Komodo and Rindja are those monstrous dragon lizards, up to 300 lbs. and 10 ft. in length, you've probably seen on *Wild Kingdom.* Plan on a 5-day safari.

Tiger safaris in South Sumatra are also on the agenda. For these and other wildlife and adventure packages (best to plan for four, six and eight persons; allow 3 months lead time), write: Batemuri Tours, Wisata Hotel Il. Figaphos Tours & Travel Il. Sudirman, Granada Bldg.; Mitra Tours, Wisma Hayam Wuruk No. 104-108. 8 J'l. Hayam Wuruk — all in Jakarta.

YOGYAKARTA
(JOGJAKARTA)

300 miles south of Jakarta is the cultural center and most important tourist destination on the island of Java — and one of the few remaining sultanates in the country.

Visit the four royal palaces, tombs, fortresses which are fine examples of traditional Javanese decor. The Sultan's palace is open to visitors on most days, but permission to enter should be obtained. The open-sided pavilions (pendopos) have marble floors, superb carvings on teak pillars and panels and painted rafters to resemble the sun. Thruout are wooden carriages, ancient musical instruments and gorgeous batiks. On the second Saturday of each month, Wayang Kulit is presented here.

Other interesting sights are the water palace at Tamansari, the Sono Budojo Museum, the Batik Research Center, the Dance Institute where in the morning you can watch rehearsals. In nearby Karang Kajen village, batik designers are working while at Kota Gede village, silversmiths are busy. In town on Malioboro St., you can shop for batiks and handcrafted silverwork.

Twenty miles from Jogjakarta is magnificent Borobudur, the largest Buddhist sanctuary in the world. Built in 850, it stands over 125 ft. tall. Terrace balustrades are elaborately carved. There are three stages to this temple dominated by the main stupa on top with an unfinished statue of Buddha. On entering the gallery, turn to the left so that you pay tribute to the gods; turning right means you are paying off evil spirits.

Just east of Borobudur are the Mendut and Pawon Temples. Mendut lies amidst bamboo groves, and it is from here that worshippers start their walk to Borobudur to celebrate Buddha's birthday.

Ten miles northeast, on the road to Solo, is the largest temple complex in Indonesia, Prambanan, with 14 intricately constructed Hindu temples, dating back to the 9th century, situated within a huge courtyard surrounded by elaborately carved walls. The Ramayana classical dance festival takes place here on the nights of the full moon from June to October.

48 miles from Yogyakarta (35 from Prambanan) lies Surakarta (Solo), even older than Yogyakarta. Palace of the Prince of Surakarta is larger than the Sultan's in Yogyakarta and is known for its fine collection of instruments and holy sets of leather puppets. Next to the palace is the Royal Museum. There's an excellent handcraft center. At night Wayang Orang (opera) is performed at Sriwedari Recreation Grounds.

SURABAYA

An industrial city with little to offer touristically. Main reason for coming here is to take a rugged 80-mile trip SE to the 7,176-ft. Mt. Bromo, an active volcano. On the way you pass thru villages of the Tenggerese who worship the mountains, have an annual pilgrimage to the crater to make offerings to the God of Fire. An hour's drive from Surabaya is the town of Tretes where you can hire a pony and guide for the trip up the mountain. Only hearty souls should attempt this. During the full moon, May-October, you can watch the dances of East Java performed in the amphitheater at nearby Pandaan.

Best hotel in Tretes is the Tandjung w/50 R, dining room, bar, pool and horses. $47 AP.

If you are in Surabaya in October, cross the straits (35 min.) by ferry to Madura Island to watch the Brahmin bull races, attend the Harvest Fair.

Can reach Yogyakarta and Surabaya either by day (lvs 6 a.m., no AC) or night train. Bima departs Jakarta daily 4 p.m. arrives Yogyakarta 2:11 a.m., Surabaya at 7:30 a.m. Train has AC sleeping, dining cars. By day train you see the rice fields, many small villages.

You get to both spots quicker by air.

SULAWESI (Celebes)

Described as an "orchid set in the sea," this is an island of numerous peninsulas extending in all directions. The main city, Ujung Pandang (formerly Makassar), lies to the southwest and is the home of Muslim *bugis* (seafarers); an old fortress remains to tell of its romantic past. 15 miles away is a magnificent nature reserve and resort area with fine white sand beaches.

Some 300 miles north is Toraja Land, a comparatively unknown, offbeat tourist attraction reached by a very bumpy road. But a very worthwhile destination according to those who've been there. Offered as a 3-day package out of Ujung Pandang by Pacto Travel, 88 Jalan Cikini Raya, Jakarta. What attracts are the weird Toraja burial cliffs, the various ceremonial rites and the Toraja's fine woodcarvings and pottery.

Sulawesi's rugged mountains and beautiful lakes, virtually unknown to tourism, afford some wonderful moments of unusual splendor. Lake Tondano, near Menado in the north, is said to be superb.

There is non-stop, jet-prop air service to Ujung Pandang from Denpasar (2 hrs.) and Surabaya (1:20), jet service from Jakarta (2:10). The Grand Hotel has 65 rooms ($20).

There is non-stop, jet-prop air service to Ujung Pandang from Denpasar (2 hrs.) and Surabaya (1:20), jet service from Jakarta (2:10). There's the 39-room Pasanggrahan Beach Hotel ($23 D w/meals) and the 65-room Grand ($8 to $17 each).

Borobudur, a Hindu-Javanese monastery, was probably erected in the 8th and 9th centuries. There are 27,000 square feet of stone surface with relief carvings made up of 1,460 pictorial panels, 1,212 decorative panels — plus 504 Buddha images carved in the round. Truly a magnificent art creation.

SUMATRA

Medan, the capital, is a commercial city and gateway to Prapat on Lake Toba, a 110-mile drive via Tebingtinggi or 140 miles over the more scenic Brastagi road. The approach to the lake is breathtaking as the road winds down over crater walls to the shores.

Lake Toba is 50 miles long, 16 wide with fascinating Samosir Island in the center. Here live the Batak people in unique homes built with overhanging gables and carved woodwork. On the island are stone chairs and tables formerly used by ancient rulers. Samosir is reached by small powerboats. Definitely worthwhile. Dancing and music performances can be arranged for groups.

There's daily jet service to Medan from Denpasar or Jakarta. Garuda and Singapore Airlines fly between Medan and Singapore; SQ offers an all-inclusive tour to Medan and Lake Toba. Malaysian Airlines has a six-day tour to Medan and Lake Toba departing Kuala Lumpur and Penang; includes Brastagi Lake Tinggi, Toba Tebing and Samosir Island.

Hotel Directory

Hotel restaurants feature Indonesian, Chinese, Japanese, French and Western cuisines.

JAKARTA
(21% Service & Tax Added)

AIRPORT INTERNATIONAL — 20 min from int'l airport, few minutes from domestic. 104 AC R, rst, bar. $13-$20.

ARYADUTA HYATT (FC) — 208 AC R, several rsts; Indonesian dances nightly. Indonesian decor. Pool. 4 meeting rooms. $32-$36. Near Presidential Palace.

BOROBUDAR INTER-CONTINENTAL (DL) — Off Banteng Square on 23 acres. 899 AC R, SU in unusual 18-story design. Rsts, bars, 2 pools, cabanas, tennis, mini-golf. *Conv:* 1300-2000. $43-$53. Helicopter service to airport $33 per person.

JAKARTA HILTON (DL) — In Senayan on 32-acre complex. William Prigge, Hilton Vice-President, calls it "our most exciting hotel." 406 AC R, SU in 14-story hi-rise. 3 rsts, coffee shop, 2 bars, pool. Attractive Indonesian Bazaar surrounds lake. Executive Club has pool, tennis, golf, several rsts, sunken bar. Open-air Balinese theater. Conv. facilities from 450-800. Conv. Hall seats 4,000. $43-$55.

INDONESIA (FC+) — Older hotel has been enlarged, remodeled. 236 AC R in new wing, 430 in original. Pool w/large terrace. 2 tennis courts. Several rsts, 4 cocktail lounges, supper club. Indonesian Cultural dances Sun. evening. *Conv:* 850. $33-$40.

KARTIKA PLAZA (FC-) — Top location, 15 min. from airport. 333 AC R, some w/balconies. Rst, supper club. Pool, bowling alley. Reports say hotel needs a face-lift and better maintenance. $37-$41. Tennis & golf arranged. *Conv:* 200.

MANDARIN (DL) — 20 min from airport. 504 AC R, pool, squash court. Rst with int'l and Indonesian food, coffee shop, bars, entertainment. Opened in '78. $40-$56.

SAHID JAYA BOULEVARD (FC) — Near government offices, banks. 514 AC R. Pool, tennis. Seafood rst, grill, coffee shop. Indonesian dances. *Conv:* 800. *Rsv:* Travelodge. $33 up.

SARI PACIFIC — DT. Opened '76. 500 AC R are bright and cheerful with impractical shutters. Water in bathroom are sporadic; elevators temperamental. Several rsts, bars, cocktail lounge, discotheque. Pool. Garden setting. $38-$42.

BALI
(21% Service and Tax)

BALI BEACH (DL) — Beautifully landscaped, superbly sited on Sanur Beach. 500 AC R, patios, 2 Olympic-size pools, bars, rsts, indoor/outdoor pool dining, Bali-Hai rooftop supper club; Balinese dances, music are nightly features. Expensive dining for ordinary food. 9-hole golf course, tennis, great beach. Now quite commercial and frantic and it is said reservations not always honored. *Conv:* 1000. *Rsv: ICH. $37 up.*

BALI HYATT (DL) — 390 AC R in Balinese palace architecture. Indoor/-outdoor rsts, exotic sunken bar; beautiful landscaped gardens cover 35 acres. Pool, 2 tennis courts. Coral beach not conducive to sunning. Note: Have letter of confirmed rsv. with you. $29-$37.

BALI OBEROI (DL) — N end of Kuta Beach. 48 lanai R w/terrace, sunken tub; 14 elegant villas w/private garden. Rst, bar, cocktail lounge, pool, good beach. Lanais $45. villas $100 un *Rsv:* Loews.

KAYU-AYA OBEROI (DL) — On Kuta Beach. Intimate, luxurious and exp. 14 villas w/pools about $120 up, 48 lanais about $40. AC dining room, 2 bars, pool. Great for skin divers.

PERTAMINA COTTAGES (FC) — Kuta Beach. 156 AC R ($37 up), bungalows ($48 up). Pool, tennis, golf, beach resort. Dining room, coffee shop, bar. Boating.

SANUR BEACH & SEASIDE BUNGALOWS (FC) — Rave notices from those who have stayed here. Excellent service. 240 AC R ($32), 26 attractive beach bungalows ($43 up). 2 lovely pools and gardens. Dining room, coffee shop. Water facilities. Rates include service & tax.

For those desiring less expensive, less lavish accommodations from $20-$29D: *Bali Seaside Cottages, La Taverna, Respati Beach* — all have pools, rst, private baths. *Segara Beach* has lovely gardens, good food.

JOGJAKARTA, Java

AMBARRUKMO PALACE (FC) — 265 AC R, SU. Rsts, coffee shop, 2 cocktail lounges, nightly entertainment. Pool, tennis. Free transfer to airport/-station. $26-$30. *Rsv:* Sheraton.

PURI ARTHA COTTAGES — 22 AC (2 w/o), small, tastefully furnished R w/patio in garden setting. Rst, bar. Well run. $18 up includes breakfast.

SRI MANGANTI — 52 AC R opened in '74 with all amenities. Delightful. $22-$24.

MEDAN, N. Sumatra

DANAU TOBA (FC) — 200 AC R set in charming gardens. Rst, nightclub, pool. *Conv:* 300. $30. Airport service $2.

PRAPAT (Lake Toba)

PRAPAT — 39 bungalows w/living room, bedroom, bath (dipper-style bathing, no hot water) on shores of beautiful Lake Toba. Dining room, bar. Tennis, 9-hole golf course. Lake resort. $18-$27 includes breakfast.

SEMARANG, Java

PATRA JASA — 47 R ($31), 24 motel units ($43). Pool, tennis, bowling alley. Rst, bar. Helicopter landing strip.

SURABAYA, East Java

JANE'S HOUSE — 38 R, some beautifully furnished w/handcarved beds, chairs, etc. AC rst, bar. Regional entertainment. $23 up.

MIRAMA (FC) — 200 AC R, dining room, coffee shop, cocktail lounges. Pool. $29-$31.

PHILIPPINES

An archipelago of 7,101 islands and islets linked like a necklace along 1,150 miles, north to south, the Philippines has a total land area of 115,758 square miles with an uneven coast line of 10,850 miles, twice as long as that of the United States. Of the 11 major islands which account for most of the land area, the three principal groups are Luzon, on which Manila is located, Visagas with its sugar plantations and fishing fleets, and the Muslim provinces of Mindanao; adjacent to the latter is the world's second deepest sea (35,440 ft.), known as the Philippine Trench.

Although geographically in Asia, the Philippines is historically linked to both East and West. Nowhere is there a more unique blend of the two, yet it remains a distinct world in itself with a flavor and culture of its own.

Original inhabitants are believed to be Aetas, prehistoric tribes that roamed these islands some 250,000 years ago. Malays came in large numbers between 200 BC and 1500 AD and are the original forebears of today's Filipino — with added endowments from Indians and Chinese who sailed here to trade.

During the 15th and 16th centuries, the north was dominated by Japanese, the southern and central areas ruled by Muslims. After Magellan's "discovery" in 1521, Spain moved in and, in 1571, set up a capital in Manila, a Muslim village, from which it controlled the northern and central islands. England captured Manila in 1762, returned it to Spain several years later. By the early 1800s, the Church and members of its hierarchy had become extremely wealthy, and corrupt, landowners so that dissatisfaction among the masses was widespread. Resistance, led by Dr. Jose Rizal, resulted in Rizal's execution in 1896, but rebellion continued under Aguinaldo and Bonifacio; by late 1898, with the Spanish-American War under way, the rebels occupied most of the Philippines, and on December 10, the United States was given sovereignty (in payment of $20 million) by the Treaty of Paris, which didn't satisfy rebel forces. Not until 1901, when Aguinaldo was captured, was the revolt quelled.

Following the conquest by the Japanese and their subsequent surrender, complete independence and a republic came to the Philippines on July 4, 1946. In the last few years, a New Society has emerged that, under President Marco, has succeeded in turning the tide from a terror-ridden, politically anarchistic and economically stagnating country into a seemingly stable regime under which progressive reforms have been initiated, the economy revived. In fact, acute observers say it's actually booming. Especially tourism. In the midst of a tourist recession elsewhere, visitor arrivals in the Philippines shot up 64% in '74 to about 410,000; Manila, with over 3,000 international-standard hotel rooms (4,000 or more by October '76¹), has a chronic room shortage (90%-95% occupancy rate). Always exciting to visit, for one reason or another, today Manila and other attractions are exciting in the most complimentary sense: busy, bubbling with fun, music and friendliness, enjoying its current political stabilitv.

Manila, the capital, is also booming — particularly in the past few years with tne construction of many beautiful hotels (see page 286), a 10,000-capacity Convention Center and an adjacent Cultural Center and Folk Arts Theater — plus (and a great plus it is) Nayong Pilipino, Philippine Miniature Village, next to the International Airport. Always exciting to visit, today Manila, as well as other areas of the country, offers more: fine hotels, good and varied dining, excellent shopping and lots of fun, music and friendliness.

So, if you like the Latin touch of Spain and Mexico, you'll enjoy the ambience and warmth of the Philippines.

The limestone Chocolate Hills of Bohol, a top tourist attraction, look like an icecream cone (or a shaved head) with a fringe of trees (or hair) around the base.

THE BIG L — LUZON

The biggest island and main tourist destination is a study in contrasts. It has tropical landscapes with a smattering of cool, temperate places. Its high mountain ranges, volcanic in origin, slope to lush plateaus, valleys and river basins. A perfect cone volcano, Mayon, reigns grandly over the Bicol region. In Tagaytay City, a short way from Manila, the world's smallest, lowest volcano, Taal, squats within its own lake. You find gigantic stairways to the skies in the mountain provinces; the 2,000-year-old Banaue Rice Terraces, hand hewn on steep mountain sides, would, if stretched end to end, reach halfway around the world. Baguio City, the cool summer capital, nestles amidst pine tree-clad mountains, an invigorating and interesting destination. The Philippine Military Academy, modeled after West Point, is here at Fort Del Pilar, Loakan.

Of course, Bataan and Corregidor Island are on Luzon. The latter has the Pacific War Memorial, a magnificent monument and shrine, while on Mt. Samat in Bataan is an equally imposing memorial; topped by a massive 300-ft. cross, it is called *Dambana ng Kagitingan* — Altar of Valor.

There are many fine beaches between Bauang and San Fernando facing the China Sea. Zambales province has La Sirena Beach Resort near Subic Bay, while Olongapo City, where the U.S. Naval Base is, has more.

Seventy-five miles south of Manila, in the province of Batangas overlooking the China Sea, is the premier resort hotel, Punta Baluarte.

Antipolo, a mountainside resort town of Rizal province, is also the shrine of the Black Virgin, or Lady of Peace and Good Voyage, patroness of seafarers and travelers. May is a month of pilgrimages here. The neighboring proving of Laguna attracts tourists for the curative powers of the hot sulphur springs.

LURE OF THE VISAYANS

Southward from Luzon, in the center of the archipelago, is an old-world magic mixed with South Sea island charms. Cebu, the country's oldest city, is where Magellan planted the Cross of Christianity in 1521 (it's still there), and nearby Mactan Island is where the explorer was slain in battle by a native chieftan, Lapu-Lapu.

Tacloban City in Leyte, home province of Imelda Romualdez-Marcos, wife of the president, is where Douglas MacArthur returned; the Price mansion where he slept still stands. Narrow San Juanico Strait is spanned by the Marcos Bridge (2,162 meters, Philippine's longest), connects Leyte with Samar Island.

Bacolod is the home of sugar cane plantations and their sugar barons — in the shadow of Mt. Kanlaon, an active volcano. Bohol has the Chocolate Hills, several hundred mounds shaped like chocolate drops. It is here that a Blood Compact took place between the local chief and Miguel Lopez de Legazpi, the Spanish conqueror.

LAND OF PROMISE — MINDANAO

Here is the home of Muslim Filipinos, a vast frontier of still undeveloped resources and a standout because of the exotic pomp and pageantry of its ruling royal houses, towering mosques solemn with ancient rituals of seafaring people, descendents of a fierce warrior race of Malays and Indonesians with highly developed lore and legends.

Zamboanga, a romantic place immortalized by poets and composers, is the principal tourist destination. As a melting pot of Christian and Muslim cultures where churches and mosques stand side by side, it's both colorful and entrancing. Next is Davao, Pearl City of the Philippines, where pearl culture is a growing industry. Bukidnon plateau is pineapple-growing and cattle-breeding country where the Del Monte plantation sprawls over its scenic parts. Lake-dwelling Maranaos live along the shores of Lake Lanao at an elevation of 3,000 ft.; Mindanao State University overlooks the lake.

274

Basilan, an inland city, is the home of the Yakan tribe of Moslems noted for colorful, delicately woven cloth. It produces rubber, pepper, oil, palm, coconut and timber on its rich, volcanic and scenic terrain; there are also a chain of beautiful beaches and coves.

The more adventurous might want to explore the untamed Sulu archipelago of more than 500 islands on the Celebes Sea at the southwestern tip of the Philippines. Jolo is the principal center of this centuries-old Sultanate of Sulu. Natives are seafaring gypsies, minority tribes as fascinating as they are quaint (and fierce) in their ways. Jolo, a 40-minute, non-stop flight from Zamboanga, has a thriving market in imported merchandise.

PHILIPPINE FACTS

Airport Taxes — Int'l departure, $1.60. Domestic departure P1 (15¢) from Manila; P .50 (8¢) from Cebu and Zamboanga airports.

Bank Hours — 9-4, Mon-Sat.

Climate — Tropical. November-February coolest and best tourist season. July-October hot and humid, generally with rain, occasional typhoons. March-May is beach weather. Mountain areas cool, temperate.

Clothing — Light, informal. Jacket/tie required in nightclubs/hotels at night. Philippine national shirt for men (barong tagalog) is light, beautifully embroidered and acceptable for any function.

Currency — One Peso equals 15¢ US (fluctuates). Notes: 1, 2, 5, 10, 20, 50 pesos (P). Coins: 1, 5, 10, 25, 50 centavos. Pesos should be purchased from authorized foreign exchange agents of the Central Bank; open 24 hours at airport.

Current — 220v, AC. Hotels have 110v converters.

Customs — Two bottles liquor, 200 cigarettes or 50 cigars. Only P500 in currency may be brought in or taken out. Baggage exempt from Customs inspection.

Embassy — Phone 598011 U.S.; 861168 Canada.

Entry Requirements — Passport. No visa required for up to 21 days; extendible to 59 days. Visa valid for 1 year (US$1). Certificate for smallpox, cholera.

Gambling — Casino, cockfighting and Jai-Alai (except Sundays).

Language — Tagalog and English.

Population — 40 million. Quezon City, the capital, has 400,000.

Religion — Only predominately Christian (93%) nation in Asia; 80% Catholic.

Telephone — 25 centavos.

Tipping — Taxis, barbers, etc., 10%. Some rsts add 10% service. Airport and hotel porters get P2 per bag.

Tourist Information — Philippine Tourist Information Center, 3325 Wilshire, Los Angeles 90010; 556 Fifth Ave, N.Y. 10038. Tourism Bldg, Rizal Park, and Manila Int'l Airport.

Water — Pure .

HAPPENINGS

January — 3rd week. Ati-Atihan Festival of Kalibo, Aklan Province, commemorates peace pact between Malays and pygmies. For days, townspeople paint their bodies black with soot, wear bizarre costumes, have a mardi gras-type festival. Tour operators offer 4-day/3-night package tours. 9th — Feast of Black Nazarene, Manila's largest procession.

February — Chinese New Year, Manila. Lady of Lourdes Procession, Quezon.

March-April — Morion Festival (Holy Week). Particularly colorful on island of Marinduque, SE of Manila. Reenactment of Way of Cross, the washing of the penitents in the river. In evening, guests at hotels are showered with flowers. Moriones parade ends the festival.

May — Harvest Festival, Quezon province. Santacruzan — a month-long street pageant in most towns. Bale Zamboanga Festival held in wooded Pasonanca Park, Zamboagna, portrays art and culture of Muslims.

November — All Saints Day. Offering of flowers and candles at cemeteries. 8th — Hariraya Poasa, Marawi; Sulu. Muslim holiday. 23rd — Angono festival, 14 miles from Manila; river parade.

December 12th — Fiesta of Pagsangjan. Bamboo arches adorn the streets. 24th — Lantern Festival, San Fernando (41 miles from Manila). Christmas comes early in the Philippines. Season of gaiety and caroling starts on Dec. 16th with first of nine days of Mass.

HOLIDAYS

January 1st — New Year's.

March or April — Maundy Thursday, Good Friday. Holy Week extremely interesting as many local Catholic observances, such as flagellation, are to be seen.

April 9th — Bataan Day.

May 1st — Labor Day.

June 12th — Independence Day.

July 4th — Friendship Day.

November 30th — Bonifacio Day.

December 25th — Christmas.

December 30th — Rizal Day.

Manila's stunning Cultural Center

MANILA

The moment a lithe, exotic Filipina beauty greets the visitor at the International Airport with a garland of fragrant sampaguita (Arabian jasmine), he has, most likely, started to fall in love, Filipino style, with Manila. By the time of departure, it's usually a full-blown affair.

On beautiful Manila Bay, this teeming metropolis of 3,500,000 is the commercial, political and cultural center of the nation with both traditional and modern architecture. The streets and broad avenues have been spruced up so that they compare favorably with Singapore's. The Pasig River, which bisects them, is being desilted and face-lifted; there's a 100-seat ferry, *Turista,* in service along its course — an easy way to sightsee from downtown to Makati. Even Roxas Boulevard, an 8-mile, palm and flame tree-lined drive facing the semicircle of Manila Bay, is being re-beautified.

Legend says that the city got its name from the *nilad* flowers that bloomed by the banks of the Pasig. Spaniards built a walled city to replace the Muslim settlement, called it Intramuros. Within its walls were Fort Santiago and 13 churches, of which San Agustin still stands. Today, Greater Manila comprises all the towns, cities surrounding Manila: Pasay City, Quezon City (the actual capital), Makati, Las Pinas and others, towns of the province of Rizal and parts of Laguna and Bulacan provinces.

Though the posh suburb of Makati has become the commercial center of the Philippines (Ayala Avenue with its skyscrapers and fashionable malls is the hub), downtown Manila is still the cultural heart — extremely inviting to the visitor and easily walkable. Here's what you want to see (and how to do it):

GETTING TO MANILA

Since the 16th century when the famed Manila galleons plied the Pacific enroute to Spain, Manila has been a major hub of trade and transport. Today, of course, tourists are carried primarily by jet.

From the U.S. and Canadian west coast, Manila is quickly reached (about 15 hours) via Honolulu, provides an ideal gateway to Indonesia and Singapore, East and West Malaysia, Hong Kong and Taiwan. See Air Travel for further particulars.

LOCAL TRANSPORTATION

You'll love those colorful jeepneys — Army surplus jeeps turned into mobile folk art — that go everywhere for a few pennies. Taxis are also inexpensive: P40¢ for first 250 meters, P20¢ for subsequent 250 meters in Manila, even less in the provinces. Horse-drawn *calesas,* though, are not cheap — bargain before riding.

Hydrofoils depart from Navy Pier, Roxas Blvd., for Corregidor; yacht *Marie-Jean* also available. Ferry boat service arranged for groups.

Rental cars (and AC buses for groups) are plentiful. Luzon, particularly, has a good road network so that Fly/Drive programs make sense. AC cars and driver run $3-$5 hr.

DOMESTIC TRANSPORTATION

Philippine Airlines provides good jet service to all major cities within the archipelago.

Dona Montserrat, a 110-cabin AC ship, offers 5-day Fiesta Islands Cruise to Cebu, Zamboanga and Iloilo (US$250-$660), 4-day Emerald Isles Cruise to Sicogon and Romblan (US$130-$340). Weekend cruises from Manila to Corregidor and Ambil ($60-$105). Negros Navigation Co., 849 Pasay Rd., Makati.

Sweet Lines (Pier 6, North Harbor) has the *Sweet Home* (89 first-class, AC cabins; some with bath) on the Manila-Cebu-Zamboanga run (6-day package tours available), and *Sweet Faith* to Cebu. 13 smaller ships go to Davao and many other ports.

Compania Maritia's *Panay* (6 AC cabins w/bath) has weekly 6-day trips to Iloilo, Pulupandan and Iligan. Two other ships have 14-day schedules every two weeks to Cebu, Zamboanga, Cotabato, Dadiangas, Davao. Reservations: 205 Juan Luna, Binondo, Manila.

The return to Corregidor — via hydrofoil.

The unique Carabao Festival, held in Bulacan, features hundreds of water buffalos, or carabaos, parading through town to kneel on their forelegs in front of the church in homage to the patron saint, San Isidro.

Walking Tour No. 1 — Start on Roxas Boulevard in the Ermita section, say at Herran St., by walking east to A. Mabini St., then turning left (north). Here, for six long blocks, are souvenir and shoe shops, a variety of art galleries featuring well-known as well as obscure Filipino artists. At the end of Mabini is Manila's great landmark, Rizal Park, famed for its multi-colored fountains, beautiful Chinese and Japanese Gardens and views of magnificent Manila Bay sunsets. Here, too, is the Luneta and its monument to Dr. Jose P. Rizal, the National Hero, and a huge topographical map of the country. Across the street is the Aquarium. Not far away, on Taft Ave., you can bet on jai-alai at the Fronton. Incidentally, the Manila Hilton is just catty-corner from Rizal Park; your walk can be started from there.

There are two coffee shops in the Park, one of which has deaf and dumb waiters. Interestingly, there's also a garden for the blind designed to help them enjoy nature by smell and touch.

Best time to visit here is late afternoon when the sun isn't so intense, when Filipinos come to enjoy themselves, when vendors are selling fresh fruits and peanuts. There are twice weekly afternoon concerts.

Return to Roxas Blvd., which becomes Bonifacio Drive, and walk north to the entrance to Intramuros, the partially restored walled city, where (turning right) you'll find San Agustin Church, oldest in the Philippines, and the Manila Cathedral — only two remaining of an original 12 churches. Here, too, is Fort Santiago built (over a period of 140 years) by the Spaniards after conquering Rajah Sulayman. Thru the years, the Fort has been used not only by the Spanish but also by British, Americans and Japanese. This national shrine features Rizal House, where the hero was detained prior to his execution, and its extensive collection of Rizaliana, as well as dungeons, turrets, cannon and other reminders of a bloody past.

Walking Tour No. 2 — Central Market, in northeast Manila out Quezon Blvd., is the biggest open-air market in the Philippines and a walking tour in itself; an entire day can be spent here. You start this tour by taking a cab. Once there you walk and walk and haggle and haggle for everything from handicrafts to livestock. Remember, the first quoted price is not supposed to be the selling price; you should be able to lower it by 15% or more.

Walking Tour No. 3 — Here again you start out by cab or, if you're on Roxas Blvd., by Jeepney marked *Santa Cruz*; ride it to the end of the line and you're there — China Town. It's a huge complex, one of the few remaining places in the Philippines where you can ride in horse-drawn rigs, and a delicious blend of aromas emanating from the many restaurants, a melange of hole-in-the-wall shops and shrines. Certain sections still have those thick, adobe-walled buildings with their Capiz windowpanes of the Spanish era. That's right — in a Spanish China Town 'twas on a night like this.

While out this way, be sure to see the Chinese Cemetery; from a distance it might be a city for wealthy Chinese living in pagodas and Oriental palaces.

East and south of the downtown area are other points of interest. Beyond Makati is the American Cemetery and Memorial in honor of those who died in action in the Philippines. Near the Cultural Center, to the south, is the Zoo. Not far beyond, in Pasay City, is the Lopez Museum with a fine collection of Filipino classical paintings and extensive Filipiniana. Back downtown, the National Museum, in the Department of Tourism building, features exhibits of folk art, natural history, Muslim and pre-Hispanic cultures. Malacanang Palace, formerly housed Spanish and American governors, is now the Presidential mansion.

Undoubtedly the most popular excursion is overnight or longer to view the incredible rice paddies of Banaue.

DON'T MISS THESE:

Corregidor — By hydrofoil to the island fortress guarding Manila Bay. Battery Way, Pacific War Memorial and, as the climax of your visit, a walk thru Malinta Tunnel carved out of the island's central mountain. Half-day tour, $11.

Pagsanjan — By car for two-hour trip thru countryside. Upstream by canoe passing beautiful gorges, high mountain walls. You'll ride up the rapids to Pagsanjan Falls, where you can swim in a natural pool below the falls. Return trip is even more exciting — shoot 14 rapids. Lunch at Pagsanjan Rapids Hotel. Tip boatmen 5 pesos each — they've earned it. Wear a bathing suit or old clothes; bring a cushion (seats hard) and a change of clothes. Full day. Avoid weekends when mobbed.

Tagaytay Ridge — By car thru suburban towns south of Manila to Las Pinas Catholic Church to see and listen to its famed bamboo organ, then thru lush villages, coconut and banana plantations to top of Tagaytay overlooking Lake Taal and its active volcano-island. Lunch at attractive Villa Adelaida. Half day.

OTHER TOURS

City Tour — Highlights are the Malacanang Palace, Paco Memorial Park, Cultural Center and Folk Arts Theater, beautiful Rizal Park, Fort Santiago in old Manila (Intramuros), art gallery row at Ermita and National Museum. By AC bus or car. About $6; half day.

Suburban Tour — Wack-Wack Golf and Country Club; Mandaluyong's industrial area; Makati where many of the new hotels are located, the famous Forbes Park, Ayala Museum; American War Memorial Cemetery at Fort Bonifacio; University of Philippines; Quezon City, the capital; the shoe factories in Marikina and Philippine Village (Nayong Pilipino).

Native Cottage Tour — Woodcarving, raffia bag production, shell crafting, production of rattan furniture. 3 hours; $6. Tours Specialist, 5022 P Burgos, Makati.

Cultural Tour — Selected museums to see religious relics, Muslim art objects, artifacts from archeological diggings, a 60-diorama display portraying significant events in Philippine history. 4 hours; $7.50. Tours Specialist.

Scuba Tours — From Manila, wonders never cease aboard the 102-ft. diving boat *Seaquest*. Southwest of Mindoro, Busuanga, Colocotoc, Demipac and Lubutglubut, staggering marine life, reefs of riotous color are yours to explore. Charters also available for 10-16 divers. Write See & Sea, 680 Beach St, San Francisco 94109.

EXCURSION FROM MANILA
BAGUIO-BANAUE TOUR

Baguio is a popular mountain resort at 5,000 ft. with ideal year-'round temperature for golf and tennis. Sights here are the Presidential summer house, marketplace and fascinating Igorot village in the Botanical Gardens. At Easter School of Weaving, Igorot tribeswomen produce striking textiles on their looms. Place mats are a good buy.

Reached by 45-minute flight from Manila, by train or by AC bus departing 7 a.m. daily (except Sun.) from Inter-Continental, returning 2 p.m. daily (except Sat) from Pines Hotel ($5 OW). From June thru November, weekend hotel and transportation reservations must be made well in advance.

Baguio is better known as the jumping-off point for an 8-hour trip over rough, twisting mountain roads to view the famous Banaue Rice Terraces. These man-built terraces climb up the mountains to 5000 ft. with water dripping from each to the one below. Magnificent scenic views from Batal, Mayaoyao, Mt. Data Lodge and Banaue.

Trip to Banaue via Bontac and Mt. Data should not be made from July-Nov due to weather. Other times it is worth the discomfort. Stop at Mt. Data Lodge for lunch or overnight, take a side trip to the Sagada Caves. For those with less time, return to Baguio instead of continuing for another four hours to Banaue. The other way to Banaue from Baguio, much shorter but not nearly as scenic, is via Bagabag — you miss many of the remote spots otherwise seen.

Usually trip is for four days. Depart by early morning plane or bus from Manila to Baguio. Sightsee, shop and overnight at Pines Hotel. Following day by car to Mt. Data for lunch, then to Bontac and overnight at Banaue hotel. Third day is spent viewing the Rice Terraces which cover some 100 sq. miles. Lunch in Bontac and then to Baguio for overnight. Following afternoon return to Manila. For those not wanting to go to Banaue, a three-day trip can be made to Baguio; includes a day at Nalinac Beach Resort for fishing, boat riding, swimming, etc.

DINING FILIPINO STYLE

As a cosmopolitan crossroads, Manila not only has a fascinating cuisine of its own but also specializes in foods from around the world. It is said to be a gourmet's delight. Dinner is from 8 to much later.

Adobo, a main course of chicken or pork, possibly both, is the most famous native dish; has a Spanish flavor with an American-type sauce and is eaten with boiled rice, a chicken/vegetable thin soup and fruit. Another is *dinuguan,* an unusual combination of pork belly, pig's heart, liver, kidney, chitterlings and tripe, highly spiced, with a pork gravy. Try *Barrio Fiesta* restaurant for these.

Other Filipino specialties: *pancit, luglog* (shrimp, smoked and flaked fish, powdered pork cracklings, onion, celery, sliced hardboiled eggs, citrus juice and rice noddles); *lechon* (roasted suckling pig stuffed with leaves); *balut* (duck eggs). *Mariposa de Vida* (Butterfly of Life), overlooking Rizal Park, serves rare, exotic foods (sea snake, monkey, sea urchins, duck embryo) said to promote potency and fertility — delicious, too, once you're accustomed to such exoticness.

On the strip in Pasay City, *Luau* has fine seafood and Hawaiian-style dishes. *Royal Room* at the Plaza, Makati (huge restaurant complex) serves a good international buffet. *Sulo,* Makati, is another large, inexpensive dining complex with Filipino decor inside and out. *Madrid,* 24 de los Santos (798277) is unsurpassed for luxury and decor, top service and superb cuisine (music nightly). *Sulo Hotel,* Civic Center, offers an underwater aquatic show, dining and dancing.

For Chinese fare, best spots are *Marquina* and *Carvajel.* Japanese, Indonesian and Hawaiian restaurants are found in downtown Ermita area and in Makati. Fiesta style (buffet) dining is very popular.

Swiss Inn, near Paco Park, is a popular drinking and dining spot with businessmen — prices reasonable. *Woodshed* on M.H. del Pilar Ave. is always jammed after offices close.

NIGHT LIFE
1 a.m. to 4 a.m. Curfew

As in other cities, new hotels have changed the night scene. Their prices are higher than elsewhere — drinks from $1.50-$3, dinner from $11 — but they do have top entertainment with international floor shows, dancing and Filipine shows.

Roxas Blvd. is nightclub strip and starts to swing as early as 6 p.m. Some offer combos during the day. Dance in a discotheque or listen to live music, rock and jazz in the supper-clubs or nightclubs — dancing, too. You'll find most of the bars to be clip joints but not expensive ones. If you're looking for female companionship, no problem anywhere. In nightclubs and hotels, hostesses are paid by the hour — but observe the curfew. Hotel's house rule for tourists: be back by 1 a.m. If in a situation where you can't make it, call Metrocom (78-79-61 local 95-76-8), and you will be escorted to your hotel. But be sure to have a good reason for being late. If you are a worrier, stick to the hotels.

D'World Nightclub, Roxas Blvd. is the busiest with six bands, over 100 hostesses and several colorful floor shows; *El Mundo* features two bands at night, two combos during the day: *Old West* has good music and steaks; *Bayside* has two bands playing alternately from noon 'til closing — gorgeously gowned hostesses; Thurs. and Fri. nights a floor show is added. *Alta Vista* is quieter, serves Filipino food, has Filipino show on Wed. no hostesses.

If gambling's your thing, you'll want to bisit Manila Bay Casino, one of the world's largest floating crap games. Open around the clock, it offers something for everyone, from the slots to baccarat. A small launch shuttles patrons (no charge) between a Rizal Park pier and the ship.

Pangkat Kawayan (Bamboo Orchestra) musicians aged 8-16 use over 100 different instruments made from different kinds of bamboo each with its own distinct sound. Performances are held Tues, Thurs, Sat. and Sun. at *Igorota Rst,* Roxas Blvd. The group has performed for notables thruout the world.

Barangay Dance Troupe performs nightly at *Sulo Rst.* in Makati; Bayanihan Troupe at *Hilton* on Tues., Fri. at 9 p.m. Philippine folk dances are so graceful and troupes so good you'll be dancing after the show is over — and they show you how.

Attend at least one performance at the beautiful Cultural Center — everything from zarzuela (Spanish opera) to jazz. Or, except Sundays and holidays, watch and bet on Jai-Alai at the Fronton on Taft Ave. Can dine at *Blue Room* and *Sky Room* (old West motif) and watch Jai-Alai from there. Games start at 5:15 p.m.; last one ends at 11:30

SHOPPERS' DELIGHT

The Philippines make some of the finest handwoven cloths, table mats, abaca carpets, woodcarvings, shoes, Muslim brassware, cigars and beer in the world. And bargaining is expected in most shops with exception of department stores and shoe shops (but fine leather shoes are only about $5).

Look for Lepanto Cloth, loomed by mountain tribes in rich, shimmering, earth colors. Great for placemats, napkins, table runners, bags, drapes and as upholstery material.

You can bring home a wardrobe of high fashion dresses made from pineapple fiber or silky banana fiber. A comparatively new fabric is *Hablon,* handwoven in unusual designs, usually in silk. The *malong* worn by Muslim women is a rich, cotton fabric coated with a silky sheen that can be made into long or short exotic South Sea fashions. Give a dressmaker 24 hours, and she'll do it for you. Nor is a trip complete without purchasing the semi-transparent *bargon tagalog* men's shirt woven from pineapple fiber; in Manila, it's worn to the most formal affair.

Jusi, a finely embroidered fabric made from raw silk, is widely used in silk scarves. From the mountain provinces of Luzon come gorgeous wooden bowls and statues. Just thirty minutes from Manila is the small town of Marikina where every native is shoemaker — here fine shoemaking is still an art.

And who hasn't dreamed of owning furniture made of Philippine mahogany? Bring your designs or have them style it — you'll do nothing but save.

Rummaging thru antique shops might even turn up an early Ming piece. Such things are still here — all you have to do is look. Prices are still very, very low on most antiques. In the tourist belt, Ermita district has many antique and art shops.

Materials, shellwork, ashtrays, rings and earrings from Sulu natural pearls and black coral can be found in any souvenir shop. Less expensive are found in the Central, Cartimar, Divisoria or Quiapo Markets.

Main shopping streets with every type of shop, boutique, coffee shop, etc., are Rizal, Quezon Blvd. and Escolta (downtown). Makiti Shopping Center and Green Hills Shopping Center in San Juan, Rizal, are excellent. Harrison Plaza Shopping Mall in front of Rizal Memorial Coliseum and Cubao shopping area, near Araneta Coliseum in Quezon City, are considered good. Can easily go from one shopping center to another by bus, taxi or, if energetic, walk. For the intrepid shopper this is a paradise. Most shops sell products made in the provinces but at higher prices. The more adventurous will want to visit the Flea Market on Roxas Blvd., the colorful local markets.

Handcraft Emporium, 3300 Ramon Magsaysay Blvd. has a huge, and good, variety of handcrafts.

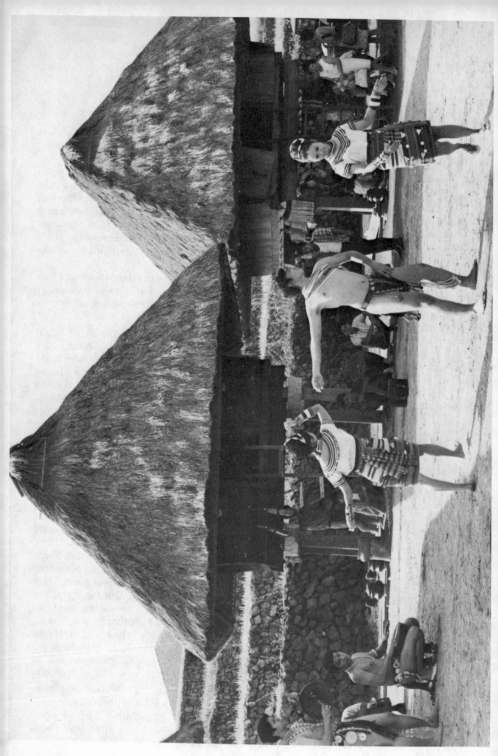

Those not going beyond Manila (even those who are) should, without fail, visit Nayong Pilipino — Philippine Miniature Village — next to the International Airport, a well-executed project sponsored by the First Lady, Mrs. Imelda Romualdez-Marcos, and a showcase of the nation's diverse cultures, arts, crafts and industries. Six major regions are represented by villages, each a perfect miniature. The Mountain Province is shown as a group of huts at the foot of the Banaue Rice Terraces; the Chocolate Hills of Bohol represent the Visayan region, a Muslim mosque and stilt houses the Mindanao region. There's a handsome Spanish colonial hacienda, a typical Filipino town reflecting early Spanish influences, authentic Bicol houses. Thruout, arts and crafts are on display, being made, sold. There are girl guides; guests are shown around in colorful jeepneys or air-conditioned buses. And a restaurant serves typical food, drinks and delicacies. All in all, an exceptional representation of the heart and soul of the country, a marvelous introduction to its many facets.

HOW TO SEE MORE OF

THE PHILIPPINES

EMERALD SUN ISLANDS
CEBU

One hour by jet from Manila to the commercial center of the Visayan Islands. As the country's oldest city, Cebu drips with historical interest. There are colorful, horse-drawn, two-wheeled carriages, grand Taoist Temple, figurine of the Holy Child, Fort San Pedro and Magellan Square, an interesting Cebu Market. At Lilang's guitar factory in Abuno, one of the country's largest, you can purchase guitars and ukuleles made of Filipine mahogany for $3 to $15.

Visit Mactan Island (by causeway) to see Magellan Monument and the mural depicting Lapu-Lapu and his tribe driving away the colonizers. Lapu-Lapu City's craftsmen make many stringed instruments, most famous being the Mactan guitar. Outside the city you can swim at Cansuhong, Pook or Poblacion Beach.

For dining there's *Celebrity Supper Club* (famous for *bulgogi,* a beef barbecue); *Diamond Tower Revolving Rst (great view); Cocina Vasca* (Spanish). Seafood is abundant.

Swinging nightclubs: *Temptation, Other Place* and *Sand Trap,* Hotel Magellan, are "in." Jai-Alai very popular — with a restaurant serving Chinese and Western food. On Sundays, cockfights start at 11 a.m., last all day.

DAVAO

1 ½ hours by plane from Manila or direct from Cebu. Situated at the base of Mt. Apo (Philippines' highest) this is an ideal fishing and skin-diving resort. A fine resort hotel, Davao Insular, and many lovely beaches make this an excellent spot for relaxing.

One of the fascinating trips is to Aguinaldo Pearl Farm on Samal Island, a half-hour launch ride. Not only are pearls cultivated here but also there's fish farming. Never have you seen such huge lobsters, crayfish and tropical fish. Allow 3 hours for the round trip. Can also explore Mt. Apo, but do so in early morning before the fog rolls in.

At the local market buy *durian,* a delicious native fruit; eat it raw or in candied form.

Dine at *Harana* in a native atmosphere complete with music or at *D'Hardin* discotheque. Rock at *Lord & Lady,* get a hostess at *Timberland* or do the two open-air nightclubs, *D'Garden* and *Sumerland,* about ten miles from town.

BACOLOD-ILOILO

Although Bacolod is the sugar capital, island-hopping here would only be of interest to those interested in antiques (visit the Espinos, Torres and Vega collections) or golf at the Country Club. Depart by afternoon ferry for Iloilo. Next day visit Iloilo Museo with its unusual collection of gold masks, pre-Spanish porcelain, elephant fossils, etc.; the Arevalo weaving district (*hablon* woven here); the Gothic-

Renaissance Church, Jaro Cathedral and Miago Church. Both cities reached by plane from Manila in an hour.

Bacolod could be included in a trip to Davao.

ZAMBOANGA

Fantastically beautiful 30-min. flight from Davao over mountain ranges, river valleys, virgin forests and Sulu Sea. Also half hour from Cebu, two hours from Manila.

Known as the city of flowers, orchids, pearls, beautiful girls, Muslim mosques and villages, it definitely has much to offer the visitor. Sail on the Mindanao Sea in colorful *vintas* (sailing canoes). Ride to Moslem villages where houses are built on stilts and boat houses; gasp at thatched roof houses covered with orchids. Enjoy the villagers dancing to native brass gongs in Taluksangkay. Return to the city via Fort del Pilar, a bastion built by the Spaniards. Shop Barter Traders' Mart at the pier for tax-free brassware, Indonesian batiks; at Shell House for dishes made of iridescent seashells and the many souvenir shops for pearls, coral, etc. To browse and bargain, don't miss the Central Market. Black coral bracelets, brass necklaces, rings, harem pants in dazzling colors and food stalls are here. Visit Sta. Cruz Island to comb its fine pink sands, snorkel to watch exotic fish.

If you're honeymooners, you can stay in a well-furnished Tree House in beautiful Pasonanca Park. It's complete with running water, toilet, stove, refrig and fully stocked larder — all free for two nights with exception of small laundry charge. For reservation, write Mayor of Zamboanga City or Park Superintendent, Municipal Offices.

Tour Packages — 3-Day Davao/Zamboanga from Manila. Overnight in Davao, then fly to Zamboanga for overnight. Return following day to Manila. Cebu can be included in 4-Day, 3-Night package, spending first night in Cebu.

Hotel Directory

Today, Manila has as many good deluxe and first-class hotels, most of them new, as any city in the world — and, as a result, a temporary oversupply of rooms, obviously to the advantage of the canny shopper. Most hotels have two or more restaurants, each specializing in a different type of cuisine; all are extremely well air-conditioned. You're sure to enjoy your stay in any of those listed in this Directory.

All Philippine hotels are licensed by the Department of Tourism to insure their meeting international class standards. 10% service and 13% tax are added to room rates — *but tax usually waived if payment is made in foreign currency.*

Those looking for either sophisticated or primitive resort life will find new resorts opening in 1979 and '80. Hour and a half from Manila, the *Puerto Azul* complex will have water sports, golf, tennis, et al, plus native-style crafts and fishing village, 1,500-room hotel, 700 villas and private homes — all on 7,000 acres. *Rsv:* Philippine Village Hotel, Manila Int'l Airport Rd., Manila.

70 miles SE at Lake Caliraya, in a national park and wildlife sanctuary, a private club, *Nayong Kalkasan* (open to public, space available), will have 20 rustic cottages — no radio, no TV, no hot water but all water sports. Write: Recreational Activities Corp., 610 Manila Bank Bldg., Makati.

Isla Pequena at Subic Bay (2½-hr. drive, 10-min. boat ride) will have 50 Tahitian-style huts overlooking the water, 50 more hillside. Restaurant to specialize in seafood. Inquiries: Baron Travel, 1365 Leon Gunto St., Ermita, Manila.

For boating enthusiasts, Houseboat Vacations Unlimited now has houseboats accommodating 6-8 overnight, 11-15 for day cruises on Laguna de Bay and Taal Lake. These 34-ft. craft have carpeting, galley, convertible dinette, show. Cost $90 per day; $60 for smaller craft accommodating 3-4 persons.

LA MALAGUENA — 30-acre Covelandia Island is 14 miles from Manila. Opened '76 with 50 Mediterranean-style R. Attractive Starcove rst, shaped like starfish (excellent seafood), and more formal Spanish rst, bar and disco. 2 pools, tennis, iceskating, bowling, lagoon fishing. Crowded on weekends with cockfight aficionados. $28-$44. Also 10 rustic cabins w/kitchenettes, $61. *Rsv:* Covelandia Island Resort, Manila Bank Bldg., Manila.

MANILA

AMBASSADOR — Faces Manila Bay. AC dining rooms, revolving rst, supper club, 2 bars; pool. $22-$31.

AURELIO — Roxas Blvd, 20 min. from airport, 5 min. from ocean terminal. 283 R (100 new). Seafood rst, luncheon buffet. Cocktail lounge. Folk dances on weekends. $35 up.

BAYVIEW — Roxas and United Nations. 350 R, most with excellent view. Dining room, Japanese rst, Tropicana bar, coffee shop. Rooftop pool. Well managed. $21.

CENTURY PARK SHERATON (DL) — 450 R, 20-story, DT hi-rise. Variety of restaurants (seafood and steak, Spanish supper club, Japanese, Theater Rst), three bars, two pools. *Conv:* 500. $32-$40.

ENRICO — Revolving rst, discotheque, 2 cocktail lounges. 231 R. *Conv:* 600. $24.

HOLIDAY INN (FC) — Roxas Blvd, opposite New Cultural and Convention Center. 369 R overlook Manila Bay. French rst, Viennese cafe, nightclub. Pool. *Conv:* 700. $30-$40.

HYATT REGENCY (DL) — 10 min from airport. 265 R w/terrace overlook Manila Bay. Excellent buffet luncheon. Top Tempura Misono room. Swinging Circuit discotheque. International floor show at 10:30 in La Concha. Pool. $39-$45.

MABUHAY — Heart of shopping district, 20 min from DT. 104 R, dining room, cocktail lounge. Pool. $15.

MANILA (DL) — New 18-story tower with 570 R, SU; old bldg restored. On waterfront near Rizal Park and golf course. Lovely grounds. Pool, tennis. $40-$50.

MANILA HILTON (DL) — 430 R, SU with great view of bay and city. Attractive Philippine decor in several rsts, bars. Top of Hilton has int'l floor show nightly. 1571 nightclub (basement) has combo, midnight show. 5th-floor pool; shopping arcade. *Conv:* 1700. $38-$42.

MANILA MIDTOWN RAMADA (FC+) — 600 R, 8 rsts w/Continental, Japanese, Chinese cuisines, 4 bar lounges; pool, tennis. $32-$37.

OTANI — Roxas Blvd. 150 R. 3 rsts, 3 bars, live entertainment. *Conv:* 400. $21-$26.

PHILIPPINE PLAZA (DL) — 700 luxurious R, SU with rfg, private lanais overlooking Manila Bay. Lake-size pool and waterfall. 4 tennis courts, putting green. Tropical gardens, promenades in natural park setting. Next to Cultural Center. *Rsv:* Western Int'l. $38-$46.

PHILIPPINE VILLAGE (FC) — At airport. 504 soundproof R, SU. Spanish-style dining room serves buffet lunch. Cocktail lounge has dancing, entertainment. Folk Art Bar features folk singers. 2 pools, tennis courts amidst lush gardens. *Conv:* 1000. $27-$35.

ROYAL — DT. 250 R. Revolving rst serves int'l cuisine. Supper club, bar. *Conv:* 600. $19-$22.

SILAHIS INT'L (FC) — Overlooks Bay and Rizal Park. 600 R attractively decorated with interesting fabrics. Marble lobby with lovely artifacts. Exterior glass elevator to rooftop Stargazer Lounge. Rst, discotheque. An excellent buy. $27-$35.

REGENT OF MANILA (DL) — Nr. Cultural Ctr, Conv. Ctr and overlooking bay. Multi-rsts, bars; pool. $32-$40.

Sulo in Quezon City with 60 R, SU decorated with Philippine craft, rst, bar and pool is mod. at $21. Executive Arms, Timberland, Sherbourne are good economy-class hotels.

IN MAKATI

INTER-CONTINENTAL MANILA (DL) — Between airport and town. 420 R. El Castelano rooftop rst has int'l floor shows at 9:30 and midnight (closed Sun). Music and drinks in Le Boulevardier Lounge (exp). Several rsts, bars; pool and cabana club. *Conv:* 900. $33-$41.

MAKATI (FC) — 15 min. from airport. Opened '74 on E de los Santos. 196 AC R (mostly SU). Several rsts one serving Singapore cuisine, three cocktail lounges, dancing nightly. Pool. $22-$32. SU to $100.

MANDARIN (DL) — 504 R, SU (Presidential SU w/pool), all with marble baths. Set amidst tropical gardens;

287

large pool and bar. Several rsts including gourmet L'Hirondelle. Candlelight dancing. Health club and conv. facilities. $40-$50.

MANILA GARDEN (DL) — Center of shopping district. 611 AC R. Two Japanese, one French rst, Spanish bistro. Japanese garden, pool. $37-$47. *Rsv:* JAL.

MANILA PENINSULA (DL+) — Built in two wings joined by 4-story center. Old world charm in new, grandiose lobby. Huge open garden and pool area. Restaurants, gourmet supper club. 256 double R, 26 SU (on top floor); refrig stocked with drinks. Filipino elegance. $56.

BAGUIO

NEW PINES — 5 hrs. from Manila by bus. 211 R mountain resort. Dining room, cocktail lounge, thermal pool, tennis. Nightly entertainment. Reserve in advance. $24-$28.

BANAUE

BANAUE — On a plateau overlooking rice terraces. 18 R, 2 SU. Very attractive dining room, poolside bar. *Rsv:* Dept of Tourism, Manila. $23.

BATANGAS

SIERRA GRANDE — Rustic mountain resort an hour from Manila airport. 42 R, dining room, bar, pool, tennis. Folk entertainment. $16.

CALATAGAN, Batangas

PUNTA BALUARTE (DL) — 23-acre resort with unspoiled charm; 2½ hours from Manila by car. Hillside overlooking China Sea. 30 new R, 45 older ones, all with rfg ($30-$32), and bungalows ($25). Decorated in traditional, rustic Filipino style. Dining room, bar, traditional entertainment. Pool, tennis, riding, polo field. Fishing, scuba diving, boating. Private airstrip. *Rsv:* Inter-Continental; Pan Am.

CEBU

CEBU PLAZA — 500 R with city views. Opens '79.

SANTA ROSA — Thatched roof cabana resort (32 AC R) on Olango Island just off Mactan. Buffet dining, cocktail lounge. Riding, fishing, scuba diving. $28. Airport transfer available.

MAGELLAN — 168 R, SU. 2 dining rooms, coffee shop, bar. Pool, pelota court, 18-hole golf course. *Conv:* 800. $16-$18.

MONTEBELLO RESORT — 10 min. from city center. 87 R. Rst, coffee shop, 2 bars, discotheque, pool, riding. *Conv:* 500. $13-$24.

SKYVIEW — Skyvue revolving rst, 3 bars, nightclub. 167 R. $8-$15.

DAVAO

DAVAO INSULAR (FC) — Suburban area beach resort, 10 min from airport. 200 R w/terrace in landscaped setting. Dining room, bar, cocktail lounge. Pool, pitch-putt, pelotacourt. Sailboats, canoes. $17-$22.

ILOILO

ANHAWAN BEACH RESORT — 7 first-class native-style cottages w/kitchen facilities and bath are amidst coco palms on a white sand beach. Outstanding seafood, Filipino delicacies. Informal resort with good scuba diving, fishing. $11-$25.

MARAWI, Mindanoa

MARAWI RESORT (FC) — Opened '75 with 20 Muslim-style units overlooking Lake Lanao. More were to be added. Pool, tennis, pelota courts, waterskiing.

TAGAYTAY

TAAL LODGE (FC) — 40 R on ridge overlook Taal lake and volcano. Features underground room to watch volcano and lake. 2 rsts, 2 bars. Pool, tennis, riding. Daily entertainment. $26.

VILLA ADELAIDA — Beautifully situated on ridge overlooking lake and China Sea. 27 R ($18), 70 bungalows ($18). Rst, coffee shop, bar. Pool, pelota court. Heliport. 1 hr. from Manila airport.

ZAMBOANGA

LANTAKA — 96 seaside R. Open-court terrace, bar, cocktail lounge, dining room. Scuba equipment available. $15, plus 25% tax.

ZAMBOANGA PLAZA (FC) — In lush Pasonanca Park. Opened in '77 with 210 R, SU. Rst, coffee shop. Pool, tennis, pelota. Shopping arcade. *Conv:* 500. $25 up.

INDIA

Sculptures that decorate the temples of Khajuraho, In Praise of Woman, are masterpieces of sensuous art.

When Aryan barbarians descended south (about 1400 B.C.) from the vicinity of present Russian Turkestan, India already had a highly developed civilization in the Indus Valley with its center in what is now Pakistan but extending over a large area.

The Aryans brought their own Vedic religion, literature, philosophy and traditions, and although they had to contend with the indigenous civilization, they absorbed much of its culture. In remote forest hermitages, Aryan mystics produced sublime poetry and philosophy, practiced the discipline of Yoga. Thus, this blending of races and cultures marked the origin of a new civilization which, despite many upheavals and alterations, has continued to this day. In fact, the 6th century B.C. in India was epochal, for it was then that the Buddha and Mahavira (founder of the Jain religion) were born to preach compassion and love and put righteous conduct above formal religion. Indeed, it was this Aryan-Indian culture that led to medieval Hinduism under the Gupta Empire (330-530 A.D.) and its successor states (to 770 A.D.).

Alexander's invasion in 326 B.C. brought India into brief contact with Hellenistic culture. Although the political impact was negligible, Indian mythology and art in the northwest was influenced for a long time by Greek tradition.

The 200 years of the Gupta dynasty is known as the Golden Age of Indian art. Supported by kings, wealthy merchants and much of the lower urban classes, Buddhism and Jainism dominated the arts which portrayed saints as supermen, gods as akin to men but on a higher level — a combination of worldly refinement and grandiose spirituality. Fortunately, much of this fine religious art is well preserved.

In the southern peninsula, a similar flourishing — particularly in the form of imposing temples — took place from the 5th to 9th centuries under the Pallavas.

The Middle Ages of India, 770-1200 A.D., were dominated by military classes that developed a Medieval Hindu civilization marked by the dominance of widespread Hindu religions, the decline of Buddhism and Jainism. Two major and three minor systems developed, "Vishnuism and Saivism, Saktism, Brahma and sun worship, fundamentally identical in general outlook, differing only on the importance of various gods, and in details of ritual and methods of salvation. . . . A rigid hierarchy of innumerable castes developed where each lower one had to pay deference to its superiors, religion abased man before the gods. Temples became mystic machines, full of magic powers, where the idol was served, like an earthly ruler, by a host of priests, monks and dancing girls. Everything . . . was supposed to be based on sacred tradition laid down in numerous handbooks. . . . The state became the monopoly of princes unscrupulously contending for supremacy, of nobles transferring allegiance to the highest bidder; intellectual culture was the privilege of a small class of conceited priests, scholars, monks and courtiers. The people, utterly exploited, became politically indifferent, merely engrossed in sectarian squabbles. The country was ripe for collapse. . . ."[1]

It came in the form of a Muslim (mainly Turks) invasion and conquest that resulted in an Indo-Islamic civilization (1200-1803), an eventual blending of Hindu and Islamic cultures and life styles and an upsurge in mystical Hinduism venerating Vishnu as a god of all-embracing love. A second conquering wave, that of the Mughals (1526-1803-1857), extended this Islamic penetration which exists today as Pakistan, then a region in western India. As a consequence, Hindu and Islamic art forms originating during that era mutually incorporate much of the other's symbolism. By the 18th century, when the Mughal empire was disintegrating, its distinctive civilization became, in general, the heritage of all of India.

---

[1] *The Art of India* by Hermann Goetz (Greystone Press). Quoted at length because the period might well have laid the foundation for the ills of India today.

Modern India (from 1803)

Led by the British India Company, which had been trading here for years, England took advantage of the Mughal collapse to consolidate its footholds, but not until around 1837 did she attempt a rapid Anglo-Christianized takeover of the subcontinent, resulting in increasing Indian opposition which exploded in the Mutiny of 1857-58 that required strenuous British Army effort to quell, after which the British government took over complete administration of the country. The status of individual states was protected, the country in general modernized, Indians gradually given high government posts and upper-class Indian social life became increasingly Europeanized. However, England finally had to yield to Mahatma Gandhi's non-cooperation movement; in August of 1947, Indian independence was proclaimed, its princely states were eliminated, and Pakistan became a separate Muslim nation.

INDIAN ART

The foregoing is detailed not so much as historical information but primarily to set the stage for understanding the periods and forms of art which you'll encounter — for these, the temples and sculptures, murals and artifacts, are certainly prime reasons for coming to this ancient land where temple carvings are as beautiful as when first sculpted, where pilgrimages are still made to places where the Buddha preached his first sermons, where tourists look down into the fortified palace of Fatehpur Sikr and see it as it was 400 years ago when Emperor Akbar played chess there using court ladies as chess pieces.

Thus, the art you'll see follows the successive civilizations: the realism of the Indus Valley; the Aryan-Indian art forms that evolved into the refinement and spirituality of the Gupta Empire; the art of the Middle Ages that started with the profoundly mystical Gupta and Pallava heritages but then becoming increasingly worldly and superficial and ending as a competition in building the largest temple with the greatest number of mass-produced sculptures; Indo-Islamic period, one of the most fascinating in the whole world of art inasmuch as two cultures, Hindu and Moslem, absorbed aspects of the other while retaining its own basic traditions; finally, modern Indian art which is searching for its own individual expression after having alternately imitated European then ancient Indian art.

That, of course, is a simplistic explanation; actually, the evolutionary processes were much more complex, involving Graeco-Roman influences, Roman-Hindu styles while Medieval Hindu art displayed different styles in various parts of the country, including, in Bengal, what's been described as Gupta Baroque and/or Rococo. Likewise, the Islamic period was divided into pre- and post-Mughal styles in both Moslem and Hindu art — to say nothing of various local styles that developed in Nepal, Java, Bali, Siam and other foreign countries where Islamic and/or Hindu religions flourished.

So, what makes a journey thru India so intensely interesting is this diversity and wealth of styles, forms, images, emotions and esthetic ideals. And yet, despite such overwhelming diversity, there is a distinctiveness and homogeneity easily identified as Indian art which, one finds, is unlike any other in the world.

ENTRY & CUSTOMS REGULATIONS

Passport, Tourist Visa or Landing Permit. Visa, good for 3 months and extendable for another 3, obtainable from an Indian Consulate General: 2107 Massachusetts Av, N.W., Washington, D.C. 20008; 3 E. 64, N.Y. 10021; 215 Market St, San Francisco, Ca 94105; 230 N. Michigan, Chicago 60601. Tourist Introduction Card and All India Liquor Permit issued free with visa. Collective visa issued for groups.

If arriving by air at Bombay, Calcutta, Delhi, Madras or Varanasi, visa not needed as Landing Permit (also Card/Liquor Permit) good for 28 days is issued by Immigration; with that, you can visit neighboring countries providing you hold round-trip ticket and total stay in India does not exceed 28 days.

Smallpox, cholera and typhoid inoculations not required by India but advised for your protection and to facilitate re-entry to U.S.

On arrival, fill out Tourist Baggage Re-export Form so you can take out your High Value Articles (cameras, binoculars, radios, personal jewelry, etc.) when exiting. You're allowed two still cameras and 25 rolls of film, one movie camera (10 reels or cartridges), a quart of liquor, reasonable personal effects. If any articles are stolen or lost, obtain a police report; without this at Customs, you could pay 100% duty on value of articles. No restrictions, within reason, on taking out your purchases (except for gold, antiques, animal skins).

CLIMATE & CLOTHING

October thru March are best months — no rain, days are pleasant, cool in the north. April to June, considered Indian summer, have nothing in common with our American version — they're hot! End of June to September is monsoon season, the wettest and greenest. These months are best time to visit Kashmir (no monsoon period); temperatures hover in the 60s and 70s.

Mean Temperature Range			Rainfall
	Winter	Summer	Monsoon
Northern	40-55F	80-105F	25"
Central	50-60	95-110	20"
Southern	75-85	80-90	50"
Coastal	65-75	85-95	80"
Kashmir*	30-45	60-70	25"

* And other mountain resort areas

From April thru Sept, only the lightest cotton clothing is needed. Synthetic materials that don't breathe are hot. For higher, cooler elevations, bring a sweater; sunglasses a must.

In the north during the winter months, particularly in New Delhi, woolen clothing is suggested for evenings. Dec. and Jan. nights can be chilly — in the low 40s.

Dress clothing for evening is rarely as formal as even a tie and jacket. Actually, the only time we needed those two items during our 12 weeks in India was at the rooftop Chinese restaurant of the New Delhi Inter-Continental.

A reminder: shoes are removed before entering temples and mosques, so bring a pair that can be easily slipped on/off. Good idea to have a pair of heavy socks in your pocket to put on.

GENERAL INFORMATION

Airport tax—$2.75.
Business hours — M-S 10-5. Sunday and second Saturday in month are holidays.
Capital — New Delhi (4,100,000 pop.).
Currency — About 9 Indian rupees (Rs)=$1. U.S. currency must be declared on arrival. No restrictions on amount that can be brought in. Keep sufficient exchange records to reconvert rupees on departure. No Indian currency can be taken in or out of the country.
Electric Current — 220v, 50c; mostly AC.
Goverment — Federal Republic.
Languages — 15 major ones; Hindi and English predominate.
Newspapers — Four in English. Int'l publications on sale in all major cities.
Population — 600,000,000.
Postage — Stamps can be bought in hotels. Get certificate of mailing for important ones.
Religion — 85% Hindu, 10% Muslim, 5% Christian, Sikh, Buddhist, Jain, Zoroastrians.
Time — + 5½ hrs. GMT.
Tipping — No to taxi drivers, yes for porters (except at hotels where it's included in service charge). Not expected by waiters but leaving small change is good form.
Toilets — Use only those in hotels, rsts.
Tourist Information — Tourist offices at major airports are generally open 24 hrs. a day. There are tourist offices thruout India: New Delhi, Bombay, Calcutta, Madras, Agra, Aurangabad, Cochin, Jaipur, Jammu, Varanasi and Khajuraho. In U.S. Gov't of India Tourist offices at 30 Rockefeller Plaza, New York 10020; 201 North Michigan Av, Chicago, Ill. 60601; 685 Market St, San Francisco 94105; 3550 Wilshire Blvd., Los Angeles 90010. Also 177 King St. West, Toronto 1, Ontario, Canada.
Water — Bottled or purified only.

Domestic Air Transportation

Indian Airlines thoroughly blankets the country, mostly by Boeing 727s and 737s. It offers unlimited travel within India for $200 for maximum of 14 days, $275 for 21 days; these Discover India fares can be purchased in the U.S. and Canada or in India (with foreign exchange). There's also a Youth (12 to 30) discount of 25% on normal fares.

Here's how long it takes to fly to various points: From Delhi to Agra, 30 min.; to Bombay, 1:45; to Calcutta, 2:05; to Jaipur, 35 min.; to Madras, 2:35; to Srinagar, 2:05 (1-stop); to Varanasi, 2:40 (1-stop). From Madras to Kathmandu, Nepal, 1:20; to Calcutta, 2:05.

Domestic Rail Transportation

Air-conditioned accommodations on Indian Railways is "as comfortable as Pullman Services in USA." Is that a positive recommendation? Anyway, you can reserve space up to 180 days in advance thru travel agencies. Foreign students get 15% discount first class, 50% on second-class fares.

292

india

Srinagar
Gulmarg ▲ ▲ Sonamarg
▲ Pahalgam
Dalhousie ●

Manali ●
▲ Kulu

Amritsar ●
▲ Simla
Chandigarh ●
Tajewala ● ▲ Mussoorie
Ranikhet ● Almora
▲ ▲ Nainital
DELHI ◉ Corbett
Sultanpur ○
Pilani ●
Sariska ○ Mathura ●
Pushkar ● Jaipur ● Kecladeo Agra
Ghana ○
Lucknow ■
Kanpur ■

Mount Abu ●
▲ Chittorgarh ■ Shivpuri ○
Udaipur ▲
Khajuraho ■ Varanasi ■
Sanchi ■
Pachmarhi ■ Kanha ○

Nal Sarovar ○

Veraval ● ○ Gir
Kodinar ●

Ajanta ●
Ellora ■ Taroba ○

BOMBAY ◉ Matheran ●
Juhu ✶ ▲ Lonavla
▲ Pune
Mahableshwar ▲
Ratnagiri ▲

Goa ✶

Chickmagalur ●
Bangalore ●
Mangalore ● Ranganathittoo ○ Kanchipuram ■
Mercara ● Mysore ● MADRAS ◉
Bandipur Vedanthangal ○ Mamallapuram ■
Mudumalai ○ Ootacamund ○
Kozhikode ● Coonoor ● Tiruchi ●
Kodaikanal ● Thanjavur ■
Cochin ● Point Calimere ○
Madurai ●
Quilon ● Periyar ○
Trivandrum ●
Kovalam ✶
Kanyakumari ✶

Sonepur ●
Rajgir ●
Hazaribagh ○

Darjeeling ▲ Gangtok ▲
Manas ○
Jaldapara ○
▲ Shill

CALCUTTA ◉
Digha ✶

Bhubaneswar ■ ✶ Konarak
Puri ✶
Gopalpur-on-Sea ✶

Vishakapatnam ✶

Secunderabad ■
Hyderabad ■

REFERENCES

BEACH	✶
MONUMENT	■
HILL RESORT	▲
WILDLIFE / WATERBIRD SANCTUARY	○
OTHER TOURIST CENTRES	●

Indrail Pass is available from authorized travel agents in India and from some railway reservations offices. First Class, AC chair seat is $35 for 7 days, $50 for 15 days, $130 for 90 days; children half price.

If AC cars are unavailable, take FC. Below FC means crowded conditions, hardwood seats.

Though network is extensive it's not rapid; average speed about 30 miles an hour. And railroad stations are hectic. At each stop, vendors sell food and drink to passengers, multitudes of people coming and going. Fascinating!

By Road

Distances are as immense as in the U.S. If you want to drive, it is cheaper and safer to rent a car with driver. No detailed road maps available so bring one along. Driving is to the left. Car with chauffeur (arrange thru car rental agency) costs about $.15 per mile. At present, self-drive cars are only available in Bombay.

City Transportation

In towns and cities, taxis and motor trishaws are metered. Bargain for bicycle rickshaws; horse-drawn carriages available in certain locations. Land Rovers in wildlife parks and shikaras (water taxis) in Kashmir.

Sightseeing buses available in towns and cities. AC bus with guide for 8 hrs, $3 per person; without AC, $1.50.

WHEN IN INDIA . . .

Sari is the flowing, wraparound dress of Indian women, and *Dhotis* are worn by men (when not wearing Western clothes). Cloths tied around the head are called, *Pugri, Safa* or *Pheta,* and ways of tying them are as varied as their colors.

You needn't hesitate to entrust your washables to the ministrations of a local *dhobi,* even though malicious gossip claims he breaks stones with your shirts. Not so.

Bargaining is in order in many smaller shops, and with all street vendors but Government and all larger stores are one-priced.

When visiting mosque, mausoleum and temple, shed your shoes at the entrance. Okay to walk into them in socks or stockings if cloth or canvas slippers are not provided.

Indian version of a handshake is *Namaste* or *Namaskar,* so spoken as the palms of the hands join in front of the chest in greeting. Serves as "Good morning," "Good afternoon," "Good evening," "Good night" and "Goodbye" as the case might be. For "thank you," say *Dhanyavad* or *Shukria.*

ADVENTURES IN GOOD DINING

Although you can travel thruout the country eating good and well-cooked Western-style food, it would be a mistake. Be venturesome. Not all Indian cooking is, by any means, impossibly pungent. Food is as varied as the regions of the country; there are 15 or more traditional cuisines ranging from the meat-based, rich dishes of the north to the countless aromatic curries of the south.

A typical Indian meal is not served in courses — a number of dishes are brought to the table at one time so you can blend and flavor according to your taste. Here are some toothsome options:

Chicken

Tandoori, a top specialty, is spring chicken baked in a simple clay oven *(tandoor)* so that it's crisp outside, moist and spicy pink inside. Eat with your hands.

Murgh Mussalum, a whole stuffed chicken subtly spiced and gentled with cream and coconut — delightful and not at all red hot.

Tikka Kabab, bite-size pieces of boned chicken brazier-grilled with onion rings, served with lime.

Meats

When in Kashmir, revel in *Wazwan,* a sensuous feast at which an array of up to 17 meat dishes may be served, such as exotic *Tabakmaz* and rich, creamy *Gushtaba.*

Elsewhere, enjoy *Mutton Do Pyaza,* tender lamb (although most mutton is goat meat, not lamb) simmered with pink onions in a golden gravy of fried onions, a hint of spice and ginger. Then there are the grilled finger foods of Islamic origin: *kababs,* meats marinated in spiced yoghurt and papaya paste, basted with ghee (semi-fluid butter, usually from buffalo milk) and grilled over charcoal. *Hussaini curry* are kabobs on bamboo skewers simmered in gravy and usually served with *parathas* (unleavened bread). Fried meat balls are *koftas* in a spicy sauce; and *korma,* meat in a poppy seed and coconut gravy; and *Palak gosht,* meat prepared with cream and coconut milk and dressed with spinach; and. . . .

Rice and Curry

Not all rice dishes are curries. Possibly the most celebrated of all Indian dishes is *Moglai Biryani* — if you haven't partaken, you haven't been to India. For it is prepared with loving care — particularly in Delhi. Tender pieces of chicken or lamb are marinated in herbs and spices, partially cooked with nuts, raisins, aromatic spices, cream and coconut and browned slowly. Alternate layers of rice and meat are laid to rest in the *biryani,* sprinkled with milk and saffron, sealed, then cooked slowly on glowing embers. It's served beautifully on a platter garnished with crisp, fried onions, nuts, eggs and potatoes — a feast for the eye and palate.

A variation of *biryani* is *pullao.* Some popular ones: *Prawn Puallo* — Pink and white, delicately spiced, shrimply delicious and popular everywhere. *Navratan Pullao* — Nine-jeweled ricefest with multi-hued ingredients; a specialty of Clarks Shiraz in Agra.

As diverse as its people, up to 20 different spices may be combined in a single curry, many of which are ideal for Westerners. A happy choice is *Rogan josh,* a nutmeg-flavored curry from Kashmir; its rich color comes from saffron and bright chilis that impart more color than fire.

From the Sea and Land

On the coast, the most orthodox Hindu eats fish — but elsewhere he's a vegetarian. You can feast on delectable giant prawns, smoked *bekti* (giant perch) and fried *hitsa* (like shad), crab curry and stuffed lobster. In Kashmir, *mahseer* (large freshwater carp) and trout. In Bombay, discover Bombay duck, an unusually prepared dried fish. Then there's *Tandoori fish* in a piquant *masala,* another specialty of Clarks Shiraz Hotel in Agra.

Pomfret (butterfish) is a great Indian favorite — with green masala (a specialty in Bombay) or smothered in green chutney and steamed in banana leaf. Prawns, soaked in crushed onion and ginger, plus chili, crisp-coated, then deep-fried, are delectable.

Many Indians continue to live as vegetarians by tradition and practice — without sacrificing good food. A superbly varied cuisine has been developed, with vegetables playing the sole, and stellar, role. Even at weddings and religious functions, food may be served on banana leaves — colorful, disposable plates. Before you leave, try a traditional South India vegetarian meal attractively served in a *thali* — served on a giant silver platter with a number of smaller silver bowls on it. Inside these bowls are a variety of vegetable dishes, lentil curry, yoghurt, condiments and sweets, accompanied by rice and puris (Indian bread of crisply fried flour).

Eat with your fingers — Indians believe that eating with implements is as unsatisfactory as making love thru an interpreter. But use your right hand only. As a *thali* meal progresses, you'll find that the various dishes complement each other: a mild dish of sprouted *gram* (chick-pea), a semi-liquid *dal* (Indian lentil), peas and potatoes in a thick gravy, sweet-sour mango dish, crisp salad, creamy yoghurt and *mithai* (dessert). *Pakoras* (vegetable fritters) are popular as a side dish. Half a dozen chutneys and pickles are available. In fact, the variety is so bewildering you understand why Indians often find eating only one course at a time so difficult.

And Then Comes . . .

For a unique experience, order *appam,* a rice and coconut pancake fermented with toddy and baked in a fired clay pot, then served with a thick middle and crisp, lacy border — for breakfast or with a chicken curry. South Indian pancakes, *dosai,* are popular in all big cities: lacy and crisp with *sambhar* (lentil curry), plain with jam and honey, or with a potato filling.

Indian wheat breads are delectable (women are complimented when termed wheat-complexioned) and varied. Implement curries with *chapatis* — round, unleavened and tortilla-like. *Puris,* round and golden, are made to dunk in curries or eat with sweets. In the north, enjoy silk-like *reshmi parathas* wrapped around a *seekh-kabab.* Discover *naan,* a bat-shaped bread baked in a tandoor — marvelous with *Moglai* meat dishes.

There is a variety of familiar and unusual fruits. Latter includes the custard apple, *toddy,* jackfruit (a single, huge fruit contains hundreds of sweet, juicy kernels), *chickoos* (nectar sweet) — plus a myriad of different mangoes. Served fresh or in puddings, dumplings and fritters.

Indian *mithais* (sweets), colorful, exotic and delicious, are served in tempting arrays in all hotels. Stop at a shop and watch orange-gold *jelabis* and *jehangiris* being made — fascinatingly patterned sweetmeats, crisp and syrupy. Carry them away with you in gay little boxes; every city and state has its specialty — like translucent *halwas* wrapped in tissue-thin silver foil (which you eat with the sweet).

Cool off with *kulfi,* a rich, saffron-flavored ice cream laced with nuts — or have a rare treat, fresh custard apple ice cream.

To mark the end of a meal — like an after-dinner mint for Americans — Indians chew *pan.* Traditionally served in a silver box with numerous compartments, a mixture of lime, betel nut and spices are folded together in a betel leaf and secured with a single clove. This mixture, repeatedly chewed, has a refreshing taste.

ALL ABOUT DRINKING

If you like your martinis and/or highballs, pay strict attention: a few states have prohibition, others have restricted areas, and most big cities have "dry days," and in all cases liquor laws are strict, so it behooves you to have an *All India Liquor Permit,* issued along with visas or obtainable by foreigners from Government Tourist Offices abroad or at Bombay, Calcutta, Delhi or Madras on arrival. It authorizes you to buy, possess, transport and consume liquor, even in prohibition states and on dry days. In Delhi, public drinking is prohibited, but foreigners in selected hotels may have drinks with meals or in bar lounges, even entertain Indian guests there (except on dry days).

Imported scotch is, of course, good and costs about same as in U.S.; bring some duty-free liquor. Avoid the local whiskey; local beers, though, are quite good. Indian red wine is good but expensive; wines are not imported. But there's plenty of native *arrack,* clear, white and potent, and *pheni,* another liquor made from the cashew apple. Indian rums are said to be good. As are some of their liqueurs. Formerly, rich nawabs and rajas vied in making them; a few are still being distilled; one of these is *asha* from either saffron or (get this) rose petals.

Incidentally, the cocktail hour is made even more pleasant in India thru the variety of snacks, munchables and waist-destroyers. Spicy mince popovers called curry puffs; *samosas* stuffed with seasoned vegetables; *vadas* — lentils ground into paste, fried to a puffy crispness; vegetable fritters (*pakoras* in the south, *bhajias* in the north). Adapted from wayside stalls are mouth-watering combinations of crisp fries drenched in sweetsour chutney with minced onion — try them in one of your hotel lounges.

On the lighter side, there are all sorts of cooling, enticing concoctions: coconut milk, icy sugarcane juice (fresh and frothy with a light taste of ginger and lemon) and fruit juices — from familiar orange and pineapple to mango and guava nectar. For a change, try a *Nimbu Pani* (fresh lime sherbet with a pinch of salt) or a tall *Lassi* (yoghurt whipped with crushed ice, syrup or salty-spiced), a kind of milk shake. Speaking of those, there are some romantically flavored ones, like *kewra. Faloola* is a pink, rose-scented, milk and custard cooler topped with ice cream; *Thandai* is a delightful almond and milk cooler. Then, hot or cold, there's always the very tasty Indian tea.

ENTERTAINMENT

Since Hindus do not drink, entertainment is generally confined to hotel restaurants, supper clubs and nightclubs where there's dancing, floor shows. Calcutta has the liveliest night life.

Musicians playing traditional Indian instruments, such as the sitar, often provide dinner music; dance groups also may perform. Be sure to see at least one dance performance as the native dance (there are four major schools, each representing a different region) is an important aspect of India's cultural life, as are Indian opera and concerts.

You'll go to bed early while here.

FESTIVALS & HOLIDAYS

When we asked an Indian friend, living in America, what she missed most about India, she replied, "Indian music, food and festivals."

The subcontinent's lunar calendar is a long procession of festivals that await the tourist thruout the year. Every region, every religion has many to offer — and each is different. No land demands more of its legends, celebrates the past so marvelously in the present. Whichever you see will be an extra bonus, both pleasurably and photographically.

Some of the main festivals are: *Holi,* thruout northern India, celebrating advent of spring (Feb. or March), is a bacchanalia of riotous character. *Dussehra,* probably the most popular, is observed for 10 days in Sept. or Oct. Based on the Ramayana epic, Rama is feted for killing the demon king Ravana (good triumphant). *Diwali* is the gayest, an occasion for great excitement and rejoicing — often marks start of New Year (Oct.-Nov.). Houses are decorated with lights to welcome Lakshmi, goddess of wealth and prosperity; originally signalled Rama's return from exile. An interesting sidelight to many of the big festivals are cattle fairs in which thousands of cows, sheep, goats, buffalo, bulls, horses and camels are for sale. Prizes awarded for best of breed.

Muhurram, a 10-day period of mourning for Shia Muslims (Jan.) commemorates the martydom of Imam Hussain, the Prophet Mohammed's grandson.

Of the national holidays, Republic Day (Jan. 26) in Delhi and all state capitals is the greatest. Festivities in Delhi culminate in a magnificent parade at which the President takes the salute; parade winds a glittering route thru the heart of the city, includes richly caparisoned horses, elephants and camels, floats and tableaux, folk dance troupes.

Independence Day is August 15, Mahatma Gandhi's Birthday October 2. Christmas is also a national holiday.

SHOPPING IS FUN

Because the merchandise is so colorful, and, in many cases, so intriguingly different, much of your time will be spent in shops, stores; better ones are one-price. You'll particularly want to shop various state and municipal government stores which display and sell the best produced in each locality. For names and addresses of these and other approved sources, get a copy of the Department of Tourism's *Where To Buy* booklet for 11 major shopping cities. Shopping hours are, usually, 9:30-5:30 M thru Sat.

Women always find the almost bewildering array of *saris* (or *sarees*), those six-yard lengths of dazzling color, utterly fascinating and irresistible as they can, if desired, be converted into a kaftan, dress or pantsuit; sari materials range from muslin and other cool cottons to rich, provocative silks from Varanasi, their borders often brocaded in silver or gold, or the light Tassar silks woven from the cocoon of the wild silk moth. And there's exquisitely delicate jewelry of silver and gold, as well as swinging sandals, shoes, handbags and belts, delightful ivory miniatures in the style of the later Mughals, Bidri-ware from Hyderabad (delicate tracery of silver on gunmetal), shawls, vard goods.

In Kashmir hand-embroidered shawls ($17); superlative papier-mache boxes ($3 up), carpets and rugs are excellent buys. India's Persian carpets cost $1,500 and rival more costly ones from Iran.

Naturally, there's an endless array of

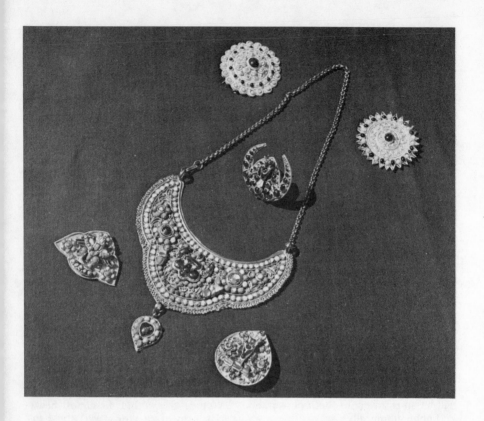

handicrafts, much of it unique to India: perfumed sandalwood carvings of animals (stunning) from Jaipur; marble inlay plates and other items from Agra; intricately crafted brassware, unusual bronzes from the south; colorful appliqued animal toys; strangely beautiful, richly inlaid musical instruments; exotic Indian Oriental rugs. Of course, you'll see much more: carved ivory, copperware, costumed native dolls, wood carvings, custom tailored garments, singing bells, precious and semi-precious stones, jade, Mughal paintings, antiques. But beware because in India, as in most other Asian countries, objects more than 100 years old are not allowed to be exported without appropriate papers from the Department of Antiquities. The U.S. Customs office has recently prohibited Asian ivory from entering the U.S. Because elephants are on the endangered species list, they hope to inhibit the elephant slaughter by restricting the import of ivory.

Thruout India, tailors quickly fashion garments for you. There is hardly a ready-made piece of clothing in the country. Everything is made to order — cheaply. Custom-made leather shoes cost $17 in New Delhi, dress shirts $5. In Delhi you'll find carpets, silk, handcrafts, semi-precious & precious stones, silver.

Agra is famed for its silks, brocades and brass products; Bombay for cotton textiles; Calcutta is known for jute products, tea, handcrafts. In Banglore, Mysore area buy batik paintings, sandalwood, antiques, silk. For bamboo products it's Trivandrum; Hyderabad is known for handcrafts, metalwork. Best quality printed silks and brocades are made in Varanasi.

Duty Free Airport Shops in Bombay, Calcutta, Delhi and Madras are run by the India Tourism Development Corp.

First-time visitors with two weeks or less to spend should choose between the North or South. The country is too vast (two-thirds the size of the continental U.S.) to see it all without losing time in transit.

The majority of the 532,000 tourists who visited India in 1976 chose the northern route, partially because the North has been better developed in terms of quality hotels, restaurants and transportation. Northern treasures include the architectural monuments built by invading Moghuls, the sumptuous palaces and forts left by the Maharajas, the city life of Delhi, the allure of Agra's Taj Mahal and the religosity of Varanasi.

Traveling in the South brings different rewards. There are less tourists, many more beautiful beach resorts such as Goa and Puri. Southern India is demonstrably more religious than the North — the most important tourist locations are the living Hindu temples of Mathurai, Bhubaneshwar and Mahabalipuram.

Game sanctuaries are located in both areas.

NORTHERN INDIA

DELHI — Tale of Two Cities

Delhi can be great fun — lots of history, good eating and good shopping. But be sure to go at the right time of year. From October to March it's fine with blue skies, temperate days; during winter, a wool coat is advisable. After April, the heat builds to an unbearable degree until the monsoon brings some relief in July. Avoid Delhi during this period of heat. An ideal time to visit is around January 26, Republic Day, when there is a grand parade down Rajpath, one of the major avenues.

Unlike many other Asian capitals, Delhi has an extensive history. Its site has been the location of seven successive cities dating back 1,000 years, which means there are more than a fair share of monuments, tombs and ruins to visit.

Today's city is a happy union of two cities: Delhi and New Delhi. Delhi served as the focal point for ancient empires. New Delhi was planned and built in the 1920's when the British decided to relocate the capital from Calcutta. The two cities have entirely different characters. New Delhi is reminiscent of Washington, D.C. — massive government buildings situated on broad avenues, plenty of green open spaces and urbane plazas. Delhi contrasts vividly: its serpentine streets and bazaar areas are crowded. As adjacent cities comprising the Union Territory of Delhi, with a population of four million, it is easy to spend at least three full days here.

The heart of New Delhi is Connaught Place where seven principal thoroughfares converge to form a large, circular park. This is a fun shopping area. When taking a break by sitting in Connaught Place, don't be surprised if an Indian offers to revive you by giving you a massage. Carrying their oils with them, these men offer skillful massages for pennies.

Shops to visit around Connaught Place include Central Cottage Industries Emporium, a large department store featuring artifacts from all over India. Better yet, if your trip to other parts of India is brief, visit the state stores southwest of Connaught Place; each sells goods unique to its area. We particularly recommend the state stores of Rajasthan, Gujarat and, of course, Kashmir.

In close proximity to Connaught Place, along Shanti Path, is the embassy district. One of the handsomest is the U.S. Embassy designed by Edward Durell Stone, who also did the similar-looking Kennedy Center in Washington. If not taking a City Tour, cruise this area by taxi as distances between embassies are great.

Center of old Delhi is Chandni Chowk, an enormous bazaar opposite the Red Fort. This major street was an imperial thoroughfare for Emperor Shahjahan. Today it is as lively a bazaar as can be found anywhere. With streets off streets leading to other streets and traffic of all kinds — vehicle, animal and pedestrian — it is indeed a lively, intriguing Indian scene. Since streets in Asian bazaars specialize in specific products, don't be surprised to find yourself, as we did, walking along a street of shops selling only plumbing fixtures — or jewelry, makeup, textiles, etc.

In Delhi, be sure to visit Jama Masjid, the Great Mosque, and the Red Fort. The former, dating from mid-17th century, is India's largest mosque, built on an imposing scale with red sandstone and white marble by Shahjahan.

Red Fort, too, was built during the reign of the emperor Shahjahan, who was also responsible for the Taj Mahal. The Fort was erected during the glittering years of the Moghul period, in 1648, and served as the administrative center and palatial residence of Shahjahan.

Located on the banks of the Yamuna River, directly across from the Jama Masjid and Chandni Chowk, the walls of the Fort are of elegant red sandstone. Inside are mosques, audience halls and royal chambers. Once the audience hall was so splendidly decorated as to inspire a Persian poet to inscribe into its walls:

> *"If there be a paradise on earth,*
> *'Tis here! It is here! It is here!"*

Even today, though the fabled Peacock Throne is gone and the ceilings have been stripped of their silver coating, the chamber is still beautiful. Each evening there's an English-language Sound and Light Show on the history of the Fort and its place in Indian history. It's very much worth seeing (and hearing).

In New Delhi, be sure to see:

Parliament House and Presidential Palace — These major structures don't look much different from imposing government buildings anywhere, but still they represent symbols of Indian authority.

National Museum — Carefully presents a representative sampling of its vast collections. Among the best: bronze sculptures, textiles and miniature paintings.

Nehru Memorial Museum, Teen Murti — The first prime minister's residence. Regular Sound and Light Shows.

Humayun's Tomb — Its architecture was a forerunner of the Taj Mahal. Built in the mid-16th century as the mausoleum of Emperor Humayun, it stands centered in spacious gardens. If you want a taste of the Taj with its bulbous dome, be sure to come here.

Qutb Minar — This 238-ft. red sandstone tower, one of the most beautiful in the world, has verses from the Koran inscribed on its tapered shaft. Built in the early 13th century by the first Muslim conquerors of Delhi, it offers, from the top, a fine vista of Delhi seven miles north.

Where To Eat in Delhi:

Some of India's best restaurants are found here. No need to restrict yourself solely to hotel dining, though there are many excellent hotel restaurants. Around Connaught Place is *Gaylord* and the *Volga. Moti Mahal,* in Old Delhi, is famed for its tandoori and Punjabi cuisines — with folk music; *Woodlands* (Lodhi Hotel) for South Indian food. *Tandoor* (President Hotel) has Indian musicians. Both Oberoi Inter-Continental *(Mogul Room)* and Ashoka Hotels serve delicious tandoori, Mogali and other elegant food. For French cuisine, *Supper Club* of Ashoka has nightly dinner dancing, Indian floor show on Sat. *Auberge,* Hotel Maidens, also recommended. Both *Cafe Chinois,* Oberoi Inter-Continental, and *Mandarin,* Janpath Hotel, are good.

STATE OF RAJASTHAN

This most northwesterly state of India, bordering Pakistan, was, prior to Indian Independence, subdivided into more than 50 principalities, each ruled by a sovereign Maharaja. The Rajputs, citizens of Rajasthan, were known for their military prowess in defending their respective kingdoms.

Visiting Rajasthan is a highlight since each of the major cities, Jodphur, Jaipur and Udaipur has a fantastic palace, museum and fort recalling the area's historic past. Further, these sites are set against a desert landscape of great beauty. Perhaps to compensate for the starkness, the people are among the most colorfully dressed of all Indians. Men might wear flaming rose turbans, women's saris are of the brightest colors. In this area, use of camels is not uncommon, nor is the sight of peacocks and vultures.

The three major cities are connected by Indian Airlines flights of less than an hour, are easily reached from Delhi and Bombay — *if you have advance plane reservations* (flights usually full). As for hotel accommodations, don't stay in anything less than a Maharaja's palace — many have been converted into hotels.

UDAIPUR

The best part of Udaipur, founded in the 16th century and sited on three manmade lakes, is not the Sahelion-ki-Bari (Garden of Maids), nor the bazaar nor even the City Palace with its tile and inlay work, as fascinating as they all are. The extraordinary experience is the Lake Palace Hotel (also known as Jag Nivas) that's situated on a rock in Lake Pichola — it seems to float on the water. It was built in the 17th century as a summer residence of the Maharaja in order to catch the cooling lake breezes. Nearby on a smaller island is a deserted palace, Jag Mandir, also erected in the 17th century and worth visiting. At one time the Moghul King Shahjahan took refuge there; the beauty of this palace may have influenced his conception of the Taj Mahal.

A launch tour (about $13 an hour) of Lake Pichola is the best way to see Jag Mandir, the buff-colored buildings at water's edge, the sprawling palace of the Maharana of Udaipur, part residence and part museum, and above all photographing the locals bathing and washing clothes on the rocks.

A half-day Rajasthan tour (about $13) takes in all city attractions and nearby historical and religious sites: fortifications, lakeside palace museum, streets that twist and climb to the old city where open-sided shops offer their wares, folklore museum, Garden of Maids and City Palace.

JODPHUR

Like Udaipur and Jaipur, Jodphur is a walled town. These fortifications were built after the capital was moved here in 1459. The Fort, built atop a rock 400 feet above ground level, is one of the most imposing and impregnable in all of India. One passes thru seven gates before reaching the inner sanctum; most of these gates commemorate various victories. Descendants of the original founders continued to govern this area until the 1947 Independence. Today, the Fort is known as the Mehrangarh Museum Fort with an excellent exhibition of the royal collections within the restored rooms. One can visit the throne room where the ceiling is fitted with mirrors and ornamental works of gold, view the coronation throne, royal palanquins, costumes and an extensive array of arms and armour.

To make your royal visit complete, stay at the Umaid Bhawan, the Maharaja's residence converted into an hotel, one of the country's most fabulous.

JAIPUR

This Pink City is a delightful visual experience: block after block of shuttered, balconied, pinkish-colored buildings frosted with traces of white; camels pulling carts, donkeys, horses, goats, bicycles, cars, trucks, vendors jam the wide streets — which also have many jewelry shops as the city is a cutting and polishing center for rubies, emeralds

Agra's famed beauty — The Taj

and sapphires.

Founded in 1727 by Maharaja Jai Singh, who moved his capital here from the 11th century, hilltop fortress of Amber, seven miles away, the city was grandly laid out in a grid pattern with broad boulevards. At Amber, you can visit the Fort, riding to the top on one of the gaily decorated, waiting elephants (about $6 per 4-passenger elephant).

Things not to miss: City Palace, now a museum, in downtown Jaipur; nearby 18th-century astrological observatory with huge, accurate, masonry instruments in triangular and circular forms; Howar Mahal (Palace of the Winds) from which court ladies could look down on street scenes without violating their modesty. India Tourism Development Corp. has tours to all main points of interest (about $5 each).

Stay at the Rambagh Palace Hotel (fabulous dining) or one of the Maharaja's other residences for paying guests.

AGRA

The Taj Mahal is completely worthy of its lofty reputation. Yet even if it didn't exist, there'd be plenty of good reasons for spending at least two nights here since the city and its environs are chock-full of Moghul treasures. Certainly no visitor should leave without having seen, at the very least, Fatehpur Sikri and Sikandra, Red Fort, the tomb of Itmad-uh-Daulah. Too, having extra time in Agra means you can return to the Taj at various times of the day (until 9 p.m.) to watch the play of light on this architectural wonder. Lucky is the visitor who's here during full moon when the Taj, open until midnight, glows in milky whiteness.

Red Fort, constructed between 1565-1573, pre-dates Delhi's Red Fort by 75 years. Built by Akbar when he made Agra his capital, the Fort lies along the Jumna River; inside are opulent palaces built by Akbar's successors, Shahjahan and Jahangir. An imposing fortress whose security was assured by two 70-ft.-high walls separating a 40-ft. moat, its most impressive areas are the Moti Masjid (Pearl Mosque of white marble built by Shahjahan) the Diwan-i-am (Hall of Public Audience whose throne room is replete with inlaid mosaics) and the Diwan-i-Khas (Hall of Private Audience).

Though less well-known than the Taj Mahal, Sikandra, Emperor Akbar's mausoleum, is another persuasive reason for visiting Agra.

Sikandra, six miles north, is Emperor Akbar's mausoleum. The setting — 150 acres of gardens — is as magnificent as the tomb, entered thru a monumental red sandstone gateway.

Itmad-ud-Daulah, just across the Bridge, is little visited, yet we found it almost as appealing as the Taj Mahal. Built before the Taj by Emperor Jahangir's wife in memory of her parents, the tomb is significant (as well as beautiful) because it was the first Moghul building fashioned totally of white marble. It is well proportioned, with small minarets at each of the four corners, and has an enormous quantity of fine quality precious stones inlaid in the marble.

24 miles west of Agra is the deserted city of Fatehpur Sikri, built by Akbar as his capital when he removed it from Agra. Constructed between 1567 and 1575, the city was abandoned after only 14 years because of an inadequate water supply. The "ruins" are in nearly pristine condition. Most interesting structures in this imposing complex: Nahabat Khana, a 134-ft.-high gateway, Diwan-i-am and Diwan-i-Khas audience halls, and the Jama Masjid. There is even a parcheesi courtyard where, allegedly, Akbar played chess using slave girls as chessmen. Astounding to learn that during its short lifetime, this sandstone city housed a greater population than London. Now, local buses leave every 40 minutes from the Red Fort in Agra to bring visitors to the once imperial city.

The best part of the Taj Mahal is to discover that anticipation is not, for once, greater than realization. Its beauty can never disappoint.

Emperor Shahjahan built the Taj in honor of his favorite wife, Mumtaz Mahal, who died during the birth of their fourteenth child in 1631. The memorial honors their love thru its faultless structure, its perfect proportions. The minarets at each of the four corners seem to anchor the building in place, while red sandstone mosques on either side lend balance, as does the reflecting pool directly in front. The tomb is inlaid with semi-precious stones — jasper, agate, lapis lazuli, cornelian and bloodstone. So fine is this inlay that it is impossible to detect seams in the marble where the stones are placed. The tombs of Mumtaz and Shahjahan are surrounded by a lacy marble screen, although their actual remains lie in a chamber directly beneath the tombs.

20,000 laborers were employed during the mausoleum's construction between 1631 and 1653.

By the way, while here, be sure to dine at Clarks Shiraz Hotel; try their Moglai dishes. *Lauries* and *Imperial* also recommended.

Agra is 120 miles south of Delhi, a 3½-hour drive or a 30-minute jet flight. Excellent train service, aboard the Taj Express, is also available. From Jaipur and Varanasi, there are daily flights (45 min., 1:50 respectively).

THE TEMPLES OF KHAJURAHO

Lying southeast of Agra, Khajuraho is a logical stop enroute to Varanasi — if lofty temples and sensuous sculptures, in praise of Woman, turn you on. These three groups of temples, built during the 10th and 11th centuries by powerful Chandella kings, are described as a "celebration in stone carving of celestial and terrestrial passion."

The best sculptures, the most intricately carved work, are found in the town itself, so quiet and small scale, now that its era of importance has passed, that it is as close to unexpurgated village life as tourists will find. Here is the Kandariya Mahadeo temple, famed for its lofty, spectacular spire; the Lakshman temple, only one to retain its complete form; Chitragupta that enshrines the image of the sun god — and many others. The two other groups lie about three miles away, as interesting for their isolated rural setting as for their sculptures.

Khajuraho has daily flights from Delhi, Agra and Varanasi, bus service from the same cities.

Hindu street worship is a common sight.

VARANASI (formerly Benares)

Called the city of "burning and learning," a reference to its dual character as a cremation site and the home of Benares Hindu University, Varanasi is one of the world's oldest cities — it is inscribed in records written 3,000 years ago. It is a holy city to the Hindus where they can bathe daily in the sacred Ganges when living and, upon death, be cremated on its banks.

During our entire stay in India, no other place left as indelible an impression as Varanasi. Shrouded bodies tied to bamboo litters are carried thru the city streets to the cremation ghats (steps) by the river's edge. The bodies are dipped into the Ganges to purify them, then placed on the ground until attendants have finished preparing the 37-lb. funeral pyre. Cows, onlookers, relatives, sadhus (Hindu ascetics) stand around the lineup of bodies. The burning goes on around the clock.

Each morning at sunrise, Hindus bathe before going to temple by immersing themselves in Mother Ganga. Doing this is a sure way to evade the cycle of reincarnation and, upon death, to become one with God. As the sun rises, thousands of people line the shore bobbing up and down in the holy water. To best view this activity, rent one of the many rowboats (with rower) and ride up and down. *Note:* no pictures of cremations permitted.

One of the most important and fascinating temples in Varanasi is the Monkey Temple where some 300 monkeys cavort among the worshippers. Hang on to your belongings — they're great thieves.

Refreshing changes from the city are visits to the 2,000-acre Benares Hindu University and Sarnoth, a site of special importance to Buddhists; here Buddha preached his first sermon, revealed his eightfold plan to enlightenment. Sarnoth, about 6½ miles from the city, is a lovely park with third-century ruins and a giant stupa.

Dining is very good at Clarks Hotel, also at *Three Aces, Elite* and *Excelsior* restaurants.

305

FABLED KASHMIR

Srinigar on the banks of the Jhelum River, the lovely capital of the state of Kashmir, where once Moghul emperors vacationed, is one of the world's celebrated and romantic destinations and a base for travel thruout the beautiful valley in which it is sited. Since it is near the Himalayas and without a monsoon season, Srinigar (5,800 ft.) and its environs stay delightfully cool and dry when it's hot and humid elsewhere in India. Mid-March to November is the time to come here, though Gulmarg, 28 miles from Srinigar, is being promoted as India's first winter ski resort. Even in May, Indians flock here to take pony rides as far as the first summit (14,000 feet) to see and feel snow.

Because of the cool climate, the vegetation is different from other parts of India. So is the architecture — buildings are mostly of wood with high, sloping roofs to allow snow to slide off. Also unlike the rest of India, residents are mostly Muslim — and there are plenty of mosques to prove it.

Within the vale of Kashmir, there is practically no heavy industry — the tourist trade is it. Here you find the finest handicrafts. Embroidered tablecloths, shawls and similar items are excellent buys. Equally fine are woolen goods, wood carvings, leather work and papier-mache. Don't miss the opportunity, even if not buying, to visit the Indo-Kashmir carpet factory which produces the finest of Persian rugs at prices below anywhere else in the world. Shops are everywhere — just walk around the city which meanders, serpent-like, along the banks of the river. A car with driver can be rented for a city tour for 40 rupees.

Accommodations in Srinagar are both unusual and pleasant; in addition to traditional hotels, one has the option of enjoying life aboard one of the many houseboats.

These floating, individual hotels are moored in either Dal or Nagin Lakes. They are 80 to 125 feet long, 10 to 20 feet wide with four, five or six rooms. The houseboat has the feeling of home, not hotel room. Our boat, *Warrior,* an A class, had two bedrooms, a dining room with antique tables and chairs, a living room complete with wood-burning heater. None of the boats have kitchens because the houseboy (always present) brings the food to you from the cook boat where it is prepared by the auxiliary staff. After our meals, we'd sit on the roof deck and look out across the lake at the snow-covered Himalayans. Perfect bliss. And the price for this luxury and contentment, including three meals and the constant services of the houseboy should be (hold onto your hats) just $20 to $22 a day.

Boats range in category and price from Deluxe to A, B, C and D. We recommend Deluxe or A classes because the boats are better maintained, more nicely decorated, better staffed and serve more interesting food. In all cases, find a houseboat on Nagin, not Dal, Lake. Nagin is away from town though easily accessible by shikara (water taxi) or bus. Houseboats are moored parallel to the shore, thus assuring the best possible views. On Dal Lake, boats are adjacent to each other perpendicular to the shore — sort of like a trailer camp.

Part of the fun of houseboating is participating in the services of your friendly door-to-door salesmen who arrive aboard shikaras. The flower vendor, shawl seller, fruit juice man, tailor and jeweler were some of vendors who dropped in on us. We bought but would have been left alone, eventually, if we hadn't.

This unusual form of accommodation resulted from a law that foreigners couldn't own property in Kashmir. So the English evaded the regulation by living on houseboats. Ours on Nagin Lake was one of a fleet owned and managed by Mohamed Wangnoo & Bros., P.O. Box 61, Srinagar, Kashmir (phone 4253).

Besides relaxing on one's houseboat, which we found the most fun, next best activity is visiting the Moghul Gardens, symmetrically laid out centuries ago by the emperors who came to Kashmir every year to escape the heat of the Indian lowlands. Shalimar Gardens were created in 1619 for Queen Nur Jahan by Emperor Jahangir; Shahjahin extended them in 1727. Each evening, April to the end of October, a Sound and Light Show traces Moghul history as well as the personalities who visited here.

Other gardens include Chasma-I-Shai, meaning Royal Spring, and Nishat Bagh or Pleasure Garden. Most pleasant way to view them all is by rented shikara; the boatman paddles you around Dal Lake to the various parks.

For one- or two-day trips, rent a car with driver (about 135 rupees per day; your houseboat owner can arrange this) and go to either Gulmarg or Pahalgam. At Gulmarg (8,500 ft.) you'll see one of the highest golf courses in the world. And if there from October to March, when there's no fog, you'll also see one of the world's highest mountains — Nanga Parbot, 28,000 ft., in Pakistan. Pahalgam, at 7,000 ft., is 60 miles from Srinagar, is an excellent spot for camping and an exquisite site for viewing the mountains and two snow-fed rivers, for walking in the pine and fir forests.

CALCUTTA

India's largest city (over 7,000,000) is the commercial hub of Northern Indiá despite being far to the east. As such, it is not a particularly fascinating tourist attraction. Most interesting facet is the city's architecture — high British.

Calcutta is an exaggeration of India's best and worst features. No one is neutral about it. Some recommend visiting the city to experience firsthand India's most pressing problems: overpopulation and lack of housing, resulting in a crush of humanity

---

TREKKING IN THE
KASHMIR HIMALAYAS

This has become increasingly popular in recent years as treks are not particularly difficult and no climbing experience is needed; however, one should be in good physical condition, not be affected by altitude and have undertaken a preconditioning program.

Leisurely trips can be arranged independently out of Srinagar, or you can take one of the trips offered by three U.S. specialists (see footnote). We understand these are lovely hikes thru meadows of wildflowers, evergreen forests and sunny birch groves, past still lakes and over high passes with views, weather permitting, of ice-covered peaks, glaciers and icefalls. Only people encountered are occasional Gujar nomads grazing their sheep and goats in the high meadows. Ponies are available for riding.

Usually included as part of, or extension to, these treks is a remote land, called Little Tibet, which India opened to foreign visitors in 1974 and where tourists are still a curiosity. Capital city is Leh in a mountainous, 11,500-ft.-high desert where the sparse precipitation is mostly windblown snow. Red-robed lamas turn prayer wheels and chant. Shaggy yaks and camels carry loads along trails lined by carved prayer stones and white-washed stupas. This area is reached by bus from Srinagar over rough mountain roads, past Muslim villages and across a mountain pass.

Hanns Ebensten Travel,
55 W. 42 St., New York 10036
Mountain Travel,
1398 Solano Ave., Albany, Ca. 94706
Questers Tours & Travel,
257 Park Ave. S, New York 10010

constantly living in the streets. Some tourists believe they will find the city too depressing and skip it altogether. Take your choice.

Calcutta was the British capital from 1757 until the beginning of the 20th century; monuments commemorate that fact. Its original importance stemmed from its strategic location as a port. In 1690, an agent of the British East India Company chose three existing villages to serve as port and settlement, procured rights to them from Emperor Aurangzeb. In 1696, Fort William was constructed to protect the port. That proved the start of British occupation of India.

WHAT TO SEE IN CALCUTTA

Take a look at the Marble Palace, a private residence with a fine collection of antiques and art. A permit from Government Tourist Office is needed for the tour. Also see Victoria Memorial Hall which houses collections of sculptures, paintings, objets d'art and historical records from Britain's long stay in India. Zoo, Birla Planetarium and St. Paul's Cathedral are all near here. Across from the Zoological Gardens, among the best in the country and famed for its white tigers, is the Residence of the Governor of Bengal, Raj Bhawan — an elegant home, built in 1804 and modeled after the English house in which Lord Curzon was born.

By car or cab, visit Parashnath Jain Temple where myriad mirrors and jewels cover the pillars, walls and ceilings. Built in 1867, it's part High Victorian, par Low Rococo.

A memorial to those who died in the infamous Black Hole of Calcutta, a prison so small that hundreds died of overcrowding, is found in St. John's Church. Indian Museum, oldest in India (1878) as well as one of the largest and most comprehensive, houses something of interest to everyone.

SIGHTSEEING OUT OF CALCUTTA

Bhubaneswar (40,000 pop.) is known as the cathedral city; at one time, over 7,000 temples stood beside Lake Bindusagar in old Bhubaneswar. Largest existing temple, Lingaraja, dates from the 11th century. Today, the city has a more modern character as capital of the state of Orissa. Quickly reached (40 min.) by daily flights from Calcutta to the northeast. It's worth a quick look, then drive 37 miles to Puri or 39 miles to Konarak. Best accommodations in Puri.

Beautifully sited on the Bay of Bengal, Puri (61,000 pop.) is one of four main pilgrimmage areas and is also noted for its fine beaches, among the best in India. Crowds mass in June for Rath Yatra (Car Festival) in which Jagannath, Lord of the Universe (reincarnation of Vishnu) is pulled thru the streets in a temple chariot. Sru Jagannath Temple, built in the 12th century in Orissian style, is one of the most frequently visited in the entire country. Non-Hindus cannot enter but from stations on surrounding roofs, one can see into the temple.

Mark Twain said that the temple at nearby Konarak is one of the world's wonders. The Sun Temple he was referring to, known as Navagraha, was built in the 13th century in the form of a chariot with 24 wheels being pulled by seven horses.

CALCUTTA DINING & NIGHT LIFE

Prince's (Oberoi Grand) is famed for fan-tailed prawn cutlets, Firpo's for an excellent variety of regional foods (has dancing, cabaret). Maxim's, Great Eastern Hotel, serves top moghlai and tandoori dishes. Typical Punjabi food at Amber, Kwality, Mocambo, Saqi. Madira known for Bengali dishes, Nanking for Chinese.

Because there's no prohibition here, there are bars, even nightclubs, in the hotels. Which means there's more after-dark doings in Calcutta than in other Indian cities, although the clubs still close around midnight. Consider visiting: 1) Prince's and Scherazade at the Oberoi Grand. 2) Maxim's at Great Eastern; dinner, show, dancing. 3) 007 Bar, In and Out Discotheque Club and Sujata Theatre Restaurant, all at the Park Hotel (has reputation of being the "in" place with wealthy Indian businessmen). 4) Le Gourmet (Spence's Hotel) has good food, floor shows.

You'll find a festival going on almost anytime, anywhere.

BOMBAY

While most tourists enter India thru New Delhi, most businessmen start here, the commercial center of India. Historic sites and other tourist attractions are at a minimum. However, like other major cities, shopping is varied and exciting. But unless your plans are to use Bombay as a jumping-off point for other cities, or to fly to Aurangabad for excursions to the temples of Ajanta and Ellora, we recommend skipping it completely. If you do go, do so during the cooler November-February season; in other months it is hot and humid due to the city's location on the Arabian Sea.

Bombay is the only modern Indian city with a substantial number of skyscrapers; usable land has always been at a premium so the trend is to build upwards. Consequently, Bombay resembles New York, though one of its delights is the architectural contrast between modern glass hi-rises and the older, more imposing, stone Victorian buildings. Victoria Terminus, the rail station, and the Prince of Wales Museum are two outstanding examples.

Bombay was once an archipelago of seven islands inhabited by Koli fishermen who called them *Mumbai* after the mother goddess Mumbadevi. When the Portuguese landed, they renamed the area *Bom Bahia* (Good or Fine Bay) which, obviously, the English converted into Bombay. For in 1661, when the Infanta of Portugal was married to King Charles II, the islands were gifted to the English as part of the dowry. Such a dowry!

The sights are generally limited to the hotel area, bounded by Marine Drive, Gateway of India and Victoria Terminus:

Gateway to India, an imposing arch at the tip of Bombay's seaport, built to commemorate George V's visit in 1911, is an active gathering point for strollers and street merchants, is one of the few public open spaces in the city. When the British "quit India," they symbolically marched thru this gateway for the last time.

Prince of Wales Museum is one of the best, most extensive museum collections in India dealing with art, archaeology and natural history; has particularly beautiful miniature paintings of the Rajasthan and Deccan schools. The building alone, as representative of Victorian architecture, is worth seeing. Next door, in a separate building, is the Jehangir Art Gallery with an interesting selection of contemporary Indian paintings.

Crawford Market is an excellent Indian bazaar selling many objects and services unknown to Americans. For example, you can get your ears cleaned by a specialist in this activity. Indian salesmen are very persistent. Of course, bargain — and bargain!

Malabar Hills is the swank residential area of Bombay; the east side, with its tall apartment buildings, is visible across the bay as one drives along Marine Drive. Hanging Gardens, a small residential park festooned with hanging baskets of flowers, is the central focus of the area. Panoramic views of Bombay from here. To the left of the Gardens, discreetly hidden, is the Parsee Towers of Silence where, in keeping with the tradition of the Parsi religion, the dead are disposed of — by exposing them to vultures.

Semi-circular Marine Drive, bordered by promenades, is a pleasant place for an evening stroll. An aquarium (adequate) is along here, as is Chowpatty Beach where, each evening, there's a multitude of street hawkers selling food and goods — plus palmists, plus balloon vendors, plus magicians and acrobats. Often, Hindu gods are sand-sculptured on the beach. Good place to mingle, not to swim.

Closest beach to Bombay is Juhu Beach, 12 miles from town and two from the airport. Crowded, particularly on weekends, the beach is not nearly as clean as those in America, but in typical Indian fashion, it bustles with humanity — good place to observe a relaxed Indian community.

Elephanta Caves are the most interesting historical attraction. An hour from Bombay by sea, the caves date from 540 to 625 AD. Legend has it that a medieval Hindu king, Pulakesin II, had the temples carved from solid rock and dedicated to the memory of shiva — for the purpose of impressing foreigners sailing into the region. The impressive sculptures were also carved from the same rock. Maheshmurti, a 19-ft.-high figure with three heads representing Brahma, Shiva ind Vishnu, is the most monumental.

Elephanta Caves are a preview of the spectacular sculptures one sees at Ellora, 200 miles away. To get to Elephanta, catch one of the sightseeing boats from the Gateway of India; guide service in English is included in the rate.

As for shopping, visit the antique shops of Chor (Thieves) Bazaar, the jewelry stores of Jhaveri Bazaar and the crowded shops of Bhuleswar. Look at the products in the fancy shops of the Taj Hotel — but buy the same things at lower prices elsewhere.

By the way, one of India's outstanding buys is prescription glasses, either sun or regular. So bring your prescriptions. For as little as $16 you get excellent lenses and frames.

DINING OUT IN BOMBAY

Be sure to try *Dhansak,* a Parsi masterpiece of meat, vegetables and Indian lentils, as well as Bombay duck, pomfret with green masala, biryanis and kabas, a vegetarian *thali* (Apollo Room, Taj Mahal Hotel, recommended; also *Chetana, Purohit* rsts.). Besides hotels, *Alibaba, Berry's, Blue Nile, Horse Shoe, Kwality, Khyber, Talk of the Town* and *Volga* are good. Many hotel restaurants have dancing/floor shows.

AURANGABAD

Important as the gateway to the caves of Ajanta and Ellora, Aurangabad is just 40 minutes (175 miles) northeast of Bombay by jet. The trip is highly recommended since the caves represent a high point in Indian art by graphically depicting the power of faith which could move men to carve monuments from mountains of rock.

At Ellora, 18 miles from Aurangabad, are temples and monasteries carved into a mountainside between the 4th and 9th centuries AD to celebrate the Buddhist, Hindu and Jain faiths. Buddhist shrines, built first, are simpler than later Hindu temples (7th to 9th centuries). These caves are unlike any tradition in Western religious art. Using primitive tools, the sculptors literally carved away a mountain of rock, created buildings of stone that included such architectural details as handrails; every building surface is intricately detailed. Altogether, there are 34 shrines to explore, of which the Kailasa Temple, 50 meters by 33 by 30, is the most outstanding. Imagine, if you can, *twice the area* of the Parthenon carved out of solid rock! A special visual delight are the many sculpted images of the gods.

The 30 caves of Ajanta, 66 miles from Aurangabad, are even more spectacularly sited. Carved into a horseshoe-shaped mountain is a succession of monasteries *(viharas)* and places of worship *(chaityas)*, the oldest dating from 200 BC to 200 AD, others belonging to the 6th and 7th centuries AD. They all celebrate Buddhism. In caves 1, 2, 16, 17 and 19 are beautiful frescos portraying the life of Lord Buddha. In caves 1, 4, 17, 19, 24 and 26 are outstanding sculptures, many of them Buddha images. As at Ellora, everything was carved from solid rock. Workers created architectural forms which resembled features in their own wooden buildings — ribbing in vaulted cathedral ceilings as well as gateways and pavilions.

Tourist buses provide daily round-trip services to each of the areas with pickups at major hotels. But don't try to visit both areas in a day — simply too much to see at both sites.

GOING TO GOA — Another Tale of Two Cities

Everyone flocks here, primarily to enjoy the beach and sun, escape the winter cold; that includes Indians from Kashmir and hippies from Europe. Atmosphere is casual, an intriguing blend of European and Indian.

Goa was a Portuguese colony for 450 years until evicted in 1961. The first Portuguese trader, Alfonso de Albuquerque, entered Old Goa in 1510, saw its strategic importance as a spice trading port and stayed. In his wake came more traders and Christian missionaries. Today, the region is 38% Catholic; baroque cathedrals attest to the permanence of their faith. Culturally, Portuguese ballads are still sung, specialty food and drinks still served.

Calangute Beach, which stretches in a four-mile arc along the Arabian Sea, looks like a dazzling movie set — with fine grained, white sand, swaying palms and other exotic props. Great spot to sun 'n' play. Other picturesque beaches: Colva, three miles from Margao, Dona Paula, four miles south of Panaji, and Vagator on the secluded northern end of Calangute.

Obviously, don't come here during the monsoon season (June-Sept.); at all other times it's an ideal 79^0, though a sweater for December and January evenings is a good idea.

If you can tear yourself away from beachcombing, visit Old Goa — not to be confused with Punaji or "New" Goa, dating from 1750 — the former Portuguese capital with excellent examples of baroque architecture and Mediterranean plazas. Explore the Bom Jesus Basilica *where St. Francis is entombed.* Built between 1594 and 1603, it's the most sumptuous of all the religious buildings in Goa. Interior is highly and richly decorated. The Saint's body is preserved in an elaborate casket made in Florence and placed within a marble chapel. St. Francis of Assisi Church and Convent is another celebrated religious structure; it was built by Franciscans, who arrived here prior to the Jesuits, and retained the porch of a pre-existing Muslim structure.

You reach Goa by flying south from Bombay to Dabolim (55 min.) — but it's another 75 min. by car from there. Ships make it to Panaji in 24 hours, a leisurely, interesting look at the shoreline and fishing villages even if the ship is not sparkling clean.

COCHIN — VENICE OF THE EAST

Cochin, India's fifth largest port (it's served as such since the 6th century BC), is a collection of islands connected by shuttle ferries. It is also known as the "Queen of the Arabian Sea" since it is a beautiful, powerful, tropical city. At sea level, it is also among the more humid of Indian cities.

Cochin's islands include the main one of Ernakulam, man-made Willingdon, containing major port facilities, airport and rail station, Gundu, Vypeen and others. On Gundu is an interesting factory where coconut fiber is woven into carpets and other useful products. On Vypeen are the Chinese nets, an ingenious, stationary fishing device. Walk from here to the nearby community, built by the English, which resembles a Tudor village. On Ernakulam, attend a dance performance/lecture at the workshop of the Kathakali dancers, one of the oldest, most stylized forms of Indian dance.

Every colonial influence in India is reflected in Cochin. The Portuguese founded the first European settlement here in the early 16th century, constructed Mattancheri Palace, still standing, which was later adapted by their successors, the Dutch, who added a tile roof. When the Indians took over, they adapted the palace to their culture with Ramayana mural scenes. The Palace, in Fort Cochin, is open to visitors.

Beautiful, baroque Christian churches are present. St. Francis, in Fort Cochin, was built in 1503. Famed Vasco da Gama, who died in Cochin, was interred there before his body was returned to Portugal. Here, too, is one of the oldest Jewish communities in the world, represented by a small, attractive synagogue, more than 400 years old, decorated with Chinese tiles from Canton. Finally, there are Muslim mosques and Hindu temples.

A harbor cruise is a highly recommended means of seeing the various islands. Convenient ferry services are also available between them.

By air, Cochin is 45-min. flight from Trivandrum, 1:45 from Madras, 1:55 from Bangalore (1-stop) and 3:45 from Bombay (1-stop).

TRIVANDRUM & KOVALAM

Trivandrum, sited on seven hills, is an attractive town, the capital of India's smallest state, Kerala, along the western coast of southern India. Scenery here is quite unlike the rest of India, more nearly resembles the tropical splendors of neighboring Sri Lanka.

Main reason for coming here, particularly when enroute north from Sri Lanka (1:15 by jet from Colombo), is to enjoy the water, sand and surf at Kovalam, 10 miles south. ITDC has built a top hotel, the Kovalam Beach, to add to your enjoyment of the crystal-clear waters, fine-grained sands and superb sunsets, the latter so magnificent that even townspeople gather in appreciation. Watching the fishermen during the day is another absorbing pastime.

South of Kovalam is Kanya Kumari (Cape Comorin), southernmost tip of India where the Arabian Sea, Indian Ocean and Bay of Bengal meet — a place of pilgrimage for Hindus as well as an astoundingly beautiful area with better sunsets, impossible as that seems, than Kovalam. And the beach is renowned for its vari-colored sands. The temple here is worth visiting.

MADURAI

Here was the high point of our visits to the temple towns of the South. For Meenakshi temple, dedicated to the Mother Goddess, wife of Shiva, is not only a center of worship and pilgrimage but also represents the epitome of Dravidian architecture. Built between 1623-1660 by the Nyak Dynasty, it is a huge complex of concentric walls, shrines, palatial hallways and holy bathing tanks. Most striking feature: 14 gopurams, sloping towers, covered with hundreds of polychrome sculptures of gods, their consorts, incarnations, servants, animals and other residents of the Hindu mythology. Looked as if a pastry chef had gone totally mad.

Yet the architecture was only a portion of the experience. Inside the temple is pure Cecil B. DeMille, especially on its holiest night, Friday. 10,000 people visit the temple each day — it is constantly alive with activity. Here's a portion of what we saw: 1) Crowds walking nine times around sculptures representing the nine planets. 2) People throwing packs of butter on sculptural figures of the Goddess Meenakshi. 3) People putting ashes (residue of burnt cow dung) on their forehead. 4) *Pure gold* sculptures of Shiva and Meenakshi displayed to the crowd on a swinging platform. 5) Women presenting offerings to the gods, particularly jasmine flowers and coconuts. 6) People bathing and brushing their teeth with a finger in the stagnant temple tank. 7) Men and women prostrating themselves before statues of the gods and, seemingly, about to be crushed by the crowds. 8) Prayers to the elephant god consisting of hitting one's temple three times, then crossing arms and hold ears while genuflecting.

The temple is the massage, the town uninteresting.

By air, Madurai is connected with Trivandrum (50 min.), Tiruchirapalli (35 min.) and Madras (1:20).

TIRUCHIRAPALLI & THANJAVUR

These temple towns come closest to revealing an ancient India as it existed before it was invaded in the north. Like Madurai, they are still unbelievably active places of worship for an intensely religious population, which differentiates them from temples in the north where there is less opportunity to view Hinduism in practice.

The temple at Tiruchirapalli (known as Trichy), dedicated to Lord Vishnu, is an enormous complex with seven concentric walls within which is an entire community of residence and bazaars. Unesco has provided funds for restoration work.

The temple at Thanjavur, 33 miles east of Trichy, was built in the 11th century by the Chola dynasty. Its most monumental feature is a cupola formed from a single granite block weighing more than 80 tons. The cupola was placed in position by moving the stone along a 3½-mile-long inclined plane.

Trichy is 78 miles northeast of Madurai.

BANGALORE

By Indian standards, Bangalore is a new city since it was laid out in the 18th century. Avenues, lined with new glass buildings, are broad and attractive. Because of its temperate climate, successful commercial status and beautiful gardens, Bangalore is a popular place for Indians to live. However, as a tourist attraction it's a bore — mentioned here merely as the jumping-off point (has good air connections with rest of India) for Mysore, a three-hour drive along good roads.

Mysore is fun. The Maharajas lived here so it's full of palaces, museums and public sculpture. The city museum houses an exotic collection of royal possessions, including antique clocks, carvings on grains of rice, photos of the royal family. The Maharaja's Palace, recently opened to visitors, has a public audience hall for 3,000, a magnificent private audience hall with colored glass ceiling, a wedding hall with paintings of royal processions.

The city is small enough to be toured on foot. Don't miss the marketplace, among the most colorful in India, and the equally bustling main street. There's a full-day tour

Mahabalipuram's famous (and beautiful) Shore Temple.

which includes the foregoing as well as the Fort and Palace of Tipu Sultan (Sriranga-patna), zoo, Chamundi Hill with an enormous sculpture of Lord Shiva's bull, Nandi, and Brindavan Gardens; latter, an hour from Mysore, is worth visiting at sunset when natural light fades and the gardens sparkle with multi-colored artificial illumination.

A full-day trip from Mysore to Halebid and Belur, the 12th-century temples built during the Hoysala Dynasty, is recommended. Exteriors of the star-shaped temples, set on platforms, are covered with friezes depicting stories from Hindu epics; the scenes, and pictures of wildlife, are intricately detailed since the sculptors were able to carve from soft, black schist which hardened only after being incised.

Bangalore-Mysore-Halebid-Belur-Bangalore can be taken as a circle trip. There is an excellent ITDC hotel at Hassan, 22 miles from Belur.

HYDERABAD — Muslim Seat Of Learning

Founded in 1589, the capital of the State of Andhra Pradesh has numerous universities, many housed in Islamic-style buildings on the banks of the Musi River which flows thru the city. Historically, Hyderabad represents the southernmost advance of the Mughal Conquerors. Today, it suffers from urban sprawl — there seemed to be no other place in India with greater bicycle congestion. The metropolitan area was made even larger when the British built a twin city, Secunderabad, on the other side of Hussainsagar Lake.

Outstanding Muslim monuments are the best reasons for visiting here. These include Mecca Masjid, one of Asia's largest mosques, that accommodates 10,000 people, and Char Minar, 1,200-ft.-high arch with four minarets erected where four main roads converge. Surrounding streets are active, exciting bazaars and particularly noted for jewelry. Other worthwhile attractions include Salar Jung Museum (vast private collection of the Nizim of Hyderabad), Nehru Zoological Park, the modern Birla temple and Golconda Fort, five miles west.

Hyderabad is 316 air miles from Bangalore, 385 from Bombay, 773 from Delhi and 329 from Madras.

MADRAS — Gateway To Mahabalipuram

One of India's larger cities, Madras is the center of classical music and dance. December and January are best months to attend performances of South Carnatic music, Kathakali and Bharat Natyam dance forms. The city is also home to India's movie industry.

Its history is the story of British involvement in India, starting with the East India Company obtaining a grant for the site in 1639. Fort George was built in 1653 (still standing and open to visitors) to house men and material for the trading settlement. Clive of India, the Duke of Wellington and Elihu Yale (after whom Yale University was named) were stationed here. Within the Fort is the Church of St. Mary, oldest Anglican church in India.

Main tourist reason for coming here is the good, one-day tour (about 130 miles RT) to Mahalipuram with a stop enroute at Kanchipuram. Latter is one of the sacred Hindu cities — and an excellent shopping center for silk fabrics. Then on to Mahalipuram where, better than a thousand years ago, the Pallava dynasty built their capital, carved and constructed cave temples, shore temples, bas reliefs and rathas. The latter are small-size models of shrines, chiseled out of boulders in the form of temple chariots; they comprise some of Mahabalipuram's chief attractions.

The tour skirts the Bay of Bengal and passes many lovely hotels, any of which provide good stops for lunch and refreshments.

Elephant herd on the shores of the lake at Periyar Sanctuary.

NATIONAL PARKS & WILDLIFE SANCTUARIES

Part of the glamour of touring India is visiting one or more of these preserves to observe the varied wildlife which is either unique to or concentrated in this part of the world.

Gir Sanctuary is the only home, and last retreat, of the Asiatic Lion. Dachigam protects the vanishing Kashmir stag, the showy snow leopard. Keoladeo Ghana Bird Sanctuary, largest and best known one in India, has over 300 types of nesting indigenous and migratory water birds, including the Siberian crane. Corbett National Park, in the Himalayan foothills, is tiger country, as is Sariska Park in Rajasthan. At Corbett, viewing is done from eight observation towers and on elephant back. At Periyar Game Sanctuary, wildlife is observed from a boat circling an artificial lake. We watched herds of elephants feeding at the water's edge; one herd even swam across the lake, passing close to our boat.

Visiting these preserves is well worth the difficulty of reaching them. Naturally, a successful park cannot be located close to urban civilization. However, those mentioned above are more accessible than some. Gir is reached out of Bombay via Ahmedabad, Dachigam from Srinagar. Keoladeo is within easy reach of Agra, Corbett by rail from Delhi and, by car, Sariska is convenient to Jaipur. Public transport to Periyar is not advised — a grueling 7-hour, uphill drive: by private car, it's at least four hours (125 miles) from Cochin, 96 miles from Madurai.

There are comfortable, if modest, accommodations in lodges and rest houses in each of the parks and sanctuaries.

BEST VISITING SEASONS:

Gir Sanctuary — Oct. to June-July. Only 13 miles from Srinagar by good road, but rest of journey is done by trekking or on pony back. Keoladeo Ghana (also known as Bharatpur) — Oct. to Jan. Corbett — Nov. to May; during rains, cannot be visited. Sariska — Feb.-June. Periyar — Feb. to May.

Char Minar, 200 feet high, is Hyderabad's outstanding example of Islamic architecture. From near the top, visitors have a great view of the winding bazaar streets below.

Hotel Directory.

Hotel bills must be paid in foreign currency, travel checks or by credit card (American Express most acceptable). However, don't expect to pay most hotel bills with credit cards; only in the biggest cities are they accepted. Change for foreign currency given only in rupees (convertible on departure with exchange vouchers).

Many of India's hotels, particularly those listed herein, are of international standards, most of them reasonably priced. Here are the well-known Indian chains:

Clarks Hotels, found in many major tourist areas, is the oldest; their hotels unspectacular but spacious and comfortable. Oberoi (see Hotel Chain Reservations) and Taj (200 Park Ave., NY 10017; 212-472-1842) are luxury chains. ITC (400 E. 85 St., NY 10028; 212-472-1842), the Indian Tobacco Co., is up and coming with attractive properties, such as the Chola in Madras, Mughal in Agra, Maurya in New Delhi. ITDC (India Tourist Development Corp.) has hotels/lodges thruout India, especially in remote sites such as wildlife preserves. ITDC manages the spectacular resort complex, Kovalem Beach, in southern India, the Ashoka in New Delhi and Lalitha Mahal Palace, Mysore.

10% to 12½% service charge added to quoted double room rates (in US dollars); also 3% to 7% luxury tax.

AGRA

CLARKS SHIRAZ (FC) — Residential area overlooks Taj. The first FC class hotel here. Long-time favorite. 140 AC R, SU have been refurbished. Dining room (delectable cuisine), 2 bars, attractive pool area. $32.

HOLIDAY INN (FC) — 1 mile from Taj. 84 AC R, several rsts. Indian classical dances. Pool, tennis. About $23.

MAYUR TOURIST COMPLEX — 22 R (some AC) in new low-rise budget hotel. Rooftop and open-air rst, bar, pool. Interesting Indian decor. Overnight camping allowed. $15.

MUGHAL (DL) — Opened '77 with 200 AC R in an unusual modern hotel with changing levels, balconies and passageways. White marble decorates lobby. Sophisticated decor. Pool, gardens, loads of flowers, waterfalls are located between different wings of hotel. Specialty rst, cafe, bar and conference room. A mile from Taj. $30-$43.

MUNTAZ — 40 R opened '77 facing the Taj.

AURANGABAD

AJANTA AMBASSADOR (FC) — 200 AC R. A bit more formal than Rama with elaborately decorated restaurants and bars. Near airport. $28.

AURANGABAD (FC) — New 65 R (replaced city's oldest), some AC, simply furnished. Open lobby overlooks lounge, rst below. Small garden. Good, moderate hotel. $20.

HOLIDAY INN (FC) — Near airport. All amenities, plus pool.

RAMA INTERNATIONAL (FC) — 150 AC modern R. Rsts serve Western, continental cuisine. 3 cocktail lounges, poolside barbecues. Tennis. *Conv:* 300. $27 up. ·

BANGALORE

ASHOKA (DL) — Residential area, 5 min. from DT. Continental rst, Indian rst, nightclub with Indian, classical, Western entertainment. Pool, tennis, 18-hole golf course. 183 AC R, SU. New and best. $26.

BANGALORE WELCOMHOTEL — Deluxe. Opens 1979.

BANGALORE INTERNATIONAL (FC) — 42 R, some AC, have view of the city, piped-in music. Modern, sleek hotel. Health spa. $15.

WEST END (FC) — 85 R (some AC) in garden setting. An older elegant hotel. Near shopping and entertainment area. $23.

BOMBAY

Reservations a must Oct. thru Feb.

AIRPORT PLAZA — 80 AC R, Skyway Rst. Take-off cocktail lounge, gardens. $21 up.

AMBASSADOR (FC) — DT. 79 AC R. Revolving rst, bar and pool. $21 up.

CENTAUR (FC+) — 288 AC R. Very good airport hotel. Attractive gardens, pool. Several rsts. $37.

HOLIDAY INN JUHU BEACH (FC) — 14 miles from DT. 210 AC R, 3 rsts, coffee shop, disco. 2 pools, tennis. $43.

NATARAJ — 82 AC R, SU. Well located on Marine Drive. Dining room, cocktail lounge. Good service. $16-$21.

OBEROI SHERATON (DL-) — Unattractive skyscraper hotel with beautiful views of the bay. 462 R, SU. Indian, French, Polynesian rsts, 3 bars, nightclub, disco. Moghul room features Indian music/dancing. Not for those desiring quiet. Pool; uninspiring shopping arcade. *Conv:* 2000. $60 up.

PRESIDENT (FC) — Off Cuffee Parade. 160 AC R w/TV, music, balcony (some with ocean view). 2 rsts, discotheque. Hotel has been modernized and restored. Pool, shopping arcade. *Rsv:* Taj. $31.

TAJ MAHAL INTER-CONTINENTAL (DL) — On waterfront with magnificent view of bay and hills, 40 min. from airport ($4). 650 AC R with stunning decor. Hotel has 2 distinct units with common lobby. Older section, the Taj Mahal, is of graceful greystone, in English colonial style, topped by a dome. Newer section is a sleek 22-story skyscraper. An international meeting place; has bazaar displaying Indian goods, medley of excellent Indian, Chinese and Western rsts, rooftop tower cocktail lounge. Beautiful pool area, shopping area. Bombay's best and *the* place to stay. Cpnv. facilities. $52 up. 10% service, plus 6% service on rooms/meals.

CALCUTTA

AIRPORT — 150 AC R with all amenities. Pool. 5 min. from airport. $30.

HINDUSTHAN INTERNATIONAL (FC) — 212 AC R, 4 mi. from center of action. 3 bars, cocktail lounge, rst, nightclub. Pleasant with pool and beautiful lawns. *Conv:* 700. $30 up.

OBEROI GRAND (DL) — Residential area, across from the Maidan. Has a new look. 60 AC R out of 300 have been remodeled, lobby refurbished. Now elegant and large with excellent rsts. New coffee shop, Chowringhee Bar. Indian Polynesian rst/nightclub, disco are new. Best here. *Conv:* 800. $52.

RITZ CONTINENTAL (FC) — Center of action. Recently opened with 118 AC R, health club, attractive gardens. $25 up.

COCHIN

MALABAR (FC) — Willingdon Island. Ideal location overlooking straits, adjacent ocean terminal, 3 miles from airport. 38 AC, large, comfortable R, 2 cottages. Efficient service. Good rst. Kathakali dances performed for groups. Pool, garden. $16 up.

NEW DELHI/DELHI

Advance Reservations Essential Oct.-Feb.

ASHOKA (FC+) — Center of diplomatic enclave. Refurbished in '77, decorated with Indian antiques. 486 AC R, several rsts, revolving tower rst, rotisserie, supper club. Pleasant gardens. Pool, tennis, mini golf. Re-equipped conv. hall, mini-theater. $38 up.

MAURYA (DL) — Midway between airport and city. Opened late '77. 350 AC R in 7-story copy of an ancient stupa. Five rsts, rooftop bar and nightclub, lounge bar overlooks waterways. Pool. *Conv:* 750. $55-$65.

NIRULA — Connaught Circle. 33 AC R, 2 rsts, cocktail lounge. Inexp and best in its class. $12 up.

OBEROI INTER-CONTINENTAL (DL) — Beautifully sited amongst gardens and ornamental lake; overlooks Delhi Golf Course with magnificent view of India Gate. 10 miles from airport ($3.50). 350 attractive AC R. Golden minarets accent Taj Rst (lunch concert and dinner dancing). Moghul Rst is like a Moghul palace. Rooftop supper club (exp, excellent food) has spectacular night view. And much more. Pool. *Conv:* 1000. $64 up.

OBEROI MAIDENS (FC) — Near historic Monuments but difficult 15-min. taxi ride from Connaught Place. 75 AC R in lovely older hotel. Pleasant service. Good French rst. Pool, tennis. *Conv:* 500. $30-$35.

TAJ MAHAL (DL)–Opened late '78 on Mansingh Rd, near India Gate. 350 R and all amenities.
These less expensive hotels are also recommended: Lodhi ($17), President ($18), Ranjit ($17; new pool).

GOA

FORT AGUADA BEACH RESORT (DL-) — Ideally situated on beachfront 9 miles from Panaji, 1¼-hr. drive from airport. Built around remains of 300-year-old fort. Pool, water sports, tennis. Attractive terraced bar with sweeping views. 120 AC R, 32 bungalows. $34 up. *Rsv:* Taj.

HASSAN

HASSAN — 28 R (some AC). 22 miles from Belur; excursions to Halebid and Belur. Good service. $9.

HYDERABAD

BANJARA (FC) — Indian rst, coffee shop; pool, tennis. AC thruout. $25 up.

HOLIDAY INN (FC) — Lake resort area. 112 AC R, dining room, pool, tennis, mini-golf. Boating, fishing. Opened early '78. $17.

JAIPUR

CLARKS AMER (FC) — 114 AC R. 2 rsts serving Continental and Rajasthani cuisine, bar. Pool, golf course, elephant rides. *Conv:* 250. $33.

RAMBAGH PALACE (DL) — 2 miles from town. 80 R (some AC) in former Maharaja's Palace. Beautiful gardens with wild peacocks, fountains, squash courts. Indoor pool. Rst. located in ballroom where Indian musicians perform. Classy polo bar (Jaipur renowned for its polo team). Riding area. Elephant, camel rides. $27 up.

WELCOMHOTEL MANSINGH (DL) — Near city center. 100 AC Rooms. Pool, health club, 3 rsts.

JODHPUR

UMAID BHAWAN (FC) — 41 R, 75 SU (some AC). Formerly the largest private residence in the world. Palace is decorated in art deco furnishings — more here than in museums. Underground swimming pool. Animals killed during the Maharaja's hunts are mounted and displayed in lobby. Unforgettable hotel where typical room can be 30-50 ft. with 20-ft. ceiling. Dining room, bar, 2 tennis courts. $32 up.

KHAJURAHO

KHAJURAHO — 48 AC R (some w/view). Attractive 1-story hotel located within easy walking distance of temples. Pleasant dining room. $20.

KOVALAM, Trivandrum

KOVALAM GROVE — 40 AC cottages w/kitchen. Pool, water sports. On beach, 10 miles from Trivandrum. Informal. Attractive outdoor dining pavilions. $24.

KOVALAM BEACH (DL) — 80 AC R spectacular hotel, perhaps the most beautiful in India. Each room has large private terrace providing fabulous ocean views. Similar views from pool area. Elegant atmosphere. Hilly hike to beach. Water sports. Yoga. Fine rsts. *Rsv:* ITDC. $24 up.

MADRAS

CHOLA (FC) — Opened '75 with 146 AC R, specialty rsts, bar. Pool, unusual ice-skating rink. Conference room. *Rsv:* A. Awal, 400 E 85, N.Y. $24-$27.

CONNEMARA (FC) — AC, 3 rst. lounges, pool. $22.

FISHERMAN'S COVE (FC) — New beachfront resort, 20 miles S at Covelang. 42 R in main building, 38 cottages in grove. Pool, riding, boating. *Rsv:* Taj.

HOLIDAY INN (FC) — Near city center. 160 R, SU. Several rsts, bar, roof garden for cocktail parties. Daily music and dances. Pool. 3 meeting rooms. $20.

TAJ COROMANDEL (DL) — Opened '77 in center of entertainment district. 240 AC modern R, SU. Indian, Chinese rsts, bar. Nightly entertainment. Pool. Conv. facilities. $27-$31.

MADURAI

PANDYAN — 57 AC R are comfortable. Rst, bar, cocktail lounge. Best here. 2 miles from temple. $14.

MYSORE

LALITHA MAHAL PALACE (FC+) — Where excellent service/food make you feel like royalty. Built by Maharaja as his guest house, the 19 R w/ceiling fans (some AC) are spacious and glamorous. Bathrooms, staircase of Italian marble. Dining room is size of a ballroom. Outside city near Chamundi Hills. $21 and up.

METROPOLE (FC) — Also a former Maharaja guest house. Though not as fabulous as above, 19 R are comfortable, attractive. In town, 5 min. from rail station. $15 up.

PERIYAR LAKE, Thekkady

ARANYA — In Wild Life Sanctuary, edge of lake. 26 R hotel, surrounded by elephant moat. Dining R, bar, boats. $15 AP.

PURI

SOUTH EASTERN RAILWAY — On beach. 32 (some/AC) R. Tennis. Excursions to Konarak. $23 up.

SRINAGAR

BROADWAY (FC) — Mountain resort with pool, tennis, adjoins 18-hole golf course. 103 R, rooftop rst. Open all year. $24 up.

OBEROI PALACE (DL) — Former residence of Maharaja; on hill overlooking Dal Lake, 20 acres of gardens. 75 R (40 more in '78). Restaurant (elaborate Kashmiri specialties), bar, pool. 6-hole golf, riding, swimming, water-skiing. $59 AP (+8% tax).

Houseboats

CALIFORNIA GROUP of HOUSEBOATS (FC) — Dal Lake. Modern facilities, bath, hot/cold water, electricity. *Rsv:* Box 19, Srinagar, Kashmir; phone 3549.

MOHAMED WANGNOO (FC) — Luxury and FC boats on Nagin Lake. 2 bedrooms, dining & living R, porch, bath, water, electricity. $20 AP includes servant. Arrangements made for game shooting, fishing, etc. Best bargain in India. *Rsv:* Box 61, Srinagar, Kashmir; phone 4253.6

TIRUCHIRAPALLI

ARISTO — 21 R, some AC, in main bldg or bungalows. Best available. $14-$16 AP.

UDAIPUR

KE PALACE (DL) — Romance of a 17th-century palace — blazing white domes and turrets. Its white walls rise from polished surface of huge man-made Pichola Lake (access by boat). 85 R, 51 elaborately decorated SU (some AC). Rst, garden snack bar, pool. Boating. Indian dances and puppet shows nightly. Stay in original, older section for palace atmosphere. $27 up.

SHIKARBADI — One-time hunting lodge of the royal family of Mewar, now a charming, small hotel and stud farm — so riding ($4.50 hr) is the thing. 10 fan-cooled R are individually, simply furnished with lovely mirrorwork, prints; each bath different. Small family-style dining room where Western and Indian food (dinner from $4) is served on silver plates, colorful tablecloths. Small disco; pool. Delightful service. $20-$26.

VARANASI (BENARAS)

CLARKS (FC) — 100 AC R need refurbishing. Facilities include two of everything, plus snake charmer — but no pool. 20 min. from airport, 10 from rail station. *Conv:* 500. $22-$24.

VARANASI (FC) — 50 new, modern AC R. Rst, bar, pool. 10 minutes from the river action. $20-$23. *Rsv:* ITDC.

NEPAL

Kingdom of Nepal, a constitutional monarchy, is an ancient land with a rich cultural heritage. Bounded on the north by the Himalayas and the Tibet region of the People's Republic of China, by India on the south, its people are of varied races and tribes speaking many different languages and dialects, wearing different costumes and ornaments. Buddhists and Hindus have coexisted here in harmony for centuries, often so subtly blended as to be indistinguishable from the other. Mysticism shapes their lives, festivals are an almost daily occurrence.

The wild, uninhabited Himalayan mountain ranges cover most of the country,

Mochnapuchore from below Dhumpus near Pokhara, Nepal.

from the perpetual snows of Mt. Everest (and six other peaks over 25,000 ft.) to the jungle area of Terai in the south where the Royal Chitwan National Park, home of the near-extinct one-horned rhino and royal Bengal tiger, is located. Thruout most of the country, there's an abundance of waterfalls, lakes and lush valleys whose terraced hillsides provide charming, beautiful landscapes. The valley of Kathmandu, at the foot of the Himalayas, contains innumerable wooden temples and shrines, many dating from the 12th century. Nepalese culture flourished here so that the temples, in the shape of pagodas, are evidence of a still active religion. The Buddha's birthplace is· in Nepal at Lumbini.

For the tourist, Nepal is an unique experience — particularly when you stop to realize that only since 1955 have visitors been allowed to enter. There is simply no place else on earth where the mountains are higher and more beautiful. Nepal is also a sobering experience since it is one of the poorest nations in the world. If abject poverty distresses you, don't come. Outside of the Kathmandu and Pokhara regions, roads are lacking. Communications and medical care are rudimentary. Foreign aid from many countries is assisting Nepal's effort to enter the 20th century — but this is still not a modern society.

KATHMANDU

Capital and largest city in the country (250,000 pop.), Kathmandu is a peculiar mixture of both old and new. It even has a twin, Patan, an adjoining city on the south side of the Bagmati River. Patan retains a greater medieval character than the capital.

Kathmandu (4,500-ft. elevation) is a pleasant and manageable size for the tourist. He feels he "knows" it after being there but a few days since the city plan is easily followed. There's the old city with its narrow, winding streets, shops and street vendors selling anything and everything, animals and taxis (painted like tigers) vying for the right-of-way (although traffic's on the left) — a bustling, colorful atmosphere. Newer Kathmandu has broad avenues and straight roads; it feels newly constructed, airy and spacious after meandering thru the old city.

You'll want to spend hours in central Durbar Square. Here are temples, palaces, statues of the gods, even erotic art. Built by the Malla kings as their royal residence in the 17th century, it was renovated by later Shah kings. Enjoy the finely carved wooden elements of architecture, such as lattice windows, doorways and balconies. Pay particular attention to:

Pillar of King Pratap Malla, who sits serenely, with hands folded, atop the pillar facing the palace temple surrounded by his sons.

Taleju Temple — 400-year-old, three-story pagoda. Foreigners cannot enter — but can gawk at the erotic statuary.

Hanuman Dhoka, historic palace of the ancient kings, guarded by the gigantic figure of Kal Bhairav, God of Terror; faithful Nepalese have plastered this hero with red paste.

Nearby Kumari Devi, House of the Living Goddess — A young girl, considered sacred, lives here until she reaches puberty. She may view the crowds from her window but may not mingle with them.

The Buddhist temple of Swayambhunath (Monkey Temple), about two miles from downtown, is considered one of the city's major attractions. Located atop a steep hill, it's a mound-shaped stupa; the Buddha's eyes, painted on the four sides of the stupa, gaze out over the valley. Reputedly the oldest stupa in Nepal (about 2,000 years), worshippers circle it in a clockwise direction spinning Tibetan prayer wheels. The site is woefully neglected and smelly from monkey droppings.

Nearby is a curious, but not compelling, National Museum with three pavilions: Nepalese sculpture and artifacts, arms and armour and one devoted solely to exhibiting *everything* associated with the royal family. Open daily, except Tuesdays, holidays, 10-4.

CLIMATE & CLOTHING

October to late March are the best months — no rain, good visibility. Woolen clothing needed for early mornings, late evenings. In December and January, temperatures drop to 35° F. We were here the last two weeks of May, during the hottest season (April-September), yet still had bright, sunny days in the 70s, though the weather was chancy with occasional rains and mountains obscured by early morning. At higher elevations, temperatures are lower. Heavy rains begin in late June; annual rainfall is 50 to 55 inches.

Good country for sturdy walking shoes and, as we've said, heavy clothing for winter months.

ENTRY REQUIREMENTS

Passport, smallpox and cholera certificate, visa. Tourist visa, good for 15 days, available at airport on arrival but that entails delay in clearing formalities; best to obtain 30-day visa in advance from Royal Nepalese Embassy, 3132 Leroy Place NW, Washington, D.C., or Nepal Mission to United Nations, 711 Third Ave., Room 1806, New York 10017.

JETTING TO KATHMANDU

One hour, 25 min. from Delhi on Royal Nepal or Indian Airlines. Popular tourist routing, via Indian Airlines, is Delhi-Agra-Khajuraho-Varanasi to Kathmandu (55 min.). Other gateways: Bangkok (3 hrs.) on Thai Int'l or Royal Nepal or Rangoon (Burma Airways, Thai).

DOMESTIC TRANSPORTATION

There are only three major roads, of which the one from Kathmandu to Pokhara is of most importance to visitors, though the Swiss Bus takes six hours — best to fly (45 min.). There's a full-day tour over the so-called Chinese Highway to the border of the People's Republic.

In Kathmandu, metered taxis available but no self-drive rental services. Frequent public minibus (reconverted Volkswagens) service to outlying areas of Kathmandu Valley, such as Bodnath and Bhadgaon. Bus schedules are flexibly, leave when they are full (painfully overcrowded by our standards) from corner of the central village green. Incredibly cheap — about 20¢ each for a 10-mile drive.

Tribhuvan Airport is four miles from city center, a 15-min. taxi ride (about $3.50).

GENERAL INFORMATION

Airport Exit Tax — Rs 40.

Banks — Closed half day Fridays, all day on Saturdays; open Sundays.

Currency — Rs 12 (Nepalese Rupees) equal $1 US 100 paias to one rupee. Hotels give official exchange rates. Upon arrival, visitors receive currency declaration form on which all money exchanges are entered; on departure, only 10% of total amount exchanged can be reconverted into dollars at airport bank. No import of Indian currency except by Nepal-Indian citizens.

Current — 220v, alternating current.

Language — Nepali. English spoken in Kathmandu and other tourist areas.

Population — 12 million. Country about same size as Wisconsin.

Shopping Hours — From 8 a.m. to 8 p.m., give or take an hour. All businesses and offices closed on Saturdays; Sunday is an ordinary workday. Government offices open 10 to 5 in summer, 10-4 during winter.

Religion — 75% Hinduism, 25% Buddhist.

Time — India Time + 10 min. (GMT + 5 hrs., 40 min.)

Tipping — None in hotels, restaurants (10% service added) nor to taxi drivers.

Tourist Information — Dept. of Tourism, Kathmandu. John A. Victor, Honorary Consul, 3630 Jackson St., San Francisco.

Water — Drink only bottled or purified.

HOLIDAYS & FESTIVALS

Note: check dates. Festival days are set according to astrological finding each year.

January 11 — Prithvi Jayanti, Kathmandu. Honors King Prithvi Narayan Shah who helped form modern Nepal.

February 18 — Democracy Day.

March 7 — Shivaratri (Night of Lord Shiva). One of the biggest Nepalese festivals; observed in all Shiva temples, particularly those in Pashupatinath.

May 22 — Buddha Jayanti (Birthday of the Buddha). Observed in all Buddhist shrines, particularly at Lumbini, his birthplace, Swayambhu and Bodnath.

August 19 — Gaijatra (Cow Festival) in Kathmandu, Patan, Bhadgaon and Pokhara to honor the dead.

September 5 — Teej Women's Festival. Hindu women fast, visit temples to worship Shiva and his consort.

September 15 — Indrajatra, Rain God Festival (one week). Particularly colorful in Kathmandu; masked dances, music and fiestas.

October 8 — Durga Puja. Most colorful and important of all. Lasts 10 days. Goat sacrifices, masked dances, prayers, processions, etc.

October 31 — Festival of Lights. Lakshmi is worshipped by illuminating the city in colored lights.

December 29 — His Majesty's Birthday. Impressive ceremonies for His Majesty King Birendra Bir Bikram Shah Deva.

RESTAURANTS & NIGHTLIFE

There are many restaurants, none great. Hotel dining is as good as any, particularly the buffet at Soaltee Oberoi and Hotel De L'Annapurna for Indian, Nepalese and continental cuisines. Other recommendations: *The Other Room,* ground floor of Crystal Hotel with entrance on New Road; western and Indian food. *Kushi Fuji* for Japanese dishes prepared before you in pleasant, casual surroundings. *Everest Cultural Society* presents Nepalese folk dances at 6:30 each evening, followed by typical Nepalese rice and curry dinner, both in an old Rana palace, downtown. Society picks up and returns guests to their hotels. If you have extra evenings, try *Indira* for Indian specialties, *Chez Armand* for French.

Casino Nepal at the Soaltee Oberoi is *the* night life in Kathmandu and particularly appealing to neophyte gamblers because of the low-key atmosphere and low betting stakes. After 9 p.m., Casino transfers visitors from/to their hotels.

THE SHOPPING PICTURE

We found the work of Tibetan craftsmen to be the most exciting purchases. Finest jewelry is made of silver decorated with semi-precious stones. Bracelets, rings and necklaces are beautiful, as are finely etched silver bowls. Patan and Bodnath are the best towns in which to explore these small, Tibetan craft shops where prices are usually lower than in Kathmandu. Other items found there include Buddhist prayer wheels, the ubiquitous cap worn by all Nepalese men, woolen garments with a rough peasant look (ideal for winters back home), religious figures.

Tibetan refugees, with government assistance, are producing the woven carpets for which they are famous. Carpet factories have been set up in refugee villages, many of them in the Pokhara Valley. Visit their salesrooms and then see how rugs are woven.

Bargaining is the rule, except at government-run Cottage Industries and Handicrafts Emporium at Judha Sadak in downtown Kathmandu. A broad, representative selection is sold there.

Finally, visit the industrial district of Patan if interested in intricate metalwork objects, such as miniature seated dogs like those guarding temple entrances.

SIGHTSEEING IN THE KATHMANDU VALLEY

Patan (150,000) is three miles southeast of Kathmandu, an easy half-hour bus ride from Kathmandu's central bus station. Founded in 298 AD as Lalitpur, this city is easy to tour on foot, starting at Durbar Square in the main market area. Nepalese architecture of previous centuries (most of the historical buildings on the Square were built under a succession of Malla kings) is the outstanding feature of Patan. Don't miss: 1) Hiranya Varna Mahabihar, 12th-century Buddhist monastery with gold-plated roof, built under the patronage of a rich Tibetan merchant. Inside are impressive prayer wheels, scenes from Buddha's life. 2) Royal Palace, identified by its golden gate, wooden and bronze windows. 3) Krishna Temple, most famous in the Square, constructed, along Indian architectural lines, of stone in 17th century. Taleju Temple is a traditional, three-story pagoda. 4) Shopping the numerous antique shops that ring Durbar Square.

Bhadgaon (Bhaktapur), nine miles east of Kathmandu, is a medieval city founded in 889 AD. Here, too, Durbar Square features temples, gates and monuments grouped around the Palace of 55 Windows. Notable wood carvings on building facades, particularly the peacock windows of a monastery near the Dattatraya Temple. You walk thru the Lion and Golden Gates, gawk at the Golden Statue of King Malla and the magnificent, five-storied Nyata Pola pagoda.

Bodnath, five miles east of Kathmandu, has a colossal stupa built on an octagonal base and inset prayer wheels. Around the base are numerous Tibetan shops with beautiful handcrafts. At Pashupatinath, three miles northeast of Kathmandu on the banks of the sacred Bagmati, are pagoda-style temples dedicated to Lord Shiva. Non-Hindu visitors, not allowed inside, can watch the worshippers from a nearby vantage point on the eastern side of the river. As in India, cremations are performed so that the ashes may become part of the sacred river. Photography not advised.

At Daxinkali, 45 minutes by car from Kathmandu thru gorgeous scenery, Nepalese participate in animal sacrifice to Goddess Kali; check for sacrificial days. Chickens and goats are slaughtered and, after the rites, skinned and cleaned in the nearby stream before being taken home for dinner. Unlike anything we've ever seen and fascinating enough to hold our attention despite the hordes of other tourists.

KATHMANDU MOUNTAIN VIEWING

October-January is the best time. During the balance of the year, peaks are apt to be clouded and fogged in, visible only at certain times of the day (like dawn). These locations in Kathmandu Valley provide magnificent view sites:

Nagargot, 22 miles east of the capital, is an easily accessible peak (7,133 ft.) from which Sagarmatha (Mt. Everest) and other snowcapped mountains of the eastern Himalayas are best viewed. And there's good hiking in the area. The hardy can stay overnight at Mt. Everest Lodge or Mt. Everest Cottage. Drive takes 1½-2 hrs.; last half hour steep.

Dhulikhel is 20 miles east along the Chinese-financed highway. Include as part of the drive to Kodari (80 miles), on the Chinese border where, at Friendship Bridge, your passport can be stamped to prove that you were *there* even if not actually *in.*

Daman, 50 miles southwest on Tribhuwan Rajpath, has a viewing tower with long-range telescope. An exciting drive over typically winding roads with great views of terraced, fertile hills.

Kakani, at 6,500 ft., is best for views of the northwest Himalayas at sunset. 18 miles northwest, a 1½-hr. drive over Trisuli road.

HIMALAYAN AIR TOURS

Early each morning, October to May, Royal Nepal Airlines has an unforgettable, one-hour flight that, at 27,000 ft., gives you eyeball to mountain top views of Mt. Everest, 14 miles away, and other eastern Himalayan peaks. Passengers take turns visiting the cockpit of this pressurized Avro jet-prop.

By 4-passenger helicopters or STOL aircraft, such as Twin Otters, one can land 8,000 ft. up to explore a sherpa village, zoom down Langang Valley between 20,000-ft. peaks, fly up to Namche Bazar, starting point for many Everest expeditions, and visit Thyangboche Monastery. Check Royal Nepal or Trans Himalayan Tours.

Most glamorous flight (45 min.) is to Everest View Hotel, Shyangboche (13,000 ft.), for one or more days; takes another 45 min. to walk from hotel airstrip to hotel (riding horses or yaks available, porters carry luggage). Namche Bazar, a neighboring Sherpa village, has excellent handcrafts; Saturday is market day . . . and really photogenic.

For land touring, local tour operators are well equipped with Japanese cars, minibuses and coaches (some AC), offer a wide variety of regular and customized tours, for individuals and groups, over 500 miles of paved roads.

EXPLORING THE POKHARA VALLEY

At 2,000 ft., it abounds in peaceful lakes, rippling streams, rural villages and bustling local bazaars, provides a closer view of the Himalayas than in Kathmandu — the Annapurna Range is only 15 miles away. It lies in the shadow of Mt. Machapuchare (22,942 ft.), the sacred Matterhorn of Nepal — and off limits to climbers. It's the most easily distinguishable sight in the central Himalayan range because of its fish tail-shaped spire.

Spring is the most beautiful time here; dense forests of rhododendrons are in bloom. It's generally slightly hotter than Kathmandu due to the lower elevation. The flight (35 min.) from Kathmandu via Royal Nepal is not as spectacular as the one to Mt. Everest but provides good mountain viewing; if you take one, you don't need the other.

Don't bother spending time in Pokhara, a dusty, one-road town. Head straight for idyllic Phewa Lake on the outskirts of town, around which are respectable, if primitive looking, outdoor restaurants. This is Nepal's second most popular tourist area. Should you stop overnight at Fish Tail Lodge and have the next day free for a mini-trek, climb Sarangkot (seen from the lake). Took us six hours round trip and, though strenuous, required only energy, not skill. Had beautiful panoramas of the Annapurna range from the top, saw a few villages along the trekking route.

Another interesting short trip, we understand, is to Henjya, a Tibetan refugee settlement. These former nomads earn their living weaving carpets and cloth, working as porters. In the evenings, you'll hear traditional chants; Tibetan folk dances can be arranged for groups.

Everything about hiking here is included in a *Walker's Guide to Pokhara*, published by the Department of Tourism, Kathmandu.

Trekking thru Trisuli Gorge village, Nepal.

MOUNTAIN TREKKING

Best during the autumn when mountains are most clearly visible, when there is no rain. Weather also good in December and January but cold with snow in the highlands above 9,000 ft. February and March, when the rhododendrum blooms, are popular. From the end of March 'til May, or the beginning of the monsoon season, it is possible to trek, but skies are hazy and cloudy; from then on, no trekking due to landslides.

Treks are run as package tours (government permit needed) out of Kathmandu and Pokhara (also Hotel Everest View) by experienced local operators, include bedding, tents, food and equipment (tables and chairs if you insist), porters, cooks and guides. Most popular are those to Annapurna and Dhaulagir ranges to view the spectacular 26,000-ft. icy peaks rising from the green Pokhara plain, follow winding trails thru orange groves and lakes. With little climbing, the less energetic can enjoy the mountains from a distance while others hike north to the Kali Gandaki River. Any Pokhara based trek (usually 20 to 25 days) puts you in the center of Tibetan and Buddhist cultures, provides marvelous mountainscapes.

Treks can be arranged for whatever time is available, will average $20 to $35 a day per person for longer ones, or for as little as $2 a day — by carrying your own pack, eating local food, sleeping in pup tents or local homes. For $7 to $9, treks can be taken by the hardy, using local inns and food and with one porter each. But a typical 15-day trek for two requires six porters, each carrying a 66-lb. load.

Deal only with a reliable, well-known, local trekking organization. Or book thru a U.S. specialist: Hanns Ebensten Travel, 55 W. 42 St., N.Y. 10036; Mountain Travel, 1398 Solano Ave., Albany, Ca. 94706; Nature Expeditions, P.O. Box 1173, Los Altos, Ca. 94022; Questers Tours, 257 Park Ave. S, N.Y. 10010; Krill Tours, 1854 S. Coast Hwy., Laguna, Ca. 92651; Himalaya Tours, 3023 Franklin St., S.F. 94123; Earth Journeys, 3400 Peachtree Rd., Atlanta 30326.

JUNGLE & RIVER TRIPS

Increasingly important in the Nepal tourism picture are visits to and thru Royal Chitwan National Park where, in jungle surroundings, the Bengal tiger and Indian one-horned rhino are protected, as are deer, bear, sloth, leopard and nearly 300 species of birds; the river trip down the Trisuli River to Tiger Tops Tent Camp is a fine birdwatching expedition.

75 miles southwest of Kathmandu, a 30-minute flight lands visitors at Meghauly airstrip where transfers to Tiger Tops Jungle Lodge are made by land rover (30 min.), canoe or elephant (2 hrs.). Here you enjoy nature walks with experienced naturalists, elephant-back safaris in search of rhinos — activities included in the cost of your room.

At carefully selected sites, a water buffalo serves as prey of the Bengal tigers; if a tiger is sighted, visitors are quietly brought to the guarded sites to observe the endangered animal — there are no more than 2,000 in the entire Indian subcontinent.

Ideal stay is two or three nights, either at the Jungle Lodge or Tent Camp — or both. Latter is best situated for jungle walks, visits to surrounding villages, fishing for mahseer, a type of tarpon.

Under the direction of Michael Yager, a licensed river guide from Wyoming, scenic float and white water trips are conducted on the Trisuli and Narayani Rivers. Crocodile, deer, rhino, waterfowl and other birds may be seen from the boats, also remote villages. These trips, out of Kathmandu, cost from $70 a day per person for 2-7 people (1 or 2 days) to $50 or less, from $55 to $44 each for a party of 8 or more. Further information, reservations: Mountain Travel.

Gaida (Rhino) Wildlife Camp is located on outskirts of the National Park. Advertised as "the ultimate wildlife experience for the budget traveler," Gaida provides elephant-back excursions and a chance to observe tigers. Accommodations are even more basic than the Tent Camp, food more spartan. But the price is right: $126 per person for three days, including air fare. Write: Manaslu Trekking, Durbar Marg, PO Box 1519, Kathmandu, or Gaida Safari Camp, PO Box 989, Kathmandu.

One-horned rhinos and Royal Bengal tigers are the attractions at Royal Chitwan National Park — if you're lucky enough to see them.

Tiger Tops Jungle Lodge, complete with private elephants.

Hotel Directory

KATHMANDU

Accommodations limited so reserve well in advance. 10% tax added to these Double rates.

DE L'ANNAPURNA (FC+) — In embassy district, 10 minutes from airport. 154 AC R, SU (60 are new). Lobby decorated with Nepalese antiques. Bar overlooks pool w/large terrace. Specialty rst, coffee shop, beauty shop, shopping arcade. tennis. $56 AP. Meeting Rs w/PA system.

DWARIKA'S — Small, intimate world "with a typical Nepali outlook and ambience." Rooms feature antique Nepali woodcarvings, deluxe baths. Reputedly good food, personal service. *Rsv:* P.O. Box 459, Kathmandu.

EVEREST INT'L (FC+) — 9-floor hi-rise opened late '78 w/154 R, 12 SU; central AC. 3 rsts, coffee shop, bars. Pool, tennis, health club, disco, shopping arcade. $40 up. Between airport/city.

KATHMANDU (FC) — 5 km north of city. Opened late '78 w/129 R (4 floors), several rsts, bars, pool and sauna.

MALLA (FC) — 3-story Nepalese bldg. in enchanting garden. 87 AC R; two cont'l rsts, bar. Pool and tennis. Just north of city center. $40-$48. British management, chef.

NARAYANI — 75 nicely decorated R, SU in 5-story modern bldg. Two rsts, coffee shop, bar; pool.

SHANKER (FC) — 148 R in former Rana Palace near French Embassy. Beautiful royal gardens. Rst, bar, pool and tennis. Local folk dances arranged on request. About $34.

SOALTEE OBEROI (DL) — With new 5-floor wing, has 289 AC R/SU in traditional Nepalese decor. Oriental restaurant serves Nepalese. Chinese, Indian, Japanese cuisines. Coffee shop, a la carte rst, cocktail lounge/-bars. Dancing nightly. Tennis, pool, gambling casino (only one in this part of the world). Conv. facilities. *Rsv:* Loews.

YAK & YETI (DL) — Modern 5-story bldg adjoins former Rana palace (now used for elegant dining in Chimney Rst). 105 beautifully furnished, appointed R, SU. Pool, lighted tennis, saunas, boating lake, gardens. $42 up.

LUKLA

SHERPA COOPERATIVE HUTS — Several 16 R huts w/modern facilities being opened along Everest trail.

POKHARA

FISH TAIL LODGE (FC+) — One of our favorites — anywhere. Reached at far end of Phewa Lake by raft. Circular pavilion dining area serves excellent western or Nepalese cuisines. AC rooms have large picture windows, exposed brick walls. During foggier times of year, front desk wakes you in early a.m. so you can enjoy the mountain views before clouded in. Room 16 has a perfect view of Machupechere. About $40 AP.

In case above is fully booked, there's the *New Crystal* w/70 AC R, rst, bar, pool, tennis. *Mt. Annapurna* has 32 AC R, rst, bar, roof garden.

ROYAL CHITWAN NAT'L PARK

TIGER TOPS JUNGLE LODGE — Makes you feel like Robinson Crusoe Deluxe in the jungle. 22 treetop, solar-heated, luxurious rooms; food flown in, including superlative beef from Calcutta. $90 a day per person, plus $45 RT air. Closed July-Aug.

TIGER TOPS TENT CAMP — 10 tents for two w/sleeping bags. Good camp-style meals. $35 daily per person, plus air fare.

GAIDA WILDLIFE CAMP — Tents w/camp cots, bedding; toilet/shower facilities. $126 for 3 days, including meals, air fare. Closed during monsoon season.

SHYANGBOCHE (Everest)

EVEREST VIEW — Highest (13,000 ft.) hotel in this part of world. For sheer dramatic beauty, none can compare. Designed by Japanese architects of native stone, Sherpas hauled materials on their backs on a 14-day climb to build this 12 R, split-level affair that perches precariously on a ridge facing Everest some 16,000 ft. above. You'll enjoy the European cuisine, drinks before a roaring fire, socializing with trekkers as they climb up or down. This bit of heaven will set you back $135 (double) a day AP. New generator should eliminate some previous discomforts (like electrical blackouts). *Rsv:* Trans Himalayan Tours, Box 283, Kathmandu.

SRI LANKA

Sri Lanka's most impressive sculptures are seen in the ancient capital of Polonnaruwa — three giant figures of the Gal Vihare: seated, standing and reclining. The one shown here is the smallest; the reclining figure is 44 feet long.

Sri Lanka (formerly Ceylon) is delightful. The people are as friendly and warm as the climate. English is spoken everywhere. Most of the island looks like a tropical paradise where plump fruits grow wild and palm trees billow in the wind. Yet the scenery changes dramatically in the center of the country where tea grows at cooler, mountainous elevations.

All this means that the visitor can spend time on Sri Lanka's extensive coast, where there are facilities for sunning and scuba diving (among the best in the world) or at the hill stations in the mountains where the English went to escape the heat. Since the country is the size of West Virginia, one can see the highlights by car. Unlike West Virginia, this small island has a population of 14 milion people.

Although Sri Lanka is located only 22 miles off the southern coast of India, its culture is completely different from its closest neighbor. Sri Lanka is a devout Buddhist country. Buddhist monks, with their saffron robes and shaven heads, are a colorful and visible presence everywhere. The ancient cities of Anuradhapura and Polonnaruwa contain monumental stone sculptures of the Buddha and dagobas, or reliquary chambers, built in commemoration of the Buddha.

Sri Lanka is very inexpensive to visit. In short, this is an undiscovered island worth discovering, particularly since it has magnificent tropical beaches and resorts on both east and west coasts. Because of the monsoons (see When To Go?), one or the other is always in season: west coast from October to April, east from March thru September.

GETTING TO SRI LANKA

There are no direct, one-plane flights from the U.S. and Canada; connections should be made, from either east or west coasts, at any of the cities listed below, all of which have non-stop flights to Colombo (except Jakarta, Tokyo — 1-stop): Bangkok, Bombay, Jakarta, Kathmandu, Kuala Lumpur, Madras, Singapore, Tokyo, Trivandrum.

Low-budget travelers can take a train in India south to Rameshwaram and ferry across the 42-mile strait to Marrar, Sri Lanka, then by rail to Kandy or Colombo.

WHEN TO GO?

Any time of the year depending on which coast you visit. There are two monsoons annually, but fortunately for tourism they affect the east and west coasts at different seasons. On the west, rainy season is May-Aug, on the east coast Nov-Feb. Because of cooling ocean breezes, temperatures rarely go above 90°.

In the hill country, temperatures are like early spring in New England — 65°-75°, though evenings can be nippy. We spent an enjoyable February evening before the burning hearth at the Grand Hotel in Nuivara Eliya, in the east highlands.

HOW TO DRESS?

Casual. We saw no tourists wearing ties and jackets anywhere. In the fancier hotels, women would often wear floor-length native batik skirts in the evening.

GETTING AROUND

There's an extensive train and bus network connecting most tourist points of interest. Train travel is not luxurious but adequate; most trains have only 2nd and 3rd class cars — choose 2nd, always. 1st class, air-conditioned cars available on a few trains, generally those with sleeping berths. There is good service south from Colombo to the Gold Coast and Galle; also from Colombo to Kandy and from there to Narvoya (for Nuwara Eliya), and to Anuradhapura, Trincomalee, Polonnaruwa, Batticola and Ratnapura.

Government transport buses go everywhere but are generally crowded, slow and uncomfortable. A luxurious and not too exorbitant way to see the country is by car (with driver), hired thru any of the travel agencies in Colombo or Kandy. We had a real bargain: a comfortable Fiat and excellent guide for 100 rupees a day, including 50 miles (2.5 rupees per mile over that), plus 20 rupees daily for driver's subsistence. For about one-third more, we could have rented a luxurious, air-conditioned Peugot, but we didn't miss the AC (and would have missed the extra rupees).

Bus tours that take you to the major sites are reasonable, include meals and lodging for several days. Government also offers special train tours in an AC, Japanese "Bullet" train. Finally, if you really want to travel in high style, the Sri Lankan Air Force picks up foreign currency by organizing helicopter tours. Unfortunately, the rates are also high.

When hiring a car, meet the driver beforehand to see if he speaks easily understandable English, will make a compatible travel companion.

HOW'S THE SHOPPING?

Disappointing. The quality of crafts is generally poor, resembling mass-produced merchandise such as that represented by the ubiquitous Kandy masks. Visit *Laksala* on York St, Fort, Colombo; it's government-run so prices are fixed. More fun is the Pettah bazaar district in Colombo, an Asian outdoor marketplace with traditional bargaining.

North of Colombo, on the west coast, is the center of Sri Lanka's batik industry. Factories employing from 10-100 girls encourage visitors. Greatest number of factories are 10 to 20 miles north of Negambo off the main road (clearly marked); here you'll be given a tour of the "production lines" and shown to the salesroom. As batik is a labor-intensive industry, don't expect terrific bargains. We paid $15 for a short cotton skirt and halter top; long skirts cost about $45. Make sure they guarantee the fastness of the dyes. Best batiks in the country are by award winner Ena da Silva, who designed the large, free-hanging batiks at the Lanka Oberoi in Colombo; batik paintings are sold at 42 Ananda Coomaraswami, Mawatha, Colombo 3. At her Mariposa Shop, 63/7 Dharmapala, Mawatha, Turrett Rd, Colombo 7, batik boxes, dresses, etc., are sold.

The real specialty of the country is precious and semi-precious gems such as star sapphires, tourmalines, rubies and cat's eyes. Best-priced gems can be bought at Ratnapura where they are mined — visit All-Ceyon Cooperative Gem Society sponsored by the People's Bank. You'll receive a guarantee of the gem's authenticity from this government store — *but you must pay with foreign currency.* Buying gems is the only reason to visit Ratnapura; otherwise all you'll see are a few small-scale holes in the ground where raw gems are mined.

There's a duty-free shop at Bandaranaike Airport.

TRIP PLANNING

Since the capital of Sri Lanka, Colombo, is both the major airport (Bandaranaike) and seaport (and the only city worthy of the name), everything starts from here. And without wasting much time — average tour group remains one day and overnight — as this is really not terribly attractive to tourists except for: 1) A nice walk on Galle Face, a park in the center of the city with Dutch cannon facing the sea; 2) National Museum's interesting collection of Sinhalese archeology and its great treasure: the throne jewels of the last Kandyan King; 3) The Zoo where elephants perform at 5 p.m. daily.

ANCIENT CITIES

Aside from the beaches, Sri Lanka's greatest tourist asset are the remains of a great civilization, centuries old, that developed under the gentle influence of Buddhism. Vast man-made lakes, parks, shrines, temples and monasteries bear testimony to the grandeur created by a proud and imaginative people.

To the northeast of Colombo are Kandy, 72 miles away, and Anuradhapura, 56 miles further north. In between, and to the east, are Sigiriya and Polonnaruwa,47 miles apart. When making this circuit by car, best place to stay, we feel, is the Village Hotel at Habarana, almost equidistant between Colombo and Trincomalee. Hotel is a two-hour drive from Anuradhapura, 45-minute from Polonnaruwa, 30 from Sigiriya. Or use the Tissawewa Hotel in Anuradhapura, Rest House in Sigiriya; there are three hotels we recommend in Kandy. Allow a minimum of four days for the Ancient Cities circuit.

KANDY — Home of Buddha's Tooth

The second largest city in Sri Lanka, and our favorite, is 72 miles by road from Colombo thru lush tropical foliage. October to April is best time to enjoy the moderate climate of approximately 77°, with July or August (depending on full moon) particularly good because of a not-to-be-missed festival (10 nights), Perahera, which celebrates the sacred relic, Buddha's tooth, brought here some 1,500 years ago.

WHAT'S WITH FOOD?

The national meal is rice and curry consisting of heaping platters of rice and from five to nine dishes of meat, vegetable, potato, prawns, fish and chicken prepared in various curried sauces. In most restaurants you can specify how spicy you like your food as curry is made with a variety of spices. Every day the mixture of dishes changes, so you'll never be bored.

On the coast, the fresh seafood, jumbo prawns and spiny lobster are delicious. Pineapple, coconut, passion fruit, mangoes are luscious.

Try the dessert buffal curds (yoghurt) and treacle (like honey).

Don't drink tap water or use ice unless made from bottled water. Most hotels provide carafes of potable water; if in doubt, inquire if water is okay to drink.

Colombo abounds in Chinese restaurants.

The best are along Galle Rd: *Chinese Dragon, Chinese Lotus* and *Golden Gate.* The best Western food is in the better hotels: *Coconut Grove,* Galle Face, *Catseye,* Inter-Continental, *Harbour Room,* Taprobane Hotel in the Fort area of Colombo. *Green Cabin,* Galle Rd, serves the best local dishes, also have excellent pastry, best consumed while drinking tea on the terrace.

WHAT ABOUT DRINKS?

Each hotel has a bar. No permit is required (as in India) to purchase drinks. Local liquors are rum and arrack distilled from coconut juice; latter, called toddy, tastes sweet but can pack a wallop. Only drink fresh toddy tapped from the coconut the same day you drink it, otherwise it ferments. The king coconut (Thambili), a popular, non-alcoholic thirst-quencher, is available at wayside stalls. Imported liquor is expensive; bring your own.

Drummers parade before the Temple of the Tooth during Perahera festivities when homage is paid both to Buddha and the sacred relic housed in the Temple.

Kandy nestles in the hills like a little Swiss village, though the mountains are only 1,674 ft. high. In the center of town is the Temple of the Tooth (Dalada Maligawa) where colorful services are held every morning and evening. A man-made lake, great for promenading, lies across from the temple.

Be sure to visit the Kandyan Arts Association, near the temple, for the best crafts of the area. Forget visiting the Elephant Baths as it's become too commercialized; police are present to control the elephant trainers who overcharge for rides.

We thought the performance of the Kandy Dancers, meant to be a ritualized dance form from previous centuries to exorcise the devil, was both overpriced and commercialized as the two-hour performance at the local Red Cross was by inexperienced, bored dancers. Supposed to be a better group at the Hotel Suisse and during Perahera.

ANURADHAPURA

An ancient city, founded in 380 BC, Anuradhapura served as the island's first capital until deserted in the 9th century under pressure of attack from the Tamils of South India. Jungles enveloped the area, and it wasn't rediscovered until 1845. Extensive restoration (not all good) of the city's monuments within its 15-square-mile area has made Anuradhapura one of the logical places to visit and experience Sinhalese culture.

The most impressive structures are dagobas, enormous dome-shaped memorials in which a relic of the Buddha (or one of his saints) is housed. The largest, Ruwanvali, is 300 ft. in diameter and over 300 ft. tall. Thuperama dagoba, built about 300 BC, is said to contain the Lord Buddha's right collarbone. Dagobas equal, and in many cases surpass, Egyptian pyramids in size. Unfortunately, the symmetry of their bell form has been disfigured by poorly executed restoration work.

Today, the city has the feeling of an enormous park studded with archeological treasures. Visit the Brazen Palace, formerly a nine-story residence for monks; only the pillars which supported the wooden structure still stand. Also see the sacred Bo Tree, reputed to be 2,200 years old. This tree grew from a branch of a Bo tree under which the

Two of the delicate, sensual women that decorate the walls of Sigiriya's rock fortress.

Buddha was reputed to have found enlightenment; the branch was brought from India in the 3rd century BC.

Because of the existence of many religious monuments, these ruins are objects of pilgrimage. The government maintains a number of rudimentary retreats as shelters for Buddhist pilgrims. When we were there, we shared our visit with Japanese Buddhists who had come there on a charter flight.

It's best to have a car when visiting Anuradhapura because of the distances between monuments. Also you'll want to see nearby Mihintale, a series of caves and shrines where monks have lived since the 3rd century BC. This is considered the cradle of Buddhism in SL because it was here that the first Sinhalese king was converted to the faith. He turned Mihintale into a monastery for his teacher, Mahinda, and his 3,000 monks. It's a 1,840-step walk up to the summit of this rock, still honeycombed with religious caves.

SIGIRIYA

It was here, in the 5th century AD, that King Kasyapa had a palace built as a fortress atop an impregnable 600-ft. rock to defend himself. Naturally, to reach this fortress in the sky, you have to climb a fairly steep distance. However, along the way you'll be rewarded by seeing Sri Lanka's most famous frescos: delicate 1,000-year-old portraits of bejeweled maidens. The surrounding jungle, as seen from atop the rock, is lush and beautiful. From here, can be seen the three defensive moats protecting Sigiriya. Foundations of the palace, council chamber, guardhouse and other structures still exist — an unforgettable experience. A city once surrounded the rock.

POLONNARUWA

The capital of Sri Lanka was moved to Polonnaruwa from Anuradhapura and Sinhalese royalty lived there from the 10th to 12th centuries, spending inordinate sums of money building a beautiful city, as evidenced by the spectacular ruins, which are better preserved than at Anuradhapura. Most imposing figures are the Gal Vihare — three Buddhist sculptures — sitting, standing and reclining — carved from a single piece of rock. The reclining figure is 44 feet long, the standing one 23 ft. high. Other treasures include the Vatadage, or round relic house with Buddhas at each of the four entrances, Trivanka Image House, Citadel, Lotus Bath and Lankatilaka; latter is the largest shrine of ancient Ceylon.

Ruvanvali, the dagoba at Anuradhapura, is rumored to have been built (about 137 BC) of cement mixed with crushed pearls, jewels and gold — hence known as the "Dagoba of the Golden Sands."

EAST COAST RESORTS

Generally, east coast resorts are more isolated, have fewer tourist groups and shops. The west coast is more built up, especially below Colombo at Bentota and Hikkaduwa, with clusters of hotels and associated tourist services. But, we hasten to add, this "congestion" is purely relative to the rest of the country; by Western standards, the most crowded beaches are sparsely populated and but a short beach walk from total seclusion.

Main east coast center is Trincomalee, one of the world's great natural harbors. As a result, the port was occupied by the Portuguese, Dutch, Danes, French and, finally, English. Today, the harbor is breathtaking, the port nearly defunct, its main purpose the storage of mothballed ships. There's an interesting Hindu temple on a cliff, some natural hot springs that come in seven different temperatures — from tepid to scalding. Best hotels are on the beach north of town. Trincomalee is reached from Colombo or Kandy by bus or rail.

South of Trincomalee is Batticaloa, still a "sleeper," though development is in the offing. Passekudah beach is lovely, the Imperial Oceanic Hotel very inexpensive.

RESORTS ALONG THE WEST COAST

The west coast, on which the capital city of Colombo is located, offers a number of opportunities for resort living. Most tour groups do just that — overnight in Colombo following arrival, then on to the beaches. Incidentally, the bulk of Sri Lanka's tourism is charters and GITs, mostly from Europe during November-March.

Besides Mt. Lavinia and Pegasus Reef, 7 and 10 miles north of Colombo, many tourists stay at Negombo, a pleasant, picturesque fishing village 23 miles north and only minutes from the airport. There's a long, thin, fire-sand beach and lots of fishermen in their homemade catamarans, sailing skiffs and dugout canoes bringing in a variety of seafood: giant prawns, spiny lobsters, seer (related to mackerel) and tiny, herring-like fish. We enjoyed the scene.

The most popular beaches are on the Gold Coast, 28 to 70 miles south of Colombo, an area that's experienced most of the country's tourist development with a number of modern hotels.

Bentota, 38 miles south, has four new hotels and a modern shopping center for Sri Lanka's best crafts. Some say it's too modern, too removed from local culture. But the village is quite beautiful, the beach peaceful.

Other major Gold Coast resort is Hikkaduwa about 32 miles farther south. Older than Bentota, it's famed for its magnificent coral reefs, world-famous diving facilities — and hippies. The reefs are only several hundred yards offshore, easily seen by glass-bottom boat or catamaran; you can rent mask, snorkel and fins, along with catamaran and pilot, for under $5 — a great see-it-yourself exploration. Colorations of coral and the schools of tropical fish are breathtaking. Scuba parties to more distant reefs are easily arranged.

Hikkaduwa's other attraction is its endless beach where at some points the sea is gentle, at others battering. European hippies have taken over the southern beach (while taking off most of their clothes). Parts of the beach provide excellent surfing; you'll see Australian and American surfers riding their boards each afternoon. During the season, the village is congested.

For serious divers, we recommend the Hotel Poseidon, run by professional divers; they'll also teach novices the basics.

Still further south is Tangalle, a quiet cove with an excellent small hotel, Tangalle Bay, in a lush setting overlooking the sea.

10 miles south of Hikkaduwa is the old walled Dutch city (1640-1796) of Galle with still-remaining examples of their architecture. We enjoyed walking the ramparts of the fort as well as the nearby beaches.

Tea pickers carry baskets on their backs into which they drop the tiny leaves.

HILL COUNTRY & TEA ESTATES

Another area that proved most appealing, and in retrospect one of our most memorable Sri Lankan experiences, was the highland region; with peaks over 6,000 ft., it offers good trout fishing, a lovely spring climate and great panoramic views. Tea bushes, together with evergreen and eucalyptus trees, carpet the mountains in rich greens.

Nuwara Eliya, 103 miles almost due east of Colombo, was the No. 1 English resort town and, as such, is reminiscent of the English lake district; buildings reflect turn-of-the-century English architecture. Other English relics: an 18-hole golf course (overrated by most) and the number of billiard tables at hotels. Hakgala Botanic Gardens are well laid out, more intimate than Kandy's Gardens, provide pleasant strolling. February (crisp), March and April is best season.

Horton Plains, 18 miles away, is another popular hill station. On a beautiful plateau, it's best in April. Excellent trout fishing.

Sri Pada (Adam's Peak), another beauty spot, is holy to Buddhists who pilgrimage there from mid-January to May. A formation on the mountaintop is believed to be Buddha's footprint, hence the pilgrims begin the fairly strenuous march at dusk in order to spend the night on the mountain, then watch the sunrise. Sri Pada is fairly inaccessible without car and driver.

A most pleasant, offbeat experience is spending one or two nights on a tea plantation in the estate bungalow of a superintendent or his assistant who are often anxious to accommodate visitors as a welcome diversion in their isolation and loneliness. The bungalow is most often a large English "cottage" surrounded by flower gardens and, perhaps, sited on the highest hill in the area. Vast tea-planted acreage lies all around, as do the rows and rows of laborers' lodgings. We loved the beautiful setting, our conversations with the estate superintendents, the tour of the plantation — a totally different travel experience.

Expect to spend between $12 to $20 double per day, including meals. A list of plantations currently accepting guests can be obtained from Sri Lanka Tourist Board offices in New York, Los Angeles.

Bathers at the ancient wells near Trincomalee have a choice of seven different flavors — tepid to scalding.

GAME PARKS & BIRD SANCTUARIES

Wilpattu National Park, the largest, is 110 miles north of Colombo on the west coast (18 miles from Anuradhapura); it can be included in the Ancient Cities circuit. Yala (also called Ruhunu) is 190 miles south of Colombo on the east coast. Elephant, leopard, bear, buffalo, deer and sambhur (large Asiatic deer with long, coarse hair) are residents of both parks. In fact, Yala looked overpopulated there were so many birds and animals. Our favorite vignettes: peacocks dancing (mating), a leopard lazily sunbathing. Best viewing times: early (6 a.m.) and late (4:30 p.m.) for a three-hour jeep ride. Jeeps rented thru your hotel for under $20 for each session; easy to share same with others and reduce the cost. Remember, though, it's purely a matter of luck how many, or few, animals you actually see at any one time.

Another park, renowned for its elephant population, is Inginiyagala (Gal-oya) east of Kandy, 190 miles from Colombo. Birds are abundant not only in National Parks but also at the sanctuaries of Wirawila and Kumạna, 32 and 25 miles from Yala.

Park bungalows, with basic facilities, can be booked in advance thru Wildlife Conservation, 54 Chatham St., Colombo. See Hotel Directory for Yala hotels. Some local travel agents specialize in nature tours. Wildlife and Nature Protection Society, Chaitiya Rd., Marine Drive, Fort in Colombo has complete details on safaris, hiking and bird watching.

Hotel Directory

Don't expect air-conditioning or hot water in most hotels *except in Colombo*. AC usually unnecessary, and it's easy to get used to cold water showers in this warm climate. Should you want hot water, call the room boy. Non-AC hotels always have ceiling fans, prove quite adequate.

10% service normally added to double room rates quoted herein (usually include American breakfast), also to meals. Extra tipping unnecessary, but if you do, a small amount goes a long way.

COLOMBO

CEYLON INTER-CONTINENTAL (DL) — 250 attractive R overlook pool and ocean. Rooftop cocktail lounge w/breathtaking views. Catseye Supper Club features int'l cuisine, music, dancing. Moonstone Barbecue Terrace Nov-April for dancing. Tennis. Bustling, modern DT hotel (45 min. from airport) catering to businessmen. $34-$41.

GALLE FACE REGENT (DL) — Old-world splendor in renovated, 150 R (some AC) English-style grand hotel directly on ocean DT. Famous Sea Terrace (great at sunset); oriental decor in rst; coffee shop, bar, shopping arcade, pool. Conv. facilities. *Rsv:* Regent Int'l. $22-$29.

HOLIDAY INN (FC) — 100 AC R; rsts, bar, pool, tennis. DT. $23-$27.

LANKA OBEROI (DL) — Beautiful DT complex w/open lobby. 366 AC R in main section (recommended) and annex. Pool, in tropical gardens, has bar, snack service. French, Eastern and Int'l dining. *Conv:* 700. $34-$42.

NEAR COLOMBO

MT. LAVINIA (FC) — 7 miles from Colombo, near domestic airport, on promontory; built into cliff overlooking sea. 200 AC R in renovated older/attractive new sections. Fantastic view from terrace pool. Highly recommended. $25-$32.

PEGASUS REEF (DL) — 10 miles north on beach. 144 AC R (some face multi-acre tropical garden). Folk dances, Sri Lankan army band concerts are great entertainment. Good rst, Lion Bar. Pool, tennis; pleasant but unspectacular beach. Bit isolated but nice to come home to. $32-$34.

ANURADHAPURA

TISSAWEWA (FC) — In old city. 25 R w/fans. Rst, gardens. $15.

BATTICALOA

IMPERIAL OCEANIC — 66 AC R w/balcony amidst palms; overlook Passekudah beach. Int'l cuisine, seafood specialties. Sinhalese decor in supper club. Glass-bottom boats, snorkeling, bicycles. *Rsv:* Hotel Tours & Trades, 89 Hyde Park Corner, Colombo 2. $32 AP.

Opened in '77 on reef-protected bay: *Sun & Fun* (31 R); *Sun Tan Beach* (20 R, cabana style). Both hotels white-walled, built to let in sea breezes, inexp.

BENTOTA

BENTOTA BEACH (FC-) — Beautifully sited between river and sea. 135 R (some AC), several rsts; pool, water sports. $30-$35 AP.

GIRITALE

GIRITALE — 42 R w/fans, rst, pool. Great view of lake, hillside. Opened '75. $34-$41 AP includes tax.

ROYAL LOTUS — Opened '77 with lake view. 54 AC R nicely furnished w/balcony. Hotel has feeling of lightness with white walls contrasted by dark woods. $17 AP, plus 10% service, 10% tax. Rst, pool. *Rsv:* Club Oceanic, Ltd., 40 Sir MMM Mawatha, Colombo.

HABARANA

VILLAGE (FC+) — 60 R w/fans in modern, attached bungalows. Stone wall bar separates open-air lounge and rst. Pool, tennis, mini-golf. Excursions arranged. Good food, efficient management. About $28 AP.

HIKKADUWA

BLUE CORALS — 30 R w/fans. Water sport, skin-diving facilities. $27 AP.

CORAL GARDENS — 48 beautiful R with magnificent sea views. Service could be improved. $35 AP.

CORAL REEF — 18 simple R w/fans. Adequate. Inexp. $15-$22.

KANDY

FC Rates: $25-$32

HUNAS FALLS (DL) — Tea plantation resort w/pool 17 miles from Kandy at Elkaduwa; reputedly one of Asia's most beautiful hotels. 23 AC R. Rst (European food), bar.

QUEEN'S (FC) — Decaying elegance, bustling with groups, in center of town by lake's edge. AC rsts, bars, nightclub; pool. 85 R w/fans. *Conv:* 500. $21.

SUISSE — On beautiful grounds slightly outside of town. 60 R w/fans (similar to Queen's), rst, bars, nightclub; pool. *Conv:* 250. $14-$23.

TOPAZ (FC+) — Excellent new hotel on hill overlooking town w/spectacular views. 48 modern AC R and all amenities. $13-$22.

NEGOMBO

BLUE LAGOON (FC-) — 53 (some AC) modern, cottage-style rooms; good food, beach and pleasant gardens. 2 rsts, bar, nightclub. Pool, water sports. $17-$21 AP.

BROWN'S BEACH (FC) — 66 AC R in long, arcaded building directly on sea. Excellent rsts, bar, nightclub. Pool. About $42 AP.

NUWARA ELIYA

GRAND (FC-) — 140 R, once-grand hotel shows its age. Rooms large, public areas immense. True to its past grandeur, serves bland English food. Though not well managed, one should stay here to experience an era long gone most everywhere in the world. About $23.

HILL CLUB — English Tudor-style club (grants temporary membership). Same bland food but more intimate (22 R) than Grand.

FARR INN (at Horton Plains) — Old hunting lodge with fireplace. Only three singles, three doubles.

POLONNARUWA

National Holiday Resort, 7 miles from Giritale, has three simple hotels: *Araliya* — 30 R, pool; *Amaliyan Nivas* — 20 R (fairly new); *Seruwa* — 41 R, pool. All $17-$20 AP.

SIGIRIYA

SIGIRIYA REST HOUSE (FC-) — 30 R w/fans. Great view of Rock Fortress. $14

TANGALLE

TANGALLE BAY — 24 R w/fans; lush setting in quiet cove. Good. $26 AP.

TRINCOMALEE

BLUE LAGOON (FC) — 40 R on beach. Natural pool, sail and deep-sea fishing boats, outrigger canoes. Dining, bar. $13.

CLUB OCEANIC (FC) — 56 AC R, modern resort on beach. European/Chinese food; bar, nightclub, health club, pool. Has "hip" reputation. $33.

NILAVELI BEACH (FC+) — 48 R w/fans and balcony overlooking sea. Open-air dining room, bars, lounge and lobby. Pool, tennis, driving range. 11 miles from Trincomalee on magnificent, deserted beach near coral reef; boat for divers, snorkelers. Excellent, friendly service. $15-$17.

YALA NATIONAL PARK

BROWN'S SAFARI (FC) — 8 R on cove. Rustic.

TISSMAHARAM REST HOUSE (FC+) — About 10 miles from park, lakeside. Quiet, clean and pleasant. Arranges jeep safaris.

YALA SAFARI BEACH (FC) — On ocean at edge of park. Clean and efficient w/42 R. Pool. Pleasant walks. About $26.

GENERAL INFORMATION

Airport Exit Tax — Rs 10.

Airport Transportation — Rs 90 per taxi. Bus service also available.

Banks — Open 9 a.m.-1:30 p.m. M-F; closed Sat., Sun.

Currency — Rate about Rupees (Rs) 15 to $1. All foreign currencies must be declared on entry; these are entered in a D Form on which subsequent money exchanges, at authorized locations, are entered. On departure, unspent Rs (up to 465) may be reconverted at the Bank of Ceylon airport exchange counter. Your valuables must also be declared and entered on D Form.

Current — 230/240v, 50 cycles AC.

Entry Requirements — Passport, *no visa for stays of 30 days or less* (but onward or return ticket needed), smallpox vaccination. If visiting areas beyond Colombo, malaria pills recommended.

Population — 14 million; 71% Sinhalese, 11% Sri Lankan Tamils. Country same 'size as West Virginia. Sinhala official language but English widely spoken.

Religion — 67% Buddhist, 17% Hindu, 15% Christian, Muslim.

Shopping Hours — 8:30 to 4:30 M-F; 8:30-12:30 Sat. As a devout Buddhist country, each full moon day of the lunar calendar is a public holiday.

Tipping — None necessary as hotels/restaurants usually add 10%.

Water — Drink only bottled, purified.

Tourist Information — Sri Lanka Tourist Board, 609 Fifth Ave., Suite 308, New York 10017; 2007 Wilshire Blvd., Room 820, Los Angeles 90057.

PAKISTAN

Because the people of this land are 98% Muslims, an area of 307,374 square miles was allotted to the new nation of Pakistan at the time of the breakup of the British Indian Empire. Consequently, the history of this Indus Valley civilization is part and parcel of what's we've already read about India. In 1940, a resolution was adopted by the All-India Muslim League demanding a separate, independent homeland which, after seven years of struggle under the leadership of the Quaid-e-Azam, Mohammad Ali Jinnah, was granted and a new sovereign state emerged on August 14, 1947.

GENERAL INFORMATION

Entry & Customs Regulations

Passport only; no visa needed for visits up to 30 days. Smallpox, cholera vaccinations necessary. *Anti-malarial precautions advised.* Normal personal effects permitted, including 200 cigarettes, 2 bottles liquor (1/3 gal.).

Currency

Rs (Rupee) 10 equal $1 US, so each rupee is worth 10¢. There are 100 paisas to the rupee. No restrictions on bringing in foreign currencies.

Airport Departure Tax — Rs 15

Capital — Islamabad, though Karachi is principal city (4,500,000,000 pop.).

Country Population — 65,000,000.

Climate — Relatively dry with warm days, chilly nights in interior and north. Summer (May-Sept.) hot, though coastal Karachi is cooled by sea breezes. Best season: Sept.-March.

Electricity — 220v, 50c AC.

Health — Drink bottled water only.

Language — Urdu and various regional tongues. English widely spoken.

Laundry & Cleaning — 24-hour service.

Newspapers — *Karachi Pakistan Times* and others in English.

Time — GMT +5.

Tipping — Hotels, restaurants add 10% service.

Tourist Information — Pakistan Tourist Development Corp., Hotel Metropole, Club Rd., Karachi. Embassy of Pakistan, 2315 Massachusetts Ave., NW, Washington 20008. Also Pakistan International Airlines' offices in New York, Washington, Chicago, Houston, Los Angeles and San Francisco.

Festivals & Holidays

Muslim holidays, based on lunar calendar, are frequent. Public holidays: March 23, Pakistan Day; August 14, Independence Day; September 11, Anniversary of Death of Quaidi-Azam; Christmas Day.

SHOPPING IN PAKISTAN

You'll enjoy it, particularly since in the bazaars and streets you'll be surrounded by women wearing traditional, full-legged trousers *(shilwar)* or saris. On M. A. Jinnah Road, the colorful bazaar section of old Karachi, you'll mingle with footpath dentists, hairdressers, fortune-tellers, faith healers and ordinary vendors — a sort of Arabian Night adventure you don't quite believe. Other bazaars, which are the main shopping centers of Karachi, are in the Abdullah Harood Road and Zeb-un-Nisa St. areas. Most popular for women: Bohri Bazaar just off Zeb-un-Nisa. Winding your way thru its narrow, crowded lanes, you'll probably wind up in a cave-like cubbyhole crammed to the ceiling with beautifully embroidered shawls and garments, tapestry-like vests and caps, silks and brocades and handprints. Gold and silver jewelry, glass bracelets are tantalizing. For the sounds and smells of typical Eastern bazaars, visit Juna Market, Jodia and Sarafa Bazaars in old Karachi.

DINING & DRINKING

Basically, cuisines are similar to those of India with emphasis on kababs and grilled or barbecued mutton/chicken prepared, of course, in the Muslim way. Flaming red Tandoori chicken is a popular favorite, as are chicken *peshaware, tikka, mussallam* and curries.

Local beer and liquors are less expensive than imported brands and reasonably good. Hotel bars are principal dispensaries. Liquor prohibited in northwestern province.

Major hotel restaurants provide dancing, entertainment.

THE MOSQUES OF PAKISTAN[1]

Islam arose from the deserts of Arabia, a country devoid of vegetation and having thousands of square miles of sheer arid sand. Its people, like its sand dunes, were always shifting their abodes; they had few possessions, and their only wealth lay in camels and sheep. Naturally, such a country could not have given birth to any architectural traditions worthy of the name. Thus, the first-ever mosque constructed after the *Hijrah* (Migration) of the Holy Prophet of Islam (Mohammad) was a makeshift structure with a thatched roof of woven date-palm fronds supported by date-palm trunks. The simplicity of the structure, its broad and bare dimensions, typified the simplicity of the "Path" — the way of life taught by the founder of Islam.

The Prophet's mosque at Medina, however, gave no hint of the heights to which Muslim architecture would rise with the spread of Islam in different regions of the world. In the 7th century, the lands around the Mediterranean and the plains of Syria, Egypt, Iran, North Africa and Spain were conquered by the Arabs. In Syria and Asia Minor, Muslims came into direct contact with Byzantine architecture, in Spain with Christian, in Iran with Persian, in Central Asia with Turkish and Mongol and, later, in what is now Pakistan and India, with Hindu architecture. They borrowed what best suited them from the individual architectural and decorative styles and evolved a practical and esthetic mode of construction which came to be known under the general term of *Saracenic Art*. In Spain, it flowered into the grandeur of the Mosque of Cordova; in Turkey it reached its artistic heights in the mosque of Sulaiman the Magnificent; in Iran it was expressed in the opulence of the Masjid-e-Shah at Istfahan, while in the Indo-Pakistan subcontinent its most outstanding creation was the Badshahi Mosque at Lahore.

Since the basic requirements of mosques were to provide a place for prayer, generally a prayer hall with a niche to indicate the direction of the *Ka'aba* (way to Mecca), a pavilion for social gatherings and a tomb for the honored dead, this structure was always given primary importance wherever Islam went.

In the early 8th century, Arabs first entered the subcontinent — a completely alien world in environment and climate. Here the broad and bare aspects of Islamic architecture came in close contact with the sinister beauty of Hindu temple architecture. It was this intricate and complicated type of architecture which was transformed into a comparatively simple, open and sunny style of construction. There could be no greater contrast than between these two architectural ideals. However, very few remains of that Arab period are extant in Pakistan today, though fragmentary remains of a mosque recently excavated at Bhambore, an early Arab settlement near Karachi, illustrates skillful reuse of older material and a then common plan in the Islamic world.

Not until the establishment of the Delhi Sultanate at the close of the 13th century did Islamic architecture have its real beginning on the subcontinent. A fine example of it is the Tughlaq period mosque on the Makli Hill at Thatta, 65 miles from Karachi, in which the outer walls show a steep batter (receding upward slope) peculiar to mud wall construction. This feature is nobly represented in the beautiful tomb of Shah Rukn-i-Alam (c. 1320 A.D.) at Multan, described as "one of the most splendid memorials ever erected in honor of the dead."

The Imperial Mughal rule (16th-18th centuries), however, was the period which witnessed the greatest architectural achievements on the subcontinent.[2] The

[1] By A. B. Rajput in *Focus on Pakistan,* Vol. 2, Nos. 3 & 4, 1972.
[2] Art historians are generally agreed that the flowering of Islamic architecture is seen in the Alhambra Palace of Granada, Spain (completed in 1391), and the Taj Mahal (completed in 1648), Islam's most famous mausoleum.

monuments of this period are remarkable for their exceptional composition and design, as well as for the richness of their decorative work, strongly influenced by the cultural traditions of the Mughals' Timurid ancestors from Central Asia and their Safavid contemporaries from Persia.

With its galaxy of Mughal architectural monuments, Lahore richly deserves the title "Queen of Cities" in Pakistan. The major group of secular buildings of this period is to be found within the Imperial Fort, outside the old town of Lahore. The Fort, in fact, is the only place in Pakistan which represents the different phases in the development of Mughal architecture.

But the real grandeur of the Imperial Mughals is best expressed in the great *Badshahi Masjid* (Imperial Mosque) built opposite the Fort in 1674 by Fidai Khan. One of the largest in the world, the mosque presents an imposing appearance, its special attractions being its bold design, solidity of structure and spaciousness. Its courtyard measures 528 ft. by 528 ft.; the four corner minarets, with an outer circumference of 67 ft., rise 176 ft. above their base. The building is mainly of red sandstone inlaid with white marble in geometric and floral patterns.

General plan and design of this mosque are identical with those of the Jami mosques at Agra and Delhi, but in its breadth, elegance and general effect it creates a new impression of the grandeur that the austere ruler, Aurangzeb, achieved for the Mughal power during his lifetime. However, the interior has a different effect. The engrailed arches (decorated with indented patterns), marble paneling with arched niches in the walls, and superb ceiling decorations in variegated colors, floral and geometrical patterns produce a soothing effect on the thousands of devotees who come here to pray.

Another of Lahore's superb monuments is the Mosque of Wazir Khan, built during the reign of Emperor Shah Jehan in 1634 A.D. Of baked brick, it is elaborately decorated with painted arabesques and lacquered tiles in true Persian style — similar to Italian frescoes. The richness and excellence of the colors add beauty to the decorations, show the renaissance of the subcontinent's Muslim architecture at its very best.

A distinctive example of Imperial Mughal style is the mosque of Mahabat Khan built in 1630 by the Governor of Peshawar — a fine, massive structure of white stone with lofty minarets in the heart of the old city of Peshawar.

Pakistan's architecture has undergone revolutionary changes during the past 28 years. The heavy influx of Muslim refugees from India, abnormal population growth and, above all, economic development have combined to make the task of architects more complex and demanding than ever before. Thus, it's not surprising, though regrettable, that there's been an increasing trend to "Western modern" and away from the traditional Mughal and local styles. Rare exceptions are newly constructed *Jami Masjid* at Islamabad, the hemispherical mosque built in the Defence Housing Society in Karachi, and the *Masjid-e-Shaheedan* on the Mall in Lahore. Here designers have made some concessions to traditional features, such as the central dome, stylized arches and minarets, in the overall, ultra-modern and simplified structure so as to give it an individuality which might be characterized by the casual observer as traditional Islamic.

Modern architectural experiments in mosque construction sans Islamic decorative motifs, bulbous, narrow-necked domes and tall, parallel minarets, will have to be conducted for years before they take root in this soil, develop a tradition of integration, balance and adjustment to suit the growing demands and changing conditions of the country.

The Folk Art of Swat[1]

It has a charm and appeal peculiarly its own since craftsmen live close to nature and thus create simple and pleasing forms which reflect the boldness and simplicity of their feelings. And the harmonious relationship between feelings and objects has an immediate humanizing impact.

To understand this art, it's necessary to know something of the history and culture of the land.

Swat, one of the most enchanting areas of Pakistan, is in the Northwest Frontier Province surrounded by gigantic mountain peaks which soar upwards to form a magnificent fan-like panorama. The River Swat, life stream of the area, flows down from Kohistan (Upper Swat) to rush thru the deep and narrow gorges between Kalam and Behrain. Winding its circuitous course southwards, the river is harnessed at Malakand by a hydroelectric project. With the help of irrigation, two good crops are harvested each year on the terraced mountain slopes and in the fertile valleys.

By virtue of its topography, the vale of Swat is divided into two parts — Upper Swat, collectively known as Kohistan, and Lower Swat, from Madyan down to Saidu Sharif. In language, social habits, ethnography and folk art, the two parts are distinctly different. Craftsmen of Upper Swat reveal a particular technique, a sense of balance between form and function and an ornamental quality quite different from the south. In both areas, inspiration comes from the encircling range of wooded mountains and snowcapped peaks, the sinuous course of turbulent River Swat, rows and rows of tall, coniferous trees, terraced patches whose designs, when seen from above, are reminiscent of those found in minor Islamic art.

To illustrate their ornaments, clothing and artifacts — which range from silver jewelry, sandals and stockings to ornately carved chairs — artisans have adopted various geometrical forms which, in ancient times, were considered symbols of agricultural fertility. Additionally, however, they have superimposed on these traditional forms floral designs, cusped arches and calligraphy; these latter forms have been employed to a great extent on mosques and other buildings to disguise the crudeness and ugliness of native raw materials.

Swat has a long and checkered history. Its people have experienced the tutelage and overlordship of many invaders, last of whom were humanitarian Muslims. They brought with them a variety of religions and cultural influences, but only Islam made its permanent home in the land and brought about a synthesis of cultural trends which became the indigenous culture. Little wonder, therefore, that the folk artist inherited influences from these varied past cultures — although the basic style remains predominately native.

However, today's gradual transformation from an agrarian to industrialized economy is having a paralyzing effect on artistic creativity. With mass production of handicrafts, the finished object is no longer an expression of the soul. But various institutions and museums, including the Lahore Museum, are preserving the ethnographical material which has been rapidly disappearing.

Domestic Air Transportation

Good jet and jet-prop service by Pakistani International. Karachi to Peshawar is the longest flight (3:15 one stop). Other flight times: Karachi-Lahore, 1:40; Karachi-Rawalpindi/Islamabad, 40 min.

SIGHTSEEING IN PAKISTAN

Most interesting cities are Karachi, Lahore, Rawalpindi and Peshawar (gateway to famed Khyber Pass), while the Himalaya, Karakoram and Hindukush mountain areas of Swat, Chitral, Gilgit and Hunza are magnificent. City and country tours are available locally; a 7-day package usually includes the four cities, while one of 12 days adds the Swat Valley, Gilgit and Hunza.

Cars/drivers can be hired thru Pakistan Tours (PTL) for about $20 a day per 3-passenger car (includes gas for 96 km), $30 for AC car. Karachi City Tours (about $4 for 3½ hrs.), offered by PTL and private operators, take in the Defense Society Mosque, Bohri Bazaar, Boulton Market and Zoo.

A new highway has been opened between Pakistan and China; mountain scenery is said to be fabulous. Northern Area Transport Co. plans a 15-hour bus trip over this highway from Rawalpindi to Gilgit in northern Pakistan.

However, most travelers to this part of the world are members of a group tour offered by a number of tour operators, many in cooperation with the Pakistan International Airlines; they normally include Pakistan along with one or more of the following: Iran, Afghanistan, India-Kashmir, Sri Lanka and Nepal.

PAKISTAN HOTEL DIRECTORY
(15% Tax Added)

Listed below are only top hotels. Pakistan Airlines and Tourism Development Corporation have already upgraded many resthouses throughout the country; within the next two years, they will enlarge and rebuild their hotels in Peshawar, Rawalpindi and the Faletti Hotel in Lahore. In Gilgit, in the north, a 50 R hotel opened in '78; in Quetta, a 150 R hotel is under construction.

Some communities add an additional 2% bed tax.

KURACHI

HYATT (DL) — Opens '80 with 400 R, all facilities, plus a 60-ft-high lobby.

HILTON (DL) — 300 R opens late '79 in new shopping center.

HOLIDAY INN (FC) — Off Victoria Rd opens late '79 w/200 R, pool.

INTER-CONTINENTAL (DL) — 306 AC R w/balcony. Next to Governor's Palace in city center. Rst, rooftop rst, bar. Poolside bar. *Conv:* 2500. $55-$60.

SHERATON (DL) — 390 R scheduled for June 1980.

ISLAMABAD

ISLAMABAD HOLIDAY INN (FC) — Opened '77 with 150 R. On Aga Khan Rd., across from government bldgs.

Built along Moghul architectural lines. Pool, tennis. Coffee shop faces pool, dining room serves Western and Pakistani cuisine. $40.

LAHORE

INTERCONTINENTAL (DL) — DT. 200 AC R, SU. Dining room, cocktail lounge, nightclub. Pool, tennis, 9-hole golf course. *Conv:* 450. $43-$50.

LAHORE HILTON (DL) — Opened fall '77 with 205 R; stunning use of inlaid mirrors and stone in lobby. Marvelous use of color throughout; furniture handcrafted. Pool. Located on Sharai Quaid-i-Alam, next to Pakistan Arts Council. $43-$50.

PESHAWAR

KHYBER INTER-CONTINENTAL (DL-) — Khyber Rd, center for Khyber Pass. 150 AC R. Pool, tennis, Peshawar Golf Club privileges. Supper club, cocktail lounge, coffee shop. Conv. facilities. $39-$44.

RAWALPINDI

INTER-CONTINENTAL (FC) — 15 min. from airport in area that is base for tours to the north. 205 AC R w/balcony on 4 floors. Elegant Kohsaar Rst has nightly entertainment, dancing. Piano bar, poolside bar. Tennis. Shopping arcade. $42-$48.

General Index

Thai Wedding Ceremony. Part of the ritual is the pouring of holy water on the hands of bride and bridegroom.

Photo Credits

Most of our personal photography was done in color, not enough in black / white for the illustrative purposes of this book. Thus, excepting miscellaneous halftones (uncredited), the majority of the photographs herein have been furnished by others. We are sincerely grateful to the following tourist organizations for their cooperation in furnishing suitable illustrations, each of which has been listed by page numbers after their names:

E & O Hotel, Penang, Malaysia — 210, 227.

Frank Heineman, New York — 172, 173.

Hong Kong Tourist Association — 2, 4, 35, 140, 142, 146, 148, 150, 152, 153, 154, 157.

Government of India Tourist Office — 40, 289, 293, 298, 303, 304, 309, 310, 316, 318, 319.

Holland America Cruises — 17, 18, 19.

Japan Airlines — 73.

Japan National Tourist Organization — 43, 46, 54, 58, 60, 67, 72, 75, 80.

Korea Tourist Bureau — 89, 93, 95.

Macau Tourist Bureau — 163-4-5.

Malaysian Tourist Development Corporation — 214, 217, 221-2-3-4-5, 230.

National Palace Museum, Taiwan — 108, 109, 112.

Pakistan International Airlines — 348.

Philippine Dept. of Tourism — 272, 278, 280, 284.

Singapore Tourist Promotion Board — 28, 239, 240, 244, 246-7-8.

Sri Lanka Tourist Board — 332-3, 336-7-8, 340-1.

Tiger Tops (John Edwards & Chuck McDougal) — 330, 331.

Tourism Bureau, Republic of China — 107, 116, 119, 120, 126.

Tourist Organization of Thailand — 5, 181, 187, 188, 190, 192, 196, 198, 200, 201, 204-5, 352.